FARMERS, WORKERS *and* MACHINES

Technological and Social Change in Farm Industries of Arizona

Harland Padfield *and* William E. Martin

THE UNIVERSITY OF ARIZONA PRESS
TUCSON   1965

Published for
The Division of Economic and Business Research
College of Business and Public Administration
The University of Arizona

TO
LAUREN W. CASADAY
Whose vision and
personal encouragement
made this study possible

CONTENTS

CONTENTS — *Continued*

CONTENTS — *Continued*

CONTENTS — *Continued*

TABLES

TABLES — *Continued*

FIGURES

Foreword

THIS BOOK is built on a simple idea, one of those obvious conceptions which has become obscured by a way of thinking based on more sophisticated ideas. This simple idea is the obvious one that a labor supply consists of men, women, and children in families with their own accustomed and often well-loved ways of living. Everyone knows this. We are all quick to say that a labor supply does not consist just of pairs of hands picking oranges or cotton or lettuce. We all know that pairs of hands are connected with a breathing reality of families seeking reasonable comfort and happiness. We know that, and yet this reality seems to fade from our thoughts once we begin to talk about matters of production and labor supply.

The conception of men in families somehow gets lost as more sophisticated ideas get into the discussion. These "sophisticated" ideas grow out of the sort of calculations which managers of business enterprises must make, if their enterprises are to survive. A business is a profit-making institution and its managers must think in terms of labor units and what must be paid each labor unit. It is an all-too-short step from this standpoint to an habitual viewing of the labor supply as composed of units — pairs of hands doing jobs. The hands must be secured, they must be kept working, they must be paid, and so the labor supply — an abstraction gleaned from the ledger sheet — becomes well-established in our thinking about the problems of agricultural production.

To bring back into our thought the realities of "labor" and "production" is not easy. Often obscuring abstractions such as these can be eliminated only through cataclysmic events, as when colonial powers not so many years ago were reminded — by revolution — that "natives" were people with political and other human aspirations. Fortunately it happens sometimes that in the cloisters of modern universities the limiting abstractions which obscure human problems are suddenly pushed aside and really new approaches to old problems are undertaken. It seems to me that this is what has happened in the present study. Instead of merely admitting, as everyone does, that farm laborers are indeed human beings and then proceeding in the usual way to talk about the labor supply abstraction, Padfield and Martin have kept their scientific attention fixed on the reality long enough to forge a new and scientifically appropriate conception. They could have taken the easy course and merely pointed out that farm laborers ought to be studied as people, but their concern was too deep to allow them to stop there.

They were not content only to talk about the desirability of such an approach. Because they were deeply interested in the urgent problems of the rapidly changing technology of farm production in Arizona and its consequences for agricultural laborers and the rest of us, as deeply interested as

[xi]

any grower, as any laborer, as any employment officer, as any legislative policy-maker, Padfield and Martin proceeded to use their new approach and carry through painstaking research. The result is a study which illuminates, as no other studies of agricultural labor in the Southwest have done, basic problems of both management and labor.

This unusual and publicly valuable contribution has come about not through ignoring existing knowledge, as might be wrongly inferred from what was said above, but rather by using with new insight the fund of knowledge — including, of course, the existing abstractions — of two important disciplines. The specialization of research on which new advances in knowledge depend has kept agricultural economics and cultural anthropology pretty far apart in our universities. Each has explored important aspects of human life and each has been immensely busy with its own kind of analysis. It was these two disciplines on which Padfield, the anthropologist, and Martin, the economist, drew in their analysis of employment problems. They came to see that their specialized approaches to the understanding of the labor supply complemented each other and, once this was seen, they were led to a fuller and unexpectedly illuminating view of the interacting factors which affect "labor problems." Their approach involved not the ignoring of existing knowledge, but instead its fuller utilization. The collaboration of Padfield and Martin points to the need for more efforts to use our relatively compartmentalized academic knowledge in joint efforts to understand and solve our human problems.

This study should help to lead us, the public, on to new ground for understanding and dealing with the dramatic confrontation between men and their technology, no less intense and no less in need of our best efforts here in Arizona than anywhere else in the world.

Tucson, Arizona   Edward H. Spicer
1965

Acknowledgments

THIS STUDY was financed by contract funds from the Bureau of Employment Security of the United States Department of Labor. It was conducted with the cooperation of the Farm Placement Office of the Arizona State Employment Service. Their representatives, Richard H. Salter, Chief of Farm Placement, and Clayton O. Kaigler, Farm Service Analyst, made available to us all facilities and data that office was able to provide. The close cooperation they rendered during the data gathering and writeup was both helpful and unbiased.

To The University of Arizona and the National Science Foundation we are indebted for the use of laboratory and office space on the research floor of the Anthropology Building. This facility was made possible by funds granted by the National Science Foundation.

We especially acknowledge the interdisciplinary administrative work accomplished by Professor Jimmye S. Hillman, Head of the Agricultural Economics Department. Interdisciplinary research needs cooperating scholars. In a large educational institution it demands cooperating administrators. Professor Hillman's efforts at every stage in the development of this project were crucial in lowering barriers which researchers inevitably face in this type of research undertaking.

To Professor Harold J. Hoflich we are grateful for patient and flexible direction in his role of Director of the Bureau of Business and Public Research. The Bureau has had major responsibility for research administration and manuscript preparation. In this connection it is appropriate to mention our debt to their Editor, Lois R. Nelson, for her editorial suggestions.

The senior author owes a special debt of gratitude to Professor William H. Kelly and Professor Edward H. Spicer — to Professor Kelly for permitting the Bureau of Ethnic Research to underwrite much of the time needed for manuscript revision and to Professor Spicer for his teaching. He is also indebted to his wife, Marianne Padfield, for contributing her time and knowledge of rural people in structuring and analyzing worker interviews.

Field researchers to be credited are Martha Farley in family studies, James Armstrong in descriptions of farm operations, and Marion Parker and James Otterness in worker interviews.

Acknowledgement is also given to the participation of Professor William C. Lawton in the early phases of the project formulation.

In a very special sense social scientists owe their greatest debt of gratitude to the individual human beings whose private affairs they intrude upon. The cooperation of each agricultural establishment involved considerable loss of their time. More significantly this cooperation involved disclosing confidential information. The trust such cooperation implies places a burden of responsibility upon the investigators which is both flattering and sobering. No less important from the human point of view are the secrets of the past, sometimes dimly remembered, sometimes disturbing in the rekindling of pain and forgotten affliction, given no less generously by the "unknown" worker. Information from *all* participants is a trust. For this privilege, most of all, we are indebted.

<table>
<tr><td>Tucson, Arizona</td><td>Harland Padfield</td></tr>
<tr><td>1965</td><td>William E. Martin</td></tr>
</table>

1 General Introduction

A BACKGROUND OF PRACTICAL PROBLEMS

TWO APPARENTLY conflicting facts have kept the "farm labor problem" in the headlines in recent years. At the same time that there is unemployment in our national economy our farmers claim that there is a serious shortage of agricultural labor. Further, this apparent labor shortage is occurring in the midst of extremely rapid labor-reducing technological change.

Two additional views further cloud the picture and lend emotional content to the issues. On the one hand agricultural workers are typified as poverty stricken victims of exploitation; on the other hand they are stereotyped as the dregs of the labor force. With these intensely conflicting views being urged upon the public, it is no wonder that there is no consensus among the various groups and individuals commenting on the farm labor problem. In fact, there is no consensus on what the problem is.

Farmers and farm oriented groups tend to view the problem as an absolute shortage of available farm workers. Socially oriented groups and "do gooders" tend to view the problem as low wages and poor living conditions for some relatively undefined group of people known as farm workers. Whether governmental agencies tend to take the viewpoint of the farmers or the "do gooders" depends on whether an agency is agriculturally or labor oriented. Action agencies such as the Bureau of Employment Security with its affiliated farm labor employment offices are caught in the middle. They must try to provide farmers with adequate, capable labor. At the same time they must try to provide jobs for everyone regardless of their capabilities.

We will not try to define The Problem. Certainly each of the problems noted above are a part of the farm labor problem. Rather, we will analyze in detail the economic, social and cultural institutions within which all these problems occur in an effort to put each participant group's problem in its proper perspective.

We will attempt to point out why technological change has occurred in Arizona agriculture and why farmers continually face an apparent labor shortage. We examine certain questions. Who are the farm laborers? Who will be affected by technological change? Who are using the present farm labor systems to their advantage? Who might be available for work under future technological systems?

We will discuss why the farmers need certain types of labor and why certain types of labor in turn need the farm.

[1]

OVERALL DESIGN OF
MANUSCRIPT AND AUTHORSHIP

Part One is devoted to a general description of the harvest systems for Arizona citrus, lettuce, and cotton. Included in this description are crop histories, harvesting and handling methods, farm organizations, and a brief view of the relationship of the various types of workers to these organizations. Part One may be viewed as an orientation for the analyses to come.

We will work from the general to the specific. Economics provides a ready-made theoretical framework with which to view the general questions of capital-labor substitution and the demand for agricultural labor. Thus in Part Two we are interested in cost pressures, the effects these pressures will have on the need for quantities of labor, a rough estimate of the timing of these needs, and a superficial view of the changing type of worker that will be required under new technological systems. An integral part of this analysis is a development of how the technologies themselves may change. Demand for labor should never be viewed independent of the possibility of technical change.

Our ultimate goal is to work toward an explanation of equilibrium. From the economist's point of view this is where the supply of labor willing to work at a given wage is exactly equal to the quantity of labor farmers are willing to hire at that wage — that is, where supply equals demand. But while the economist's theory enables him to make fairly good broad generalizations about labor demand, it is of relatively little use in explaining labor supply. Demand is related to costs, returns, and technologies. These factors are rather easily observed and measured. Supply is related to the human factor. Here much less measurable factors such as cultural institutions apply. Questions arise. Who are these workers? What are their backgrounds? How do they fit into the systems? What are their goals?

Thus Parts Three through Five take the cultural view of the farm labor problem. The factors lying behind the economist's simplified view of supply are viewed in detail. Further, labor demand is not in fact independent of labor supply. While it is often convenient and useful to view demand independently, the more complete explanation also involves the cultures and institutions of the potential labor force. The technology adopted for use is directly related to the attributes of these people.

Part Three consists of a description of a sample of workers employed in the crops in question. Six hundred and three workers were included in the sample. Data were obtained by means of standardized, pretested, and precoded interview schedules. All interviews also provided information in depth which was used in the analytical portions of the study.

Part Four is an analysis of the subcultures in Arizona farm labor. Each subculture is seen to have certain core institutions which are important in the participation of the worker in agriculture. These are referred to as *participant institutions*. The members of these core institutions participate in agriculture out of needs peculiar to their distinctive institutions and cultural backgrounds.

Finally, in Part Five we return to the concept of equilibrium — but in terms of social equilibrium. Again we are looking behind the useful but simplified concept of supply and demand where people are viewed simply as quantities of workers. Here, the generalized farm harvest system is viewed as a common mechanism of exploitation born out of the needs of each participating group analyzed in Part Four. The role of each group in that system and the function of the system itself for each group is analyzed. This leads to hypotheses about the social effects of changes in technological systems, and conversely the technological and economic effects of changes in the nature and availability of the participant social groups.

The division of authorship is fairly obvious once one realizes that Harland Padfield is a cultural anthropologist and William Martin is an agricultural economist. Parts Three, Four, and Five are culturally oriented; Part Two is straight economics. The description of Part One also fell to Harland Padfield as the project director and principal researcher.

However, since we are not only research cooperators, but also good friends, every part of the research and the manuscript was discussed time and again at all hours of the day and night over the past three years. The final chapter, containing our recommendations, is a joint effort arising from these interminable conversations.

PREVIOUS STUDIES OF INDUSTRIAL LABOR

The Inadequacies of Commonly Used Viewpoints

Even the most casual observer of the farm labor force must be keenly aware that he is not dealing with *a* population, but *many* populations. The specific clusterings of human characteristics and behavior will depend upon the era, the region, and the industry. More basically, they depend upon the idea of human groupings which the observer consciously or unconsciously has in his mind. This is fundamental because the limitless complexity of human experience forces everyone — participant and observer alike — to operate on implicit assumptions about how people are organized and motivated. These assumptions constitute his social framework. This social framework, through which an observer sees others, automatically sensitizes him to certain social values and activities while at the same time blinding him to others. Depending upon his level of awareness, he may or may not refer to the part he is not interested in as *given*. Regardless of this, the effect is the same — one type of social reality will manifest itself through one method of analysis while another type of social reality which tends to emerge through another frame of social organization is obscured, obviated, or lost entirely.

It is common to view workers through the frame of formal management structure. This view tends to regard workers as interchangeable units whose output depends upon the manner in which they are formally arranged in relation to their physical surroundings, their tools, and their raw materials as well as in their relation to structures of authority. Social reality so perceived is reacted upon by management with policies that will, according to their logics, increase production by elimination of unnecessary motions, streamlining of lines of communication, and removal of tasks and employees performing those tasks which efficiency studies reveal as superfluous.

On the other hand many agencies, governmental and private, tend to approach employment problems in a census framework. While this view may take into account educational, vocational, and psychological factors it still does not differ from the person-as-a-unit concept. Jobs are regarded as demanding certain of these qualities of an employee. After determining the number of jobs available and the education and skills required, it remains simply to locate an equal number of workers with these required qualifications. Moreover, where labor demand and labor supply are unequal, it remains simply to change the educational level and skills of such and such a number of workers to quantitatively equate them with the jobs which are unfilled. The census view shares with the efficiency view one profound deficiency: both are unequipped to deal with the sociological dimension.

The Importance of Industrial Labor Studies and the Mayo School

The sociology of the workshop emerged as an unexpected by-product in research designed to increase assembly line efficiency. Born out of sheer necessity, these factory studies began in England during World War I. The industrial age had long since become sophisticated in the mechanics of production, but in the sustained emergency of the almost unlimited demands of modern warfare, attention became more and more focused on the human factor of production as the ultimate bottleneck. At first, industrial personnel studies were conducted from the implicit viewpoint that workers were physiological carbon copies of machines and that a simple causal sequence for production slumps could speedily be discovered. This viewpoint is evident in the inventory of subject matter headings that appeared during the first 12 years of study by the British Board of Industrial Fatigue:

I. Hours of Work, Rest Pauses, etc.	10	reports
II. Industrial Accidents	5	reports
III. Atmospheric Conditions	9	reports
IV. Vision and Lighting	5	reports
V. Vocational Guidance and Selection	7	reports
VI. Time and Movement Study	10	reports
VII. Posture and Physique	4	reports

But, ". . . the single discovery, the simple remedy, the one best way, had failed to materialize. The situation that had actually revealed itself was that of multiple factors closely interrelated and all potentially important in the control of industry" (Mayo 1960: 5-6).

Mayo goes on to describe in historical detail the course of the exploration of multiple factors. The physiology of tiredness was explored under controlled conditions. The effects of minute changes in pulse, blood pressure, and lactic acid were measured under varying conditions of position and work-pause rhythm among workers with differing levels of motor skills. Physiological concepts metamorphosed into concepts of monotony which are more psychological than organic. Thus the human-extensions-of-machines concepts began to give way to concepts more distinctly human (Mayo 1960: 1-32). Nevertheless, both the early physiological and psychological approaches to worker behavior still had one thing in common. They were individualistically oriented. They tended still to view workers as interchangeable (albeit complex) units who, when grouped by physiological or psychological types, would react uniformly to physical and structural changes in assembly line organization.

As the physiological approach led utimately to psychological considerations framed by the context of monotony and boredom, investigations in the latter area disclosed still another dimension to industrial worker behavior. By the late twenties, studies of the Industrial Research Boards in England had begun to delineate a social dimension. A study of monotony by S. Wyatt and J. A. Fraser in 1929 disclosed, in addition to the fact that boredom varied with the intelligence of the worker and the degree of mechanization of the task, that it also varied with the social conditions of work. They discovered that workers produced more when they were allowed to work in compact social groups (Mayo 1962: 32).

Industrial labor studies in the United States began in the twenties independently of the British studies. Significantly, these studies which began with the same objectives and methods but without communication with the investigators in England, were driven step by step to similar methods and conclusions (Mayo 1960: 41). A comprehensive document of one of the best known and most thorough inquiries is *Management and the Worker* by Roethlisberger and Dickson (1943). Harvard University began the study in 1927 in the Hawthorne plant of the Western Electric Company. It was concluded in 1939. The 12 year study led the investigators to view workers as physiological units, then psychological units, and finally as members of social organizations. For our purposes, it is necessary only to sum up the culminating viewpoints of what has come to be called the "Mayo School" of industrial relations.

The workshop is seen as a social organization in a state of dynamic tension between management and workers. The aims and logics of management are projected in what Roethlisberger and Dickson call *formal organization,* while the sentiments and social and psychological needs of workers are framed by and receive expression in *informal organization.* Workers within the plant were found to have their own groupings with definite membership and status positions. Workers' attitudes, motivations, and performances in the production system had to be understood in terms of these groups to which they belonged — in spite of the fact that membership was not formalized by lists of names, duties, and statuses. Group standards, values, and attitudes operated in very real fashion as guides to the behavior of the worker. For example, much the same situation exists within a school system. It has a formal organization of superintendent, principal, counselors, teachers, secretaries, and students. It has formalized standards and sanctions of grades and punishments. But a teacher who thinks the classroom behavior of a 14-year-old can be determined and explained entirely in terms of the formalized school system would be naive. Standards for classroom conduct come from informal peer groupings, just as standards for production behavior of a worker are governed by the informal social organization of the department or section of which he is a member (Roethlisberger and Dickson 1939: 551-568).

For our purposes there is no reason to go into the controversies which have centered about the Mayo school in the past 20 years (see Landsberger, *Hawthorne Revisited,* 1958). The Mayo school of industrial labor must be recognized in this study because it contributed a major concept to the theory of industrial labor: workers behave as members of their own social units. This is essentially an institutional concept and in its most fundamental sense has application to farm labor. The view that workers in a cotton field or a citrus grove behave in a social framework is a necessary beginning in understanding farm labor problems.

The Limitations of the Mayo School in Farm Labor Studies

Beyond this point it is necessary to make an important departure from Roethlisberger and Dickson. While they framed their inquiries *within* the work organization(s) entirely, one cannot limit a study of farm labor to those social groupings which occur within the farm harvest organization without excluding the larger part of the iceberg. To be sure informal congeries of workers tend to form around their job groupings, such as crew membership, common job tasks, piece rates, etc. But this application of the concept of the worker society does not go far enough. Workers — especially farm workers — are members of active organizational systems which operate *outside* the work situation. These systems or institutions cluster around their ethnic affiliations. These include, in the case of Arizona farm industries, Mexican-American, Negro, Indian, Filipino, and two types of Anglo. The institutions which integrate members of an ethnic group come first. The workshop comes second. The former have a continuous historical tradition. Behavior patterns of the latter are recent and change frequently. In the case of a farm harvest system, the membership of the workshop varies from one day to the next. It is less stable, less continuous, and less binding upon the behavior of its members than the institutions they return to at night and within which they continue to interact, even in the fields.

The Mayo school succeeded in adding a second dimension which up to its time had been largely overlooked: human efficiency *within* the production system. However, by its own frame of viewing a factory system it was walled off from considering the wider (outer) problem of a social efficiency in terms of human resources. Examining the cultural background and the community institutions of the worker permits the broadening of industrial-employment research so that it may more fully answer questions with respect to the behavior of workers on the job. In addition, it enlarges the scope of investigation beyond considerations of production efficiency. It brings to the subject of industry and labor questions of the impact of technologies upon society, and the impact of society upon technologies.

NEW WAYS OF LOOKING AT FARM LABOR

In order to move our vantage point to human groupings outside of the workshop, something must serve as the focus. An outer but interdependent field is needed — a field which is changed when we interfere, a field which is affected when a worker's occupation is changed or forfeited entirely. It must be stable, it must have continuity, it must have definable bounds, and it must be observable. Such a field is not adequately or precisely encompassed by the term "ethnic group." It is conveyed by the concept of *culture*. A worker's cultural background is his blueprint for behaving. This blueprint for behavior can be traced back generation after generation and has provisions for its own perpetuation in future generations. A worker's cultural background is important at all levels of consideration. It is important in job placement, job training, work organization, and behavior. A worker's cultural background is especially important when it differs radically from the culture of the majority or dominant society.

The Anglo middle class American employer, union leader, or employment counselor is a member of both the majority and the dominant group in relation to all of the major segments of farm workers. When he deals with another middle class Anglo-American, he can do so automatically. He can expect the other man to do the "natural" thing. When he deals with an ex-sharecropper Negro, an Apache Indian, a Mexican-American, or even an Anglo alcoholic, he cannot operate with his full set of unconscious and implicit assumptions about workmen. If he does he is operating blindly. When he enacts a policy determined to produce a given social or economic result, it more likely than not will produce an entirely unexpected result — one which both surprises and frustrates him.

Viewing the major segments of farm workers as separate subcultures will focus upon the blueprint which determines their behavior — specifically behavior affecting their participation in farm work. We cannot go much beyond this, however, without a second focus, one which will enable us to see the action and interaction of living persons. For this the blueprint idea is too general. We need an idea which focuses upon the workmen themselves in the act of following their guides to behaving. We need a *social* concept. The concept of *institution* embraces both the blueprint and the persons-in-action idea. The concept of an institution is used to convey the idea of *people* arranged in relation to one another in *set* ways following *standards* that have been handed down by their culture for a specific situation.

Thus proceeding from the cultural view to an institutional view serves to specify: (1) the situation, (2) the persons involved, (3) the behavior guides or standards for the occasion, and (4) the relationships of one member to the other. The institutional concept belongs in a cultural context, but it is a more dynamic conceptual tool which will enable us to observe interaction and change. Thus, when a machine is introduced into a farm organization we can be more specific about *how* it changes the culture of the worker. We can point to a specific institution — e.g., his family. We may observe that this machine alters his relationship to his wife or his children. We may observe further that a behavior standard or norm — e.g. frugality—is affected by his higher salary if he becomes the operator of the machine. Or a standard of stern independence may be affected by his unemployment and subsequent dependence upon welfare if he is replaced by the machine. The institutional concept therefore provides us with a frame that discloses interaction, equilibrium, and change.

Employers, union leaders, and public agencies have not, on the whole, been unaware of the cultural and institutional backgrounds of farm workers. Knowledge, however, has been implicit, largely unconscious, and at times erroneous. This general discussion hopefully has served to point up the social fallacies commonly held by many employers and social agencies, the history of the emergence of the social dimension in studies of worker behavior, and the need for an outer orientation in understanding industrial labor—especially farm labor. We have urged the use of the culture concept to provide this outer focus and, for the purpose of analyzing social and technological dynamics, the more specialized culture concept, the concept of the institution.

PART ONE

CROP HISTORIES
and
HARVEST ORGANIZATIONS

2 Past and Present

EACH INDUSTRY has its peculiar pattern of interests and concerns. These patterns in many instances lead backward in time to specific events which have their own logical continuity. Although we commenced gathering descriptive material without delving into the history of each industry, it soon became obvious that a systematic gathering of background information was desirable. In the chapters to follow, this historical emphasis is denoted under *Background,* although the clues which led to an examination of the histories of these technologies emerged originally in the descriptive phases of the research. These clues are apparent in the Organizational Structure of Harvest Activities and Experience Accounts. Many of the anecdotal accounts are studded with references to decisive events from which stemmed, at least in the informant's mind, this or that specific set of circumstances.

In citrus, managers feel up against it because they depend completely upon the method of picking which has remained fundamentally the same since the dawn of horticulture. Our technology has propelled humans into space and instruments to Mars, but we pick oranges the same way the Ancient Malaysians picked them — by hand. This fact is essential in understanding the frustrations and anxieties of growers and packers when they face the cost-price squeeze with a labor market becoming more competitive every year. Lacking a breakthrough in picking man-hour requirements, they experiment in short cuts in boxing, hauling and storage systems.

Citrus worker types and worker traditions reflect a continuity that matches the antiquity of hand picking. A rich lore continues to grow about their experiences while at the same time their numbers diminish.

Lettuce is a booming industry. It exhibits almost complete technological uniformity. Yet growers and shippers are uneasy and defensive. A backward glance tells why. Mexican labor displaced union labor. From the standpoint of the union, the battle is lost only temporarily and the sheds, centers of union power, cast baleful shadows across the vegetal landscape teeming with braceros in their wide-brimmed hats and the sounds of raucous radios blaring *rancheras* and Mexican commercials.

In cotton, technological uniformity is also evident but mechanization did not inundate the industry. The flow of change meandered. In contrast to citrus and lettuce, those who have achieved a role in the new technology see a relatively secure future. The technology is stable. On the other hand, those who have not made the economic or occupational transition are painfully aware of their obsolescence. They vary only in their reaction to this knowledge. Each year is the year of decision for many who have forestalled a change of occupation for the last time. Still others will return compulsively season after season like tired migratory birds to the dried marshlands of a bygone age.

Crop technologies are dynamic. Therefore their labor populations are dynamic. What jobs did workers now occupying the top positions in the present technologies have before these technologies came into play? What jobs did those now in the lowest positions have? This introduces the whole question of mobility — the mobility of workers moving from one industry to another as well as from lower status jobs to higher status jobs in the same industry. The past is necessary to establish a picture of these dynamics just as it is to show the corresponding changes in crop technologies.

Thus the individual histories of the growth and development of the cotton, citrus and lettuce industries and societies set the stage for the dimensional significance of these technologies and organizations today.

For these background histories we used different methods because the crop industries studied were in different stages of development. Since changes in cotton have evolved over a long period of time, written historical documents are available. Citrus harvest methods tend to be highly individualized. Sketches of citrus methods are more or less an outgrowth of descriptions and discussions of each company. We simply extend these discussions to include the past. Change came dramatically, abruptly, and recently in lettuce. No complete historical documentation of these technological events is available. Therefore, in the case of this industry, informant accounts were used to construct the pertinent background. The question of where to begin and end always arises in such cases. In our case we began with those primarily responsible for the design and implementation of the technological innovations. In addition, accounts were obtained from secondary sources such as associates and former employees. Such methods are more traditionally ethnographic than historical, but they served to project the point of view of the informant and establish sufficiently reliable background to lend perspective. In each of the industries we made systematic observations of all technical and organizational systems as they were operating.

The chapters on the industries follow basically the same format. First the range of variation of the technical systems in harvest activities of each crop is discussed. Each company studied is presented in accordance with the technical system it represents. Each major heading introducing another management unit has a hyphenated title telling which type of system it uses.

A short profile of the company is followed by an inventory of its harvest equipment. Then there is a detailed discussion of the organization of its harvest activities. These discussions give the number, size, composition, and makeup of crews and positions and duties of its personnel. This is followed by a discussion of the company's wage system. A complete step-by-step description of operations follows. Technical and organizational aspects are blended in a sort of a motion picture sequence. The descriptions of each company-harvest system unit is concluded with Experience Accounts. These are texts taken from key management personnel — managers, superintendents, etc. — who have been intimately involved in their company's development and adaptation of the specific technology in question.

There are many aspects to the harvest operations which are not discussed here because they are described primarily from the viewpoints of management. The viewpoints of other participants in these systems will emerge in appropriate portions of the study.

Although the present tense is generally used in the descriptive passages, changes are likely to have occurred in some company practices since 1962 and 1963 when the field studies were conducted.

3 The Citrus Industry

BACKGROUND

AT THE TURN of the century, a picker, field box, sack, and ladder constituted the harvesting system for Arizona citrus. The "standard field box" was 3,115 cubic inches in volume with slight variations in shape depending upon the packing house. It held from 45 to 47 lbs. of grapefruit, 50 to 55 lbs. of oranges, and 60 to 62 lbs. of lemons. Field boxes were carried through the groves on small wagons pulled by teams of horses. They were unloaded, filled and re-loaded by hand.

Wagons were pulled to the sheds by teams until trucks began to make their appearance in the 1920's, carrying boxes back and forth between the groves and sheds. However, boxes were still distributed through the groves by teams and wagons. Wagons met the trucks at the end of the rows where fulls were transferred to trucks and empties transferred from trucks to wagons. In the latter part of the 1920's and early 1930's, harvesters began to eliminate this operation by taking the trucks directly into the groves. As one authority puts it, "The development of that technique follows pretty closely the development and improvement of trucks" (Higleman 1964). Also during this period the field box began to assume a variety of sizes and shapes with the introduction of new packing houses. However, all field boxes had one essential element in common — they were designed to be handled by hand, thus setting an absolute limit on the size. One field box was considered to be equivalent to two packed boxes. Later, with the advent of the carton, three field boxes were considered equivalent to four cartons.

Bulk methods, as the descriptions will illustrate, assume numerous versions. All have eliminated the field box. The picker dumps his sack of fruit directly into a large pallet box, a low-slung trailer, or onto a conveyor belt carrying it into a truck. Bulk methods of low-slung trailer and the belt and truck variety, both essentially for tree-ripened grapefruit, first made their appearance in Arizona in the mid-1940's (Higleman 1964). They were probably used even before 1940 where sheds were located in the midst of groves with no hauling distances, and when sweating or shed ripening of fruit was not needed. Pallet boxes came into use several years later. They represented an extension of the bulk principle to fruit needing shed ripening.

This provides background for harvesting operations selected for study. Inasmuch as almost all companies in our sample have played instrumental roles in the development of harvesting technologies, the history of harvesting operations from the 1940's on is documented by the sample companies themselves. Before the companies are described, additional background information is provided on the overall structure of the Arizona citrus industry existing during the 1962-63 season.

Maricopa and Yuma Counties account for all but a tiny fraction of the total citrus production in Arizona. Almost the entire citrus crop in the state is harvested by packing houses rather than by the growers. The non-grower packing houses — 17 in Maricopa County and four in Yuma — are divided into "commercial" packing houses and "cooperative" packing houses. Commercial houses are owned by an individual who packs on a custom basis at so much per box or on a contract basis for an entire grove. The owners of the groves have no say in the management of the shed or harvesting operation. Cooperative packing houses, on the other hand, are owned by grower members. Each owns a share in the enterprise and has a voice in the operations through his board of directors. They are administered by a salaried manager.

Harvesting systems for all citrus operations may be put in two general categories. In the standard field box system the boxes are handled in the groves manually. In a bulk system power equipment is needed to raise the picked fruit to a bin or truck or to raise and lower bins for pickers to put the fruit into. All bulk systems may be considered variations of four general types: bulk trucks with conveyor belts, bin or pallet boxes handled in the groves by forklifts, bins towed through the groves in especially designed trailers, and bins handled in the groves by trucks with special racks and tailgates to lower, raise, and revolve them. More detailed descriptions of these systems follow. The sample of six harvester-packers represents both commercial and cooperative harvester-packers, and all technical harvest systems. Acreages range from 792 acres to 5,284 acres. In Maricopa County the sample (four companies) accounted for 6,059 acres of a total producing citrus acreage of 12,721 (Hill and Hillman 1964) or 48 percent. In Yuma the sample (two companies) accounted for approximately 9,345 acres of a total of 10,008 producing acres (Hill and Hillman 1964) or approximately 93 percent.

The companies are discussed roughly in the same order as the chronological sequence of their developments. We begin with a description of a company whose operation is still basically the old field box and truck system.

A COMPANY—STANDARD FIELD BOX SYSTEM

A Company is a commercial packing house which harvested 1,413 acres of citrus on a consignment basis during the 1962-63 season. They had 880 acres in oranges, 395 acres in grapefruit, 43 in lemons, and 95 in tangerines. Their groves were scattered over a large area and ranged in size from 5 to 80 acres. Fairly large blocks of 20 to 40 acres were the rule, however.

Mechanical Harvesting and Handling Equipment

  4—1½-2-ton flat-bed trucks
  1—bus

> 1—ladder trailer
> 3—grove trailers
> 1—tractor used to get through the groves when trucks cannot
> 1—field power conveyor belt
> 11,000—field boxes
> —and enough bags (standard field box size), ladders, clippers, and sizing rings to provide for as many as 100 pickers

Organizational Structure of Harvest Activities

During the 1962-63 season A Company used domestic workers only. They had two crews picking. The main crew was made up of 25 to 32 men hired directly by the company. The supplementary crew ranged from 12 to 18 pickers. These two crews differed radically in their composition and formal articulation with the company. The larger crew was made up almost entirely of older single Anglo males (between 50 and 65) most of whom referred to themselves as "fruit tramps." We refer to them as "Anglo-isolates." Their foreman was also an experienced fruit picker and an Anglo-isolate; although he was younger than most of his pickers. The foreman's chief duties are to pick up his crew each morning in the company bus at an informal gathering spot in the south part of the city, to supervise them in the field, and to maintain his crew at working size by keeping posted of their whereabouts when they are not working. He also attends to their needs for small loans between pay periods. Most of his duties are carried out informally. These duties will be analyzed later as part of a general pattern.

The second crew was composed almost totally of Mexican-American families from Texas, many of whom could not speak English. Their foremen were a father-and-son team, also Mexican-Americans from Texas. Most of the crew had recently settled down in a predominately Mexican-American community, a fringe settlement of a larger Arizona town. The role of this foreman, in addition to keeping his crew up to size and supervising them in the field, differs from the role of the Anglo foreman since he and his father also owned and supervised a hauling operation for A Company.

Briefly the field operations are structured as follows. The general manager for the company is in charge of all operations. Directly under him is a salaried field superintendent. He sees to the over-all operation of the harvest activities. This includes giving directions to pickers and directing the drivers, swamper (loader), and second swampers. Some of his other duties are to recommend fertilizers to growers, estimate the number of boxes of fruit by size and grade, set up drives, clear ahead for pick, and tell the plant foreman and the crews when the grove will be ready. Crew foremen answer to both the field superintendent and the general manager, whoever is more convenient.

Drivers, in addition to duties detailed in the description of operations below, have responsibility for the care of their vehicles as well as the proper handling of the fruit. The first and second swampers' and pickers' duties are discussed in the description of operations.

Wage System

P, foreman of the small crew, gets 8 cents a box on all fruit that his trucks haul from the groves. Out of this he pays two loaders and one driver each 1 cent and 1½ cents a box, respectively. With the 4½ cents a box remaining after paying swampers and driver, P and his father average about $60 per day for their hauling operation. Out of this they pay for and maintain their two $7,000 GMC trucks.

P gets an additional 2 cents a box for his responsibilities as foreman. This nets him about $24 a day with which he has to purchase, operate, and maintain a bus as well as supervise and recruit pickers.

In citrus P calculated about the amount his workers would make at 1,200 boxes a day. His driver would make $18 and swampers $12. If his 20 pickers each averaged about 60 boxes of oranges in good picking at the A Company rate of 16 cents a box, they would earn about $9.60 for a seven-hour day. Of course some pickers would pick less and others would average more. Under conditions of bad weather, scattered small groves, or low-yield trees earnings would be much less.

For its "regular crew," A Company has what its manager refers to as "adjustable pay rates" for pickers. The rate depends upon the condition of the grove, size of the trees, amount of desired fruit on the tree, and frequencies of movement from one field to another. The going market price of fruit is also a determining factor.

Generally the rate paid pickers per field box (50 to 60 lbs.) of fruit is as follows:

Oranges	17 cents
Lemons	75 cents ring picking (just a certain size)
	50 cents strip picking (all fruit on tree)
Grapefruit	15 cents ring picking
	10 cents strip picking
Tangerines	75 cents color picking

The regular foreman gets 2 cents for each box produced by his crew for supervision in grapefruit and oranges and 5 cents a box for supervision in lemons and tangerines. Drivers are paid 2½ cents for each box they handle in regular picking. The first swamper, the man who helps the driver set up boxes on the truck, gets 1 cent for each box loaded. The second swamper picks up surplus boxes in the groves and helps load at the grove location. He gets paid $12 a day.

Production rates collectively and individually were extremely variable from one day to the next due to factors which varied enormously: size of trees, size of the fruit, yield per tree, whether the grove had trees to be picked mixed with a variety not yet ready, how many times a crew had to move from one grove to another, how far apart the groves were, the condition of the weather, the worker himself, to name a few. The problem of control of these variables was so important that research designed especially for this would be necessary before these production data would be meaningful. The foreman's estimates of picker averages were as follows: 14 boxes per hour per man for grapefruit strip-picking and from 6 to 8 boxes per hour for strip-picking of oranges. Our observations during orange harvest indicated these estimates were a little high for most pickers on these particular crews.

Although pickers are not paid for time lost in moving from grove to grove, A Company has two systems which work to the advantage of the picker. They use a special cleanup crew for tiny groves or tag ends, thus reducing moving time loss. Second, they have field men tag target trees in groves that have mixed, easy-to-confuse varieties, e.g. Valencias and Sweets.

Description of Operations

At the plant the driver and first swamper spend about 30 minutes loading and securing 340 empty field boxes on 2-ton flat-bed trucks. Six boxes at a time are hand-carted onto a truck from the loading dock. Precautions are taken to get boxes loaded in good shape so that none will be lost in transit to the grove. After securing two cables to hold the load in place, the driver and first swamper depart for the grove. Upon arrival at the grove, the truck is driven down between two rows and the first swamper distributes the boxes on either side of the truck. From 13 to 20 boxes (depending on anticipated yield) are dropped off at each stop on either side of the truck. When all the empty boxes are distributed, the truck is ready to be loaded with full boxes.

The crew foreman transports some of the workers and all equipment to the grove. Many of the pickers drive their own vehicles to the grove since some of the female pickers bring along small children. The pickers go about picking the fruit without much direction from the foreman. He selects a tree, places a ladder against the branches of the tree, and with a canvas bag, large enough to hold a box of fruit, hung diagonally across his chest and shoulders, climbs to the top of the ladder, picking the fruit of the size and color desired and dropping them in the bag. When the bag is full, and often before the bag is full, the worker descends the ladder and, unhooking a latch at the bottom of the bag, drops the fruit into a field box.

With the field box method, the worker need not concern himself about a full bag because he is paid by the box rather than the bag. This is to his advantage since he can pick all the fruit within reach of one placement of the ladder and does not have to climb to the top of the ladder on the next placement with a heavy, partially filled bag.

The worker must stay with one tree until it is completely picked. Frequently husband-wife teams will pick together as a unit, which allows the woman to stay on the ground and leaves the climbing to the husband. A worker or worker team will stack several to a dozen field boxes in one central position and leave his slip of paper on this stack of boxes before moving to another part of the grove.

The foreman spends most of his time filling partially empty boxes and tallying the number of boxes per picker. He also checks to see that each picker's tree has been picked clean before the picker moves on. The pickers often do not fill their boxes full enough so the foreman fills those boxes which are not full and records the number of filled boxes. A particular picker's boxes are all located at one truck drop so the foreman just uses one of the partially filled boxes to fill up other boxes at this point. This operation consumes a large portion of the foreman's time.

In loading the full boxes on the truck to be hauled to the plant, the truck driver puts the boxes on the truck bed and the first swamper stacks them. If the foreman does not have the boxes checked, then both the driver and swamper assist him. If many boxes have to be filled and checked before they can be loaded, it takes from one to two hours to load the truck with 252 field boxes (oranges only) and to secure them. If all boxes are checked ahead of the loading operation, then the actual loading operation takes the driver and helper about a half hour. Average travel time is from 25 to 35 minutes from grove to plant.

When the fruit arrives at the packing plant, the driver and helper unload with hand trucks. Six field boxes are handled at a time and are wheeled into the sweat room. Usually a third man, employed at the plant, also helps unload. When three men unload the fruit, the operation consumes about 15 minutes.

Experience Account

According to B, the manager, the field box system is better because the workers are happier and production is better. B said that A Company gets the best pickers because they are using the old field box method. He said that he is considering some sort of bin system, but his workers would have to be compensated for the fact that picking in bins cuts their production.

B also insists that growers are resentful of bulk systems because they like to know per-tree averages and can see them with the field box methods. Moreover tractor hauling, needed for some bulk systems from one grove to another on small scattered groves, is too expensive.

Still, B says if he had close hauls he would go to bulk in a minute. He considers the ideal system one in which the shed is close to the groves and pallet boxes on two-wheeled trailers are used. He also has the feeling that if they ever renovate their plant from the ground up they might go to some kind of bulk system. Evidently his apparent favoritism for the field box method may involve some rationalization because that is the system A Company is presently using.

B COMPANY
BULK-TRUCK AND BIN-TRAILER SYSTEM

B Company is a harvesting and packing cooperative. During the 1962-63 season they had 5,284 acres of producing citrus and 135 members. Its nine-member board has a president and vice president and a salaried general manager who is hired annually. H, the present manager, has been with the co-op since 1944.

B Company's 5,284 acres were made up roughly of 1,068 acres of grapefruit, 1,980 acres of oranges, 2,124 acres of lemons, and 112 acres of tangerines. Most of their groves are concentrated in large blocks only moderate distances from the plant — 10 to 15 miles. Most of their groves are young, especially their lemons. In 1959-60 their lemon harvest increased from 25,000 boxes for the previous season to 210,000 boxes.

The company uses two variations of the bulk method — bulk trucks with portable power conveyor belts to carry the fruit dumped from pickers' sacks over the rear panels and the bin-trailer system involving the use of pallet boxes on two-wheeled trailers which are towed through the groves. The bulk trucks are used for all their grapefruit harvesting. During sweating (fruit ripened in storage) season the bulk trucks simply transfer the green fruit to pallet boxes at the plant. The bin-trailer system is used for the orange and lemon harvests.

Mechanical Harvesting and Handling Equipment

    11 — 1½-2-ton bulk trucks
     5 — power lifts (conveyor)
     2 — fork lifts
    24 — especially constructed two-wheel trailers to carry four pallet boxes or bins arranged two by two, and with two tier steps on each side whereby pickers reach the bins and which fold up for highway travel
     8 — pickup trucks to pull the above trailers on the road
     8 — tractors to pull the above trailers through the groves
2,000 — bins or pallet boxes which have a capacity of 25 standard field boxes
     3 — reconditioned school buses
       — and enough ladders, picking bags, sizing rings, clippers, canvas sleeves (to protect pickers' arms from thorn injuries and infections), gloves, and water cans to provide for as many as 500 pickers

Organizational Structure of Harvest Activities

During the 1962-63 season B Company relied heavily upon Mexican Nationals. Generally they did not have enough domestic workers to make more than one crew. Although their policy is to assign domestics to the same crew, sometimes it was necessary to complement this crew with Nationals. The domestic workers they had were placed through the Farm Labor Office "involuntary day haul" (IDH) system, requiring employers who use Nationals to use available domestic workers first. These men are referred to by management as "farm office boys."

The size of crews, depending upon harvesting needs, ranges from 10 to 30 men each. During November, the peak of the season, the manager says they run between 25 to 30 men each. All crews work directly under company personnel and are paid and supervised through a standard system. Of the 19 domestics interviewed, one was a Mexican-American foreman. The remaining 18 were Anglo-isolates.

The company has four permanent foremen, three of whom are Mexican-Americans. One foreman has been with the company six years, another 15 years, and the third 20 years. The other permanent foreman is a Negro who has been with the company 20 years. The company elevates other workers to foremen as the numbers of crews increase in the season. Among these are three Negro foremen and one Filipino. The foremen's duties will be spelled out in the description of operations.

Directly over the foremen are the field superintendents. B Company has two — one for grapefruit harvest, the other for orange-lemon harvest. They are concerned mainly with the mechanics of picking — tentative picking schedules, fields being ready, equipment being ready, drivers getting to areas properly and rapidly enough, the allotment of paraphernalia to crews, buses, meals, etc. Each superintendent may have as many as 12 to 14 crews in his particular crop. The field superintendents are not ordinarily involved in which groves are picked and when except as ground conditions are concerned.

Directly over the field superintendents is the general manager who deals with the growers and determines the size, variety, grade, and quantity of fruit to be picked as well as which grove is to be picked. Also under the general manager are the superintendent of the grapefruit processing plant, the superintendent of the lemon-orange processing plant, and the superintendent of the cannery.

B Company has a special position of general assistant manager for the son of the general manager. He assists the manager in all administrative activities, especially in the field operations. M speaks fluent Spanish which enables him to function effectively in dealing with their Mexican-American foremen and Mexican National pickers. There is some degree of tension inherent in this structural feature as there is an inevitable flow of information from the top of the administrative pyramid to the bottom (pickers) which bypasses the field superintendents.

B Company requires no swampers (helpers on trucks) since they do not use the standard field box for any of their harvest operations. All truck drivers answer directly to the relevant field superintendent. Their duties are confined specifically to the care and fueling of their vehicles and their operation between the groves and plant.

Wage System

B Company pays its pickers by weight rather than by volume (field box). Actually it has eliminated the field box entirely as any form of measure, even for marketing. As H, the general manager puts it, "It eliminates boondoggling because buyers pay by the weight, so why shouldn't growers and pickers be paid by weight rather than volume? Figures won't lie, but liars will figure!"

The total tonnage for the crew for the day is recorded at the scales at the plant. At the end of the pay period each crew has a total weight and a total earnings figure. The individual picker is reimbursed according to the number of full sacks of fruit that he has contributed to this total weight for his crew. A counting board is kept mounted on the side of the trailer. There is one counter on the board for each individual picker. Each time he dumps a sack into the bin he punches a counter and a buzzer sounds. The sacks are simply a unit of standard measure whereby the pickers can divide up the tonnage total. Full sacks are expected and are enforced by foremen and the pickers themselves.

It is interesting to note that when B Company first switched over to bulk, they reimbursed the crews simply by dividing the crew total by the number of men in the crew. This worked well and still works for the Mexican Nationals, but for domestic workers the counter system became necessary. Another complication is the Adverse Effect ruling of the Department of Labor governing the use of Nationals. This requires growers or companies using Nationals to pay a 95-cent hourly "adverse effect wage" to their braceros (Nationals) as well as to all domestics working in the same crop activity. If an individual's production amounts to an hourly figure less than 95 cents, regardless of the method of paying workers, then that worker gets the 95 cents an hour for the day or days that his piece rate production was low. In some picking, production is inevitably lower than that necessary for the workers to earn the hourly minimum through piece rates. Then the counting of each individual's sacks is a secondary matter, whether they are domestic or National.

Rates are as follows:

Variety	How Picked	Tonnage Rate	Estimated No. Field Boxes Per Ton	Field Box Rate (in cents)	Remarks
Oranges	strip picking	$ 4.00	40	10	
Grapefruit	strip picking	3.75	50	7½	No counters used
Lemons	strip picking	8.25	33	25	
Lemons	strip clipping*	9.90	33	30	
Lemons	size clipping	11.55	33	35	

*Using clippers

The field box rate is a function of the number of field boxes per ton. Other estimates of boxes per ton run as low as 36 and 44 boxes for oranges and grapefruit, respectively, and as high as 37 boxes for lemons. These would imply field box rates of 11 cents and 8.5 cents for oranges and grapefruit, respectively, and rates of 23 cents, 25.5 cents and 32 cents for the three types of lemons.

Average daily output per worker again could not be determined. We made one random observation of a 13-man crew of domestic workers requiring two hours and 20 minutes to fill four bins (100 field boxes). We esti- mated a total of approximately 30 man-hours for this operation. The field box rate of 10 cents would earn them $10 (not considering the adverse effect wage), or approximately 34 cents per man-hour. Another nine-man crew, again domestic workers, required three-and-a-half hours for the same opera- tion. Again the total man-hours were about 30 and the per man hour earning the same. These observations were made in a very dense and very old grove with high, hard-to-reach tops.

Picking cost data from this company's annual report showed that actual picking costs were over twice the quoted piece rate costs. Therefore, the adverse effect wage must have been in effect most of the time.

Pickers are not paid for time lost in moving from one grove to another in the middle of the day. This applies to the guaranteed wage. When the company computes the production of the crew against the number of hours they pick to see whether the piece rate or minimum wage applies, time lost in moving is not considered. Drivers and foremen are paid $1.25 an hour. Drivers have no time docked for lunch but foremen are docked 30 minutes.

Description of Operations

The driver of a ½- or ¾-ton pickup truck leaves the packing house pulling an especially constructed two-wheeled trailer which accommodates four empty bins with a total capacity of 100 field boxes. At the grove the trailer is unhitched from the truck and hitched to a field tractor operated by the crew foreman, to be pulled through the grove during the picking and loading operation. One-way travel time from packing house to grove varies from 5 to 25 minutes. Fifteen minutes is about average.

The foreman pulls the trailer into the grove between the third and fourth rows so that three rows on either side of the trailer are picked simultaneously. The foreman's main responsibilities are to move the tractor and trailer to facilitate the picking operation and to see that trees are picked clean. These two responsibilities do not keep the foremen fully employed. The only other function performed by the foreman is to record the totals from the pickers' counters for each picker each day. When three of the four bins are filled, the foreman locates the trailer strategically and unhooks from the trailer. He then goes to the roadside and picks up another empty trailer which the truck driver has delivered following the initial trailer delivery. He locates it in the grove so that as soon as the first trailer is loaded the pickers can dump into the second trailer. He unhooks from this second trailer and rehooks to the first trailer. The loaded trailer is then ready to be pulled to the roadside and picked up by the truck driver for delivery to the packing house. Before the loaded trailer is pulled from the grove, the counter board (the board holding an individual counter for each picker and its electrical supply) is transferred from the first to the second trailer. This transfer is usually done by one of the pickers. After moving the loaded trailer to the roadside, the foreman then hooks on to the second trailer he already had located in the grove and the process is repeated in accordance to needs and time.

The picking crew is transported to the grove by means of a school bus operated by the foreman. Ladders are taken to the grove on the bin trailers by the truck driver. Pickers operate basically as they do in any citrus picking operation with one exception. In this system they do not dump their full sacks into their own individual field boxes, but into one of four bins mounted on a two-wheeled trailer instead. To do this they must step up two steps on an especially constructed steel stair. All pickers dump into the same bins. The individual workers do not work on sets (a number of contiguous trees) or trees assigned to them. Trees vary in quantity and quality; hence in B Company's operation, as many men as desire can work a tree and share or switch off in picking on the ground and climbing the ladders. This cooperative method eliminates the carrying of near-full sacks up ladders.

At the packing house empty bins are placed on trailers by a towmotor. The bins are loaded from the trailer rear and as another bin is loaded, the previously loaded one is pushed forward. This operation consumes three to five minutes. This especially built trailer has three series of rollers incorporated in the trailer bottom to facilitate loading and unloading bins. As a bin is unloaded, the driver is able to push the next loaded bin back into unloading position. The unloading operation consumes about five minutes.

Experience Account

H, B Company's general manager, gave the following account of the development of their system:

> It's always hard to walk up to a Board of Directors and say 'let's throw away 30,000 field boxes.' The fire answered that (the fire at Christmas 1944 which burned down the Company plant in Yuma). When we began to rebuild, we used this opportunity to begin shifting to a new system. At first we built a conveyor to handle bulk in the field—one which would convey the fruit dumped at its base to the top of a truck. The first ones were too small and finally we ended up with one which takes two men to handle. We wanted bulk because it was difficult to get anyone to handle field boxes — swampers and drivers. Also upkeep on field boxes in the desert region of Yuma was phenomenal. Time needed in setting up for picking and clearing the fields after the pickers went home amounted to sometimes as much as two hours before picking and three hours after picking. Now they start the same time the crew does and come in at least 30 minutes after the crew finishes picking. The first year alone we pointed our finger at $30,000 in savings — labor, trucks, and box repairs.
>
> After the fire we had enough boxes to finish the season but the fire had also eliminated the box handling machinery. The first season (fall of 1945) we installed temporary bulk handling conveyor equipment. This equipment was adequate until toward the latter part of the fifties when our lemon crops and sweet oranges began to be harvested in great amounts.

We favored a bin system but at first started with what few field boxes we had left. During 1957-58 and 1958-59 we packed 25,000 boxes or so of lemons. During 1959-60 our increase in lemons was from 25,000 to 210,000 boxes and, consequently, we had a great incentive to begin considering some bulk system for lemons. The problem in lemons is bruising the fruit, but still they can handle them much rougher than the industry thought they could years before this. I won't say you *can't* do anything! The old-timers would turn over in their graves if they could see the way we handle lemons today! They used to handle them entirely in trays and if you dropped one you'd had it.

We considered flat trucks with bins or bin-to-a-man system as well as little bulk trailers. Packing house men came to us with ideas. At about that time a competitor started the fork-lift bin-to-a-man system. I didn't like this because I had seen it on grapefruit and it involved too many trips through the field, and too many trips cause compaction. I have seen it where the grower needed to plow after this. We knew that Central California growers had bins on wheels with many variations, and we went to see _____(C Company's) version of this. After much consideration we finally picked the bin-trailer system because there is less compaction, the fork-lift tractor for bin-to-a-man system is too expensive, supervision is much less with the bin on a trailer system because the pickers stay localized around the trailer, and the trailer system is a lot easier on bins. They are never set off in the fields. We have three trailers for each crew and each trailer has four bins.

The first season — 1959-60 — that we began the bin-trailer system, we used field boxes side-by-side with the bin system about a month or two. We wanted to check the sweating and decay problems — my mind was made up practically, but I wanted to test this. The proof was evident in a few months. So we switched over entirely to bins. The only modifications were counters installed in 1960-61 whereby each picker could tabulate his sacks, and the trailer and steps were strengthened for a more sure footing for the pickers.

(In response to the query on worker response to their new system) — The first season in using the bulk truck method many of the old fruit pickers quit and went to another outfit using the old field boxes, but they began to compare pay checks and after a couple of pay days began drifting back — actually it's easier to pick bulk.

C COMPANY
BULK-TRAILER AND BIN-TRAILER SYSTEM

C Company's bin-trailer system is essentially a variation of that used by B Company. For tree-ripened grapefruit, however, C Company uses bulk trailers rather than bulk trucks. C's bulk trailers operate on exactly the same principle as their bin trailers. Both are mounted on the same chassis. The only difference is that a platform is mounted on the chassis to accommodate three bins for the bin system and a padded bed is mounted on the chassis for the other. Also, the bins or pallet boxes must be removed at the plant with a fork lift whereas the padded bed is simply tilted in dump truck fashion to allow the grapefruit to pour over the side.

C Company is a cooperative organization. During the 1962-63 season it had 57 member-growers and approximately 1,092 acres of bearing citrus— 796 in oranges, 245 in grapefruit, 40 in lemons, and 11 in tangerines. Its plant is centrally located. Most groves are within a 20-mile radius. Their groves tend to be large and concentrated with very old trees.

Mechanical Harvesting and Handling Equipment

  36 — bin trailers, narrow and especially designed to carry three pallet boxes close to ground
1,000 — bins or pallet boxes, 24 field box capacity, 25" x 58" x 45"
  36 — bulk trailers (same chassis as bin trailer)
   6 — trucks, 1½-ton, especially equipped to tow trailers on highway
   5 — tractors, small, to tow trailers through groves
   6 — used school buses to carry crews from plant to groves
   6 — ladder trailers which are towed behind buses on way to groves
   2 — fork lifts used at plant to unload bins from trailers
     — sufficient ladders (aluminum), clippers, rings, and picking bags to supply up to six crews of 16-20 men at peak season
Note: C Company's picking bags are slightly more than one-half field box capacity rather than one, as some companies use.

Organizational Structure of Harvest Activities

In peak season, November-December, C Company employed six crews of from 16 to 20 pickers each. At peak employment only about one-third of their labor demand was met by braceros — two crews. C Company keeps one Mexican-American foreman primarily to handle braceros. Shortly after peak activities, at the time observations were made, C Company had three crews operating at capacity — all of them domestic.

Of the 50 employees interviewed, all except nine were Anglos. They averaged about 40 years of age, with 14 above 50. The average education of the group was above 8th grade with 28 of the 50 workers having 8th grade diplomas. Eight of the 50 were drivers and 42 were pickers. Exactly half of the pickers interviewed were Anglo-isolates. The other half were living in family units. Of the eight drivers and foremen, six were Anglo and only two were Mexican-American.

C Company's harvest activities were headed by a field superintendent whose biographic profile shares basic features with the rank and file of their more steady workers. He was born on a sharecropper farm in Arkansas. His family sold out in the 1930's and he came to Arizona and worked as a fruit picker from 1935 to 1938 — the last two of these seasons for C Company itself. In 1939 he went on as driver for C, their only driver for two crews. In 1942 he took over as field foreman and is now functioning in a key role in the field operations. He has a face-to-face relationship with all except the most itinerant of their employees as well as with the grower-members of the co-op.

H's duties begin at the plant in the morning as foremen load their pickers on buses and as truckers get their equipment ready. He makes minor adjustments in the crews, attempting to keep them constant in size and membership. He gives grove directions to drivers, generally keeping them with the same crews throughout the season. During the day H will make first hand observations of each crew's operations at least once, and usually twice. At the same time he will exchange information with growers and their foremen on such things as fertilizers, freezing protection, quality, yield of their fruit, and the timing of harvest activities with non-harvest activities. In the evenings H meets his foremen and crews at the plant and collects their time and production sheets. These are the records of the hours and number of field boxes each worker has accounted for. He advises crew foremen of the groves they are to pick the following day.

Drivers and foremen perform roles quite similar in nature to those peculiar to the citrus industry as a whole. (See Description of Operations.) C Cooperative generally picks their drivers and foremen from their most dependable pickers. If the worker force drops down so that there are too many drivers and foremen, they go back to picking. Those drivers and foremen having the least longevity in their positions are put back first and so on.

C Company has a "checker" whose duties are described in operations. Directly above the field superintendent is the general manager. Under the latter is a position parallel to the field superintendent — that of plant superintendent.

Wage System

C Co-op has an adjustable pay scale as follows:

Oranges	15-18 cents a field box
Grapefruit	9-12 cents a field box
Lemons and tangerines	45-60 cents a field box

Factors which establish the pay rate are these: (1) size of the tree—bigger trees are more difficult and thus give the workers a higher pay rate, (2) amount of fruit on the tree, and (3) whether or not the fruit is concentrated or scattered. Judgments are made by the field superintendent. When the company uses braceros, the adverse effect wage of a 95 cents minimum per hour applies.

Pickers' productions are recorded by a checker who records each bag that a picker dumps into the bin. C Company requires pickers to use specially sized bags — just over one-half field box — because, according to management, "It makes it easier for the surplus and shortage adjustments which will show up in the bin system." This way there is always an overage, i.e., when a tandem trailer unit which has a capacity of 144 field boxes is filled, the tally sheets for the crew will show something like 120 boxes. The overage, 24 boxes, is then distributed equally among the pickers. Also they do not use full field box bags because the one-half box bags are more convenient for the pickers and they do not bruise the fruit as much.

C Company offers certain advantages to workers in terms of more concentrated groves which, in combination with their system of a special tag-ends crew, means a minimum loss of time to pickers. This advantage was partly diminished by the fact that their groves tended to be very old with large trees, thus requiring a lot of ladder work and walking to get to the bins.

In addition to their regular pay system, C Company has what is called a bonus system. The worker gets 2 cents a box for every box of oranges and 1 cent for every box of grapefruit that he has picked throughout the entire season—provided he remains throughout the season (around the middle of February to the beginning of July). Allowances are made for sickness and emergencies. The worker gets the bonus figure from the day that he starts, regardless of when he starts, and receives it in the last check.

Checkers receive $1.10 an hour. Drivers are paid $1.30 an hour from the time they start their trucks in the morning to the time their equipment has been serviced and parked late in the evening. They are paid through their lunch hours. Foremen receive $14 per day flat rate. On fractions of days foremen receive half pay for half-days or less and full pay for over half-days.

Description of Operations

The truck driver leaves the plant pulling two especially constructed trailers which accommodate three bins each. The truck is especially constructed so that the front wheels of the forward trailer are carried on special racks on the truck. Individual bin capacity is 24 field boxes. The combined capacity of two trailers is 144 field boxes. On arrival at the grove, the trailers are unhooked from the truck and hooked onto a farm tractor. This tractor pulls the trailers and bins through the grove for the harvesting process. The foreman transports the workers and equipment to the grove in a company-owned school bus pulling a ladder trailer behind. All equipment is owned by the Company. If there are no filled trailers to go back to the plant, the truck goes back empty to bring two more trailers to the grove. The tractor which pulls the trailers is operated by the crew foreman. He moves and locates them in accordance with the pickers' need. The checker sits on one of the trailers and tallies the number of bags picked by each picker. When a picker finishes picking a tree, he calls for a check by the crew foreman. He does not move to another tree until the foreman approves. The foreman assigns a definite tree to each picker and when the tree has been picked clean he assigns another tree to the picker. The foreman and the checker pick out and discard foreign material and bad fruit as it is dumped into the bins. The foreman's responsibility seems to be broader and more definite than under other systems of harvesting.

When the six bins are full, the trailers are pulled to roadside and left there to be picked up by truck for the haul to the plant. The tractor then hooks onto two more empty trailers and the above process is repeated.

The average time for hauling is 30 minutes from grove to plant. At the plant, one towmotor or forklift unloads the full bins and stores them in the sweat room while, at the same time, the truck driver is loading empty bins on the trailers with a second towmotor. This unloading and loading process takes from seven to eight minutes.

The operation for tree-ripened grapefruit or juice fruit is identical (when the trailer chassis have the padded bulk beds mounted on them instead of the platform for the bins) except for the plant phase discussed earlier.

Experience Account (field superintendent)

We started a bulk trailer system in Chandler Heights in 1946. Although at this time growers hadn't considered any particular need for using the bulk system in general in their other areas, we started using it in Chandler Heights because of the short distances involved. We thought that it would bruise the fruit. It was in using bulk trailers in the Chandler area that we found we could use them on the long haul. In fact, we found that this system bruised the fruit less than using the field boxes.

At Chandler Heights we also worked out the dumping technique necessary for bulk handling. In 1948 Chandler Heights formed its own independent co-op and we started building bulk trailers for use in long haul in Mesa. We also started changing over the house systems for the use of bulk trailers. (J, the plant superintendent, designed them and as far as H knows their co-op was the first to use bulk systems in citrus anywhere.)

Some of the advantages of the bulk system are:

1. One driver can haul as much fruit as two drivers and a swamper using the field box system.

2. At the plant one man receives and feeds whereas in the old system of using field boxes, three or four receivers, two feeders, as well as two men in the yard stacking empty boxes were needed.

3. So far as bruising was concerned, our padded bulk trailers eliminated squashed fruit.

4. The bulk trailers require very little repair. Every year we needed up to six men for one month to as long as six weeks repairing field boxes.

Still in the late forties and early fifties we used field boxes for green fruit, and bulk trailers were used only for fruit that was ripe on the trees.

In '45 and '46 we tried an elevator system for the 1½-ton truck (a type of bulk system), but it didn't prove satisfactory because there was too much bruising.

In 1957 or a little before, it was becoming apparent that our field box system, still in use for green fruit, was becoming sadly obsolete. We were faced with the problem of modernizing our plant facilities for the field boxes or shifting our system completely for a type of pallet box. The thinking was that if we had to go to the expense of modernizing our field boxes we might as well be done with it and change our plant over for the bin system entirely.

Maybe modernizing for field boxes would have been less expensive than changing to the bin system but other reasons pressed. We were finding the big trees in the groves were being damaged by the flat bed trucks necessary for the hauling of the field boxes. By this time we had been using a bulk trailer for ten years. We had ten years' experience in seeing fruit being damaged more with field boxes than with a bulk system. Also the switch-over problem necessary every year on our trucks, that is changing from handling the field boxes to pulling the bulk trailers, was quite an expense.

In 1957 J (plant superintendent) and I went to Porterville, California, to observe the pallet box system at a well-known packing house there. When we got back J began designing a little different type of basket for use on the same kind of trailer chassis that we were already using for the bulk trailers. We used a standard basket or bin which is ordered in parts and assembled at the plant.

(Asked about pickers' reactions) — The pickers didn't like the bulk trailers at first and started leaving to go where field boxes were still being used. I would say we lost 50 percent of our old pickers. The new pickers worked in all right. We started the sack counting system as soon as we switched to bulk and it was this aspect of this system which the old-time pickers objected to. We would like to do away with the checker and have a communal system of total boxes divided at the end of the day by the number of pickers, but we can't get a crew of pickers even enough. We have discussed this with the pickers. The slow pickers go for it, but the fast pickers don't want any part of it.

(Asked about whether or not C Company has a policy of discussing any of these changes with their workers) — The company just took the item into the field and told the workers what to do. We told the foreman beforehand, but we just took the trailers out with a checker and started. Other than the grapevine, they didn't know of it.

D COMPANY — BIN-FORKLIFT SYSTEM

The forklift method, described more fully in the operations section, solves field box problems by hauling big pallet boxes on 2-ton flat bed trucks to the groves, unloading them at the groves, and positioning them throughout the groves with a forklift tractor.

D Company, like A Company, is a commercial house harvesting, packing, and shipping fruit on a consignment basis. During 1962-63 they had 4,061 acres of citrus with approximately 1,301 acres of oranges, 291 acres of grapefruit, 2,453 acres of lemons, and 16 acres of tangerines. Most of their groves are in large concentrated plots within 10 to 15 miles of the plant. Most of their groves are young, and newly producing.

Mechanical Harvesting and Handling Equipment

12 — 2-ton flat bed trucks to carry bins from shed to groves — 12-bin capacity

2 — flat bed transport trailers to pull behind trucks during rush season — 12-bin capacity

2,600 — bins or pallet boxes — 25 field box capacity

7 — forklift tractors used to transport bins in the groves

2 — towmotors used at plant to load, unload, and transport bins

10 — crew trucks or buses

6 — ladder trailers

— sufficient ladders, sizing rings, clippers, bags, gloves, and canvas sleeves to supply 350 pickers in peak season

Organizational Structure of Harvest Activities

D Company's harvest operation was all but shut down during the period of observation due to damages from freezing weather. They had one crew operating at the time with only three domestic pickers — Anglos. Ordinarily during their peak season, November, they will employ as many as ten 35-man crews — all braceros. According to management, they seldom get over 25 domestic pickers.

The crew operating during the time of our observations was composed primarily of Mexican Nationals. The company had Mexican-American drivers, one of whom was schooled in Mexico, and a Mexican-American foreman, who could not speak English. The field superintendent was a bilingual Arizona-born Mexican-American. This ethnic structure in combination with 350 Mexican Nationals at peak season (90 percent of their picking force) makes the D Company harvest organization essentially Mexican.

The duties of the personnel are standard. D Company has forklift drivers instead of swampers. Their functions will be detailed in the operations section. D Company does not use checkers. Bins are assigned to a specific picker or a pair of pickers.

Directly above the field superintendent is the general manager. Parallel to the field superintendent, in a different administrative line, is the plant superintendent.

Wage System

Rates are as follows:

	How Picked	Tonnage Rate	Estimated No. Field Boxes	Field Box Rate (in cents)
Oranges	strip picking	$ 4.50	40	11
Grapefruit	strip picking	3.75	50	7½
Lemons	strip picking	8.25	33	25
Lemons	strip clipping	9.90	33	30
Lemons	ring clipping	11.55	33	35

Drivers, forklift operator, and foreman get $1.35 an hour.

Description of Operations

A 2-ton platform truck with 12 empty bins (total capacity 300 field boxes) is driven from the plant to the grove by the truck driver. Bins are stacked two high, two wide, and three long by a towmotor prior to departure from the packing house. This takes five to eight minutes. When the driver arrives at the grove he leaves the truck at the roadside and returns to the packing house, either in a truck already at the grove or with the supervisor. He takes the second truck as described and returns to the same grove. Thus one truck driver has two trucks assigned him. While he is hauling a load to the plant on one truck, the other is being loaded at the grove. One-way travel times average from 20 to 25 minutes or from 40 to 50 minutes for the round trip.

Empty bins from the transport truck are unloaded at the grove roadside and distributed throughout the grove by two forklift tractors — two to each picking crew. The forklifts provide three services, (1) they unload empty bins from the truck, (2) they distribute the bins in the grove, and (3) they gather and load the filled boxes on the waiting truck. One forklift is operated by a person hired solely for this purpose but the second forklift is operated by the crew foreman.

Bins are identified by the picker's name or number, or both, recorded at the receiving dock of the packing house. If two pickers wish to share a bin, each gets credit for one-half bin.

Supervision is somewhat closer than was observed at B Company located in the same area. Each picker is responsible for a specific tree and does not move to another until foreman approves. The crew foreman is kept busy checking trees and operating the second forklift. The operator of the first forklift is not fully employed. He serves no other function except to move field trucks during the loading and unloading operations.

The picking crew is transported to the grove by means of a crew truck, a converted field truck not considered capable of field work any longer. Ladders, bags, water cans, and all necessary picker equipment are transported to the grove by this means. The crew foreman usually operates the crew truck.

Experience Account

W, the General Manager of D Company, had this to say about their harvest system:

> It's the only thing that would do the job in our particular groves. It prevents serious damage from trucks in the groves, it provides bigger pay loads, and much less cost in terms of box repair and replacement, swampers, box-handling time in the house, storing, and automatic dumping.
> This is the first packing house in the industry designed solely and completely as a bulk operation. We started plans in February 1947. In fact, we had to build our own dump for a bulk box.

There was none made. I had to fight the company to make the capital expenditures for this operation. People in the industry were aware of these innovations only to a point at this time. Now a lot of people would like to go bulk, but the conversion costs would be prohibitive. Now all these innovations are accepted. We have three automatic dumps and have no problem getting any expenditure for_____(D Company). Our company is building another plant in Florida and is taking all data from us. Our company considers this a better or the best operation.

(W objects to the bulk truck and conveyor belt system for grapefruit because of fruit damage in the bottom layers. He also objects to the revolving bin system of F Company because of tree damage. As for the bin trailer system of C Company, W objects for only one reason — low hauling capacity) — There is one advantage to the trailer bin system that I like very much. There is no damage to the bin. We'll just have to go along and see which is best — but God Almighty, if I went to a trailer operation with 2 million boxes of lemons, Jesus God Almighty, I'd have this country run over with trailers!

E COMPANY — BIN-FORKLIFT SYSTEM

E Company in the 1962-63 season had 792 acres of citrus, a little over half of which the company owned. The rest it harvested, packed, and shipped on a cost-plus basis. Almost all of its acreage was in grapefruit, 638 acres, with only 143 acres in oranges, and 11 in tangerines. Most of its groves were concentrated in large blocks, but they were located on the average from 25 to 30 miles from the plant.

Their mechanical system resembles closely that used by D Company, and will be discussed only briefly.

Mechanical Harvesting and Handling Equipment

Because of their system — similar to A Company in this respect — of using independent trucker-foremen, E Company furnishes only the following:

   2 — forklift tractors to load, unload, and position bins in groves
450 — bins or pallet boxes, 47" x 32" x 47", with a 22 field box capacity
   1 — bin dumper, especially constructed to enable the forklift to dump contents of a bin into a bulk truck for juice fruit
   1 — towmotor to load, unload, and transport bins at the plant
      — sufficient ladders, sizing rings, clippers, and bags to accommodate 50 pickers

The trucker-foremen furnish four 2-ton flat bed trucks, two small buses, and two trailers, and provide maintenance for the forklift tractors.

Organizational Structure of Harvest Activities

At peak season E Company employs two crews from 12 to 18 men each. The ethnic, education, age, and marital profile of this group of workers closely resembles that of the Anglo crew of A Company. Twenty-four workers and two foremen were interviewed — 26 in all. All but three of these

26 were Anglo-Americans: 19 were above the age of 50, eight had less than an 8th grade education, and all but six were Anglo-isolates. Morale among the pickers was unusually high. Most said they would not work for anyone else. They were happy with the arrangements and felt devoted to their foremen.

The older of the two Anglo foremen, J, is approaching 80 and has been in the fruit harvesting business most of his life. He has been a foreman since 1929. Both he and the younger foreman have known most of their pickers personally for years — they know their lore, their hangouts, and their devious, informal channels of communication. On the other hand, the general manager of the company has virtually no direct contact with the pickers. The company pays the foremen for so many boxes and they pay the pickers. They are hired, managed, and paid by the foremen. Thus E Company's organizational system can be classed as the old Anglo fruit picker system, similar to that of A Company.

The trucking and supervisory setup for E Company is uniquely intricate and informal. One foreman, T, and the field superintendent, L, are partnership owners in the trucking enterprise. In this respect they occupy dual roles for the company — that of supervising as well as owning and maintaining four 2-ton trucks, two buses, two trailers, and maintaining two forklift tractors. T's supervisory duties as foreman include driving the bus to pick up his crew, supervising a crew in the grove, and operating the forklift tractor in the grove. L's supervisory duties are to oversee the entire harvesting operation. In addition to these two roles, L has still a third role — that of custom farming the groves which E Company owns.

The second foreman, J, simply picks up his crew and supervises them in the field.

There are two drivers. Their duties differ. One of the drivers is T's father who operates only the trucks for T's crew — hauling empty and full bins to and from the plant. The other driver, X, serves J's crew. In addition to driving a truck, he operates the forklift tractor.

Wage System

For the complex network of interlocking entrepreneur and supervisory activity, E Company pays 10 cents a field box for all the boxes picked by both crews — "For the whole ball of wax," as the general manager puts it. Moreover, the general manager has no precise idea how this 10 cents is divided among its five recipients. As nearly as field researchers were able to determine the 10 cents is divided as follows:

owners of trucking enterprise, two men (T and L)	5 cents
driver of truck (T's father)	1 cent
supervising, driving bus, and forklift for crew (T)	1 cent
supervising and driving bus for crew (J)	1½ cents
driving truck and operating forklift for J's crew (X)	1½ cents

The pickers are paid 15 cents a box for strip picking oranges and 10 cents a box for strip picking grapefruit. There are no checkers. Each picker simply puts his mark on a bin and picks into it until it is full.

Description of Operations

The driver leaves the plant with a load of 16 empty bins. Usually there are already some bins at the grove which were dropped off the night before. The load of empty bins is unloaded at the roadside by means of a forklift tractor. The tractor is operated either by the picking crew foreman or the truck driver. The crew foreman picks up pickers at a special rendezvous and transports them to the grove. The crew foreman shows the men where to start picking and then proceeds to distribute the bins in strategic spots throughout the grove. Each picker has his own bin(s) and, as he moves away from it, the foreman moves the bin so that carrying bags is minimized.

As the bins are filled, the foreman moves the filled bins with the forklift to the roadside and stacks them, two high. Two filled bins are then loaded on the truck in one lift. Usually a full load of bins is loaded at one time, in about 15 minutes. Sometimes, however, the truck stays at the grove and, as the bins are roadsided, it is loaded. The latter procedure usually takes about two hours for 16 bins.

There is no direct supervision of the pickers; the foreman devotes most of his time to moving empty and full bins to and from the roadside and moving partly filled bins to accommodate pickers. The pickers move from tree to tree at their own discretion without any checking by the foreman. It appeared that there was more fruit left on the tree and on the ground than we observed under closer supervision systems. The foreman tallies each picker's bins either when he roadsides them, loads them on the truck, or at day's end. The picker's name is on each of his bins so the foreman merely multiplies the number of bins for each picker times the bin capacity (22 field boxes). This is the simplest means of tally observed in any method.

When the truck has been loaded it proceeds to the packing plant. The average haul takes about 30 minutes but varies from 15 to 45 minutes. When the truck arrives at the packing plant, it is unloaded by a towmotor in about 10 minutes. The towmotor then loads the truck with empty bins for its return trip.

Most of the volume handled by this company is from its own groves. From 10 to 20 percent is harvested on a custom basis. This operation is unique for its informality. One gets the impression this is just a big, happy family operation.

Experience Account

E Company moved gradually from a field box to a bin system. In the 1957-58 season they made their first step by building an addition to the plant for storing bins. A special clamp was the key to their policy of gradual change. It allowed lift trucks and automatic dumping equipment, designed primarily to handle bins, to handle field boxes as well. In 1959-60 they started building bins, bought a field forklift tractor, and put one of their two crews on the bin system. The following season the shift was completed. A, the general manager, gave the following reasoning:

> Trees were getting too big and the flat bed trucks carrying the field boxes were causing damage more and more every year and growers were putting the pressure on to get out of the groves or use some other method. Several growers flatly said, 'Either you get a system in here to not tear up the trees or you're not going to pick any fruit.'

> The second incentive was the increasing problem of getting labor to handle field boxes — truckers, drivers, and swampers. Also repair and replacement of field boxes was terrific.

> (A, commenting on other methods) — We rejected the bin-trailer system used by_____(C) Company, because our average haul distance is 25 to 30 miles. Six baskets or 144 boxes is an awfully slow process. Our present method allows trucks to haul an equivalent of 352 field boxes. Another disadvantage to the bin-trailer system is that their workers have to work bunched up with a checker. In our company every man is on his own. We like our pickers to be independent. Actually at the time we began switching over there were no other bin systems around. We just devised it as we went along.

> (Asked about workers' preferences) — Our pickers had no objection whatever because it eased up their job and the old fruit pickers running their circuit had been getting exposed to the bin system in apple picking. All liked it. We have always paid the going rate, and as a result of this and using one bin to a picker, it has worked to our advantage in getting the old-time fruit pickers.

F COMPANY — REVOLVING BIN SYSTEM

The most recent development in citrus harvesting systems is the "revolving bin system." This system (described in operations section) was developed cooperatively by the general manager and the plant superintendent of F Company.

F Company is a harvesting, packing, and shipping cooperative, which had, in the 1962-63 season, 107 member-growers with 2,761 acres of producing citrus. Of this, 1,793 acres were in oranges, 416 acres in grapefruit, 494 acres in lemons, and 58 acres in tangerines. Their groves were widely scattered over great distances. This factor, in combination with their system of picking members' groves by percentage, required a great deal of crew moving. Tree sizes in most of their groves were about average.

Mechanical Harvesting and Handling Equipment

    14 — 2-ton trucks with especially engineered hydraulically operated
         bin racks
 1,500 — bins, 40″ x 34″ x 72″, 27 field box capacity
     7 — 1 ½-ton platform trucks with canvas tops and seats for haul-
         ing crews
     2 — bin racks for loading bins on trucks at the plant
       — sufficient aluminum ladders, sizing rings, clippers, and bags
         to supply 200 pickers

Organizational Structure of Harvest Activities

F Company has as many as seven crews during peak season. Their crew sizes vary enormously due to the great numbers of itinerant domestic workers whom they hire on the involuntary day haul system. During the week of November 28 through December 4, 1962, F Company had six crews in operation. Two of these crews were made up of Mexican Nationals with 23 men each. Of the four domestic crews, one was referred to as their permanent crew. It was made up of 18 men — ten Mexican-Americans, six Yaqui Indians, and two Mexican aliens. All, including their foreman, were from the same community. The other three crews, although having a small nucleus of permanent pickers, were supplied primarily through the involuntary day haul system. One had 33 men, one 34 men, and the other 42 men. According to the field superintendent, each had a turnover of 20 pickers, 21 pickers, and 20 pickers respectively during the first week of observation.

Of the 31 domestic workers interviewed in the latter three crews, Anglos predominated. The remaining were about equally divided between Mexican-Americans and Negroes. Nineteen of the 31 had above 8th grade schooling, and all but four of the 31 were isolates, i.e., living alone. Their average age was 34.

The mechanic, six foremen, and 12 truck drivers for F Company were Mexican-American. Only one foreman was an Anglo. Of the 12 of these who were interviewed, all were attached to family households. Their average age was 32. Their average schooling was slightly below 8th grade. F Company also had a young Mexican-American assistant field superintendent. He is a high school graduate and speaks fluent English and Spanish. His bilingualism was an important asset because the field superintendent did not speak Spanish.

The pickers for F Company may pick either in one-half box sacks or in full box sacks. The sacks, however, must be full before dumping into the bins because there is only one bin for the entire crew. Trees are not assigned, nor must the picker's tree be checked before he moves to another tree. Pickers who are used to working together may cooperate on the same tree, thus saving one another the task of climbing ladders with partially full bags.

The foremen supervise the picking in every respect. They are responsible for instructing new pickers, the condition of the fruit as it flows into the bins, the way it is handled by the pickers, and whether or not any fruit is left on the trees. The foreman must also record each picker's production. He is often assisted by the truck driver. This responsibility carries over into the adjustment of "overages" and "shortages." These terms refer to a daily accounting procedure. All fruit trucked into the plant is received and credited to the particular crew it is from. Although the fruit is received in bins, the number of bins is always multiplied times 27 field boxes — the capacity of each bin — and this total count of field boxes is supposed to equal the total number of field boxes that each foreman reports his pickers having picked for the day. If the received amount is more than the picker production report turned in by the foreman each evening, then the difference is called an "overage," and it must be distributed among the pickers for that day. If this difference is the other way around, it is called a "shortage" and must be made up by docking a fractional amount from each picker that day.

It is the foreman's responsibility to make these picker production adjustments. According to management, overages are given to the pickers "who consistently pick extra full sacks," and shortages are made up among the pickers "who consistently pick short sacks." Just how this is done varies with the foreman and the individual picker. Field observations disclosed that some foremen simply say nothing to a rather productive picker who consistently shorts, but simply skip a mark for him now and then to make up for it. As one foreman said, "This guy always does it, but I skip a mark every now and then; he's happy — he stays with me all season — a steady picker." Other foremen are more formal about it.

Other duties of F Company foremen include the transportation of their crews and the inventory and care of all worker equipment. They assist the field superintendents in making picking-time and production estimates in their groves. Also management expects them to look for permanent workers on their own. The foreman of the permanent crew is aided in maintaining his crew by his rather prominent role in the Mexican-American and Yaqui community from which they come. He has *compadres* as well as kinsmen among his pickers. He belongs to the same religious organizations that are active in the community and is a co-worker with many of them in the community's secular activities. In addition some of the truck drivers and supervisors also have interlocking community and kinship relationships. F Company's middle management structure can be considered an extension of Arizona Mexican-American social organization. More will be said about this later.

F Company's field superintendent, a middle class Anglo-American, is an integral part of upper management organization. He communicates on a face-to-face basis with the grower-members of the co-op. He arranges picking dates in conjunction with growers' normal grove activities. He knows their groves intimately — their sizes, grade, and variety and their approximate potential yields. It is up to him to maintain the correct percentage balance of pick for each of the members. As an example, if the co-op has orders for so many thousand boxes of a particular variety, grade, and size of fruit, he is supposed to see to it that all of the groves which have the specified fruit contribute to this demand proportionately. He keeps in touch with the plant superintendent. At the end of the day he goes over the next day's orders to set up the next day's picking plan. He designates the area best able to supply the desired fruit and the best combinations of crews for the particular picking job. He is responsible for the over-all organization of the foremen and the pickers' equipment, buses, and trucks. Also he has the responsibility of coordinating daily with the farm labor office on involuntary day haul quotas. On picking days he contacts every crew at least once.

R, the assistant superintendent, also contacts all crews, but he generally works in an area where P is not. Thus each crew is contacted in the field twice in the day — once by the superintendent and again by the assistant. R's contacts are of a different nature than P's, however. R does not communicate with growers as much as their foreman does. His relationships to F Company personnel vary. Some he relates to by virtue of his position only. With others, especially those in his own social milieu, he functions as a go-between for management. His real asset to the company is no doubt the fact that he plays a significant role in the society of many of their key personnel, especially the drivers. R does not make decisions as much as he phrases personnel problems for the attention of management. From management he interprets decisions to personnel. Another thing to be considered is that, although most of their Mexican-American personnel can speak English, R is more acculturated to Anglo business management than the others. His more sophisticated English enables him to communicate with management at more levels.

The field superintendent and the plant superintendent answer directly to the general manager. He in turn answers to a seven-member board of directors. Drivers' functions will be described more fully in the operations section.

Wage System

Pickers' piece rates are as follows:

Oranges, strip picking	15 cents a box
Grapefruit, strip picking	12 cents a box (for juice only, pickers are paid 10 cents a box)
Grapefruit, size picking	15 cents a box
Lemons, strip clipping	40 cents a box
Tangerines, strip clipping	40 cents a box

During the time that F Company uses braceros, they must, of course, guarantee their pickers a 95 cent adverse effect wage. Moreover, they must hire all workers assigned by the farm labor office on the involuntary day haul system. However, by agreement with the local farm labor office, the co-op is protected from having to pay pickers who fall (in production) substantially below their hourly minimum. At the end of three days, the company may with "just cause" — in this case lack of production — fire the worker. Production records are turned in daily to meet this situation as well as to pay off domestic workers quitting before the end of the weekly pay period.

When the co-op does not use Mexican Nationals, the piece rates alone apply. The company has a fixed rate policy which holds regardless of working conditions, e.g. moving from grove to grove during the day, or picking in groves with mixed varieties, big trees, low yield, etc. According to management, the company occasionally pays pickers $1 an hour when a crew has extremely poor picking. Also, they try to rotate bad picking fairly among the various crews. More comment on this follows in the description of operations.

Drivers are paid $1.20 an hour with overtime after ten hours. Drivers are also given credit for time spent waiting at the plant for weather to clear so that operations can begin. Foremen are paid a flat $16 a day.

Description of Operations

The driver leaves the plant with the truck, equipped with an especially built rack, hauling nine bins. Average travel time for the truck is 30 minutes. The longest haul takes from 55 to 60 minutes and the shortest from 10 to 15 minutes. The crew foreman gets the worker transport truck from the plant. After checking the equipment, he picks up the crew and drives on to the grove. At the grove each picker unloads his own ladder and bag and begins picking. The truck driver locates his truck between the rows and lowers the first bin for loading. The truck driver and crew foreman tally the number of bags picked by each crew member as they are dumped into the bin. Supervision of picking is, in general, by the crew foreman but the truck driver helps when not moving bins or the truck. Usually a picker is assigned to a specific row to facilitate tree checking. Either the truck driver or foreman inspects the fruit as it is dumped by the picker into the bin. Any foreign material is picked out along with inferior fruit and thrown away. The truck is moved at certain intervals to keep up with advancing pickers. Slow pickers have to carry bags farther because the truck is moved ahead in accordance with the progress of the larger number of pickers. Two trucks and equipment are assigned to each crew, except on the longest hauls. Then a third truck is usually provided.

As a bin is filled the driver locates it on the truck by means of hydraulic lifts and chain conveyors and moves an empty bin down to loading level (ground level). When loading the truck with empty bins, one is placed on the bottom row, four on the second row, and four on the top row. At the plant, empty bins are placed on an especially constructed loading rack by a towmotor. This rack coincides with the three-tier rack on the trucks so one man simply pushes the bins from the rack onto the truck. The time of this operation is about three minutes. The one bin on the bottom is filled first. Then, as three more bins are filled, they all are placed in the bottom row. The next four to be filled are placed on the middle row, and the last bin filled goes on the top row front. This arrangement allows hauling the maximum legal load per axle.

When all nine bins are filled, the driver locks the bins into place and leaves for the packing plant. The other empty truck then takes its position for loading. When the loaded truck arrives at the plant, the driver unlocks the bins and backs up to the unloading ramp. A towmotor removes each bin as it is placed in unloading position by the driver. This is all mechanical. The driver operates a series of clutches to move bins into unloading position. It is ten minutes from the time the truck enters the gate loaded until it leaves the same gate with empty bins.

The time required to fill the truckload varies greatly due to the experience of the picking crew, the type of fruit being harvested, and the yield of the grove along with several other more minor reasons. Observed times varied from one hour to one hour and 45 minutes.

The movement of the truck over the ground does compact the soil. Operators and F Company feel, however, that travel over the same ground has been minimized; thus the net effect is less compaction than with most other methods. They estimate that 50 percent of the traffic in the grove is eliminated, as compared to their previous systems.

Additional Observations

1. As all pickers do not pick at the same rate, the slower ones have to carry their fruit excessive distances.

2. F Company has groves scattered over a very wide area and a system of picking groves by percentages. These two factors make it necessary to move crews more frequently than with the other systems observed, thus curtailing picker production.

3. Although rotation of "bad picking" is a sincere goal of management, their paucity of permanent experienced pickers tends to place the burden of "bad picking," usually requiring more skill, upon the one permanent crew they have. In this respect, what is considered to be more efficient from one set of factors tends to be inefficient from the standpoint of another set of factors — viz. by discouraging the very pickers which they sorely need.

Experience Account

The following text was given by B, the general manager, a key figure in the innovation of the F Company system:

> It was a combination of factors that triggered the change. First, an excessive amount of damage and decay of fruit being handled in field boxes because of a decline in attitude of help on trucks; second, the difficulty of getting truckers and swampers; third, excessive overtime needed by truckers and swampers in handling field boxes — these were little things gnawing at me all the time; and finally, the company was faced with a problem of, within one year, building an increase in sweating capacity (for ripening fruit in the shed) amounting to 50 percent. The lowest bid that we could get on building this addition was $120,000.
> We were looking for value received in this problem — how many birds could we kill with one stone. The more I thought about it and the more I talked with the board, the more we were convinced that we wanted to get away from the field box method. We had 12 years experience in bulk handling, since 1947, by using semi-trucks and feeders for the latter part of season picking. We knew the depth to which fruit could be handled by bulk methods. Moreover, I had done experiments in fruit coloring and knew from these that the deeper the fruit is in the bins the more uniform is

the coloring process. We began to figure out box and bin shapes to put to best use the available capacity that we already had. I had seen other bins used by other companies and saw that they lost room in storage as well as on the trucks because of the shapes of the bins. In the space of one month I worked up about 40 bin equations of different sizes and shapes.

The factors which had to be considered in the design of a bin were as follows:

1. The state highway requirements relating to height of vehicles and gross axle loads on trucks

2. The width of the drives in the groves

3. The center of gravity on the trucks

4. The cost of the containers

5. The most important of all from our standpoint — gaining the utmost capacity of available space in our sweat rooms. This involved airflow, shape and capacity, labor and handling in shed — with the old field box method one man could lift 50 lbs. at a time; with the present method, one man lifts and handles 1600 lbs. of fruit at once.

We considered mechanical equipment no real bother because we can always make mechanical innovations anytime. We had first to get the box design before any other changes. I started out with a bin that would hold eight boxes — you can imagine the amount of wood that you could get in a sweat room and, of course, that's what we don't want. So after I had met all the five requirements of our bin design — working it out so that we needed not one additional square foot of floor space, I then contacted machinery companies for plant equipment designed to handle these bins. They had the answer in a matter of days; however, it did take a lot of juggling.

The next problem was the trucking problem. I worked with the plant superintendent closely on this. First, I came up with the idea of two tiers. Second, the plant superintendent came up with the idea of the elevator on the end of the truck dropping box bins from either of these tiers. Third, I could see then that those bins were never going to come off the truck. I could see that we wanted power. First, I tinkered with the idea of a gravity system whereby the bins could be dropped or rotated from front to the back to get to the elevator, but that didn't work so well. My first move was to go to the _____ (National Co-op) engineering department. I said we would like to hire their engineers, that we would be willing to pay for them ourselves and that I would stay there overnight, live there, sleep there, until the job was done. They turned me down cold. They said they didn't want to be connected with it because it was too radical an idea — it might not work. Then they made reference to '. . . old _____(E) down there; maybe he'll do it.' This was rather in a kind of disparaging manner.

I went to see old _____(E) who is known as a radical in the industry. He has one of the finest minds in the industry. He is an eccentric but I like him. We have always clicked. This was something _____(E) liked. I had the load factor, all the specifications. We went to work at once. By four p.m. I had given him all I had. I went out of town but called at noon the next day and he said, 'Let's go!' He didn't give a damn what I was going to do with it; he had a problem, that's all he wanted. The_____ (National Co-op) attitude has really changed since then.

Results: The system cost the company actually a little less than the $120,000 they needed, or would have needed, for the additional sweat room capacity using field boxes. Costs were: $45,000 with rigs on the trucks, $35,000 on bins, and $40,000 on dumps and forklift trucks in the sheds. The company did get its extra sweating capacity without building another square foot of floor space, and everything else it got was a plus. The advantages were no swampers, no overtime, less turn-around time on trucks, therefore fewer trucks needed, less traffic in the grove by 75 percent, and the elimination of the drudgery of the pickers having to handle field boxes in the groves.

(Asked about worker sentiments) — This had been partially worked out before since we had been using a bulk-truck loading system during the latter part of the seasons for ten years before the revolving bin system. This involved the same tabulating system for the pickers and the picking bags. From the company's standpoint, this bin system eliminates the problem of pickers dragging behind the crew and also makes it so they can't fudge on field boxes. In '47 when the company started its bulk system for ripe fruit some workers left at that time, but generally it was the type of worker who would object to anything — the loud-mouth type. Also every year during the middle of the season, when the switch-over began (from bulk-truck to field box), there were always arguments as to who was going with what system. This way they know that we use one system and that's it. If they don't like it they can go down to the employment office and work for another outfit. We don't stand over them with a club! As far as I was concerned we had an abominable situation to begin with as long as we were forced to take everything from the employment office, so I just figured out the economic factors and ignored the other.

(B making reference to the fact that his experience in the past as a fruit picker had caused him to consider the drudgery angle) — I thought of chasing field boxes when I was a picker and it seemed better to me from that standpoint. It certainly took a lot of drudgery out of the field operation. When I was a kid I used to dump everything by hand, and I would say, 'This is the last box I can lift,' and I said, 'By God there are machines to do this, and I'm going to use them!'

SUMMARY — CITRUS

Summary tables of citrus harvesting systems follow:

Table 1

Summary of Citrus Harvesting Operations

Company	Size in Acres	Type of Business	Mechanical System	No. Crews	No. Crews Braceros	Size of Crews
A	1,413	Commercial	Standard field box	2	None	25-32 & 12-18
B	5,284	Cooperative	Bin-trailer	25	All	10-30
C	1,092	Cooperative	Bin-trailer	6	2	16-20
D	4,061	Commercial	Bin-forklift	10	All	35
E	792	Commercial and Grower-harvester	Bin-forklift	2	None	12-18
F	2,761	Cooperative	Revolving-bin	7	2	18-40

Table 2

Summary of Citrus Pay Systems

Com-pany	Oranges Strip	Grape-fruit Strip	Lemons Strip	How Computed	Compensation Moving Time	Drivers	Foremen
A	17¢	10¢	50¢	Actual field box	Especially paid, small crew for remnants	2½¢ box	2¢ box oranges 5¢ box grapefruit
B	10¢	7½¢	30¢	1 box sack unit of measure paid by tonnage weight	None	$1.25/hr.	$1.25/hr. (given 30 min. lunch)
C	15-18¢	9-12¢	45-60¢	½ + box sack tallied by "checker"	Adjustable pay scale	$1.30/hr.	$14.00/day
D	11¢	7½¢	30¢	1 box sack unit of measure paid by tonnage weight	None	$1.35/hr.	$1.35/hr.
E	15¢	10¢	—	Sack — size unimportant as paid by the bin (22 field boxes)	Virtually no moving necessary	Informal division of a total box rate for production of all pickers	
F	15¢	12¢	40¢	1 or ½ box sack tallied by foreman	None	$1.20/hr.	$16.00/day

4 The Lettuce Industry

BACKGROUND

LETTUCE HARVESTING operations revolve around one basic technology. This is in sharp contrast to the citrus industry which is characterized by enormous variations in factors which seem to justify a variety of methods. To compare the two is to compare a standardized technology with one which is highly individualized. It would be a mistake, however, to allow the prevalence of one technology in lettuce harvesting to obscure underlying manifold indications of instability and change. There are lingering evidences of competing systems representing the clash of economic interests which may have only temporarily subsided, and there are tensions inherent in the prevailing patterns themselves which have motivated expensive experimentation. However (at the time of this writing) these experimental changes have established little more than waning beachheads.

The Shed Pack

The birth of lettuce as an industry — distinguished from the pushcart and fruit-stand enterprises of pre-World War I days — is attributable to the synthesis of the old-fashioned icebox and the railway car. As in the case of many technological innovations, early experiments in this direction had their share of financial disasters and heart-breaking failures. Because of the fact that ice stored, handled, and crushed in tremendous tonnages was the key element in lettuce packing and shipping, the industry and the permanent, stationary packing shed developed as an inseparable complex. A brief discussion of harvesting, grading, and packing in a 1923 Colorado Experiment Station Bulletin illustrates the fundamental interlocking features of the field portion and the shed portion of the harvesting-packing operation which prevailed until the mid-1950's:

> The plants are cut just below the head in such a way that all the leaves are left intact. One who is experienced in harvesting lettuce can tell at a glance what heads are ready to cut. The heads are put into field crates as soon as cut with the bottom of the head up, and should be taken to the packing shed at once. Everything possible should be done to keep the heads cool and prevent wilting by sun and wind. Putting crates in the shade as soon as filled or covering with canvas will be of advantage in this particular.
> At the packing shed the lettuce is trimmed, graded and packed into crates which are at once loaded into refrigerator cars. The

standard crate used in Colorado is what is known as the Los Angeles crate and measures 13x18x24½ inches. The crate is lined with paraffin paper and the heads packed two to four or even five dozen to the crate, depending upon the size of the heads. Crushed ice is placed between the layers of heads in the crate, about 35 or 40 pounds being used for this purpose.

Many growers are beginning to recognize the need for strict grading of the lettuce shipped and urge that a high standard be set (McGinty 1923: 22-23).

At this period in the history of the industry (the 1920's), the loosely packed field crates were loaded on horse drawn wagons in the field, pulled to the ends of the rows, and transferred to "large auto trucks at the edge of the field" by which they were hauled to the sheds (Jones and Garthwaite 1925: 26). A variation of this method was developed by pioneers in the Arizona lettuce industry in Yuma (this according to an oldtimer in lettuce, now the field superintendent of one of the older lettuce shippers in Yuma):

> A dump cart took the place of field crates which was also drawn through the field by a team as cutters threw heads into it. The cart was pulled to the end of the row where its contents were packed in field crates, loaded on trucks, and then taken to the shed where it was trimmed, graded, iced and packed.

A later sequence of developments is given by the same informant:

> The L. M. McClaren Company in 1935 began the use of wide-track trailers pulled by tractors straddling two beds. After being filled (again by the cutters), the trailers were pulled to the ends of the rows where they were hitched to trucks and towed to the shed where the above operations took place.
>
> In the late forties, the wide-track trailers were replaced by wide-track trucks carrying large, heavy metal-strap baskets through the fields, with the rest of the operations the same.

The 1940's witnessed the multiplication of minor technical and organizational variations, each suited to the individual circumstances of this or that company or grower-shipper partnership. A 1944 extension bulletin mentions some of these:

> Harvesting is done by hand. A gang of men go down the rows, cutting the matured heads from the two rows adjacent to a furrow and tossing them onto trucks *or* trailers. The cutters may place the heads in windrows, from which *another crew* following toss the heads into large steel-framed crates *or* baskets on trucks *or* trailers. . . . These baskets, having four small wheels on the bottom, can be rolled from the vehicle to the packing table. . . .
>
> In the *larger* lettuce-growing sections, *mechanical loaders* are in general use. The conveyor, mounted on a truck body, moves at right angles to the rows just ahead of the harvesters. Each man cuts from the two rows nearest him, placing the heads on the moving belt, where they are elevated and drop into 'baskets' on a truck *or* trailer. The apparatus covers eight to eleven beds (Knott and Tavernetti 1944: 30; italics ours).

In summary, lettuce could be thrown into crates, baskets, or conveyor belts. It could be thrown by the cutters themselves or a special crew of "tossers." Finally, the heads could be carried through the fields and to the sheds in either trucks or trailers. One fundamental feature remained nevertheless. The lettuce was packed for shipment in a packing shed.

Thus in the beginning lettuce was packed in sheds. It is packed in sheds to some extent to this day. It was inevitable that the persistence of this 50-year-old tradition which reached its zenith at the dawn of the 1950's should have made it the common cornerstone of worker subcultures and of financial empires. The interests of the participants in this system — the shed pack — must be taken into account before the technological events of the last decade can be thoroughly understood.

The Field Pack

In the 1930's another tradition developed in the lettuce packing and shipping industry. This system was referred to as the "field pack" or the "field dry-pack." It originated as a field operation designed for short hauls to local markets. Yuma and Imperial Valley became important in field packing because of their proximity to coastal markets. Shippers' crews would cut in the cool, early hours of the morning, pack the lettuce in half-size *crates*, lid them, and load them directly on vans. The load was then top-iced and trucked to San Francisco or Los Angeles without further ado. There was a natural tendency on the part of shippers motivated by the obvious economic advantages of the field pack to stretch shipping distances farther and farther. Long distance shipping of field dry-pack lettuce was practiced especially by Eastern growers. In fact, for two eastern varieties — Boston and Romaine — this was considered to be the only profitable method (Platenius 1940: 8). However, as distances increased, lettuce wilted and buyers grumbled.

Methods of precooling by refrigerated storage were developed specifically to extend the shipping and shelf life of dry-packed lettuce. This allowed growers to dry-pack far beyond the "cool, early hours of the morning." In fact, a Cornell University Experiment Station Bulletin cites one eager grower as mounting an ice crusher on a truck to follow his cutting and packing crew in the field in order to add ice to his field *dry*-pack (Platenius 1940: 8). Nevertheless, the technical limitations of the control of temperature operated as an ultimate barrier. It continued to reinforce the traditional outlook by interests in the industry that field packing was not an acceptable way of handling top-grade lettuce. Therefore, throughout the 1940's, field pack got second-grade lettuce. First grade lettuce was reserved for the shed. Thus it was that field packing of lettuce developed not as a competing but as an alternate tradition in the industry.

The fact that for over a decade this tradition persisted in a complementary but *subordinate* role meant that it would become the craft of a different class of workers. The more sought-after shed jobs were filled by the elite of the migrant stream, whereas the lower-paying stoop jobs in the fields became the crafts of immigrant classes which varied according to the decade — Japanese, Filipino, and Mexican — wetback, green card, and American. This fact must be taken into account in setting the stage for the revolution which followed the synthesis of two relatively unrelated developments — cardboard packaging and vacuum cooling.

Another component in the setting at the turn of the decade (1949-50) was the rising costs of material and labor. The shed tradition was more susceptible to these costs for two reasons: it required a war-critical item (lumber) and its class of workers, comparatively sophisticated and well-organized, stood at the top of the industry in wages.

United States Department of Agriculture Marketing Service Reports and Agricultural Experiment Station Bulletins of the early 1950's supply the bare statistics which disclose the transition of the field-pack tradition from a complementary role to a competing role. A 1952-53 cost survey of lettuce harvests in California and Arizona was designed specifically to compare costs between these two methods. A recap of the authors' view of the situation is pertinent:

> Until a few years ago practically all lettuce harvested in the desert areas of southern California and Arizona during the winter and spring and in the Salinas-Watsonville area of California during the summer and fall was packed in large packing sheds. For many years the *Los Angeles crate* was the principal shipping container. It was supplanted by the *WGA crate* in 1951. Both of these containers were of sawed and nailed construction and accommodated either four or five dozen heads. Crushed ice . . . was the principal means of refrigeration.
>
> Building of vacuum-cooling plants in the various producing areas to flash-cool the lettuce and the subsequent introduction of the fiberboard carton as a lettuce container have brought extensive changes. Now a high percentage of the lettuce grown is dry-packed in cartons (two or two-and-a-half dozen heads) in the field and cooled by placing the field-packed containers in a vacuum tube until the temperature of the lettuce has been lowered to 35° F . . . (Voegeli *et al.* 1955: 1).

A terse statement of comparative costs follows:

> The cost of shed-packing lettuce in WGA crates with ice exceeded the average cost of field-packing the same quantity in fiberboard cartons by $0.50 or 29.4 percent, in the Salinas-Watsonville district in 1952, and $0.32, or 17 percent, in the Arizona-Imperial Valley area. Most of the economies realized . . . resulted from lower costs for containers and container components, lower labor costs for packing, handling, and loading, and lower overhead costs for facilities and equipment (Voegeli *et al.* 1955: iii).

With this sudden technical breakthrough, the dominance of the field-pack system was not long in the making. Reports and bulletins of the late 1950's document the ascendency of the field-pack tradition as a *fait accompli.* One study devoted to a more efficient use of shed facilities in house-packing western lettuce flatly states in its "Foreword," "The 1956 volume of house-packed lettuce (in Salinas) could have been processed through a single packing plant of either 420- or 630-crate-per-hour capacity" (Enochian *et al.* 1957).

This breakthrough turned on the key element of cheap labor. Labor in the form of the traditional field-pack worker was augmented by the bottomless reservoir of unsophisticated but vigorous braceros, who had been used as cutters for shed-pack lettuce through the late 1940's. By 1960, instead of motley crews of Filipinos and Mexican-Americans cutting and packing second-grade lettuce for a limited market, swarms of Mexican Nationals — trained by row bosses recruited from the ranks of the old dry-pack crews — cut and packed the cream of the crop in slick cardboard cartons which were hustled to vacuum cooling chambers, "instantly cooled," loaded on sided refrigerated cars, and highballed to the hungry metropolises of the East.

This standard field-pack system, in operation at the time of our field observations, is described:

The work day in the lettuce fields begins around 5:00 a.m. or after frost melts, which may be as late as 10:00. At this time the crews are lined up and told which type of lettuce to cut.

The size of the crews is regulated by the number of lettuce packers. Under average conditions there are 18 packers, 36 trimmers or cutters, four sprayers, eight carton closers, eight windrowers, three loaders, and three foremen.

The cutters lead off the crews spread among 30 to 36 rows of lettuce. They determine the quality by either size or firmness with the help of the two cutter foremen. Normally, only the premium or top grades of lettuce are cut first. After the cutters cut the lettuce they trim off excess leaves and place it stem-side up on the top of the row.

Following the cutters are the packers. They use "humps" or small tables made like a wheelbarrow to hold the cartons while they are being packed. They pack the lettuce into cardboard cartons with either 24 or 30 heads per carton, depending on the size. Naturally 30 packs are inferior heads and are usually packed either the second or third cutting. The packers pick up three heads of lettuce at a time and gently squeeze in two layers of lettuce per carton with 12 heads per layer. The last layer is placed stem side up.

The empty cartons come by the pallet with 640 cartons per pallet. These come flattened out and the bottoms must be stapled. In the initial operation the folder picks up a carton, folds it together, and drops it on the stitching machine. The stitcher runs 16 staples in the bottom of the box. The boxes are then stacked on a platform and spread out among the lettuce heads. The stitcher truck moves down the rows at the same speed as the cutting crews.

After the packers come the sprayers, who spray fresh water on the cut stems to wash away the milk to keep the top heads from turning brown. They place a small piece of cardboard on the top to cover the gap left by the carton tops when they are closed.

The closers follow the sprayers and close the cartons by squeezing the carton tops with an especially made hand press. Then they staple the tops with a large gun-like hand stapler and leave the cartons in the rows for the windrowers.

The windrowers collect the closed cartons and move them toward the center of the operation. They stack the cartons on end in two single rows, approximately four rows apart, to allow the especially-constructed Fabco Widetracks to drive in between. Three men load the trucks — two on the ground handing up the cartons and one man stacking the cartons. There are 640 cartons to a car-of-cartons (a railroad car). The Fabco trucks hold ten pallets of 32 each, or one-half a car-of-cartons. Upon reaching the coolers the trucks are unloaded in one operation by an especially-constructed forklift that will handle the entire ten pallets of lettuce in one load.

The lettuce is cooled from approximately 70° to 36° in eight minutes in the vacuum tube, then loaded by a power lift on refrigerated cars or semi-trucks.

Lettuce Machines and Prepackaging (Wrap)

More than one method of field packing lettuce was developed during the years of the packing shed's decline. One group of growers in the Salinas-Watsonville area during the mid-1950's tried dry-packing cartons on a "dry-pack machine." An Agricultural Marketing Service Report briefly describes this operation:

> The cutting and trimming for machine-packing is the same as for other methods of field dry-packing. As the dry-pack machine moves over the trimmed lettuce, trimmed heads are picked up and placed on a packing platform on the moving machine. The lettuce packers riding on the machine select and pack either 2 or 2½ dozen heads in the cartons, and the packed container is placed on a conveyor that moves toward the stitching machine. After the closing operation the containers are placed on a moving truck to be carried to the vacuum-cooling plant or refrigerator car . . . (Voegeli *et al.* 1955: 10).

Another variation of the mobile packing shed idea was a trailer-packing system:

> With this method . . . the cutter-trimmers are followed by a truck-trailer packing unit. The trailer unit contains positions for 4 packers and a carton-stitching machine. It is equipped with gravity conveyors for passing empty cartons from stitcher to packer and for transferring packed cartons to the truck. The packed carton top is closed and stapled as the cartons pass along the conveyor to the truck. Packed cartons are stacked on the truck and, when a truck is completely loaded, the trailer unit is drawn to the roadside and parked. A second truck-trailer unit moves in immediately after removal of the first unit. The packers on the trailer are supplied with lettuce by 4 pickup men who range over the harvest strip and hand-transfer trimmed heads from the ground to the packers' work table (University of Arizona 1954: 6-8).

All mobile packing shed systems faced the same bottleneck, however. They could move only as fast as their slowest packer. One report established that of three variations of the field pack — ground crew, packing machine, and packing trailer — the machine and trailer were more efficient in high density lettuce by about 2 cents a carton. However, in low density lettuce, the ground crew was more efficient than either of the two by approximately 5 cents (University of Arizona 1954: 14). Therefore, the ground crew system of field-pack has predominated.

Until the invention of an effective wrapping film at the end of the 1950's, machine field-packing could not seriously challenge the efficiency of the ground crew system. Wrap allowed significant savings in shipping costs to offset the higher packing costs. Film-wrapped lettuce made it unnecessary to ship waste material in the form of wrapper leaves to protect the heads.

The idea of prepackaging lettuce is not new. Experiments on a commercial scale were carried on as far back as 1946 (Abshier and Wood 1949). However, these differed from present practices in two fundamental respects. Lettuce was packaged in cellophane, and it was packed in the sheds.

Until the chemical industry developed a film that allowed the plant to expirate, wrap was not commercially feasible. One of the largest growers and shippers in the industry pioneered such a process in 1959-60. By the 1961-62 season as many as ten shippers in the Imperial Valley, California and Yuma, Arizona area were using some form of prepackaging. For that season Arizona shippers shipped a total 877,718 prepackaged cartons of a grand total of 23,928,179 cartons (Arizona Fruits and Vegetables Standardization Service 1962).

The publication of an Agricultural Marketing Service market survey devoted exclusively to "prepackaged lettuce" (USDA 1962a) documents the significance of the trend. Some of their findings may have been harbingers of the decline that followed. The report stressed three general complaints by buyers, principally chains: lack of uniformity of size, discoloration of leaves showing through the permanent wrap, and consumer dislike for the brittleness of the film (USDA 1962a: 1-2). The 1962-63 season in Arizona showed a decline of over 50 percent in prepackaged lettuce with virtually no decline (less than three percent) in the grand total of cartons shipped (Arizona Fruits and Vegetables Standardization Service 1963). All indications are that the 1963-64 season will show an even greater decline.

In brief, the lettuce harvesting systems of Arizona (and the Western region) evolved from the old field-pack tradition as opposed to the shed-pack tradition. Although the ground crew version of the field-pack tradition is the rule, some shippers prepackage lettuce using a modification of the older dry-pack machine. Moreover, one grower-shipper is prepackaging on a very limited basis in the shed, using the traditional shed system with a shed labor union. In the light of this background, we drew a purposive sample of four companies. The first of these companies (G Company) was primarily responsible for the revolutionary shift from the shed pack to field pack. Also, this company is playing a pioneer role in the development of prepackaged field-pack lettuce. The second company (H Company) also played a key role in the development of the carton and vacuum cooling system. The third company (I Company) was one of the last companies in Arizona to abandon the shed ice-pack. The fourth (J Company) was one of the few companies in Arizona with a field operation including an independent crew of Filipinos from the old field dry-pack tradition.

Following is a comparison in terms of acreage and production between the sample and Arizona as a whole.

Company	Acres in Arizona	Cartons in Arizona	Acres as Percent of Total Arizona	Cartons as Percent of Total Arizona
G Company	3,135	1,587,019	5.5%	6.8%
H Company	2,597	1,577,904	4.6	6.8
I Company	1,688	423,182	3.0	1.8
J Company	2,575	1,057,784	4.5	4.5
Total, Sample	9,995	4,645,889	17.6	19.9
Total, Arizona	56,919	23,343,262	100.0	100.0

Thus, the sample companies farmed a total of 9,995 acres in Arizona accounting for 17.6 percent of the total lettuce acreage in Arizona in 1962-63. They produced from this acreage approximately 20 percent of all the cartons shipped from Arizona in that same year.

Moreover, these companies collectively accounted for approximately 13 percent of all lettuce shipped in the United States (USDA 1963a). Therefore, in addition to providing excellent case studies in the organizational and technical transitions that have taken place in the last 15 years, they represent a significant percentage of the total production of lettuce in both the state and the nation.

G COMPANY — FIELD PACK AND FIELD WRAP

In 1949, when the shipping of shed-packed lettuce was reaching all-time highs, two blacksheep of the industry met to seal a bargain on a process that was to revolutionize the industry which had largely rejected them. One was a compulsive inventor in trouble for his ideas and the other was an independent-minded shipper desperately looking for new ideas. Rex Brunsing, the inventor, had been kicking around the idea of vacuum cooling for a number of years. As far back as 1940 a man by the name of Kasser had been experimenting with a vacuum chamber as a means of injecting substances into fruit and vegetables. It was from Kasser's experiences with these experiments that Brunsing got the idea of using a vacuum chamber as a mean of precooling fruits and vegetables. In the words of B, the principal owner of G Company:

At that time Brunsing was traffic manager for the Garin Company. Rex was pushing it with Garin, 'The Old Gentleman.' Then when Garin died, the young crowd at Garin booted him out because he was always pushing some scheme. That's when we got into it (1949-50). We were trying to buy an ice plant because we were spinning our wheels. We had one bought but they backed out of the sale the last minute. All coastal markets were dry-pack in those days. Eaton in Watsonville did some precooling in a cold storage room, but still used ice cars.

(Asked who did the contacting) — Rex hustled me. Rex had been around our business many, many years. Keikefer Container Corporation lent money to finance the 'Vacuum Cooling Corporation,' that Rex and some fellows in San Francisco formed. This included Webb, Kasser, and the White family.

Rex tried dry-pack crates with vacuum cooling at Rex's pilot plant (1948-49). Rex and National Container Corporation came up with the carton idea. Another thing, crates were going up. They needed our business like a hole in the head! They could put it in housing (referring to Korean War shortages). When we set up to give it a whirl, Zellerbach and Kiekefer were going to give us cartons, but they were hard to get. August, 1950 we got cartons from Kiekefer and I traded my shed property for my part in the vacuum cooling plant. The first vacuum cooling plant (for commercial use) was built on our (G Company's) property in Watsonville, and the "Vacuum Cooling Corporation" shipped the first carlot of vacuum-cooled cartons in the spring of 1950.

We started packing cartons in the fields and the shed both, just to find out which was best. It took a couple of weeks at the most to find out. In the shed the union wanted outlandish prices and all kinds of bull___. Also we were handling merchandise too much. I kept a complete file to prove it but there was still resistance — shook companies and competition resisted it. In the fields we started packing with Filipino dry-packing crews. Then we started using Nationals. We were the first to use Nationals in packing cartons. We made bosses out of Mexican boys who worked in Filipino crews.

In 1951 and '52 most produce companies fought it. Hell, a committee of influential businessmen called on me and told me what was going to happen to the industry, and all the men it would put out of work, and all the ice companies going broke._____(D, owner of H Company) was with them. But in 1953_____(D) promoted a vacuum cooling plant of his own. We started law suits, but Kiekefer wasn't satisfied with Rex._____(D) contacted me when he was getting closer to court and wanted to buy into the company. So I went to Kiekefer and Rex with an offer and bought him out. Vacuum Cooling was paid $3,000,000. Their debt was over $2,000,000. We (D and B) gave Rex $500,000 for his rights. Rex and the others (San Francisco investors) got $800,000. Then the_____(G and H) Cooling Corporation was formed.

(Asked why he went with D) — I was still interested in the lettuce business (as opposed to the cooling business) and I needed _____(D) for his dough and financing ability and_____(D) needed me to put a deal together. He knew I was the only one that could do it. We were going to give plants (shippers) an interest for costs — ___, we couldn't even give it away! Only very few places we put a deal together — Blythe and Phoenix. We offered it to everybody in the business. Just like you standing out there and giving 10-dollar bills for a dollar. They just couldn't believe it! It's pretty near god-dam unbelievable the story! By 1952 the changeover began fast. But there was ice packing as late as 1957. There's none now.

In 1960_____(G and H) split up. By then there were a lot of companies using it. We never brought any law suits. We sold patents to the industry for what we paid for them. Now patents belong to the industry. Any outfit that wants to can build its own cooling plant. (Some growers and shippers have their own. Others form a co-op and others use commercial coolers. G Company has continued to do its own cooling.)

In the 15 years since then, G Company has mushroomed from strictly a packing-shipping (and some say near-bankrupt) operation with partnership agreements on 2,000 acres of lettuce to a *growing*-packing-shipping company with 11,835 acres of their own land, growing celery, cabbage, and broccoli in addition to lettuce. Accounting for more than seven percent of all lettuce shipped in the United States, they have some justification for their claim as the world's largest shipper of lettuce.

Setting aside the factor of size, the chief characteristic of G Company which accounts for their importance in the industry is their constant experimentation. This is the outstanding characteristic of the owner. The relaxed, undisciplined atmosphere of his management organization encourages a fierce loyalty, colorful expressions, and a stimulating dialogue of ideas. At quitting time evening after evening we observed their raucous seminars with two or three long-distance participants — one in Washington, another in Salinas, and another in El Centro — while B and his field boys were gathered around the big table in Redrock chewing up the lines. B will listen for as long as ten minutes without a word. Then he will challenge a particular idea, usually with the enthusiastic support of a majority with an axe to grind. At the end, consensus or no, he will defer to the one who has the ultimate responsibility over the operation in question. As one participant put it, "The idea may be screwball as hell, but B'll give it a whirl!"

Results are the determining factor in B's unorthodox methods. The idea may be to manufacture a $15,000 piece of equipment from scratch. It may be to replace a semi-manual stitching machine with an automatic box gluer, to try one row boss to a crew instead of two, to organize a field crew around three packing machines instead of one, or to employ an entire crew of Negro workers on an experimental basis. If the idea works they keep it. If it doesn't, they don't. A complete record of all G Company's "trials and errors" in the last five years would have required a full-time historian.

The nucleus of one such major innovation came to B's attention in the fall of 1959. This was a synthetic film specifically designed for prepackaging fresh fruits and vegetables. It was developed by Dobeckman Chemical Company, a subsidiary of Dow, and called "Trycite." B had been close to Dobeckman for years buying celery and carrot bags. B brought workers in from the fields to the cooling plant to run some tests on the wrapping of lettuce. They took cartons of field-packed lettuce, retrimmed the heads, and wrapped them in Trycite. Hot-air blowers were used by hand to shrink the film. The lettuce was then repacked. These first tests were conducted at their Holtville cooler plant in the winter of 1960-61. B had an agreement with Dobeckman to have prior, but not exclusive, rights on their supply of Trycite.

In July 1961, G Company ran more extensive experiments in Salinas. At this stage they began designing and manufacturing special equipment in order to field wrap the lettuce. These first machines looked like land planes. Girls sat on them, reaching down to retrieve the cut and trimmed heads. But as B said, "This didn't work because one worked while the other sat." Next, the company bought old dry-pack machines. These machines were mounted on a conventional wide-track chassis with wings on either side extending out at right angles over five and a half beds of lettuce. From the tip of one wing to the tip of the other the machine covered 13 beds. Each wing held four packers and folded back behind the chassis while on the road. B's engineers modified the packing stations into wrap stations, installed film rollers, film-cutting devices, and shrinking ovens.

A period of intensive experimentation followed in the fall of 1961. Most of it centered around the film-dispensing and cutting devices at the individual wrap stations. The first cutting device was a kind of shuttle that slid back and forth on a bar at right angles to the film feed. The cutting was done by a conventional single-edged razor blade clamped in the shuttle. A far more elaborate system was tried in the field at the same time. It consisted of a waffle iron-like machine installed at each wrapping station. Both the base and the hinged top had matching elements which met perfectly when the top was pulled down. Two rolls of film were mounted, one below the elevation of the base and one above the elevation of the base. They fed through the cutting machine, called a "Vanco." The ends were fused together, making a kind of envelope into which a head of lettuce was placed. When the top of the Vanco was pulled down, the matching heating elements met in a circumscribed pattern to cut and seal the envelope like a cookie cutter around the head. The top was lifted up, the head tossed on the belt to take it to the shrinking oven and the process repeated.

The Vancos soon proved too delicate and complex. Also these contraptions did not make an attractive package. The original system was kept with a simple motion-saving modification of the shuttle cutter. It was replaced with an electrically-heated wire that is automatically brought up against the sheet of film when the wrap girl puts the head of lettuce in place to wrap. The weight of the lettuce depresses a platform which raises the taut hot wire by means of pivoted levers.

Many other modifications were tested and discarded — machines with electric drives, machines that maneuvered by pivoting in the middle of their chassis, and automatic box gluers in place of stitchers. In the fall of 1961, during the peak of their experimentation, we observed as many as four different machines in the field at one time. Almost daily changes in the duties of personnel were an inevitable result. There was griping, bickering, and an unusual amount of turnover — especially among machine operators, crew foremen, and truck drivers. A more complete discussion of personnel factors will follow in the organizational section.

In the 1963 season, a machine and its complement of workers operated in this manner. The lettuce is cut, trimmed especially close for wrap, and placed in the traditional manner by a crew of 12 "cutters" working sometimes far in advance of the machine. The self-propelled wrap machine follows with "set-up" men walking behind wings, two to three to a side. They pick up the trimmed lettuce and place it on a platform beside the "wrap" girls. There are three to a wing standing on a platform facing the chassis of the machine. The wrapper pulls the Trycite film over her working platform to a specified length. As she is doing this with one hand, she picks up a head of lettuce being piled either to her left or to her right, depending upon which wing she is on. She places the head directly in the center of the square of film now exposed. As the head is placed the hot taut wire is raised and severs the square of film from the roll. The square is folded at the corners around the head of lettuce much like a diaper, with four overlapping corners instead of three. The package, with the film enveloping the head, is then touched, butt end, to a hot plate to seal the four corners together. The package is quickly tossed onto a conveyor belt moving parallel to the wings, mounted on the side opposite to the set-up platform. The belt moves the enveloped heads toward the chassis through butane ovens which shrink the Trycite to form a tight bag around the head. The conveyors from both wings move toward one another and dump the completed packages onto a central elevator at their juncture. It elevates the packages up and to the rear to the packing platforms. There three "packers" or "fillers" fill especially sized cartons with 18, 20, 24, or 30 heads. A "gluer" walking along behind the platform glues and stacks the cartons on the ground as they are filled. From here the operation is identical to the standard field pack. The cartons are trucked out of the field on wide-wheelers to the coolers and then fed to refrigerated cars or vans.

G Company's first carlot shipments in the summer of 1961 were an immediate success. As B put it, "The chains bought it right off and wired for more!" In September of 1961 G Company began shipping wrap in volume. They reached a peak production of wrapped lettuce in Redrock in the fall of 1961, shipping as many as 30 cars a day. Their total volume of wrap for Arizona alone for the 1961-62 season amounted to over 600,000 cartons. By the 1961-62 season, however, competitors were shipping their versions of wrapped lettuce. In addition to G Company, the other three companies forming the basis of this study accounted for over 134,000 cartons of wrapped lettuce shipped in Arizona.

Carlot totals for the following season (1962-63) document the quick decline of wrapped lettuce. G Company itself dropped from 600,000 to less than 300,000 cartons shipped in Arizona. The other three companies dropped from 134,000 to less than 40,000 for Arizona, with one company abandoning it entirely. When asked about the decline in wrapped lettuce, B refused to view it as a decline. When asked why it did not go as big as he originally thought, he replied, "Because the industry never pushed it hard. It's coming!" He also blamed the fact that some used it for second quality lettuce. During the 1964 spring season G Company was still shipping 20 percent of their lettuce wrapped. They still had regular customers who bought nothing but wrapped lettuce.

Although we collected data on G Company over a period of three years, intensive observations were carried out principally during the 1963 spring harvests in Pinal County. At this time and place G Company harvested 1,120 acres of lettuce. G Company farmed a total of 3,135 acres. It shipped 1,587,019 cartons of lettuce in Arizona in 1962-63. This accounted for 5.5 percent of the total acreage and 6.8 percent of the total production in the state. This corporation also has farms in Imperial Valley, Salinas, Watsonville, and Firebaugh. They also occasionally buy up crops in Aguila and Willcox, Arizona.

Except for historical data to point up developmental trends, all descriptive data following pertain to G Company's Pinal County spring harvest operation of 1963.

Mechanical Harvesting and Handling Equipment

  9 — wrap machines, made as described above
  5 — stitcher trucks, each serving a ground crew
 17 — Fabco wide wheeler trucks to haul cartons from field to plant
  8 — crew buses
 10 — ½-ton pickups for foremen and field superintendents
  2 — ½-ton pickups for mechanics
  3 — large portable parts houses
200 — humps, flatbed wheelbarrows for packers in ground crews
200 — clamps, used by box closers in ground crews
150 — spray cans, 5 gallon, used by waterboys to spray top layer of lettuce in cartons before lids are closed
150 — staple guns, used by closers to staple shut cartons
500 — knives, used by cutters in all crews

Organizational Structure of Harvest Activities

In 1963 G Company had five ground crews and three machine crews operating at peak cutting in Redrock, Pinal County. The organization of each type of crew will be discussed separately. The ground crew system of field pack was described in the Background. G Company uses the standard system. Their Redrock harvest ground crews, which would vary slightly in numbers of workers per position, had on the average the following breakdown:

 40 — cutter-trimmers
 20 — packers
  6 — closers

```
4 — water boys
3-4 — box spreaders
  6 — windrowing and loading
  1 — stacker or folder
  1 — stitcher-driver
  2 — pushers or row bosses
  1 — foreman
```

In their other operations ground crews are usually made up of 60 Nationals who cut and pack exclusively, while locals (usually 16 in number), fill the remaining positions. However, in Redrock G Company had 80 Nationals on each ground crew to allow for the fluctuations in the number of locals. The extra Nationals were put on cutting and packing when the company had enough locals and on spreading, windrowing, spray-pad, closing, and loading in that order when they could not get enough locals. As the field superintendent said, "Monday, no locals; Tuesday they're all there." Thus, the ground crew sizes for G Company in Redrock varied from 80 to as many as 100 men.

The ground crew field pack system in operation at G Company was organized around a stable core of Mexican Nationals who were schooled to perform the most strategic jobs. Of the 34 non-Nationals who were interviewed on the ground crews, their profile is as follows: Twenty were Mexican-American, eight were green card Mexicans (immigrants), three were Negro, and three were Anglo. Twenty-two of them were below the age of 30, 18 of them were educated beyond the 7th grade, and all except seven were members of households. Perhaps the most significant fact is that 28 of these 34 were of Mexican descent. Another ethnic priority for positions was evident. Those of Mexican descent were engaged almost exclusively in closing (lidding), windrowing, and loading and were readily distinguished from "farm office boys" who were usually — depending upon how long they stayed with the company — given spray-pad and box spreading.

The foremen and row bosses for G Company's ground crews were all Mexican-American with a few green card Mexicans working as row bosses. Of the few Anglos who were working in skilled jobs in the ground crew system, all were stitcher-drivers, i.e., they drove the stitcher truck and made boxes for the crew. Stitcher-drivers were about evenly divided between Anglos and Mexican-Americans.

G Company's machine crews point up even more strongly the Mexican-American and green card Mexican ethnic pattern. Some historical digression is needed at this point, however. When G Company first began to use their present lettuce machines they planned on building up a steady, permanent harvest force for the company. B felt that the machine would make this possible by eliminating most of the stoop work and saving in shipping costs, thus allowing higher wages for machine crews. Moreover, G Company had volume lettuce year-round, guaranteeing steady work for those who were willing to move. B was even talking about getting FHA financing for a fleet of house trailers to house his corps of permanent "migratory" workers. He talked about a $1.50 minimum wage for the most menial tasks in his machine harvest crews.

G Company's first trial in human organization, in an avowed effort to recruit more steady workers, was the hiring of husband and wife teams on his machines. B's thinking was that married workers are more steady workers and that male workers would tend to be more responsible with their wives working where they could watch them. This policy proved a partial failure since it could not be followed consistently. Many good workers simply did not come this way. Furthermore, a great deal of fighting developed when husbands objected to orders given their wives by the foremen. This policy was eliminated as an aim, although many husbands and wives still work in the same crews and even on the same machines together. Another plan which soon required modification was the company's effort to make up entire machine crews from local workers. After a few unsuccessful trials, they had to draw the line at cutting and trimming. FHA financing was never obtained for mobile housing and the $1.50 minimum was never attained, even in the peak wrap year. But it did reach $1.19 (ASES 1962a: 27), considerably higher than the required minimum.

In the fall and winter of 1961, G Company had machine crews made up of one machine per crew. Mexican Nationals cut and locals performed all other tasks. Each single-machine crew had one foreman (most of whom were Anglos) and one row boss, all of whom were Mexican-Americans or green card Mexicans. Also we observed that almost all of the machine drivers were Anglos with a mixture of Anglos and Mexican-Americans doing the remaining tasks. Wrapping was done primarily by women but occasionally by men. Women occasionally performed other tasks such as putting scraps of film in sacks on the Vancos, and infrequently set-up (retrieving cut heads). Machines varied in the number of wrapping stations. As many as eight could be seen or as few as four. During 1962 organizational fluctuation became less, but an equilibrium had still not been reached. This was perhaps a reflection of the mechanical experimentation still going on. The Mexican element became more pronounced and the Anglos fewer. G Company had eliminated the one-foreman-per-machine pattern and was running two machines per crew, referred to as "tandem-machine operations" in the *Arizona Lettuce Production Survey* (ASES 1962a: 28).

By the spring of 1963, during the time of intensive field observations, mechanical as well as organizational equilibrium had been reached. All Vancos had been eliminated. There was only one standard type of machine to be found. Moreover, there was no talk of further innovations. This was in striking contrast to the past two years when the air was electric with scuttlebutt and changes occurred almost daily. Now the basic pattern was as follows:

There were three machines per crew with each machine having:

    10-12 — cutter-trimmers, all Nationals
       4 — set-up
       6 — wrap
       3 — fillers (packers)

1 — gluer
1 — stitcher-driver

Each crew of three machines had, in addition to the above men multiplied by three:

2 — loaders
1 — row boss
1 — foreman

The total number of workers per crew ran from 79 to 85 — 30 to 36 Nationals and 49 locals. The cutters were all Nationals. Each machine had six wrap stations, all operated by women. No women were at any other tasks. Set-up jobs were reserved almost exclusively for the farm office placements.

The Mexican-American pattern was now complete from the foreman down. The exception was the farm office placements who were generally Anglo or Negro. Of the 73 machine crew workers who were interviewed, all but 12 were of Mexican descent — 40 were citizens and 20 green carders. Over 50 were below the age of 50. Almost half had over a 7th grade education. Forty-six of the 73 were part of households, with most of these forty-six from the Mexican element. Two of the three machine crew foremen and all row bosses were Mexican-American.

The only skilled positions in which Anglos or non-Mexicans could be found in any numbers were driver-stitchers and truck drivers. These jobs were about equally divided between the two ethnic groups. A high percentage of these workers were working for G Company the year-round. Moreover, all wage workers, including even the field hands, now belonged to the Teamsters' Union. The exceptions were a few workers who worked for G Company in Arizona only. Nevertheless, regardless of union organization, patterns of conduct between positions — how people were arranged in their tasks, who got what tasks, who did the teaching of tasks to newcomers — were based largely on informal, interpersonal, and interfamily relationships, a natural outgrowth of the ethnic and class characteristics of the young Mexican element. This will be developed in more detail in the worker section of the study.

Although B has not realized his vision of a vast, centrally housed, mobile community of an elite class of migrant workers, he has accomplished two things which might give him an edge in the non-bracero times ahead. He has a commercially proven field pack system which has as its nucleus an integrated class of local workers. Secondly, a relatively high degree of stability has been achieved in the relationship between the company and these workers.

Wage System

Wage rates are expressed in two ways. First there is a guaranteed hourly minimum which varies by the particular job task the individual is performing. Second there is a per-carton piece rate calculated on a per-crew basis, whereby a crew as a whole gets a total amount of earnings from the total number of cartons it produces. These earnings are divided up among the crew on the basis of the job task performed. Each job task group has its fractional portion of the crew's per-carton piece rate; e.g. the piece rate for a crew may be $.21 per carton, but the sprayers and spreaders may get only $.0098 per carton, the lidders and loaders $.0516 per carton, and the cutters and packers $.1388 per carton. Theoretically the variations in guaranteed hourly minimum rates and the variations in piece rates per task groups should be on the same scale. For instance, if a cutter makes a certain percentage more than a spreader in terms of minimum hourly wage, he should make the same percentage more than the spreader in terms of the piece rate. To quote from the *Arizona Lettuce Production Survey*: "This method provided a scale of rates for the various task groups which were graduated upward from the less skilled tasks, and which also provided hourly guarantees and overtime pay" (ASES 1962a: 4).

Following are job descriptions for each type of job, the number of workers per job group, the guaranteed hourly minimum, and the piece rate per carton as specified in the job order for G Company. The ground crew system and the machine crew system are given separately under the headings "Ground Harvest Operations" and "Machine Harvest — Hand Wrap Operations," respectively.

[G Company]
LETTUCE & CABBAGE HARVEST
MASTER ORDER TO
THE ARIZONA STATE EMPLOYMENT SERVICE
THE CALIFORNIA DEPARTMENT OF EMPLOYMENT
EFFECTIVE MARCH 1, 1963

The following are conditions of employment offered by [G Company] for lettuce and cabbage harvest in California and Arizona and the descriptions are outlined in the terms of lettuce but references to "lettuce" are also references to "cabbage," since the work is the same for both.

I. *Ground Harvest Operations:*

The wage offered is 21 cents divided among the crew and underlying hourly crew guarantees applicable to group job classifications as follows:

Job Description	No. of Workers	Guaranteed Hourly Wage	Piece Rate Per Carton
Cutter-Trimmer-Packer	60-72	$1.12 per hour	$.1388
Carton and/or Crate Spreader	2	1.26 per hour	.0098
Water Spray & Pad Man	2	1.26 per hour	.0098
Field Lidder*	4	1.40 per hour	.0237
Field Loader*	5	1.40 per hour	.0279
			$.21

*Workers in a 9 man team share wages on equal basis as combination may be 5 lidders and 4 loaders depending on work.

The hourly guarantee is applied on a field basis and applies to the over-all crew average of piece rate earnings. Crew is set up on a basis of 73 to 78, but may change to coincide with work to be performed as required and established by employer. Jobs will be filled in each crew from field loader positions up as shown above.

Definitions:

Field Loader: Includes only those employees who carry-over packed cartons or crates to the windrow and lift the packed boxes up to the bed of the trucks and stack such boxes in the load.

Field Lidder: Includes only the employees who center top pads and close the cartons or crates by stapling, hand nailing, or gluing.

Field Spray & Pad Man: Includes only those employees who wash or spray the lettuce and place pads on the top of the commodity packed in the container.

Cutter-Trimmer-Packer: Includes only those employees who pick the correct size of lettuce by cutting the roots of the lettuce with a knife and trim the outer leaves according to instructions and place the trimmed head on top of the bed (planted rows) according to instructions. The packer then comes and picks that trimmed head and places it in the carton or a container.

II. *Machine Harvest — Hand Wrap Operations:*

The wage offered is 20.388 cents per carton, divided among the crew with the piece rate and underlying hourly crew guarantee applicable to various job classifications as follows:

Job Classification	No. of Workers	Guaranteed Hourly Wage	Piece Rate Per Carton
Cutter-Trimmer-Set Up*			
(in rotation)	36	$1.12 per hour	$.08666
Wrapper, Hand*	24	1.26 per hour	.06999
Carton Filler*	9	1.40 per hour	.02784
Container Gluer &			
Sealer-Stacker-Loader*	6	1.40 per hour	.01939
			$.20388

*Machines operate in combinations to accomplish the work required and Container Gluer and Sealer-Stacker-Loaders work together as a team for the machine combination.

The hourly guarantee is applied on a field basis and applies to the over-all crew average of piece rate earnings. Crew is set up on a basis of 75 workers, but may be changed to coincide with work to be performed as required and established by employer. Jobs will be filled in each crew from carton sealer up as shown above.

Definitions:

Cutter-Trimmer-Set Up: Includes only those workers who select the proper quality and size of lettuce and cut the head of lettuce from the root with a knife and trim the outer leaves and place the trimmed head of lettuce on top of the bed on leaves, all in accord with instructions. The pick up then lifts the head from the bed and makes a critical examination of each head to determine that trimming is proper, that there is no decay, broken leaves or such other damage or defect as instructed, whereupon the head is placed at the wrapping station. Workers work in rotation either cutting-trimming or picking up.

Hand Wrapper: Includes only those workers who work to wrap the head of lettuce in film in a manner prescribed and upon instructions while sitting or standing at a wrapping station and the machine.

Carton Filler: Includes only those workers who fill cartons with wrapped lettuce in a manner and/or in a pattern as prescribed and in accord with instructions from time to time.

Container Gluer & Sealer-Stacker-Loader: Includes only those employees who glue, seal or otherwise close filled containers, move filled containers to the ground, apply glue or otherwise close the box, stack the filled boxes and load the boxes onto a field truck in combination, one man from each machine glues and stacks while the two others load the packed and sealed containers.

Drivers, stitchers, and stitcher-drivers for G Company receive an hourly rate of $2.925 with overtime allowed (after crew shut down). Row bosses earn $2.39 with no overtime. Foremen earn a monthly salary between $600 and $750. No wage distinction between ground or machine crew is made in these categories.

There are two hidden factors which are not apparent in this formalized breakdown. One operates to favor certain groups of workers under certain conditions. The other operates to favor G Company workers in general over workers in other companies. The first factor is a result of the fact that the number of workers per job classification varies according to field conditions. Some variations from the formalized job descriptions have become permanent. The formula for converting minimum hourly wage rates to piece rates is simple; at a given ratio of production the minimum hourly wage for a task group equals the piece rate for that task group *divided* by the number of workers in that particular task group *when* the conversion was originally made. If the number of workers for a given task group is reduced with no adjustment in the piece rate for that task group, then the remaining workers in that task group will exceed their minimum hourly wage at a lower level of production than the workers in other task groups. For instance, originally there were eight wrappers per machine (24 per machine crew). At the time of our field observations there were only six per machine or 18 per crew. This lowers the minimum number of cartons at which piece rates will begin for wrappers.

Actually, such differentials have become formalized for the task groups in the machine crews as follows: Wrappers begin to earn piece rates when the crew's production has reached 2,700 cartons per eight hours. Loaders and gluers cut in at 3,500 per eight hours, fillers at 3,600, and cutter-trimmer and set-up do not begin to earn piece rates until the crew has produced 12,000 cartons per eight hours. For the latter group piece rates are virtually meaningless. They receive minimum hourly wage rates only. No one is cheated. But, the actual amount earned by the workers in the different task groups does not vary from group to group in the manner represented by the guaranteed hourly wage figure. The workers in the crews are keenly aware of this. Incentives for this or that group operate in accordance with a net result of a combination of factors rather than in accordance with just the posted hourly minimum. This is borne out to a certain extent by the *Arizona Lettuce Production Survey* which shows wrappers in Pinal County 1962 spring harvest making the highest hourly earnings of any task group in the machine crews (ASES 1962a: 27); yet their guaranteed hourly wage figure would seem to put them midway between the lowest and the highest in earning potential.

The second factor is that G Company allows the computation of piece rate for fractions of full work days. They go by the field. When a crew goes to another field in the middle of the day, the crew gets another crack at exceeding their hourly wage figure. The company allows the computation of piece rates on the basis of the number of hours in that particular field for the remainder of the day. Thus, if the crew spent only one hour in a field, the wrappers would be allowed to earn more than their guaranteed $1.26 providing the crew's production for that hour in that field exceeded more than 337.5 cartons, even though the crew's production may have been far below that hourly rate in another field. The company may underwrite low production throughout one portion of the day, yet pay a piece rate wage *above* the guaranteed minimum for another portion of the same day.

Experience Account

To present a clear focus of a grower's opinion or attitude toward harvest systems has a tendency to distort the grower's *whole* view. This is especially true of lettuce growers because the field pack system, as it is now practiced, is inextricably associated with the Mexican National program. Owing to the fact that for over a decade braceros have been used in such massive numbers in this key technological role, it should come as no surprise when growers are digressive, vague, and sometimes contradictory about technical and organizational adjustments they are planning. They do not present any single answer because they do not see any single clear cut result. They see rather a host of interdependent variables, all of which are enormously altered by the repeal. This is more apparent as the time comes closer. Prior to 1964 discussion was likely to focus spontaneously upon the relatively simple problems of technical or mechanical systems. As the time moves closer, they seem more compelled to consider human or organizational aspects. This leads inevitably to bewilderment and differences of opinion. Because of their tendencies to view labor problems in terms of technical or mechanical factors, they are on unfamiliar ground when faced with the organizational impact that loss of such a huge labor reservoir is likely to have.

At the risk of arbitrarily reinforcing this awkward dichotomy in the thinking of lettuce growers, we now abstract from their involved accounts only those discussions which have to do with technical systems or mechanical aspects of their harvest systems. Their thinking toward the human aspects of their problems are given in a later section (Part Four). As with other participant interests, managements' accounts tend to be more emotional and more subject to controversy when human aspects of labor systems are discussed. It is important to provide management with the same anonymity provided for all participants in the farm labor system. That degree of anonymity is not possible in this portion of the study.

A year ago at G Company, B and most of his management personnel were unanimous about the labor-solving potential of the machine-wrap system. Today this unanimity is gone. Perhaps this is due in part to some of its fundamental technical problems. H, a district manager of a large lettuce company in the Salt River Valley, a previous associate and a long time admirer of B, had this to say about the machine wrap system:

> Wrap does help carrying qualities, but other times it doesn't. There are three disadvantages to it. (1) If there is any loss or any deterioration in the head, rather than losing a leaf or two, the total head is lost. (2) Quality is far more critical in the harvest operation. (3) There is less bulk involved hence less money changing hands and less profit to work with on the part of buyers.
>
> However some form of this is coming. Chain stores showed an interest in the wrap lettuce. Their disposal problem is solved, but the jobbing trade resists it. They resist any change because the competition is so intense. For instance they're opposing moving markets out of town, out of the dust-belt area just because it is a change. They fought the carton and vacuum pack, but the chains bought it immediately. They liked it because the cartons were half the size and weight of the crate and women could handle them. Also the lettuce had a much longer shelf life.

H considers the most serious problem of the machines to be the fact that they

> . . . led _____(B) right back to the same trap which caused the machines in dry-pack not to work — namely being inflexible so far as adjusting to the individual differences between one bed of lettuce and another. The ground crew system with Mexican Nationals offers maximum flexibility with respect to this; whereas on the machines if one side is lighter than another the people on that side do nothing . . .
>
> There is some entrenchment against going to any other system, but _____(B) pushed it over before. He is probably the guy to push it over again, but there are more sophisticated processes involved now. The point is that before (going from shed pack to field pack) we went from heavy investment to light, but now the problem is in going the other way.

B, himself, still feels that it will come to some form of prepackaging. However he does not dwell so singlemindedly upon wrap as he used to. Now he considers other alternatives as well. When asked how he was going to face the repeal of P.L. 78 he responded:

> We'll do something — we'll pay our cutters three or four dollars an hour and get some bums to throw it in a truck. We'll go to filling — just a bulk deal, by weight and volume. Liddin' and packin' is a lot of bull__! They (referring to present ground crew system) make too much work for themselves. They make it hard. Hell, there doesn't have to be that much work to packing lettuce!

(Asked about going back to the shed) — Give me a hundred good cutters and the rest bums, to throw it in a box, and we can get a better product in the field because there's too much handling in the shed.

(Asked about losing space in shipping) — They are building bigger cars all the time. You can get 1400 cartons in some — before you could only get 640. And we can trim closer. Most shippers are against bulk because any farmer can go shipper. We're also thinking seriously about growing lettuce in Mexico — going where the labor is.

Others at G Company say that B is thinking about pushing low-weight wrap lettuce through airlines freight for overseas markets — Canada, The Netherlands, and South America. Still others say that he will do something simple, like recruit and pay top wages to cut and pack the old (ground crew) way.

H COMPANY—FIELD PACK AND SHED WRAP

H Company is one of the pioneers of the Arizona lettuce industry. Along with Knowlton and McClaren, H played a major role in the development of Yuma as an important lettuce producing area. They were in the thick of the experimentation going on in the late 1930's and early 1940's, shifting from hauling crates to steel baskets, and from trailers to trucks to conveyors (see *Background*). H Company was the first shipper to begin using the carton field pack and vacuum cooling system in Yuma. They did so in 1953, directly after they went into partnership with G Company and formed the "G and H Cooling Corporation." They had begun independently to use vacuum cooling earlier in El Centro. This had sparked the legal controversy between H and G Companies that led ultimately to the cooling corporation partnership.

The forces that pushed H Company into field packing lettuce are discussed from the viewpoint of their harvest superintendent (now retired). J cites these reasons for the shift:

(1) We were feeling the cost of labor in the shed. We were pressing ourselves out of the business. We had a two dollar crate and couldn't make it! (Asked if there was a sudden increase in wages at any one period) — No, there was more of a trend. We were one hundred percent union, and we tried to argue with them. They wouldn't listen, wouldn't even hold it. Our men were getting increases practically every year. They were absolutely refusing to hold the price and we were caught in a squeeze. A lot of shippers went under. Every year three to four went out.

(2) There was also an increase in the price of lumber. A crate used to cost 10 cents and when we stopped using crates and went to cartons (1951), crates were costing between 50 and 60 cents apiece. Now a crate costs 75 cents. So we figured it out that at 25 cents for a carton, we could buy two cartons for one crate. This savings is tremendous. Last year for instance, we used 1,500,000 cartons just in Arizona!

(3) The trade began demanding this pack. Not so much the pack itself, but the liking for an easier package to handle in the store. The stores were using women help and they couldn't handle crates but they can handle cartons.

(4) It cuts out the hauling of culls and excess handling. In the field, culls simply are not cut.

On the opposite side, J says:

The shed gave a little better control of the packing operation and also allowed the shipper to have better control of the market. This way anybody who can afford to lease equipment and lease ground, can grow as much lettuce as he wants to because all he has to do for labor is to license for Nationals.

J maintained that they did not have immediate success because:

. . . We were all new to the game. We were using people who were connected with the shed pack in the field in an attempt to teach the packing to the Mexicans and there was friction. They didn't want to get out from the sheds to the fields because they knew it would be a job loss. And there was a certain amount of resentment of Mexicans. Also, there were complaints from buyers because at first it gave the appearance of being a very good thing but it flooded the market. There was no study of loading and storage and handling problems of lettuce handled in this fashion. The trade was not ready for the change just then.

In cantaloupes the struggle is going on right now. Two years ago some companies started using cartons in the shed and the workers refused to do it, and we had to abandon it. They threatened to strike.

Asked how Mexican Nationals worked out in the field for packing, J said:

We started with white packers, but they were not subject to the control that we can put on Mexican labor. They were out to get the quantity — go, go, go — they don't care about the product. With the Mexican, he didn't care about being slowed down, not so driven with money-lust. Whites were late, drunk, and unruly, and after all, they were out to stop this field pack. We had 30 to 40 white cutters and packers. We had to let them go. They were absolutely uncontrollable.

H Company does not emphasize experimentation as much as G Company. Their organization is not set up for it. They have a highly formalized organization that fits the blueprint of industrial management. In the two recent technological changes, they responded to demand rather than stake their reputation on pushing a first. This was demonstrated in the role they played in the field carton pack. It was demonstrated again in their response to the most recent development in the industry — film wrapped lettuce. H was not *the* first, but *one* of the first shippers of film wrapped lettuce. They did not use Trycite, tested by G Company, but a competitive version of it — Cello Wrap — developed by Du Pont. As D, the general manager of their Arizona Division, sums it up: "Competition forces you to do many things and this was one of them."

H Company began wrapping as a field operation in 1961-62 in Imperial Valley. In their field operation, H used a modified bracero bus as a mobile packing shed to house 14 wrappers and two packers. The mobile shed was preceded by cutters who were all Mexican Nationals. Inside the mobile shed were a mixture of Anglos and Mexican-Americans, all domestics. The wrappers were all women, wives of other H employees, and the packers were men who were taught by packers from the ground crews. The company wrapped in the field this way for a year, then moved to the shed for prepackaging on a "limited demand" basis. In the shed the proper selection could be controlled — "quality control," D calls it. He adds, "On a pioneer deal like this there has to be some sacrificial lamb._____(G Company) went big into this field with a mobile packing operation but this is not the way. The shed is more experienced and it may come to it even though it is union."

H's wrap operation, as it now stands, is identical to the shed pack operation in the ice-pack days, viz. in the field, cutters (Mexican Nationals) toss heads into large metal baskets mounted on wide wheelers. The trucks haul to the shed where the metal baskets are rolled off the trucks, lifted by power, and tilted onto conveyors which carry the heads first to the trimmers, wrappers, shrinking ovens, finally to the packers. The packers fill standard cardboard cartons which are then sealed, vacuum cooled, and loaded on refrigerated vans or cars. All shed workers, except foremen, are union.

H Company was shipping as high as 15 to 20 percent of their lettuce prepackaged. In the 1964 spring harvest they were shipping about five percent. This was for the company in both Arizona and California. In Arizona they shipped almost 14,000 cartons of wrapped lettuce in 1961-62. In 1962-63 they shipped 11,865.

Their two divisions — California and Arizona — farmed a combined total of 5,597 acres of lettuce in 1962-63 and produced a combined total of 3,277,904 cartons of lettuce. This accounted for approximately four percent of all the lettuce shipped in the nation. In addition to lettuce, this corporation produces grapes, strawberries, safflower, broccoli, romaine, cauliflower, melons, cotton, alfalfa, bermuda seed, and cattle. Their Arizona Division accounted for 4.6 percent of the lettuce acreage and 6.8 percent of the cartons shipped in the state in 1962-63. Their lettuce acreage for that year breaks down as follows: Yuma, 1,311; Harquahala, 600; and Aguila, 650. All field observations were made at their Yuma operation in the spring of 1963.

Mechanical Harvesting and Handling Equipment

    4 — Fabco trucks converted to stitching trucks to serve ground crews
    7 — Fabco wide wheeler trucks to haul cartons from field
    5 — ½ -ton pickups for foremen and field superintendents
    1 — ¾ -ton pickup, power chassis for mechanics' tools
    1 — 1-ton flat-bed truck hauling cartons and water
    3 — crew buses
    3 — wide track trailers

      10 — gas engines, emergency power for stitching machines
      35 — box presses or clamps used by box closers
      40 — staple guns, used by box closers
     100 — humps or portable packing tables
     250 — lettuce knives
      12 — foremen knives

Organizational Structure of Harvest Activities

The Arizona Division of H Company is headed by a general manager. Under the general manager are four ranches and the following supervisors: a supervisor of vegetable and melon growing; a cattle superintendent; a cotton superintendent; a supervisor of small grains and grain feed; a supervisor of purchasing, labor procurement, and payroll; and a harvesting superintendent. Under the harvesting superintendent is the following hierarchy: an assistant harvesting superintendent, a cutter-packer supervisor, four crew foremen, 12 row bosses, and 300 harvest hands. Also under the harvest superintendent are seven truck drivers, a mechanic, and a service man.

The system in use at their Yuma lettuce harvesting operation during the time of our observations was the standard field pack system. The harvest superintendent was a young Anglo college graduate with a degree in agricultural economics. He had worked for three years as assistant harvest superintendent under J, the old timer shed pack and field pack veteran who had just retired. The cutter-packer supervisor was Anglo, also with experience in the shed pack tradition. The assistant harvest superintendent, alternating as a crew foreman, was a 29-year-old Mexican-American with 11 years experience in the field pack tradition — four years packing, four years as row boss, three years as foreman, and now part-time assistant harvest superintendent. The last five years he worked for H Company.

All foremen were of Mexican descent—three of them Mexican-American and one a Mexican immigrant (green carder). The Mexican row bosses were predominantly green card Mexicans. Nine out of the 12 were immigrants and the other three citizens. Each crew was organized around a stable nucleus of Mexican Nationals who performed all of the cutting and packing. During the week of March 11 through 16, 1963, Crew One had 53 Nationals, Crew Two had 57, Crew Three had 57, and Crew Four had 58. Each crew varied in the number of domestics from 12 to 25. During the above week, H Company had a maximum of 100 locals with a minimum of 78.

Taking a maximum of 79 men, 54 Nationals and 25 locals, the job-task breakdown of an H Company ground crew in average density first cutting lettuce is as follows:

      36 — cutter-trimmers
      18 — packers
       3 — water boys (spray-pad)
       6 — closers
     3-4 — box spreaders
     2-3 — windrowers
       4 — loaders

1 — stacker or folder
1 — stitcher-driver
3 — row bosses
1 — foreman

Nationals are put on cutting and packing first. If there is a surplus, they are put on the other jobs in the following order: spreader, closer, windrower, spray-pad, and loader.

Of the 49 local or domestic workers interviewed, 25 were Negro, 13 were Anglo, eight Mexican-American, and only two green carders. Thirty-four or almost 70 percent of these men were not attached to any households. Twenty-four were above the ages of 40, and 37, or three-fourths, had above a 7th grade education. Nine were high school graduates and four had gone to college! These 49 were all harvest hands occupied in this order of frequency: spray-padding, spreading, closing, windrowing, and loading.

With the exception of the equipment operators, all of whom were Anglos, positions of importance from cutting, packing, row bossing, foremen, on up to assistant harvest superintendent were, without exception, Mexican.

Wage System

Harvest hands receive a $1 an hour guaranteed wage or an equal division among *all* workers of 24 cents a carton. The H Company has by agreement with their local farm labor office a "pool system" for their piece rate. This means that the total production of *all* crews for the day is used in determining whether the workers get piece rate or minimum wage. For instance, four crews of 75 men each working for an eight-hour day would earn $2,400 at the hourly wage figure. Regardless of the production of any given crew, under the "pool system," all four crews would collectively have to produce 10,001 cartons before the piece rate would take effect. Then it would take effect for all workers in all crews equally.

Management considers this system superior to the individual crew system because variations in the quality and density of lettuce from field to field are equalized and "the penalty of having to hire locals is equalized." The latter means that one crew will not object to getting more locals — whom they consider to be unproductive — than another crew.

Stitcher-drivers get $2.925 an hour and $4.2125 for overtime. Folders and drivers get $2.575 an hour and $3.8625 overtime. Row bosses get $1.75 an hour. Foremen are salaried at $100 to $135 a week.

Experience Account

H Company's experience with wrap differed from G Company's. First, H was not the innovator. They went into it only as a result of demand. Secondly, they did not make the tremendous investments in wrap equipment that G Company did. Therefore they are not as committed to film wrapped lettuce. They were more ready to talk about the decline in wrap. D, the general manager, blames two things — the use of wrap for inferior quality lettuce and consumer resistance. Since outer leaves could be taken off, some growers took advantage of this to harvest what was not marketable in the regular carton. D developed his thesis about consumer resistance by pointing out that quality is critical in the introduction of prepackaged produce because the housewife instinctively distrusts it. "She examines wrapped items more critically than the ones not wrapped because she thinks the store is trying to sell inferior fruit." Another drawback, according to D, is the crinkly sound of the plastic film. In the main D would agree with G Company on the future of wrapped lettuce. He cites the fact that the chemical companies are beginning to break through the "sound" problem, and are coming up with a breathing *soft* film. Also, he thinks that the industry generally is now more quality conscious in wrap packing. D sums it up by saying, "It will all be wrap five years from now."

As to alternatives to the bracero-centered field pack system, D generally seems to be thinking in terms of moving back to the sheds (H Company has already done this for their wrap), ". . . which would require a general upscaling of costs whereby the consumer would buy less, but pay more." On the other hand, his reservations also are apparent when he points out that

> . . . Arizona lettuce is not localized around a shed operation investment. We farm Aguila and Harquahala and this scares me. If this goes to shed then outlying districts are cooked geese — *our* (H Company's) cooked geese — there's no domestic labor force— the investment for such a short shipping season in these outlying areas would be fabulous. Aguila, Harquahala, and Willcox came about because of the shift from the Salt River gravity irrigation system to pumping. These are field packing areas. They would collapse or become one central cooperative. There would be tremendous changes.

I COMPANY — FIELD PACK

I Company is smaller and simpler than the other three companies. It is headed by one man, J, who began in lettuce in 1942. J started in dry-pack before anything else but he packed and shipped first cutting and first grade lettuce. This was an exception to the ordinary dry-pack procedure.

In 1947 he bought the American Fruit Growers shed in Yuma but processed his *second grade* lettuce in the shed rather than the first grade. In 1956-57 he abandoned the shed pack altogether. According to N, his field superintendent, he was the last man in the Yuma area to abandon the shed pack for lettuce. As N put it:

> . . . There's no doubt the biggest saving in dry pack in cartons, or crates either for that matter, as a field operation compared to a shed operation is in the labor. If the unions had laid off making demands, I know they would now still be in the shed. The growers wouldn't have abandoned such an investment. What it boiled down to was staying in business. It meant go to the fields and stay competitive or stay in the shed and go broke!

According to N, shed packers were getting $2.50 to $3 an hour. This compared to the going rate in field operations of 50 cents an hour.

In 1961-62, J moved heavily into film wrapped lettuce. He shipped over 95,000 cartons that year, almost a quarter of his 1962-63 production. He used Dow Chemical Company's Trycite — the same used by G Company. Rather than a field operation, however, he used a shed system about identical to H Company (see above). Their trimmers and wrappers were women, all the other workers were men. Although many of the workers were too young to have been working in the sheds during the ice-pack days a number of them had shed-packed before. The workers were mostly Anglos, with Mexican-Americans numbering about one to three. The workers were union members on "withdrawal." This means they were inactive and were not paying dues at this time by permission of the union. This is normal procedure for shed workers during the winter season.

By the following season (winter 1963), J was shipping no wrapped lettuce whatsoever. According to his management it was difficult to get premiums to make it pay. "Wrap has to get fifty cents more. You could do it on a four dollar market, but on a buck and a buck and a quarter, it gets kind of tough." Also cited was the fact that latent defects do not show up until after shipment. Then the receiver has to unwrap the defective heads, trim off the defects, and rewrap it. J since has sold most of his wrap equipment.

At the time of field observations, I Company was farming 1,688 acres of lettuce and shipped, during the 1962-63 season, 423,182 cartons accounting for 1.8 percent of the total shipped in Arizona. In addition to lettuce, the company also grows and ships cantaloupes. Their entire operation is in the Yuma area.

Mechanical Harvesting and Handling Equipment

    5 — Fabco widewheeler trucks
    2 — ½-ton pickups for foremen
    4 — crew buses
  75 — humps, flatbed wheelbarrows or packing tables
  25 — clamps, used by box closers
  15 — staple guns, used by closers
    9 — hatchets used for crates for special orders
100 — knives
  72 — files
  12 — water cans
    1 — stitcher truck, modified from a Fabco widewheeler

In addition, I Company leases the following:
    1 — stitcher truck
    4 — stitching machines

Organizational Structure of Harvest Activities

I Company's entire field operation, including harvest, is organized under a field superintendent. Directly under him are a tractor foreman, an insect and fertilizer foreman, and an assistant field superintendent. Under the assistant field superintendent is the irrigator foreman and the field foreman for harvest or cutting operations. Under the latter are two harvest crews each headed by a foreman. Each crew foreman has an assistant called a "helper," "assistant row boss," or "pusher." Generally 185 to 200 men are employed in the harvest operations. They are split into two large crews.

I Company uses the standard ground crew field packing system organized around Mexican Nationals. A social profile of the force engaged in harvest activities runs as follows. The field superintendent was an Anglo, in the lettuce packing business almost 20 years. He knows both the shed pack and the field pack. The key man directly under him was the assistant field superintendent, a 42-year-old Mexican-American in lettuce field harvest systems for 22 years — virtually all of his adult life. In 1940 this man was doing contract thinning at so much an acre. In 1942, when Mexican Nationals began to be used, he started supervising thinning-and-cutting crews by helping his brother and father, crew bosses. He has been "pushing Nationals" for I Company for 15 years. The cutting foreman directly under him was an old Filipino directly from the old dry-pack tradition. One crew foreman was a Mexican-American with a green card assistant. The second crew foreman was a green card Mexican with a Mexican National assistant. The latter, however, was sponsored for citizenship by I Company and was in the process of getting his immigration papers and work permit — green card.

I Company had a total of 95 Nationals, 58 green card Mexicans and 36 non-green card domestics. (Technically green carders are considered domestics.) Of the 36 non-green card domestic workers interviewed, 19 were Anglos, eight were Negroes, six were Mexican-Americans, and three were Apache Indians. Twenty-seven, or three-fourths, were isolates and exactly half were over 40. All except five had above a 7th grade education. Eight were high school graduates and three had a college education.

J's crews, generally 90 men each (99 men counting foremen, stitcher, folder, and loaders), break down as follows:

48 — cutter-trimmers
24 — packers
 2 — waterboys (spray-pad)
 8 — closers
 4 — spreaders
 5 — windrowers
 4 — loaders
 1 — folder
 1 — stitcher
 1 — row boss or assistant
 1 — crew foreman

The usual job-task hierarchy prevails. Cutting and packing are considered most important. Their most experienced Nationals or green carders are used in these tasks. Spraying, spreading, windrowing, and closing in that order are given to their itinerate workers or "farm office boys" as they are called — those placed through the involuntary day haul system. Loading and folding are considered choice jobs and are handed out to the domestics with more longevity with the company.

Of the three drivers interviewed, all were Anglos. Of the two stitching machine operators, one was an Anglo and the other a Mexican-American.

Wage System

The harvest hands are on a 22 cents per-carton per-crew piece rate, with a guaranteed 95 cents an hour wage. Loaders, folders, and, of course, stitchers, drivers, and row bosses are not included in this system. Loaders collectively, for the entire operation, get 2½ cents a carton. This 2½ cents is generally divided among eight men, sometimes among six. Folders get $1.25 an hour. Each stitcher gets 1¼ cents per packed carton his crew produces. Drivers collectively get 2 cents for all cartons produced by both crews. This must be split among four. Pushers or row bosses get $12 a day. Foremen are salaried at $84 to $100 per week.

Experience Account

In the winter of 1963, when J was asked about trends at the packing and shipping end of the industry, he said:

> Hell, it'll go back to the shed if the buyers would let it! (Asked what was causing it)—These locals! That's the reason the Mexicans can't make anything now. They are carrying up to 50 locals on their backs — carrying boxes around and pads and stuff. The shed can beat it because there they will make up on piece rate. (Asked about the union) — Hell, we've always had to put up with them in one way or another!

As of this writing however, he has no plans to move back to the shed when the Nationals go. They have no definite idea as to what they are going to do, except to start as usual in the fields with the expectation that they can get enough harvest hands to use the field pack system. They are joining with the Western Growers Association in their plans for recruitment of locals.

J COMPANY—FIELD PACK AND FIELD WRAP

J Company is the youngest of the four companies studied. They *began* four and a half years ago as a field pack operation using the standard carton and vacuum cooling. This company is the only one of the four which made a practice of using independent packing crews. They were packing a film wrapped lettuce using a machine operation similar to G Company's.

Their first experiments with wrapped lettuce began in Yuma in December 1962. Due to killing frost, they did not get into full production. Because of a lack of enough acreage to justify moving their equipment for the remainder of that season, J Company did no more wrap packing. However, they were planning to wrap part of their 1964 Harquahala crop.

J Company's wrap system centers around a Conveyco dry pack machine altered with wrapping stations very similar to G Company's. They use a film manufactured by Union Carbide. Their crews have cutters, set-up, wrappers, fillers, box gluers, and a stitcher. Wrapping is done by women. Their machine crews are composed primarily of Mexican-Americans.

In the 1962-63 season J Company harvested a total of 2,575 acres of lettuce in Arizona and shipped a total of 1,057,784 cartons. This was 4.5 percent of the state's production. The company farmed 1,303 acres of lettuce in Yuma, 760 acres in Harquahala Valley, 287 acres in Willcox, 135 in Aguila, and 90 acres in Salt River Valley. All field observations and worker interviews were made during their spring 1963 harvest in Salt River Valley and Harquahala Valley. In addition to these above crops, J Company also farms cantaloupes and cotton and grows lettuce out of state.

Mechanical Harvesting and Handling Equipment

These data were not available.

Organizational Structure of Harvest Activities

At the time of field observations, J Company had three ground crews working but no machine crews working. One of these ground crews was an independent crew made up of a nucleus of Filipinos augmented by green card Mexicans. The other two crews were the standard type composed almost entirely of Mexican Nationals. One of these crews was under the supervision of an Anglo foreman, the other was under a Mexican-American foreman. Both crews fluctuated around an average of 90 men each.

The Mexican-American's crew had an actual count of 86 men. The breakdown is as follows:

41 — cutters
23 — packers
8 — closers
4 — spreaders
3 — water boys (spray-pad)
2 — windrowers
1 — folder
1 — stitcher-driver
2 — pushers
1 — foreman

All except seven men were Nationals. These seven were the foreman, two pushers, one folder, one stitcher-driver, and two water boys.

The Anglo foreman's crew had an actual count of 90 men assigned as follows:

44 — cutters
24 — packers
7 — closers
4 — spreaders
3 — water boys
2 — windrowers
2 — folders
1 — stitcher-driver
2 — pushers
1 — foreman

All except seven men were Nationals—the foreman, two pushers, one stitcher, two folders, and one waterboy.

The harvest operation was headed by an Anglo field superintendent. Under him was a field foreman, also an Anglo. As mentioned, one of the crew foremen was an Anglo, the other was a 34-year-old Mexican-American. The Mexican-American was born in the United States but schooled in Mexico. He had a 5th grade education and came from an occupational background entirely in field harvests. Ten years ago he began working as a harvest hand in lettuce and apples.

The four pushers have almost identical social profiles. They were between 20 and 33 years old. One had a 4th grade education, two went to the 8th, and one the 9th. All four were Mexican-Americans born, raised, and educated in the United States. All had families.

The six truck drivers and one mechanic fit a different mold. All seven were born or raised in Mexico. Five were still green carders and two had recently gained citizenship. Their level of education ranged between 3rd and 6th grade, all in Mexico. All were living with their families.

The two stitchers fit a third pattern. Both were in their early twenties. Both were Anglos with higher than average levels of education—one 10th grade and the other two years of college. Both lived with their families.

A fourth pattern was exemplified by the two folders and two water boys, involuntary day haul placements from the farm labor office. Four were in their late thirties and one was 54. All were isolates (living alone). Two had a 7th grade education, one a 10th, and a fourth had a Bachelor of Science degree. Two were Anglo and two were Negro.

The independent harvest crew had a 49-year-old Filipino crew leader. Like many of his workers he had immigrated to the United States in 1930 and had begun working in stoop labor in vegetable crops while still in his teens. His father, who did not emigrate from the Philippines, was a sub-sistence farmer and fisherman. Of the 15 other Filipino workers in his crew, all were in their late fifties or early sixties. All had less than an 8th grade education. All schooling had been in the Philippines. Nine or 60 percent of them had less than 4th grade schooling. All except one reported speaking the Ilocano dialect. Three spoke Tagalog and one Sebuano. All of them had emigrated in the late teens or early twenties. Many of them stopped off in Hawaii for a year or two before landing in California. All had begun work in vegetable crops and had adhered almost exclusively throughout the decades to this crop-harvest pattern. They spoke only their dialects (chiefly Ilocano) in the fields. Many of them had difficulty in conversing in most casual English. They referred to their legal status in the United States as "permanent residents."

Of the eight non-Filipinos interviewed on the independent crew, seven were green card Mexicans and one was a naturalized Mexican-American. All but one ranged in their late twenties or early thirties. One had one year of school, two had two years, four had five years, and one six years—all in Mexico. Six were living with their families and two were isolates.

J Company almost invariably reserved first cutting, top label packing for their National crews. The independent crew got second, third, or even fourth cutting, almost always with second label. The independent crew worked for piece rates only but the National crews operated under the adverse effect guaranteed wage of $1 an hour.

Wage System

J Company workers are paid either 24 cents a carton (on a crew basis) or a guaranteed hourly wage of $1. Management reported that each crew decided which system they wanted and then were paid by this system regardless of fluctuations in production. The $1 hourly rate or 24 cents piece rate applied to the cutters, packers, closers, spreaders, water boys, and windrowers.

Each folder receives ½ cent a carton, each stitcher gets 2 cents a carton, loaders get 1 to 1½ cents per carton divided between two. Each truck driver gets 2 cents for each carton that he hauls.

Pushers or row bosses are paid anywhere from $75 to $150 a week and foremen's salaries range between $500 and $750 a month. Foremen also get a pickup and in some cases a car for family use with gas and oil credit cards as well as phone expenses.

Experience Account

Management indicated that they have no special plans to cope with the cancellation of the bracero program except to "play it by ear." They may cut back on their acreage or go completely to independent crews. They also indicated that they may use more green carders. "We would not consider going back to the sheds!"

The attitude of management toward independent crews agrees with the stereotype we encountered with all growers sampled on the subject. They say that independent crews pack only for quantity, do not "take pride" in their pack as the Nationals do, and are not selective in their choice of heads. Management claims independent crews pack heads as they come to them rather than wasting motion in walking up and down the beds looking for the right quality and size.

5 The Cotton Industry

BACKGROUND

COTTON AS AN INDUSTRY is older than either citrus or lettuce. Its origin extends back into precolumbian antiquity. There are references to its cultivation in the colonies as early as 1621 (McGowan 1961:1; Smith and Jones 1948: 34). Also unlike citrus or lettuce, slave labor formed the basis of its technology. Perhaps because of more than a century of slavery and still another century of sharecropping, technological changes in cotton have come about comparatively slowly. A Texas experiment station bulletin brings the time aspect into focus:

> Cotton was grown for its fiber in the United States for approximately 170 years before a young Southern widow inspired Eli Whitney to invent the cotton gin. More than 100 years passed before the invention developed into the modern gin plant. The first mechanical cotton picker was patented in 1851 and almost 100 years passed before this invention developed into a successful machine. The mechanical cotton stripper was first patented in 1871 and 75 years passed before the tractor-mounted stripper came into extensive use. Thus, we can see that mechanical harvesting and processing of cotton has been slow in comparison with the development of the automobile, airplane, radio, radar and the atom bomb (Smith and Jones 1948: 34).

A 1937 National Research Project Report focuses on the economic aspect of the slow evolution of cotton mechanization:

> Even though a mechanically successful and economically feasible cotton picker may be near at hand, its spread will probably be gradual rather than sudden. This view is strengthened by the history of the introduction of other agricultural machines. Rapid mechanization has occurred only where the financial rewards have been high or labor shortage acute. Therefore, as long as there is an abundance of cotton pickers willing to pick cotton for 75 cents to 1 dollar per 100 pounds, and as long as other prices maintain their present alinement, the mechanical picker cannot be expected to take the Cotton Belt by storm (Horne and McKibben 1937: 18).

Hand picking still accounts for almost a third of the cotton harvested in the United States (USDA 1963b). As recently as 1958, Arizona, heading the nation in cotton harvest mechanization (Barnes 1963), harvested more than half its crop by hand (ASES 1959: iv). Not counting experimental and individual grower versions, manufactured stripper harvesters have been available for 33 years. Manufactured spindle harvesters have been on the market for 22 years. Thus in cotton fundamentally different technologies—hand picking and machine picking—have persisted side-by-side for over three decades. It compares in this respect to the contemporaneous shed pack and field pack in the lettuce industry prior to 1950. However in lettuce these two technologies occupied *complementary* roles. In cotton, hand picking and machine picking are fundamentally *competing* technologies. In lettuce, when the field was thrown into direct competition with the shed pack by the sudden appearance of the cardboard carton and the vacuum cooler, its harvesting technology was *completely* revolutionized in eight years. In cotton, more than three decades have witnessed men and machines competing in a seesaw struggle whose outcome must be regarded as an inevitable trend more than a revolution.

This factor helps distinguish cotton technology from that of citrus and of lettuce. Each industry discloses its peculiar history of change, and each in turn has instigated different types of occupational and social adjustments. The relatively long period of cotton mechanization is a most important factor in the understanding of its effects.

The Mechanical Stripper

Although the first cotton stripper was patented in 1871, 1914 is the year of the first recorded attempts at stripping cotton. It occurred in the High Plains area of Northwest Texas. D. L. Jones gives an account of this event in a 1928 circular:

> The first attempts at stripping cotton bolls by mechanical means probably were made in 1914. Conditions at that time were ideal to develop such an innovation. A large yield was produced, the price was very low, making the cost of hand-picking too great to leave any profit. The first attempt . . . was done by use of a picket fence. The picket fence such as used in this country is made of wooden pickets that are held together with several strands of wire. The picket fence was pulled by a team across the cotton rows, stripping off the bolls. When this cotton was taken to the gin, it was refused on account of its having too much trash and many unopened bolls, which would not allow the gin to successfully handle it. The farmers who attempted this refused to be so easily discouraged on this road of progress, and took the cotton to a thresher and had it threshed. This threshing broke open the unopened bolls and removed some of the trash, and it was then returned to the gin and handled more satisfactorily (Jones *et al.* 1928: 5-6).

From this experience, farmers in the High Plains area developed box shaped sleds with V shaped slots formed by a wooden inclined plane descending from the floor of the box to the ground. Other machines had teeth, some metal, some wooden. For a number of years sled stripped cotton was run through threshing machines before ginning it. In 1926, gins in the High Plains stimulated by a bumper crop and an acute shortage of labor (Jones 1948: 37) developed extracting equipment, eliminating the threshing step. Hundreds of bales of machine stripped cotton were ginned that year (Smith and Jones 1948: 37).

Improvements followed. Wheels were substituted for runners. Two sets of teeth were installed for two row work. According to Smith and Jones (1948: 34), farmers used such a large number of strippers in 1926 and 1927 that the farm machinery manufacturers became interested and sent their engineers to develop commercial machines. John Deere was one of the manufacturers who participated in the development of the mechanical stripper. Their participation began in 1927.

By this time Don Jones (cited above) of the Texas Agricultural Experiment Station was developing improved varieties of cotton for easier stripping. Defoliation experiments were being conducted. John Deere began experimenting with improved models in the Delta as well as the Plains. In 1930 John Deere manufactured 50 mule-drawn strippers, five 1-row tractor-mounted stripper cleaners and five 2-row tractor-mounted stripper cleaners. The depression hit, money became scarce, and labor became cheap. John Deere ended up closing out their carry-over stock of mule-drawn strippers at $15 each in 1941 (Neighbour 1948: 76).

During the depression and pre-World War II years, John Deere continued experiments for the improvement of cleaning and green boll separation — two of the principal problems in stripping. Also, Jones of the Texas Station continued experimental design and testing of strippers throughout the 1930's. He developed a successful field extractor and the roller type stripper which became the basis of design for most commercial roller strippers. By the early 1940's the Morris or "Marco" cotton stripper and the Boone stripper had developed successful commercial models from the results of Texas Station experiments (Smith and Jones 1948: 40).

The radically changing labor situation brought on by the war was first felt shortly after the John Deere Company had closed out their stock in 1941. Mr. Leonard Neighbour, chief engineer of the John Deere Spreader Works, recalled this sudden turn of events:

> In a visit with Don Jones late in 1942 on a trip to Lubbock to see an experimental cotton picker, we learned that there was a growing scarcity of help due to the war and that the strippers recently disposed of for $15.00 were being resold for $150.00 to $200.00.
>
> Other things were happening to cotton. Mr. Macha, a farmer of Tahoka, Texas, had discovered, recognized its significance and preserved a new storm proof boll type mutation in a field of 'Hi-Bred' cotton which he further developed and which was now receiving wide acceptance on the Plains. The American Cyanimid Company was making promising demonstrations of defoliation of green cotton plants. Mechanical cotton harvesting was again a live issue.
>
> Tractors had replaced mules, so we developed and built two-row tractor mounted cotton harvesters and tested them in 1943. Production quantities of our No. 15 two-row harvesters were built

and sold in 1944. Mechanical harvesters by other manufacturers also began to appear in fair numbers . . .

In 1944 and 1945 our No. 15 cotton harvesters began to show up in Georgia and the Carolinas, the Delta, Arizona and California. These had been bought from dealers and users on the Plains and taken to territories in which we were not yet ready to recommend their use (Neighbour 1948: 76).

Although machine stripping is now firmly established, it is confined almost exclusively to Oklahoma, Texas, and New Mexico. By 1962, 58 percent of Texas cotton and 60 percent of Oklahoma cotton was machine stripped. The national average for 1963 was 20 percent (USDA 1963b).

It is yet to be proved that the mechanical stripper has significant application to the cotton varieties and cropping patterns in Arizona. According to M. D. Cannon of the Cotton Research Center, Tempe, one of the original John Deere strippers tested in the state in 1944 and 1945 is rusting on a farm near Tucson. In 1956, 1957, and 1958, 60 machine strippers, designed and manufactured by a machine shop near Kyrene, again proved impractical in Arizona cotton. However, a manufacturing company in Wichita, Kansas has the patent rights on a double brush-roll type of stripper. They have been testing it in the Willcox area for the last two years and plan to sell it in commercial quantity in the 1964 season (Cannon 1964).

The Mechanical Picker

INTERNATIONAL HARVESTER — Although other types of machine picking have been tried, the mechanical picker of the spindle type is the only one that has proved successful in Arizona so far.

As nearly as can be determined, the first attempt to develop a mechanical cotton picker was made by S. S. Rembert and J. Prescott of Memphis, Tennessee, September 10, 1850 when patent No. 7,631 was issued to them. Their machine was equipped with both picking cylinders and picking discs, the cylinders being placed upon vertical shafts and the discs on horizontal shafts. They had a clear vision regarding the future development of cotton culture in mind as they made the following statement in their patent claims: 'Our cotton picking machine may be multiplied and extended to such a width as to embrace several rows of cotton plants at once' (Smith and Jones 1948: 53).

This is one of the ideas in the family of invention and patents that led to the spindle type of picker developed commercially for the first time by International Harvester.

At the Second Annual Beltwide Cotton Mechanization Conference in Lubbock in 1948, the Vice President of International Harvester Company, R. C. Archer, traced the ideas that "were combined" in their picker back to two "outstanding pioneers"—Angus Campbell and John Appleby. Campbell working in the late 1890's in the experimental department of Deering Harvesting Company developed many of the features of what later was known as the Price-Campbell spindle cotton picker. In the early 1900's John F. Appleby, an associate of William Deering, developed a machine with spindles that entered the plant vertically. Experiments in upland or short staple cotton indicated that it was capable of picking an entire crop at one time with ". . . some degree of success" (Archer 1948: 79).

According to Smith and Jones (1948), who make no mention of Appleby, Campbell's early patents (including his first in 1895) were assigned to the American Cotton Picker Company of Pittsburgh, Pennsylvania. T. H. Price is mentioned receiving a patent on a cotton harvester as far back as 1904, assigned originally to the Utility Cotton Picker Company of New York. Campbell's name appears in the patent records again November 19, 1912, this time in partnership with B. C. White. This patent, No. 1,004,611, was assigned to the Price-Campbell Cotton Picker Corporation of Wilmington, Delaware. Smith and Jones go on to explain:

> . . . It appears that Price and Campbell joined in forming the Price-Campbell Cotton Picker Corporation a short time prior to the granting of the patent in November 1912. They interested the late J. A. Kemp of Wichita Falls, Texas, and formed the Mechanico-Agricultural Company for the purpose of manufacturing the Price-Campbell Cotton Picker. One of the machines this organization made was on display at the Texas State Fair at Dallas about 1920. Several years later, the International Harvester Company acquired the patent rights held by this organization and developed a rear-mounted tractor cotton picker (Smith and Jones 1948: 53-54).

To pick up the story again from International Harvester's Archer (1948):

> . . . With the acquisition of the Price-Campbell Picker, International Harvester continued the development of the spindle type machine and concluded experiments with the suction type picker. In the same year a machine was built that incorporated many of the Price-Campbell features. The early results were again disappointing. The machine was complicated and expensive. It left too much of the cotton unpicked and too much on the ground. It damaged the oncoming unripened cotton in sections where several pickings were necessary because of the long ripening season.
> . . . In 1925 a small, less expensive machine was built. An unsatisfactory drive mechanism for the picker drums, doffing difficulties caused by long straight spindles and a constant problem of keeping spindles clean and free of plant sap retarded its success. Experiments were channeled toward making a more continuous operating machine . . . With each change our engineers were coming closer to what they knew could be done.
> . . . Before 1939 experiments had been carried on with self-propelled trailer type and attachment type machines. The change in tractor models in 1939 from F-20 to Farmall H and M was an important development in the progress of the cotton harvester. After that change, experiments were confined almost exclusively to attachment type pickers. With the short picking season, the attachment type machine was to prove more economically sound since the tractor could be used for other farm purposes during

> the rest of the year. The mechanical pickers needed high clear-
> ance tractors because of the tall cotton plants grown in the . . .
> Delta area and in the irrigated section of Arizona and California.
> Special wheels with extra large diameters elevated the . . .tractor
> to the required clearance . . .
>
> In 1940 for the first time the attachment picker was mounted
> on the new model tractor to be driven in the reverse direction—
> a design that has remained basically the same. This permitted
> the cotton plants to enter the picker unit before the bolls could
> be knocked from the plants by the tractor. The picker drum box
> remained in relatively the same position. The basket was placed
> behind the operator over the hood of the tractor to insure clear
> vision. This location also permitted a large capacity hydraulically
> operated basket that could be dumped into wagons or trailers . . .

Archer exposed detailed lists of mechanical problems facing International Harvester — the size, shape, angle of penetration, taper, and the
positioning of the spindles. The cotton-catching barb of the spindles was a
particularly critical problem. They tried individually inserted phonograph
needles, steel wire points, saw blades, and barbs raised out of a metal cone.

Other major design problems are enumerated—the doffing mechanism
consisting of rubber lugged discs revolving at right angles and counter to
the spindles came after many types had been tried. The problem of keeping the spindles clear of sap was finally solved with a separate rubber
moistening pad for each of the 20 rows of spindles. Also, the basket
receptacle that distributes cotton evenly—without the aid of an extra man—
and the mechanism for driving the picker spindles required experimentation.

After the machine had been sufficiently developed to pick dependably
and efficiently in terms of physical units, improving the grade of machine
picked cotton became the most critical problem. International engineers
tried adding cotton cleaners to the picker with limited success. Cleaners on
portable trucks were tried. Finally research on the mechanical picker was
extended to gin operators and cleaning machinery manufacturers.

Cooperation on growing was required also. Clean fields, the use of
varieties of cotton adaptable to machine harvesting, improved planting
methods and defoliation all contributed.

Finally there was the economic aspect:

> Until 1941, the development of a machine that could be kept
> operating continuously without stoppages caused by plant or field
> conditions had been regarded to be economic as well as engineer-
> ing problems. There were times when an abundance of low price
> hand labor minimized the importance of a mechanical machine.
> With the full development of a picker that could operate continu-
> ously and satisfactorily, the economic problem also cleared. An
> increasing scarcity of labor and increasing high farm labor rates in
> 1941 created a mounting demand for a mechanical cotton picker.
>
> In 1941 our company first released the mechanical cotton
> picker for sale on a limited basis. Twelve machines were made in
> 1941 and 1942 on a laboratory production basis, 15 in 1943, 25 in
> 1944, and 75 in each of the next three years. . . . Since the war

and the completion of a new factory at Memphis we have been able to produce the machine in quantity. Our schedule this year (1948) called for approximately 1,200 machines (Archer 1948: 79-83).

Forty-eight percent of the nation's crop was harvested by machine pickers of the spindle type by 1962. California ranked highest in 1962 with 90 percent of its crop machine picked. Arizona ranked second with 82 percent. Because of the fact that Arizona had the highest percentage of machine ground scrapped cotton (ten percent), the total machine picked cotton in Arizona (92 percent) put it neck-and-neck with California's combined total of 94 percent (USDA 1963b).

THE RUST PICKER – The Rust brothers stand out in the history of mechanical cotton pickers for two reasons. Their picker design was a recognized success earlier than any other spindle picker. Second, they intentionally inhibited the exploitation of their own invention.

James Street, in *The New Revolution in the Cotton Economy* (1957), outlines in biographical detail the ambitions of the brothers. It recalls their experiences in crawling through their father's fields picking cotton, their frustrations in attempting to use their invention to the benefit of the poor sharecropping farmer, and finally to the belated quantity production of the machine.

John Rust, an itinerant farm hand equipped with only a correspondence engineering course, became a designer and superintendent of construction for a thresher company. This background, along with boyhood days spent in the back-breaking drudgery of cotton picking, led him to design a spindle picker as early as 1924. A flash of insight on the application of moisture to the spindles brought a breakthrough in his design. He filed a patent in 1928, shortly afterward. The picking principle of this original design was kept throughout all modifications. Street states:

> . . . The picking unit which he designed embodied an endless belt fitted with vertical rows of moistened smooth spindles that rotated as they entered the cotton plant. The backward movement of the belt was synchronized with the forward motion of the machine, so that the rows of spindles would come into contact with the cotton in a relatively stationary position and thus avoid injury to the plant. As the loaded spindles traveled on their circuit they were stripped clean by pairs of traveling steel ribbons, and the cotton was conveyed to a storage basket (1957: 124).

John's brother Mack joined him in 1928, at the time of the filing of the patent. From this time throughout the depression years of the 1930's continuous modifications brought it to widely publicized acclaim, ". . . for it appeared to show conclusively the labor-saving potentialities of the picker and thereby to cast an ominous shadow on future employment prospects in the (Delta) region" (Street 1957: 125).

The Rust brothers stood at a crossroads. They had been stimulated primarily by social motives from the start, and had been financed in part by humanitarian investors. Street speaks of them:

> As socially minded individuals with an intense sympathy for the impoverished cotton farmers whom they saw around them, the Rust brothers were now faced with a perplexing set of problems. They were eager to see their machine put to use, but they did not wish to be responsible for encouraging the trend toward large-scale mechanized farming at the expense of small farmers. They were afraid widespread labor displacement would result if the sale of their machine were unrestricted. . . . They resorted to one plan after another in an effort to resolve these dilemmas (1957: 126).

They adapted the machine to the needs of the small farmer by running counter to their efficiency principles. They designed a small pull model selling for less than $1,000 that could be drawn by a utility tractor. Other plans included marketing under restricted conditions, making it available for self-help cooperative farms, and even introducing it in the Soviet Union.

Street goes on to say that toward the end of 1937 they shifted to new plans to raise capital, again with philanthropic motives. They planned to limit their share in returns to ten times that of their lowest paid employee. All remaining personal profits were to finance a foundation devoted to helping displaced cotton farmers and fostering cooperative farming.

World War II inhibited manufacturing and by 1942 the Rust brothers reached rock bottom. They sold the shop tools to pay off obligations. Their charter was revoked. John and Mack parted. Mack took several demonstration machines to California and Arizona to establish a custom picking business.

John set about redesigning the machine to make it more durable, keeping mass production requirements in mind. But this time both John Deere and International Harvester had the lead in commercially feasible, quantity produced machines. It was not until the late 1940's and early 1950's that Rust pickers began to appear in quantity through the manufacturing companies of Allis Chalmers, Ben Pearson, Inc., J. I. Case, Massey-Harris-Ferguson, Inc., and under the Rust name itself (Street 1957: 125-127).

Arizona Cotton

Emil Haury, an eminent authority on Southwestern archaeology, cites numerous data indicating the prehistoric cultivation of cotton and the development of cotton textiles among the Hohokam in the Salt and Gila River valleys of Arizona as far back as A.D. 900. Moreover, according to early pioneer accounts and aboriginal weaving forms found among these native dwellers of desert river valleys of Arizona (Haury 1950: 446-448), this prehistoric aboriginal industry continued through historic times among the Pima-Papago peoples of the Gila and Salt prior to the introduction of Egyptian varieties. It is an irony of history that one thousand years later, at the center of this prehistoric aboriginal civilization with its sophisticated cotton textiles, a cotton research center was established devoted to the testing and development of an exotic variety of cotton—American-*Egyptian*. For 50 years, from 1907 to 1957, the Cotton Research Center at Sacaton on the Pima Indian Reservation was the center of extra-long staple cotton experimentation in the United States and the home of development for all the American-Egyptian varieties (McGowan 1961:55).

According to McGowan's *History of Extra-Long Staple Cottons* (1961), scientific cotton breeding in the United States started in 1898. The first experiments concerned imported varieties of Egyptian cotton and were conducted in the humid portions of the cotton belt, then the center of the cotton industry of the United States. Early tests confirmed that these varieties were not suited to the climate of the cotton belt. By 1901 research on long staple varieties had shifted to the arid portions of the Southwest (p. 51).

In 1901 Egyptian seed reached Arizona and California. From this seed Doctor A. J. Chandler grew the first cotton in what was later to become the center of a large cotton-growing district — Chandler, Arizona. Some was planted at the territorial farm, an early University of Arizona experimental station located two miles northwest of Phoenix. A third lot was planted in Imperial Valley, California. The following year the Bureau of Plant Industry established a test station in Yuma as an area most approximating the climate, soils, irrigation methods, and growing conditions in the Nile Valley of Egypt. Tests in the development of an American-Egyptian variety continued there for the next five years. By 1907 an extra-long staple variety was considered sufficiently good and productive to submit to cotton mills using imported Egyptian cotton. The tests were favorable. As a result of this,

> . . . the possibility of establishing an Egyptian cotton culture on a commercial scale in the irrigated valleys of the Southwest received increased consideration. Officials estimated that with new reclamation projects under way as authorized under the Newlands Act of 1902, there would soon be 600,000 acres of land under ditch in the Yuma, Salt, Imperial, and Gila Valleys, and that if one-fifth of this acreage could be used to grow Egyptian cotton, production would equal annual imports from Egypt (McGowan 1961: 51-57).

In 1908, the largest acreage to that date (19 acres) was planted at Sacaton under a cooperative arrangement between the United States Department of Agriculture and the Bureau of Indian Affairs. Five acres were put in at Yuma, two acres were planted at the Indian School farm at Phoenix, and about four acres were planted by individual farmers in the Gila Valley, west of Phoenix. Three more years of experimental work followed before seed was considered ready to be distributed to farmers for commercial use. By 1912 American-Egyptian cotton was ready for commercial planting on a small scale. In addition to 181 acres in California and 30 in Mexico, 303 acres were planted by 32 farmers in the Salt River Valley and 29½ acres were planted on Indian land at Sacaton. Acreage increased gradually. Five more years were required before ginning facilities, oil mills, uniform market grades, and storage warehouses were developed sufficiently to support a cotton industry in Arizona. By 1917 Arizona's cotton industry was firmly established. Its 333 acres of long staple cotton had grown to 33,000 and its production from less than 300 bales to 15,900 bales (McGowan 1961: 60-65; Seltzer and Pfuehler 1959: 28). Thus, at two independent points in time separated by a thousand years, Arizona's climate and exploitable river water had become the basis of a cotton ecology.

An all-time high of 200,000 acres of Pima (long staple) cotton was planted in 1920. But the end of the war and the subsequent dumping of 485,004 bales of Nile-grown Egyptian cotton on the American market brought the cotton market crash of 1920. However, another chance factor operating to the detriment of the upland cotton producing areas of the United States—the boll weevil—helped mollify the consequences of the 1920 crash on Arizona cotton farmers. Upland (short staple) prices rose whereas Pima prices did not. More and more Arizona cotton growers turned to short staple and by 1923, for the first time in Arizona's cotton production history, the acreage of upland surpassed that of Pima. Upland has not been exceeded by Pima since. As McGowan states, "The ideal of the one-variety community was lost never to be regained" (1961: 37-38).

Arizona's cotton acreage, productions, and yield have fluctuated considerably in the four decades since 1923, but it has consistently ranked as one of the nation's leading cotton producing states. Its all time highs were attained in the non-allotment Korean War years, reaching a peak in 1953 of 648,500 acres of upland and 41,500 acres of Pima for a combined total of 690,000 acres producing 1,070,000 bales (Seltzer and Pfuehler 1959: 28). In the 1962-63 season Arizona produced approximately six percent of the cotton produced in the United States (USDA 1963b). It led the nation in per-acre yield of upland cotton by averaging 1,114 pounds (University of Arizona 1963: 16).

Within the state, cotton is the basis of a $166,000,000 economy and in the ten-year period from 1952 to 1961 accounted for 38 percent of all crop and livestock income (based on cash receipts) produced in Arizona (University of Arizona 1963: 3).

Arizona Cotton Labor

Arizona agriculture had its beginnings with the advent of mechanized farming. In the spring of 1867, seven years after McCormick reapers had reached mass production, the first commercial crop in the Salt River Valley (excluding Indian crops) was sold by a Y. T. Smith to Fort McDowell. It was part of a hay contract and consisted of wild grass growing along the banks of the Salt River. It was harvested by a Mexican crew of wage workers. That same year a commercial canal building company was formed, new canals dug, and ancient Indian canals retrenched. Arizona commercial agriculture was on its way (Park 1961: 168). By 1880, the United States census reveals the number of Arizona farmers had reached

1,725. The 1880 census also discloses that ". . . a large percentage of Phoenix residents gave their occupations as operators of threshers and headers, indicating that considerable agricultural machinery was already being used in this locality" (Park 1961: 173). This fact is further confirmed by indexes of volume of farm power, machinery, and equipment which show a 132 percent increase in the two decades between 1870 and 1890 (Cooper *et al.* 1947: 7). By the time cotton was grown on a large scale in Arizona (1920) the mechanization of certain portions of crop production was already well established.

Mechanization proceeded unequally among the differing phases of crop production. This was especially true of cotton. To quote a *Mechanization of Cotton Production* bulletin, "The advent of the row-crop tractor in the 1920's . . . created an unbalance of labor in that one man could grow much more cotton than he could harvest. The problem of obtaining enough day laborers for chopping, hoeing, and harvesting grew steadily until it became very acute during and following World War II" (Colwick 1953: 3).

This disparity in mechanization is apparent in the following statistics. In the century between 1800 to 1900 man hours per acre *before* harvest in cotton had shown a decline from 135 to 62. Man hours per acre for harvest (50) show no decline whatever during the same period. The period from 1900 to 1940 shows a continuation of the *pre-harvest* man hour drop, a decline of 62 to 46 man hours per acre. However harvest requirements — 52 man hours per acre — remain what they were a century and a half before (Cooper *et al.* 1947: 3).

A seasonal pattern of labor input, characteristic of the Arizona cotton industry, was exhibited from the beginning. The February low and the October peak in cotton production employment varied by ratios as large as 28:1 (ASES 1960a: 8). The concept of "labor scarcity" became almost a fixed idea in public and private policy concerned with recruitment of labor. Even before the first small scale commercial plantings of Arizona cotton in 1912, a labor scarcity for harvest was anticipated. McGowan cites this as one of the first problems of the "Infant Pima Cotton Industry":

> Labor problems at best, were provocative and as acreage and volume increased became more so. In the first years the Salt River Valley Egyptian Cotton Association in cooperation with the Southwestern Cotton Committee was able to get the cotton picked by the white settlers from Texas and Oklahoma, Mexicans, and Indians from the Pima and Papago reservations. Later, labor problems were assumed by the Arizona Cotton Growers' Association, formed especially for that purpose (McGowan 1961: 68).

This concern for the recruitment and nature of cotton harvest labor is attested to by a special publication of the Arizona State Employment Service titled *Arizona Cotton Harvest 1950:*

> The position of cotton in Arizona's economic picture is dependent to a large degree on the agricultural labor .available to

plant, cultivate, and harvest the crop. The 1950 crop required approximately 40,000 hand pickers during the peak of the harvest. It is a historical fact that Arizona must depend on migratory farm workers to pick its cotton crop. Every year, commencing in late August and ending in mid-December, a wave of migratory workers originating in Texas, Oklahoma, Arkansas, and other neighboring states, descends into the cotton fields. This wave reaches its peak in October and November, during which time as high as 2,000 cotton pickers arrive in Arizona every week. According to records kept by the United States Employment Service Agricultural Information Station at Benson, between 20,000 and 25,000 agricultural workers arrive . . . traveling as members of crews, family groups, or singly (ASES 1950: 2).

An all-time high for cotton hand pickers in Arizona of 48,500 was recorded in 1952 (ASES 1960a: 2).

In summation, although Arizona inherited an industry which had flourished for centuries in the Southeastern United States, it was founded on fundamentally different labor institutions. Whereas the growth of Cotton Belt agriculture was based historically upon chattel labor, the cotton industries of Arizona and the Southwest developed around mechanized technologies that alternated seasonally with massive labor populations not attached to the land.

Arizona Cotton Mechanization

Barring the rather obscure references to the testing of mechanical strippers in Arizona in the 1944-45 season (Neighbour 1948; Cannon 1964), the first machines to move into commercial harvesting of Arizona cotton appeared in 1946 (Barnes 1963: 44). In 1949 they appeared in sufficient quantity to test. As might be expected early results were disappointing. To quote Barnes (1963: 44):

In early tests, machines did not show up well in comparison with hand pickers. Losses from spindle pickers were high. In 1949, tests showed 18.7 percent loss from spindle pickers compared to only 4.8 percent loss from hand picking. . . . There was a whole grade difference in favor of hand picking. Even as late as 1958, 31 pounds more of machine-picked seed cotton than of hand-picked seed cotton were required to make a 500-pound bale of lint.

But in 1959, the following year, the balance swung over decisively in favor of machine picking. Figure 1 illustrates the trend in percentage of machine picking in Arizona from 1950 to 1963.

With the exception of the seasons from 1954 through 1956, there has been a steady percentage increase in machine-picked cotton in Arizona. The three-year decline in machine picking is probably due to the fact that from 1951 through 1953, when allotment free acreages rose by 250 percent — from 275,000 to 690,000 acres (Seltzer and Pfuehler 1959: 28) — machines could only augment the enormous quantity of hand pickers needed for the all-time peak harvests. The *Arizona Cotton Harvest 1952* points out that without picking machines in the December peak, 46,000 hand pickers would have been required in addition to the near Arizona record of 41,550 hand pickers already working (ASES 1953a: 6). The rise in machine picking from 1951 to 1953 could therefore represent a premature adoption of mechanical alternatives under unusual conditions. This explanation is further supported by the abrupt 60 percent drop in acreage in 1954 (Seltzer and Pfuehler 1959: 28), by the continued arrival of abundant quantities of hand pickers in 1954 — 43,300 are cited by the *Arizona State Employment Service* (1964a) — and by a University of Arizona Agricultural Experiment Station cost study in 1953 which states:

> . . . The lower direct picking costs with machines, coupled with the lack of sufficient hand pickers during the peak of the season (1953), has accelerated the adoption of mechanical pickers in Arizona.
>
> Recently, however, some growers have become alarmed concerning field losses with machine pickers. Losses as high as three-quarters of a bale per acre have been reported by growers who have gleaned by hand after mechanical pickers. Some growers are now thinking of returning to hand pickers entirely. Others report little or no field loss and plan to continue using machines exclusively. This study is aimed at indicating under what conditions of acreage covered, yield and field loss it is profitable to machine pick (Vanvig and St. Clair 1954: 1).

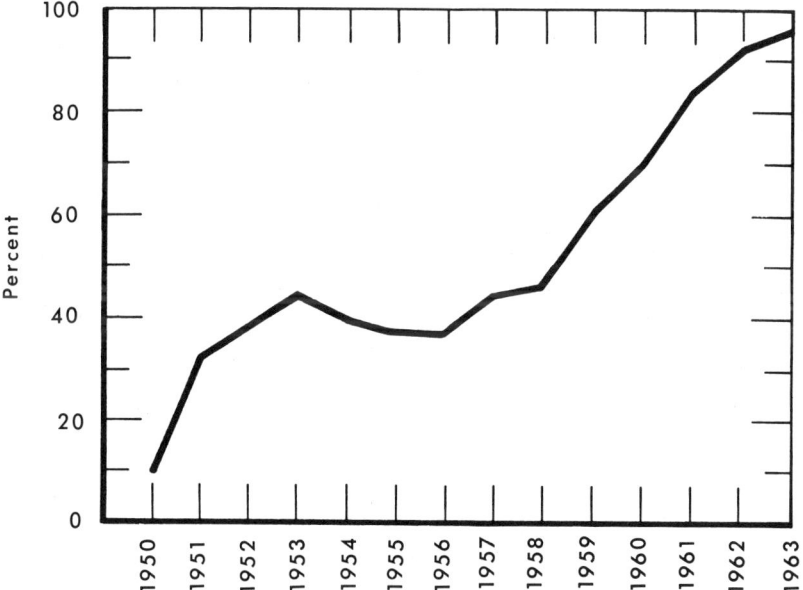

Figure 1. Percent of Machine Picked Cotton in Arizona by Year
(Arizona State Employment Service 1951; 1952; 1953b; 1954-
1959; 1960b; 1961; 1962b; 1963; 1964b)

Be that as it may, since 1956 the rise in machine picking has been steadily reaching a near "saturation point." This increase is due to a combination of factors, none of which is independent of the others. Some of the factors Barnes cites are the continued improvement of picking machines, the continued development of specialized ginning facilities oriented toward machine-picked cotton, increased knowledge in the application of machines, development of machine-suited varieties of cotton, and development of machines to salvage ground-loss cotton (Barnes 1963: 44). While these factors are technical in nature, they each have a corresponding effect on cost. Another contributing factor is the reduction in available hand labor caused by stricter regulations of interstate picking crews requiring insurance and specifying seating standards for their buses (ASES 1957:22).

The salvage machines, usually in the form of the Rood Harvester, began to make their appearance in the late 1950's. The *Arizona Cotton Production Survey 1959-1960 Harvest* makes reference to the Rood in connection with that season's harvest. It is described as a highly efficient machine. The report continues, "If this machine lives up to its promise, it heralds the end of large scale hand scrapping in Arizona" (ASES 1960a: 63). These predictions have been borne out. The USDA Economic Research Service reports made first mention of percentage machine scrapped cotton for Arizona for the 1961-62 season. During that season nine percent of all the cotton ginned in Arizona came from machine scrappers (USDA 1962b). In the 1962-63 season it was ten percent (USDA 1963b).

In terms of human factors the dramatic climax to the near saturation point of machine-harvested cotton in Arizona is reflected by comparing the all-time high of hand pickers in 1953 (48,500) to the peak quantity employed in the 1963 season (5,300) (ASES 1964a). This is nearly a 90 percent drop.

In looking back over the 18 year period of the change, however, two important characteristics stand out. As with the cotton industry as a whole, Arizona has required a relatively long period of time for these changes in its cotton technologies; moreover, hand technologies in cotton still persist. The number of seasonal workers required, especially in thinning and weeding, is considerable. This number (5469; ASES 1963b) still exceeds the peak numbers required in either lettuce or citrus. This certainly is not to minimize the impact of change nor the fact that cotton hand technologies are obsolete technologies. Nevertheless, unlike changes in the production systems of other industries, old methods still exist as alternatives for management and as stop-gap employment or supplementary income for thousands of workers who need more time to make the enormous social adjustments necessary. This is not to mention the social residue who will never have any occupational alternatives.

Three cotton farm operations were studied. The first grew 350 acres of cotton. The second farm, although part of a large state-wide operation, operated as a unit with 918 acres of cotton. The final farm company had a total of 4,718 acres in cotton. All acreages apply to the 1962-63 season. All farming operations were located in Pinal County. The companies were selected on the basis of gradation of size and the prior rapport gained with these companies in preliminary survey work.

Collectively these three operations cropped 5,624 acres of upland or short staple cotton, about four percent of the total upland acres in Pinal County. Their total collective upland yield for the 1962-63 season was 14,940 bales with a per-acre average of 1,330 pounds. Their collective Pima acreage was 362 yielding 569 bales with a per-acre average of 785 pounds. Their total collective production for the season was 15,509 bales, accounting for 1.6 percent of the all-cotton figure of 942,000 bales for the state (University of Arizona 1964a: 11). These three farm companies hired between 120 to 150 workers throughout the year.

In addition to these farms, eight independent chopping and picking crews were studied and a sample of their workers interviewed. These crews are independent employment units since their personnel are not hired by the farms the crews work for. The farm companies have no records of individual workers because they do not pay them as individuals. The company hires the crew leader and pays him for the work of his crew on a piece rate basis. The crew leader then pays his individual workers. Only the crew leaders themselves and local farm labor offices have any idea of the individuals who make up these crews. Moreover their membership changes to a certain extent every day.

As there is no licensing- of crew leaders in Arizona, there is no complete precise listing of them. Hence there is no universe from which a random sample can be drawn. Three of these eight crews were contacted while working for one of the sample farms. Five of them were chosen at random in the course of traveling throughout Pinal County. The total membership of these eight crews was 225 workers, each taken at the time its crew was studied. A certain amount of information was obtained on all 225 of these workers. However, interviews were administered to only 76 (or 34 percent) of these 225 choppers and pickers.

In addition to these eight independent chopping and picking crews, one other non-independent chopping and picking crew was studied. Each of its chopper-pickers worked directly for the farm, each was paid a set hourly rate and received his wages on a weekly basis from the grower. This crew was supervised by a foreman who also worked as a regular employee of the farm. This crew is included among the personnel inventory of this farm company — Company K — even though it was doing the same kind of work as the other eight.

Although farms and crews were studied during the thinning and weeding season instead of the harvest season, the known practices of the different job groups in cotton production—equipment operators, general hands, and crew workers—indicated that each job group played a role in the harvest season that was an occupational equivalent of the role it performed throughout the growing season. All sample farm managers and owners reported that during the harvest season their tractor drivers generally operate picking machines, their equipment foremen act as picker operator foremen, their tractor mechanics act as picking machine mechanics, and the independent crew leaders used for chopping are generally used for picking.

Following is a breakdown of the harvest season jobs of the cotton workers interviewed in the spring of 1963. Sixty-two or 86 percent of the 72 choppers interviewed indicated that they had hand picked the previous season. The remaining ten had worked at other farm hand jobs. Eight or 53 percent of the general hands or irrigators reported hand picking, four operated equipment, and three did general farm work.

Twenty-five fell in the "skilled" category during harvest season. Three foremen were foremen and two mechanics were mechanics. Of 13 tractor drivers, all except one, who acted as a foreman, operated machinery. Of the seven crew leaders, four ran picking crews, two operated equipment, and one hand picked.

Thus the supervisors, equipment operators, and hoe hands worked basically in the same capacity in both the weeding and the harvest season. The irrigators, however, appear to be a transitional occupational group. Most reverted to hand picking after layby (the end of preharvest activity) and others filled in as equipment operators. These latter are referred to by management as "our top irrigators."

K COMPANY — 86 PERCENT MACHINE HARVEST

During the 1962-63 season, K Company farmed 350 acres of cotton yielding approximately 1,000 pounds per acre. K had the following acreages in addition: 15 acres in wheat, 50 in safflower, 160 in barley, and 250 in maize.

Of the 700 bales K Company harvested, 100 bales or 14 percent were picked by hand, mostly ends and corners. Approximately 400 bales or 57 percent were picked by machine and 200 bales or 29 percent were scrapped by machine — Rood Scrappers. This gives K Company a total of 86 percent machine picked cotton which is significantly below the state average of 95 percent machine. All cotton was machine picked twice and scrapped three times.

Mechanical Harvesting and Handling Equipment

2 — 2-row John Deere cotton picking machines
1 — Rood scrapper
10 — wire cotton trailers
2 — ½-ton pickups
1 — 2-ton truck
4 — wheel tractors (2 Farmall, 1 John Deere, and 1 Case)

Organizational Structure

K Company is essentially a family farm. P, the owner-operator, is directly in charge but uses a 40-year-old Anglo as a "working foreman." Below the foreman level, P has Papago Indians exclusively. About six are general hands and 20 to 25 picker-choppers. These Indians have worked on-and-off for P from 10 to 20 years. All are from Santa Rosa village which lies just across the range of the Sawtooth Mountains. Many are related by blood or marriage. The more seasonal workers of the group occupy the farm camp from late spring through fall but go back to their village during the late fall and winter.

Four younger males, although referred to by P as "general ranch hands," are principally equipment operators. Two of the older men are hand laborers only. One of these, a very old Papago who cannot speak English, is the village messenger for Santa Rosa. He performs an important role in the ceremonial feasts still held in that village. Another of the younger men is the son of the ceremonial leader of the village — "Keeper of the Smoke" (Underhill 1939). At the time of field observations the village leader had just died and his son, who had been driving tractor for P for ten years, was leaving the farm to move back permanently to the village.

At the time of observations the picker-chopper crew had the following membership: F, supervisor, general ranch hand, and key family figure in the crew; his wife, daughter, and younger brother; his father's sister and her mother-in-law; and his father's brother's daughter and her son.

Other families were: the A family—husband, wife, daughter, and wife's sister (the wife and her sister are cousins to F above); the V family—husband and wife; and the I family—husband and wife.

Wage System

Picker-choppers receive $3 a hundred pounds for picking and 70 cents an hour for thinning and weeding. General or irrigator hands are paid 80 cents an hour, equipment operators 90 cents an hour, and the ranch foreman receives a salary of $75 a week with a $25 raise in the offing.

All workers have free housing, water, electricity, and added privileges of transportation when they need it. If they can drive, they use the farm pickup for Saturday trips to Eloy or Stanfield.

P is proud of his Indians. He knows them. He adapts to their ways by keeping a surplus of hands to offset their visiting and ceremonial patterns which do not necessarily coincide with the crop cycles. This arrangement is a unique inter-institutional adaptation which has developed over several decades. This kind of pattern was established between these families and this farm before P bought the farm.

L COMPANY — 100 PERCENT MACHINE HARVEST

In 1963 L Company's Pinal County, Maricopa Farm grew the following crops:

849 acres of short staple cotton
69 acres of Pima cotton
380 acres of safflower
172 acres green manure crops
124 acres of barley
22 acres of wheat

The 849 acres of short staple yielded 2,462 bales with an average of 2.9 bales or 1,450 pounds to the acre. The 69 acres of Pima yielded 145 bales with a per-acre average of 2.1 bales or 1,050 pounds.

One hundred percent of their cotton was machine picked and scrapped. All cotton was spindle picked twice. Custom Rood Scrapping accounted for approximately 740 bales or 30 percent of their short staple and about 17 bales or 12 percent of their long staple.

Mechanical Harvesting and Handling Equipment

1 — John Deere 2-row picker
3 — International Harvester 1-row pickers
15 — cotton trailers
3 — ½-ton pickups
1 — ¾-ton service truck
1 — 1½-ton winch truck
1 — 1½-ton water truck
1 — 1½-ton flatbed truck
2 — 400 International Tractors
2 — 300 International Tractors
1 — 200 International Tractor
1 — DC Case Tractor
3 — International Harvester M's

Organizational Structure

At the top of the corporate structure of L Company is the Board of Directors. Directly responsible to the board is the president and gin manager. Under the president are four parallel positions — the feedyard superintendent, the Pima County superintendent, the Maricopa County superintendent, and the Pinal County superintendent (F). Under F is the Maricopa Farm foreman, a young, college-educated Anglo.

Under the farm foreman is an irrigator foreman. This position was filled by a 31-year-old Texas Mexican-American. His mother is a Mexican immigrant. In the past he worked as a seasonal migrant with his family picking cotton, onions, tomatoes, and Michigan sugar beets. He and his father went from there into the produce hauling business. In 1952 he came to Arizona and began to work his way into farm equipment, operating tractors, cats, and picking machines.

Under him are seven irrigators. All were Indians—two Papagos and five Pimas. All of the Pimas and one Papago lived on the Sacaton Reservation and commuted to work. The other Papago lived in the L Company's housing. As a rule when irrigating got slack, most of the Indians stayed on the reservation, except for one Papago who drove tractor.

In addition to the irrigators, L Company has seven equipment operators. They operate tractors and caterpillars in the growing season and cotton picking machines during the harvest season. With one exception, they were all Mexican-American.

All picking, thinning and weeding for L Company's Maricopa Farm is done by the independent crew system. The independent picker-chopper crew working at L Company during field observations is included in the descriptive section of this chapter dealing with independent crews.

Wage System

L Company uses both ditches and overhead sprinklers for irrigation. Irrigators are ordinarily paid 80 cents an hour. Those who work with the sprinklers, however, have to work harder and therefore have a different wage system. Their hourly wage varies by the crop, the season, and the size of the pipe.

Cotton, 3″ line beginning season	$1.25
Cotton, 3″ line maturing season	$1.50
Cotton, 4″ line beginning season	$1.50
Cotton, 4″ line maturing season	$1.85
Barley, 3″ line	$1.25
Barley, 4″ line	$1.50

The irrigators have the choice of working in either system.

Equipment operators make $1 an hour during growing or harvest season. The cat driver gets $1.05.

The irrigator foreman earns $1.10 an hour, perquisites, and a pickup.

The ranch foreman earns a monthly salary of $500 and owns a modern house and pickup.

For thinning and weeding L Company pays 70 cents an hour to the worker and 10 cents a man-hour to the leader. For hand picking the Company pays $3.30 per hundred to the crew leader.

F, the superintendent, plans to continue 100 percent machine harvesting. Next season, however, he is planning to custom harvest. He claims he can do so for 1½ cents a pound. He also plans to eventually eliminate hand thinning by "planting to stand" rather than overplanting. L Company also invests heavily in chemical weed controls.

M COMPANY—98 PERCENT MACHINE HARVEST

M Company sprawls over a 10 by 13 square mile area northwest of Stanfield, Pinal County. Although the total acreage of the company goes by the names of several farms, personnel and equipment are employed over the operations as a whole.

M Company's 1962-63 land use is as follows:

4,425 acres of short staple cotton
 293 acres of Pima cotton
5,400 acres of barley
3,600 acres of maize

The 4,425 acres of short staple yielded 11,779 bales with an average of 2.66 bales or 1,330 pounds per acre. The 293 acres of Pima yielded 423 bales with a per-acre yield of 1.45 bales or 725 pounds. Total cotton acreage was 4,718, total production was 12,202 bales.

Management reported that only 250 bales were picked by hand, slightly over two percent. All cotton was machine picked twice. Having been scrapped entirely by 16 Rood machine scrappers, none of the cotton was hand scrapped. Although management has no record of the total amount of scrapped cotton, they reported scrapping all cotton between machine pickings and at row ends for a total of from four to eight times.

Mechanical Harvesting and Handling Equipment

 10 — John Deere Model 99 2-row cotton pickers
  7 — International Harvester 220 D 2-row pickers
 16 — Rood scrappers
 27 — International Harvester 560 wheel tractors
200 — cotton trailers

Organizational Structure of Harvest Activities

M Company is headed by a Board of Directors. Directly under the board is the general manager. Answering to the general manager are four different departmental units, the office administrative personnel and three different sections of the farm, each under a ranch foreman. All foremen are Anglos.

One farm section was headed by two Anglo foremen. This section generally works six equipment operators and ten irrigators. All operators in this section were of Mexican descent, all irrigators were Indian.

A second farm section headed by an Anglo foreman generally employs six equipment operators and 12 irrigators. These workers were about equally divided between Anglos and Mexican-Americans. The shop unit employs two full-time mechanics — one for pump engines and the other for moving equipment. Both were Anglos. Neither of these specialists has a farm background. The pump mechanic has a background of heavy equipment training in the military service and nine years with compressor engines with a natural gas company. The equipment mechanic has an occupation background as a millwright in the lumber industry.

The largest farm section was headed by an ambitious young Anglo with less than a high school education. He learned farm management in the field under several very successful farm operators in the boom-town era of Pinal County's cotton industry. Under him are 15 to 20 tractor and machine picker operators, 15 to 30 irrigators, four irrigator foremen, and one tractor foreman.

The equipment operators were made up about equally of Mexican-Americans, Indians, and Anglos. One Negro was an exception. The irrigators were predominantly Indian with a third or more of Mexican descent.

All of the seven machine operators interviewed at M Company are in their twenties or early thirties. Two were Mexican-Americans from Texas, two were green card Mexicans, and three were Indians. The tractor foreman was an Anglo with a 7th grade education. He was born on a 200-acre family farm in Alabama, went from there to sharecropping in Missouri, and immigrated to Arizona in 1948. He picked cotton the first fall, operated equipment the next season, and in ten years worked up to foreman with four years as a shop mechanic in between.

Of the six irrigators interviewed, three were Papago Indians. One Papago is from the Arizona reservation. The other two are Sonora Papagos from Caborca. Two of the irrigators were Mexican-Americans from New Mexico. The family of one still lives in Mexico. The father of the other died in Mexico and his mother immigrated. The sixth irrigator was a green card Mexican.

The one irrigator foreman interviewed was a Papago born in Kom Vo village on the reservation. His father raised cattle and flood-plain farmed. Fifteen years ago the foreman began off-reservation cotton picking. In a six-year period he worked his way up from hand picking to irrigating and general farm work. He moved off the reservation to farm-furnished housing. He has been a water foreman for nine years. All 15 years were spent on the same farm.

All equipment operators run picking machines during the harvest season, along with several of the "top irrigators." All hand picking and chopping that M Company does is done by independent crews, several of whom they allow to occupy abandoned cotton pickers' camps that exist on company premises.

Wage System

M Company pays $3.35 per hundred for hand picking, $3 an acre for thinning, and 80 cents an hour for weeding. The crew leader is paid the total wage bill on the bases of total weight, total acreage, or total man hours. He in turn pays his crew members after taking out his "commission" which may run as high as 20 percent.

Irrigators get 80 cents an hour, tractor drivers get $1 an hour, cat skinners and picking machine operators get $1.25.

Irrigator and tractor foremen get $100 per week.

Ranch foremen get a monthly base salary plus a bale bonus of $1 a bale. Perquisites are furnished all workers. Their value varies in the order of rank.

INDEPENDENT PICKING-CHOPPING CREWS

A crew by crew breakdown and discussion follow. The symbols used to indicate relationships are:

fa — father
mo — mother
hu — husband
wi — wife
so — son
da — daughter
bro — brother
si — sister
au — aunt
neph — nephew
ni — niece

Crew 1

No.	Family or individual	Relationships	Ethnicity
8	J family	fa, 4 so, 2 da, and 1 da-in-law	Choctaw-Anglo
6	A family	fa, wi, 2 so, and 2 da	Yaqui
3	S family	fa, so, and da	Pima
3	Sh family	fa, wi, and da	Anglo
2	M family	fa (foreman), and so	Mexican-American
2	AJ family	hu and wi	Mexican-American
2	V family	hu and wi	Papago
2	AA family	2 bro	Yaqui
4	individuals	single males	Anglo
1	individual	married male	Anglo
1	individual	single female	Anglo
1	individual	single male	Negro
1	individual	single male	Mexican-American
36			

Descriptive trait	No. or Am't.	Percent if applies
Family workers	28	78%
Individual workers	8	22%
Anglo	17	47%
Indian	13	36%
Mexican-American	5	14%
Negro	1	—
Males	24	67%
Females	12	33%
Workers' pay	$ .25 a row (thinning)	
Leader's pay	$3.00 an acre	

The crew leader is a 58-year-old Mexican-American from Texas who works year round as a crew leader during picking and chopping season.

His parents were "five cent immigrants"— i.e., they paid 5 cents to cross the border. Before World War II he sharecropped with his father in Texas. During the war he worked as a construction laborer. In 1952 he came to Arizona and has been pushing cotton crews ever since.

The crew and leader occupy an old abandoned cotton camp on one of the farms in return for which they pick or chop on a priority basis for that farm company. We refer to this kind of housing throughout the study as "obsolete farm housing." Most of the crew members have their own cars; those who do not, ride out in the leader's pickup from the camp. He furnishes hoes.

Crew 2

No.	Family or individual	Relationships	Ethnicity
6	S family	fa (leader), wi, and 4 da	Mexican-American
4	SP family	fa, and 3 so	Mexican-American
10			

Descriptive trait	No. or Am't.	Percent if applies
Family workers	all	
Mexican-American	all	
Males	5	50%
Females	5	50%
Workers' pay	$ .45 a row (thinning)	
Leader's pay	$3.00 an acre	

This is essentially a family crew. The father of the first family acts as a crew leader. He is a 55-year-old Mexican-American from New Mexico. He has been in migrant seasonal work most of his life, working in sugar beets in Colorado and picking cotton in Texas. He came to Arizona six years ago, drove tractor for two years, and has been chopping and picking with his family for the last four years.

This crew also occupies obsolete farm housing for priority work for this farm. Twelve family members live in two rooms.

Crew 3

No.	Family or individual	Relationships	Ethnicity
6	L family	fa, wi, 2 so, and 2 da	Anglo
4	W family	fa, wi, 1 so, and 1 da	Negro
3	A family	fa, wi, and so	Negro
3	K family	fa, wi, and da	Negro
2	H family	2 bro	Mexican-American
2	J family	mo and da	Papago
2	S family	bro and si	Mexican-American
2	N family	2 bro	Negro
2	SA family	fa and so	Negro
2	SH family	fa and so	Mexican-American
2	RC family	hu and wi	Negro
1	individual	single male	Papago
1	individual	single female (fa irrigates for co.)	Mexican-American
1	individual	single male	Negro
1	individual	single male (leader)	Anglo
1	individual	single male	Negro
1	individual	married female (hu irrig. for co.)	Negro
1	individual	married female (hu irrig. for co.)	Negro
37			

Descriptive trait	No. or Am't.	Percent if applies
Family workers	30	81%
Individual workers	7	19%
Negro	20	54%
Mexican-American	7	19%
Anglo	7	19%
Indian	3	8%
Males	22	59%
Females	15	41%
Workers' pay	$ .70 per hour (thinning and weeding)	
Leader's pay	$ .10 per man-hour	

The leader of this crew is a 54-year-old Anglo. He was born in Tennessee, later worked as a general hand on his father's farm in Arkansas, sharecropped in Missouri, and migrated to Eloy, Arizona in 1947. There he operated machinery for five years, supervised Nationals for a year, and has alternated between equipment operation and crew supervision in cotton for the last 12 years.

Most of his crew occupy obsolete farm housing for first priority work on the farm they are now working on. Many of the others, however, live in their own or rented houses and cabins in Eloy and drive out to work in their own cars. A bus is furnished for the farm housing workers.

Crew 4

No.	Family or individual	Relationships	Ethnicity
5	J family	fa, wi, si, so, and da	Pima
3	G family	1 bro and 2 si	Mexican-American
3	O family	fa and 2 so	Mexican-American
3	B family	fa and 2 da	Mexican-American
3	L family	fa, so, and da	Mexican-American
3	LJ family	fa (foreman) and 2 so	Mexican-American
3	N family	mo and 2 da	Pima
2	GT family	bro and si	Mexican-American
1	individual	single male boy	Pima
26			

Descriptive trait	No. or Am't.	Percent if applies
Family workers	all except one	
Mexican-American	17	65%
Indian	9	35%
Males	13	50%
Females	13	50%
Worker's pay	$. 70 per hour (thinning and weeding)	
Leader's pay	$ .10 per man-hour	

The leader of this crew is a 38-year-old Mexican born in Tamaulipas but raised in Laredo, Texas. He obtained green card status in 1939. He has been in migrant seasonal work most of his life, working in onions and tomatoes in Texas, January through May; in sugar beets in Wyoming, May through August; and in cotton in Arizona, from August through January. In 1946 he settled down in Pinal County, cat skinning and tractor driving in the growing season and contracting picking-chopping crews in between.

This crew is not centrally housed. Some live in rented or owned housing in Maricopa; others live on different farms for which other family members work full time; and most of the Indians live on the Sacaton reservation. All workers furnish their own transportation.

Crew 5

No.	Family or individual	Relationships	Ethnicity
3	C family	mo. so, and bro-in-law	Negro
3	CR family	mo, da, and so	Negro
3	B family	mo, so, and si	Negro
3	T family	2 si and 1 bro	Negro
2	M family	mo and da	Negro
2	W family	au and neph	Negro
2	D family	2 si	Negro
2	R family	2 bro	Negro
2	W family	2 si	Negro
1	individual	married male (leader)	Negro
3	individuals	single females	Negro
2	individuals	married females	Negro
2	individuals	single males	Negro
30			

Descriptive trait	No. or Am't.	Percent if applies
Family workers	22	73%
Individual workers	8	27%
Negro	entire crew	
Females	19	63%
Males	11	37%
Workers' pay	$ .70 per hour (thinning and weeding)	
Leader's pay	$ .10 per man-hour	

This crew is headed by a 41-year-old Negro who was born in Arkansas and lived part of his early life in Texas. He has been a farm field hand, a sawmill machine operator, a dock loader for trucks in San Francisco, a railroad section hand in Wyoming, and a truck driver in New Mexico. He migrated to Arizona in 1950 and picked cotton for his uncle, who was a crew leader at the time. He alternates between foundry and metal work in Phoenix, and labor contracting in the Coolidge area.

Most of this crew's personnel are augmenting income of husbands who are engaged in non-farm work. Most of them live in owned or rented *rural*-urban fringe slum-type housing and come to work in car pools.

Crew 6

No.	Family or individual	Relationships	Ethnicity
6	H family	fa, 4 so, and 1 da-in-law	Mexican-American
5	G family	fa, 2 da, and 2 so	Mexican-American
3	R family	fa, wi, and da	Mexican-American
3	P family	hu, wi, and bro	Papago
2	T family	hu and wi	Mexican-American
2	H family	fa and so	Mexican-American
2	individuals	single males	Mexican-American
1	individual	single male (leader)	Mexican-American
1	individual	single female	Mexican-American
25			

Descriptive trait	No. or Am't.	Percent if applies
Family workers	21	84%
Individual workers	4	16%
Mexican-American	22	88%
Indian	3	12%
Males	17	68%
Females	8	32%
Workers' pay	not determined	
Leader's pay	not determined	

A 73-year-old Mexican-American heads this crew. He was born and raised in Texas on a cattle ranch where he worked most of his life as a cowboy. After a serious injury in 1955, he moved to Arizona, already an old man. He has alternated since in general ranch and farm work, doing a little picking, ditch cleaning, irrigating, and crew pushing.

Most of the members of this crew live in owned or rented houses in Casa Grande or Stanfield. A few live in obsolete farm camps and work on other farms when chopping or picking run out on their home farm. Most furnish their own transportation to the particular farm where they are working.

Crew 7

No.	Family or individual	Relationships	Ethnicity
5	W family	mo, 2 so and 2 da	Anglo
2	P family	hu and wi	Papago
6	not determined	males	Papago
6	not determined	females	Papago
5	not determined	males	Mexican-American
5	not determined	females	Mexican-American
2	individuals	single males	Negro
12	individuals	single males	Anglo
1	individual	single male (leader)	Anglo
44			

Descriptive trait	No. or Am't.	Percent if applies
Family workers	precise No. undetermined	
Individual workers	precise No. undetermined	
Anglo	18	41%
Indian	14	32%
Mexican-American	10	23%
Negro	2	4%
Males	29	66%
Females	15	34%
Workers' pay	not determined	
Leader's pay	not determined	

This crew is headed by a long-time Anglo professional labor contractor. He originally came from the South and has been in the Eloy area since the forties. He is strictly independent, hauling all of his workers from a central pickup point in Eloy. The majority of his workers live in rented cabins or cot houses in Eloy and load up on his bus every morning. A few belong to families working permanently on farms in the area. The latter members drive to the field the contractor is working in their own cars.

Crew 8

No.	Family or individual	Relationships	Ethnicity
12	S family	fa (assistant leader), 4 so, 3 da, 1 bro, 1 si-in-law, and 2 ni	Negro
2	W family	mo and da	Negro
2	L family	si and bro	Mexican-American
1	individual	single female	Negro
17			

Descriptive trait	No. or Am't.	Percent if applies
Family workers	all except one	
Negro	15	88%
Mexican-American	2	12%
Females	10	59%
Males	7	41%
Workers' pay	$. 70 an hour (thinning and weeding)	
Leader's pay	$ .10 per man-hour	

This is for all intents and purposes a one-family crew with a few hangers-on. This is the pattern of many of the crews in the area. The father or assistant crew leader is called an assistant because he works as part of a larger crew. He manages the crew in the field, receives payment from the grower, pays workers, and drives a bus.

S, the assistant leader, is a 52-year-old Negro born on a sharecrop farm in Texas. He himself sharecropped from 1931 to 1944. In 1944 he migrated to Arizona where he has chopped and picked for the last 19 years. He supplements his cotton work with tractor driving, gin work, and construction work.

Most of the crew own or rent in Eloy and ride to the fields in the bus.

Summary of Independent Crews

Four of the eight crew leaders are of Mexican descent, two are Anglos, and two are Negroes. All except one are from Texas or the deeper South and all are from vocational backgrounds rooted in cotton culture.

Most of the 225 crew members live independent of farm housing. Most crews are paid by the hour. About half get to work in crew leaders' buses and half in private automobiles.

Of the 203 crew members classifiable as working in family units or as individuals, an overwhelming majority (78 percent) worked in family groups.

The average crew size is 28, significantly smaller than the average crew size of 38 reported for Pinal County picking crews by the *Arizona Cotton Production Survey 1959-1960 Harvest*. Also, our crews averaged 43 percent female as compared to 19 percent female in the 1959-1960 survey (ASES 1960a: 24). This indicates a trend that can be expected as seasonal cotton work becomes more and more a supplemental income to local families.

PART TWO

THE ECONOMICS
of the
TECHNOLOGIES

6 The Theory of the Firm

THEORY IS USEFUL since it provides a simplified view of a complex set of relationships. By observing the "real" world through the simplifying lens of theory we are able to recognize facts that are obscured by the flow of unsorted details.

We begin our analyses of the harvest systems described in Part One by outlining the basic economic theory of the firm. Then, immediately following, we show its relevance to and implications for Arizona's farm mechanization and labor problems.

THE BASIC PRINCIPLES

The "theory of the firm" as applicable to the farm labor problem rests on three basic principles. They are as follows:

1. Farmers are in the farming business to make a profit. Individual farmers may have no inherent desire to maximize profits; yet, since farming is a competitive occupation and returns always tend to approximate costs, farmers must continually adjust to changing input and output prices to remain in business. Thus, farmers will tend to *act* as if to *maximize profits* because of the competitive nature of their occupation. Their only alternative is to be forced out of business.

2. The law of diminishing returns is operative in agriculture. This law states that as more and more of a given resource is applied to another resource which is fixed in quantity, one may be sure that over some range, total output will be increasing at a decreasing rate. This is the area of resource combinations in which a firm trying to maximize profit will operate. The practical application of this law is that as the price of an input rises (if the production technology remains unchanged) less of that input is used. Thus, as wages rise, less farm labor is hired, even if production methods remain essentially unchanged. This follows from the farmers' desire to maximize profits in order to stay in business.

3. There is always an alternative method of production. Particular production methods are used only because the farmer believes that these methods make him the most profit under his resource conditions and the expected input and output prices he faces. Because of the diversity of resource situations that individual operators face there can be no one least-cost method of production; but, to the extent that certain costs rise and fall for all operators, general tendencies in production methods occur. The practical application

of this principle to the farm labor problem is that as wages rise, production methods will change so as to use more capital (i.e. machinery) and less labor. Moreover, since production methods change, an entirely different type of labor may be required. Farmers will make these changes no matter if they are liberal or conservative, anti-labor or pro-labor. They must in order to stay in business.

THE PRINCIPLES ILLUSTRATED

These three principles are illustrated in Figures 2 and 3. Imagine that Figure 2 is an input possibilities map for the production of oranges. The curves show the alternative ways to produce given quantities of fruit from a given acreage. For example, Q_{10} could be produced with 17 man-hours of labor and 80 dollars of capital. Another alternative would be to produce Q_{10} with 36 man-hours of labor and 40 dollars of capital. Since the curve Q_{10} is continuous, many other capital-labor combinations exist for

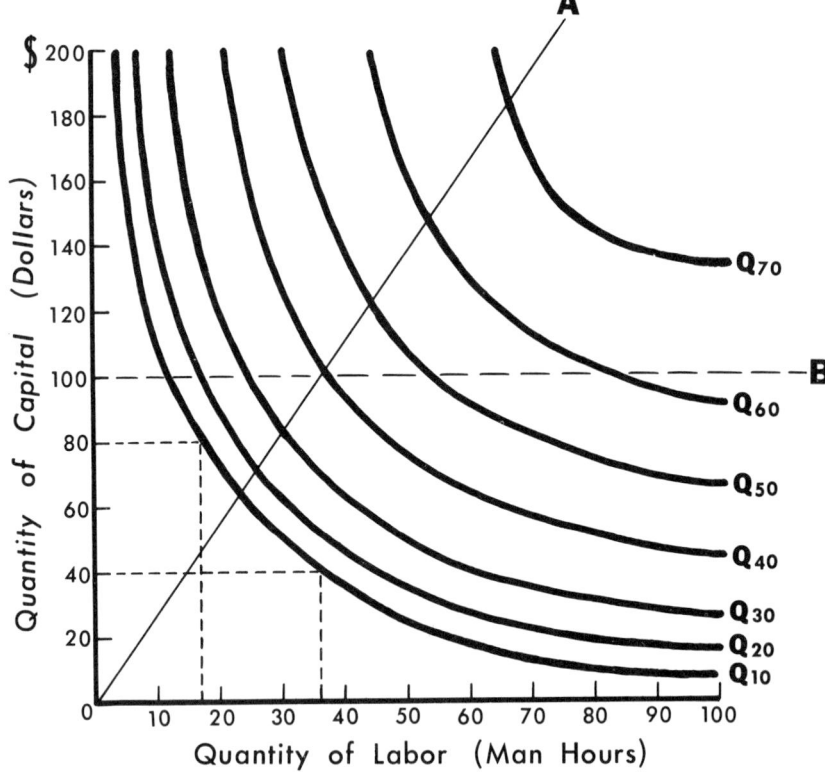

Figure 2. Hypothetical Input Possibilities Map

producing this given output. Higher output levels may be reached by increasing both capital and labor (acreage remaining constant) rather than by substituting one for the other.

Note that with capital held constant (e.g. at 100) it takes larger and larger quantities of labor to reach the next higher output level. (Read along line B.) The same is true of capital quantities when the quantity of labor is held constant. It is also true that as both labor and capital are increased simultaneously (e.g. along line A) it takes larger and larger increments to increase output. Eventually a maximum output point would be reached (not shown). The fact that larger and larger quantities of the inputs are needed to produce an additional unit of output shows that the law of diminishing returns is operative.

So far only physical relationships have been shown. Diminishing returns and alternative production methods are purely physical concepts. Figure 3 combines these two concepts with prices to illustrate profit maximization.

Assume that the going wage for labor is one dollar per hour. If the operator had 100 dollars to spend on production, he could either spend it

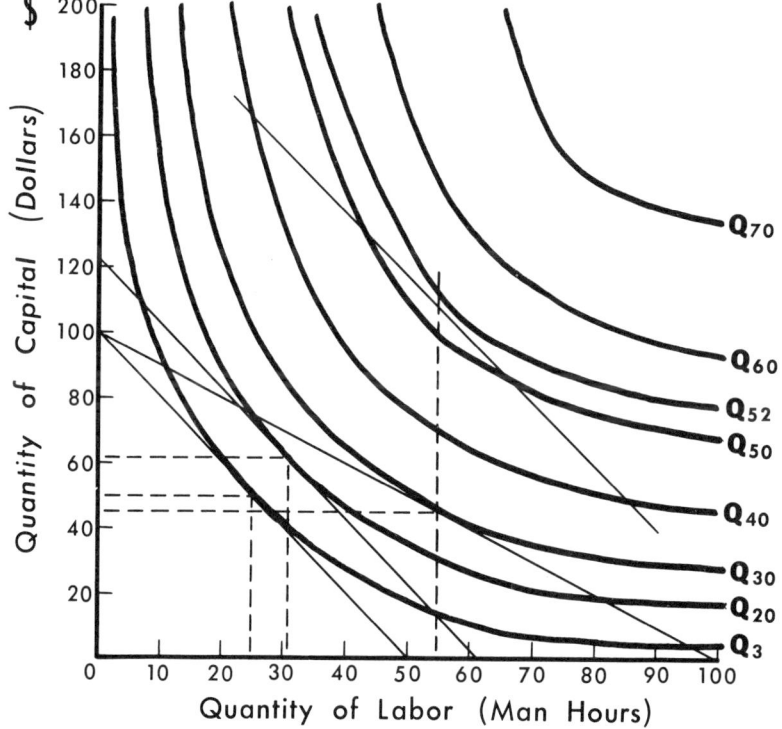

Figure 3. Hypothetical Input Possibilities Map Showing Maximum Profit Positions

all for machinery ($100 worth of capital equipment), or all for labor (100 man-hours), or any intermediate combination of machinery and man-hours. These combinations are illustrated by the straight line between 100 and 100 in Figure 3. Since the operator is trying to maximize profit, he will wish to obtain the highest possible output for this given expenditure. Q_{30} may be obtained using 55 man-hours of labor and 45 dollars of capital machinery. No other capital-labor combination totaling 100 dollars will give this large an output.

What must happen if wages rise? Assume wages become two dollars per hour. The 100 dollars could now purchase 100 dollars of machinery, 50 hours of labor, or any intermediate combination of the two. These alternatives are represented by the line between 100 (capital) and 50 (man-hours). The maximum profit combination is now 50 dollars of capital with 25 man-hours of labor producing output Q_3. Output has decreased, labor use has decreased and investment in machinery has increased.

In reality, there is no reason for the total expenditure to remain constant (at 100 in our example) as wages rise. Higher production costs will cause operators to reduce production but their motivation is to maximize profits not to maintain constant total costs. As total production falls, the price received for their product will tend to rise inducing some reexpansion of ouput. The new equilibrium output will be somewhat less than before the wage hike but higher than illustrated. By equilibrium output we mean the output that will maximize profits for the firm.

Perhaps it turns out that Q_{20} is the maximum profit output for this firm. (Selection of the exact output would need further analysis involving the price of the product.) It is the *ratio* of the price of labor ($2.00) to the price of capital ($1.00) that determines the slope of the expenditure possibilities lines. This line will be parallel to the line between 100 and 50 (ratio 2:1). It will be tangent to the curve for output Q_{20}. It intersects the axes at 124 units of capital and 62 man-hours of labor (ratio 2:1). We find that the equilibrium input combination is 62 dollars of machinery and 31 hours of labor for a total expenditure of 124 dollars.

The rise in wages caused a decrease in labor hired, an increase in capital expenditure, an increase in total expenditure, and a decrease in total output. The wage increase could not be absorbed by the industry without a reduction in the original labor force of 55 man-hours unless demand for the product increased to require a maximum profit output of around Q_{52}. For this to happen consumers would have to be willing to buy very much larger quantities of the product and at a much increased price—an obvious contradiction.

Of course, consumer demand will increase slowly over time due to population increases, rising standards of living, etc. Eventually, the higher wages for an equal size work force would be possible — but not for some time after the wage hike.

PRACTICAL APPLICATION OF FIRM THEORY TO ARIZONA FARM LABOR PROBLEMS

The practical application of this discussion to the farm labor problem in Arizona is as follows. Any change in the ratio between the price of labor and the price of machinery will cause adjustments in the quantity of labor hired and the quantity and type of machinery used. Since different types of machinery would be used, different types of labor would be necessary. A rise in wages not only causes operators to shift to other known technologies but hastens the search for new technologies. In the face of rising wages any acceptable new technology will be labor reducing in terms of man-hours though not necessarily in terms of the total wage bill.

Even if wages remain constant the competitive nature of agricultural enterprises with their low profit margins forces operators to search for cost reducing methods. Many of these methods will be labor reducing. Machinery companies and agricultural experiment stations are dedicated to aid farmers in this search.

This tendency to use more capital and less labor in agricultural production will not be reversed as long as agricultural businessmen tend to attempt to maximize profits—and the profit motive is the basis of our free enterprise system.

The social results of this tendency are both good and bad. A cost-efficient agriculture produces inexpensive, abundant food. A labor-efficient agriculture frees our labor force to produce the many other nonfood items that we desire. But certain unsophisticated segments of our population need opportunities for simple, often seasonal, labor that agriculture has provided in the past. The only other alternative for many of these people in our modern, complicated society is a subsistence existence on welfare. This introduces another system of complex problems having psychological and social as well as economic aspects.

In the following sections applications of firm theory will be discussed relative to the capital-labor substitution problems involved in citrus, lettuce and cotton harvesting in Arizona. Later chapters will treat the problems of farm laborers themselves as they are affected by this substitution process.

7 Citrus Harvesting and Handling

EACH OF THE SIX citrus harvesting operations described in Chapter 3 may be thought of as having their individual input possibilities map (see Figures 2 and 3). The shape of each map is defined by the physical resources with which they have to work, for example, the age of each orchard, how the orchard is pruned, the hauling distances to the packing shed, and the type of citrus.

The output line is defined by the number of groves that the firm has contracted to harvest. (This number is affected by the cost-price ratio of the firm but we may neglect this complication for this report.) The capital-labor combination that most efficiently lets the firm operate on this given output line is defined by the relative cost of capital and labor. Since each firm's input possibilities may be different, firms of the same size (that is, harvesting the same output) could have different capital-labor combinations even though the price of labor facing each firm is the same. Thus, each of the several harvesting systems in use may be a perfectly rational economic choice for that particular firm.

Where resource conditions are fairly similar, however, certain harvesting systems will be more efficient than others. A detailed study comparing costs and efficiencies of several handling systems for deciduous fruits was made by Stollsteimer in 1960. With a little interpretation, his results may be adapted to the Arizona citrus harvest.

CITRUS HANDLING COSTS

Stollsteimer analyzed four bin handling methods and five lug handling methods. Figures 4 and 5 present his results for the methods that are most comparable to the methods used by the Arizona citrus harvesting operations of our sample. Two bin methods and two field box methods are included. Figure 4 shows total hourly handling costs as a function of the rate of output in boxes per hour and the one-way hauling distance. The cost of the containers is not included. Figure 5 presents the same data with container costs included.

The handling methods are defined as follows:

F-1—Field boxes are hand loaded on low-bed trailers in the orchard and pulled directly to the packinghouse behind a tractor.

F-2—Field boxes are hand loaded on flat-bed trucks in the orchard and hauled directly to the packinghouse.

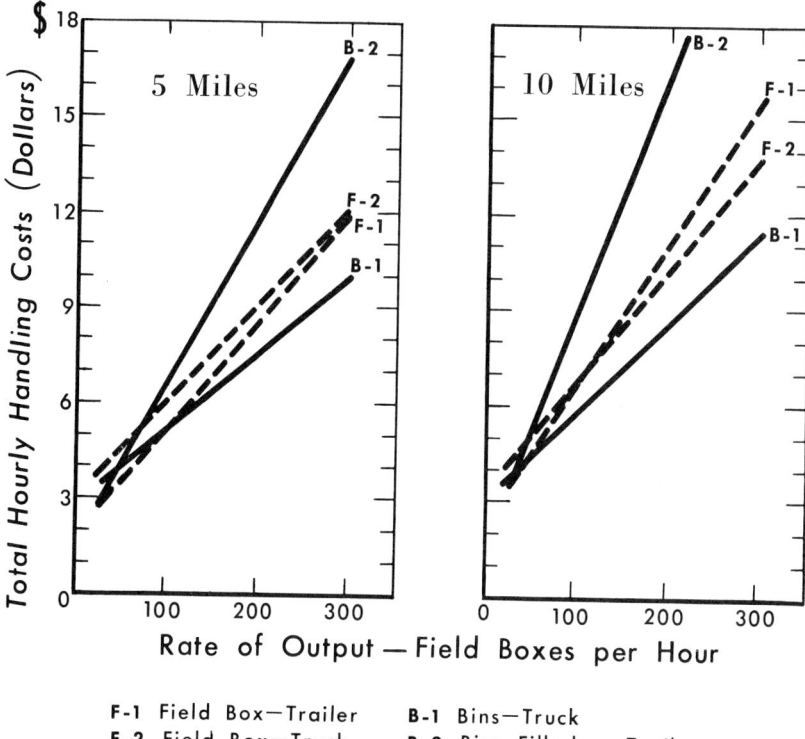

F-1 Field Box—Trailer   B-1 Bins—Truck
F-2 Field Box—Truck   B-2 Bins Filled on Trailer

Figure 4. Total Hourly Handling Costs with Alternative Handling Methods in Relation to Rate of Output and One-Way Hauling Distance; California, 1959

B-1—Bins are handled in the orchard with forklifts and transported to the packinghouse on flat-bed trucks.

B-2—Bins are filled while still on a low-bed trailer and pulled to the packinghouse behind a tractor.

Field boxes hand loaded on trailers (F-1) is the low-cost hauling method up to three or four miles hauling distance, providing output rates are below about 200 boxes per hour. With five miles or more the bin-forklift-truck method (B-1) becomes low cost except at very low output rates. Field boxes hand loaded on trucks (F-2) becomes the lowest cost box method with more than about six miles hauling distance if output rates are above 100 boxes per hour. With hauls of more than ten miles F-2 becomes the least cost box method and B-1 the overall least cost method no matter what the output rate.

The cost of the box method is as low as the least cost bin method only at low output rates or low hauling distances. With long hauling distances the bin and box methods are comparable only at very low output rates.

HANDLING AND CONTAINER COSTS

While hauling costs alone are part of the total handling cost picture, they are not as crucial in selecting citrus handling methods as they are for deciduous fruits. Deciduous fruits are normally harvested by the grower himself. The grower does not own the containers nor must he handle or store the containers once the fruit reaches the plant. Since citrus is harvested by the packer who not only hauls the fruit but owns the containers and must store the fruit at the shed, the cost picture for citrus is more complicated.

Figure 5 shows the combined hourly handling and container cost with alternative handling methods in relation to rate of output and length of haul.

The bin-truck method (B-1) is still by far the least cost method except

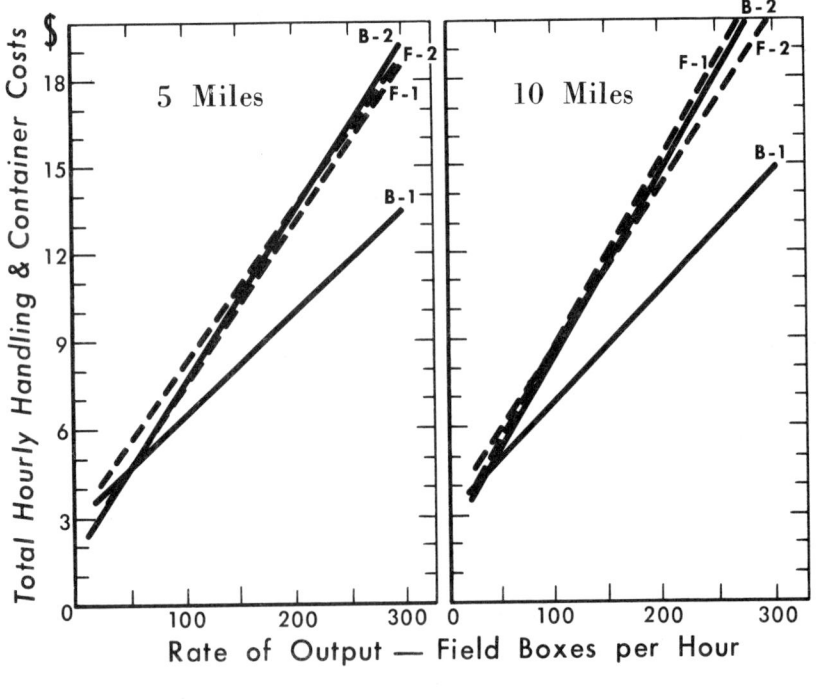

F-1 Field Box—Trailer   B-1 Bins—Truck
F-2 Field Box—Truck   B-2 Bins Filled on Trailer

Figure 5. Combined Hourly Handling and Container Costs with Alternative Handling Methods in Relation to Rate of Output and Length of Haul; California, 1959

at low output rates and with low hauling distances. Bins filled on trailers (B-2) or field boxes on trailers (F-1) are the low cost methods at distances below five miles and output rates below 100 boxes per hour.

Bins filled on trailers (B-2) is a high cost method when container cost is not considered. When container cost is included, B-2 costs about the same as do the two field box methods. B-2 is better at low output rates than at high output rates.

Arizona citrus handlers using methods similar to B-2 have modified the method to fit their conditions of long hauling distances. This modification is to use trucks to pull the trailers on the highway instead of tractors. Therefore, the bin on trailer method as used in Arizona citrus has lower costs than shown in Figure 5 and is more efficient than the field box methods.

Further cost savings by using bins occur at the packing shed where less labor is needed to receive the fruit and stack the empty containers, and less plant space is necessary to store the fruit.

CASE STUDIES COMPARED WITH THE COST MODELS

This section discusses how well the operations studied fit the theoretical cost models.

The field box method used by A Company corresponds exactly to method F-2. As with all the citrus operations studied, A Company faces relatively long hauling distances—at least an average of ten miles one way. Therefore, while the field box method used is the least cost box method, A Company would be better off with method B-1 unless their output rate rarely gets above 50 boxes an hour. This low rate occurs only when their small crew is working in lemons or tangerines which comprise only ten percent of their acreage.

This company already has the necessary trucks for the bin-forklift method (B-1). New purchases would involve forklifts, bins, and reorganization of the packinghouse. Note, however, that the difference between methods B-1 and F-2 is not as large when container cost is neglected. This means that as long as they already have their boxes, there is little reason to make the shift until major container or equipment replacement becomes necessary. They will surely make the shift to bulk handling at that time.

The "bin filled on the trailer" system used by B Company differs from the model in that in method B-2 the bin-trailers are pulled to the plant with tractors while B Company uses pickups. B Company is the largest outfit studied. It faces relatively long one-way hauls (up to 15 miles) and has a high hourly output. In addition to using pickups to pull their trailers on the highway, they use bulk trucks for their grapefruit harvest. These two modifications pull their costs down closer to method B-1.

C Company operates the same as B Company except that they use specially modified trucks to pull their trailers rather than the pickups. This enables them to haul the equivalent of 144 boxes rather than 100 boxes as does

B Company. C Company's harvest includes longer hauls than B Company so this extra capacity is essential.

The bin-truck-forklift method used by D Company corresponded almost exactly to method B-1. D Company hauls an equivalent of 300 boxes per load while the model assumes only 288. Therefore, D's costs may be slightly lower than shown. D is a large company with a high output rate per hour. Method B-1 should serve them well.

Company E is a small firm using small crews but has long hauling distances (up to 30 miles). Method B-1 is the obvious choice under these conditions. However, E Company's set up differs from B-1 in that all trucks, truck drivers, buses, bus drivers, supervisors, and forklift operators are contracted for at a flat 10 cents per box. The company furnishes the forklifts. Examination of Figure 6 shows that 10 cents per box is rather expensive no matter what system is used if the output rate can be maintained above 50 boxes per hour or

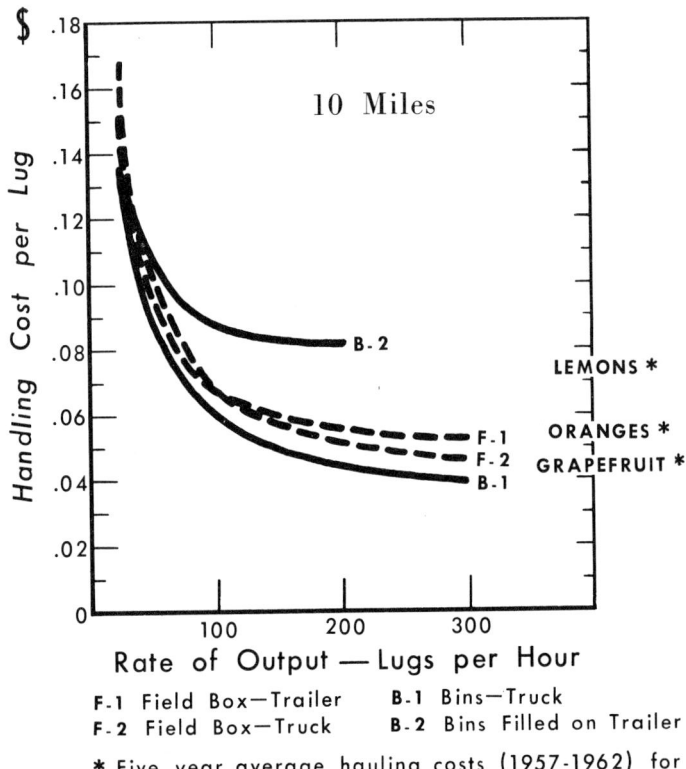

Figure 6. Handling Costs Per Field Box for Citrus in Relation to Rate of Output for a 10-mile Haul — Also, Average Handling Costs by Type of Citrus

unless a 30 mile hauling distance (with an output of 100 boxes per hour) is more typical than the ten mile distance shown.

Figure 6 shows how the four handling methods compare on a per field box basis at alternative output levels. While it is suspected that Stollsteimer's method of allocating overhead costs makes these figures slightly high for efficient citrus operations, average hauling cost data from the California Citrus League's records show the cost curves to be quite reasonable (California Citrus League, 1963). The average cost levels are drawn on the right side of Figure 6. Lemons have the lowest output rate and thus the highest costs. Grapefruit has the highest output rate and thus the lowest cost. Average costs approximate those that could be maintained by an efficiently operating firm using the field box method.

The Revolving Bin

Company F uses the revolving bin system. This system is not covered in the Stollsteimer models but roughly corresponds to a combination of methods B-1 and B-2. It has the advantage of eliminating the forklifts (as with B-2) yet achieves a relatively large load on a rapid traveling conveyance (as with B-1). The load is nine bins or 243 field box equivalents — B-1 carries from 264 to 300 boxes.

Disadvantages are the possibilities of soil compaction in the orchard, having to trim the orchard to fit the truck, and having to have the truck wait in the orchard all the time the pickers are filling the bins.

Comparison with the bin-forklift method involves a balancing of forklifts and forklift drivers against more trucks and truck drivers. Table 3 presents a comparison between D Company using the bin-forklift method and F Company using the revolving bin method. If both companies were efficiently organized and had the same crop mix, it would be a good comparison of efficiency of method. Since the relative efficiency of the two companies' organization is not known and D Company harvests a much larger percentage of lemons than does F Company, the comparison is only rough.

The revolving bin method shows overhead (fixed) costs per acre of $7.50 compared to the bin-forklift system of $6.67. In addition, F Company uses 1.72 more trucks per acre than does D Company (338 ÷ 197). Presumably, F Company's variable trucking costs would be 1.72 times those of D Company if wage rates were the same. Actually, F Company pays $1.20 per hour for its drivers while D Company pays $1.35. D Company must run forklifts while F Company does not.

Variable costs per hour per comparable machine crew total $2.59 for D Company and $2.56 for F Company. If F Company had to pay comparable wages, however, its total variable cost per hour per crew would be $2.82. Thus, the revolving bin system of F Company costs 23 cents per hour more per machine crew to run than does D Company's forklift-bin system if the same wage rate is paid. In addition, F Company's fixed costs are 83 cents per acre higher than D Company's. It appears that the bin-forklift system is the

least cost harvesting system for citrus. Thus, we may expect this citrus handling system to become predominant unless capital investment costs of the
revolving bin systems are reduced. This analysis does not mean that the revolving bin may not be the least cost system for F Company itself. Special circumstances, as described in its experience account in Chapter 3, may make
the difference in their special case.

Table 3.

D Company (Bin-forklift) Compared to F Company (Revolving Bin)

	D Company	F Company	
Bearing Acres			
Oranges	1301	1793	
Grapefruit	291	416	
Lemons	2453	494	
Tangerines, etc.	16	58	
Total	4061	2761	
Annual depreciation of transportation, equipment, lifts, and bins	$21,378	$16,429	
Interest on investment on transportation equipment, lifts, and bins (at 6%)	$ 5,703	$ 5,693	
Total fixed costs (Depreciation plus interest on investment)	$27,081	$20,716	
Fixed costs per acre	$ 6.67	$ 7.50	
Number of acres per truck	338	197	
Number of forklifts per truck	.58	—	
Variable costs per hour per machine crew[a]			
Truck (gas, oil and minor repairs)	$ .29	$ .50	or $ .50
Truck driver	1.35	2.32	2.06
Forklift	.17		
Forklift driver	.78		
Total variable costs per hour	$ 2.59	$2.82[b]	$2.56[c]

[a]Computed as follows:
  D Company — 1 truck and truck driver, 5/8
         forklift and forklift driver
  F Company — 1.72 trucks and truck drivers
         (338 acres per truck divided by
         197 acres per truck)

[b]Wages computed at $1.35 per hour so as to be comparable to D Company.

[c]Wages computed at $1.20 per hour as F Company actually pays.

IMPLICATIONS FOR THE DEMAND FOR LABOR

Mechanization of citrus handling systems will not greatly affect the total demand for farm labor. The handling system selected does not demonstrably change either the number of pickers needed nor their wage rate. It is in picking that the great majority of harvest labor is used.

The switch from field boxes to bin systems eliminates swampers and some packinghouse receiving men but may add the job of forklift operator. While some capital-labor substitution occurs the main change making the bin system more profitable is a substitution of one form of capital for another. Bin costs are substituted for packinghouse space and box costs.

8 Lettuce Harvesting, Handling, and Packing

IN CONTRAST to the situation in citrus where resource conditions dictate a variety of harvesting and handling systems, resource conditions in lettuce appear very similar. We would thus expect a single least-cost harvest-handling system to predominate. In actual practice, this single system has been the Mexican National ground crew.

The shed pack fell by the wayside because of rising labor costs. The machine field-pack has been largely discarded since the ground crew was more efficient in low density lettuce — and lettuce is often of low density. The experiments in field-wrapped lettuce did not reduce production costs but rather aimed to create a premium priced product. The ultimate success of this system depends on maintaining quality control and gaining consumer acceptance.

In the meantime, the end of the Mexican National program will cause further changes in lettuce harvest and handling systems.[1] This section will explore possible effects on both grower-shippers and hired labor from the economist's point of view.

LABOR EFFICIENCY VS. LABOR COSTS

The change from shed pack to field pack was a rare example of the substitution of labor for capital. The normal trend in our society of rising labor costs is the substitution of capital for labor. The capital-intensive system uses less but more productive labor.

Smith, (1961) showed that

. . . labor requirements (in terms of *man hours*) with field pack are actually from 7 to 42 percent higher than with house pack . . . the lower labor costs (in terms of dollars) with field pack *did not result from increases in labor productivity*. These lower labor costs must be attributed solely to the lower wages paid the workers in the field pack method. The weighted average for field pack workers was $1.07 per hour as compared to $1.82 for house pack workers . . . Actually, had the same wage been paid in both methods, labor costs (with field pack) would have been from 7 to 42 percent higher than with house pack depending on harvest density. For average conditions they would have been 13 percent higher.

Because field packing labor is somewhat less productive than that employed in house packing operations we would expect wage

---

[1] Public Law 78 expired on December 31, 1964. Congress has thus far indicated that the Mexican National program will not be renewed.

differentials to exist. However, the difference far exceeds that which might result from differences in productivity (at least as measured here). For example, with average conditions, the labor requirements per unit of output with field packing are 13 percent higher and, therefore, labor productivity 13 percent lower . . . than with house packing. On the other hand, the wage of field packing workers was 41 percent less than paid packinghouse labor. This large difference undoubtedly reflects the manner in which the two wage rates were determined . . . the field wage rate is determined pretty much by the unilateral actions of the employer group. In short, they control the wages paid field workers. Packinghouse wages, on the other hand, are derived from collective bargaining between a strong union and a strong employer association. In the years immediately preceding the shift to field packing it appears that the union was dominating the negotiations. Vacuum cooling, therefore, provided shippers with a means of getting out from under union domination as well as almost completely controlling the wages paid. It was this control of wages rather than any technical improvement which was the basis for the cost saving with the new method of shipping point processing operations.

Thus we saw a shift from an efficient, capital-intensive system to a relatively inefficient labor-intensive system in response to a rise in packing shed labor costs. The Mexican National labor program provided the low-wage field labor. The invention of the vacuum cooler provided the technical breakthrough that made the widespread use of this low-wage labor force possible.

PROJECTED REACTIONS TO RISING COSTS

With the cessation of the Mexican National program, lettuce packers again face rising wages. Two basic questions arise: (1) How will the lettuce farmers and packer-shippers react to the new conditions, and (2) What effect will their actions have on the demand for domestic labor?

This time no alternative supply of cheap labor appears on the horizon. Therefore, unless they follow their old cheap labor supply to its source in Mexico they must shift to a more capital-intensive system, if such a system is available. The only such system presently available is the shed pack. As noted, this system is less expensive than field pack if labor costs are comparable.

But both the field pack and the shed pack require field workers for cutting the lettuce. Both systems as previously operated required that the heads be selected for maturity before they were cut. This has traditionally been a Mexican or Filipino craft. With the Mexican National program discontinued and the old Filipino crews dying out, will there be enough cutters left to operate the shed system as it was run before? Even though the shed system needs only about one-half as many cutters as the field-pack system (since the lettuce is not trimmed in the field), the answer is probably no. The quantity of workers could probably be obtained (at a higher wage) but the quality of lettuce packed could well suffer.

In the old shed-pack system the lettuce was selected for maturity, cut, and thrown untrimmed onto a conveyor to a truck. The lettuce was trimmed and packed at the shed. Judging from the ability of the type of domestic field labor attracted by the prevailing wage, a shed system using such labor for cutting would have to do considerably more selection and sorting at the shed than was done under the old shed system in the late forties. Labor efficiency would be lower and more waste would be hauled to the shed where it could create a disposal problem. Nevertheless, such a system appears to be the most likely alternative as an interim solution while lettuce harvesting machines are being developed.

A further problem is that packing sheds do not exist in the new lettuce areas such as Aguila and Willcox which opened up after conversion to the field pack was complete. This problem will remain even after the lettuce harvesting machines now under development are put in service. As presently designed, these machines select firm heads, cut them, and elevate them to some receptacle. The lettuce must still be trimmed and packed by hand. The labor saved is only the number of cutters needed under the shed-pack system. Whether the machine or the cutters best select the proper quality of heads is still open to question.

A possible answer to the packing shed problem is to construct mobile packing sheds on semitrucks. These truck-sheds could be stationed at the ends of each field to receive the baskets of lettuce cut by either the machine or a domestic hand-cutting crew. These truck-sheds would solve the problem of lack of shed space in the newer lettuce areas and could be moved from one area to another at will. There are advantages of such truck-sheds over the present field packing machines. They would be more mobile, less unwieldy, could be more compactly designed, and would eliminate some of the soil compaction due to machine travel in the field. A truck-shed would surely have a more efficient output per man than the present field machines since output would not be directly related to the rate of cut in each row. In short, it would provide the efficiency features of the shed pack as well as the mobility necessary to work the small, isolated lettuce areas.

LETTUCE HARVESTING MACHINE COSTS AND ITS EFFECTS ON LABOR

The new lettuce cutting machines will obviously be adopted as fast as they become available whether or not Mexican National labor is still available. A simple rough calculation will show why.

Agricultural engineers give $35,000 as a rough estimate of the original cost on the first two-row lettuce harvesters now under development. This price would include service and repairs for the first year while the "bugs" are being worked out of the machine. If we assume that the machine is completely depreciated in three years, one year's depreciation would be $11,667. Interest on the average value of the investment would be $875 per year using five percent as the interest rate. Therefore, fixed costs total $12,542 per year. Repairs may be negelected because they are included in the purchase price. Operating costs for the machine would be similar to those of the field trucks and drivers necessary under the other systems.

It is estimated that this two-row machine will cut 400 cartons of lettuce per hour if a 50 percent cut is available. This cutting rate would require about 22 men cutting under the shed-pack system and about 40 men cutting and trimming under the field-pack system. If cutters can be hired for one dollar per hour the shed-pack system would cost $22 per hour for cutter labor alone. In addition, foremen and pusher labor would be required. A harvesting machine would have to work only 570 hours per year to reduce its fixed cost to $22 per hour. Operating costs may be neglected since they are comparable to the operating costs of the trucks and conveyers. At eight hours per day, 570 hours is only 71 days work per year. If the machine could be kept at work for 300 eight-hour days, the comparable cost is only $5.22 per hour.

Obviously tremendous savings are possible even if the price of labor is no higher than $1.00 per hour — the present guaranteed wage for the Mexican Nationals. Further, no camp costs nor compliance with governmental regulations are necessary with the machines. The conclusion is obvious. Machines will replace cutter labor as soon as the machines become available whether braceros are available or not.

Since the first machines will be ready within a year to a year and one-half and more machines will thereafter be forthcoming, termination of the program at this time can only cause confusion and turmoil within the lettuce industry for the two-to-three-year period before machines become commonplace. In addition, lettuce production will no doubt decline in the interim with a corresponding increase in lettuce price. Further, total jobs will decline as producers move to the more labor-efficient shed type system. Field hand labor will decline tremendously. Where a typical crew now uses 40 cutters, 20 packers, four sprayers, and six windrowers and swampers, a shed-pack crew will use about 20 cutters only. Since domestics presently fill only the sprayer, windrower and swamper positions, such a shift would double the demand for domestic field labor during this interim period if lettuce production did not decline. However, as we have pointed out, such increased demand for labor will be extremely short lived as the producers rush to get machines into the field.

Trimmer and packer labor will still be required whether the lettuce is cut by men or machines. However, this will be shed or truck-shed labor rather than field hand labor. Women will be able to fill many of the positions. The lettuce packers will again find themselves dealing with the unions.

FURTHER CHANGE

Obviously, the process of mechanization will continue. University of Arizona agricultural engineers are already developing a mechanical trimmer to be adapted to their cutting machine. This device will trim the lettuce in the field, eliminating the disposal problem at the shed and the job of the trimmer. The development of automatic filling (packing) systems should not be far behind.

Even the new lettuce cutter machines themselves are already on the way to obsolescence. If the problems involved in developing uniform lettuce stands with uniform maturing dates can be solved, a simple clear-cutting (mower) machine will replace the expensive "selector machine." Whole fields will be cut at one time while mechanical trimmers and graders process the heads and discard the trim and culls in the field. Thus, from the farmer's point of view, availability of labor problems are rapidly diminishing; from labor's point of view the problem of diminishing farm jobs has barely begun.

9 Lettuce Prices, Costs and Quantities

IF THE MEXICAN NATIONAL program is not renewed there will be an interim period of one to three years during which harvest labor exactly suited to present technologies will be in short supply. This period will end as lettuce harvesting machines become commonplace. During this period the different quality of farm labor will cause wages for hired farm labor to rise. What will be the effects of these actions on the quantities of lettuce produced, the price of that lettuce, and the lettuce producers' gross farm income? Further, how will these variables affect the demand for labor?

Consumer demand for lettuce is related to the consumers' willingness to pay. Consumers will purchase a small quantity of lettuce at a high price, larger amounts of lettuce at lower prices. These alternative actions are illustrated as the demand function DD in Figure 7.[1] This function shows the different quantities of lettuce that would be purchased at alternative prices. Prices and quantities may change but *demand* (the entire schedule) remains constant unless there is a change in income, population, tastes and preferences, etc. (To say that demand has changed would imply that the whole line DD would have shifted either to the left or to the right.) Thus, demand is independent of the lettuce producers' cost picture. Demand is given.

The supply function for lettuce is directly related to producer costs. The industry will be willing to furnish a small amount of lettuce at low prices and larger amounts of lettuce at higher prices. This function is shown as line S_1S_1 in Figure 7.

The intersection of these two functions is the equilibrium point of supply and demand. Producers are willing to furnish quantity B at price A and at this price consumers will clear the market. A higher price would call forth a greater supply but induce consumers to purchase less. The surplus would drive the price back down to equilibrium. A lower price would make consumers wish to purchase more while producers furnished less. Competition for the available produce would drive the price back up to equilibrium.

As the price of labor rises, each firm's cost function per unit of output will rise and the industry supply function will shift upward and to the left. This new supply function is shown as S_2S_2 in Figure 7. Costs must necessarily rise even though the growers shift to a new method of production. If this

---

[1] A demand *function* shows the *functional* relationship between quantities and prices. It shows what quantities will be purchased at various given prices. The supply *function* shows what quantities will be offered at various given prices.

were not so, the growers would have shifted to the new method before wages rose.

PRICE ELASTICITY OF DEMAND

The price, quantity and income results of this rise in wages and consequent shift of the supply function depends on the structure of consumer demand, that is, the slope of the demand function for lettuce. If the demand curve is as shown in Figure 7, the new equilibrium position shows that lettuce prices would rise considerably, yet consumers would purchase only a little less total quantity. (The price would rise from A to C while quantity falls from B to D.)

Gross return to the producer would be greater than before the wage hike. Gross return is price times quantity. This is shown on the graph as the area under the price line and to the left of the quantity line. Note that area OCFD is larger than area OAEB.

Such a situation is known as an "inelastic demand." Where demand is inelastic the percentage change in quantity is smaller than the percentage change in price. Under these conditions a smaller quantity sold will return a larger gross revenue.

If the demand curve is as shown in Figure 8, however, a cutback in supply could be very large with little resulting increase in price. Gross revenue declines even though prices have risen. Figure 8 shows S_1S_1 as the original supply curve and S_2S_2 as the supply curve occurring after the rise in wages. Prices rise from A to C while quantity drops from B to D. The area OCFD is smaller than area OAEB.

Such a situation is known as an "elastic demand." The percentage change in quantity is larger than the percentage change in price. Where demand is

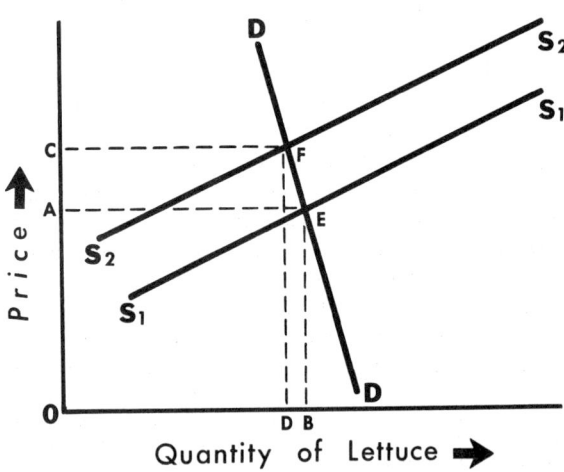

Figure 7. Lettuce Supply and Demand at the Farm Level (Hypothetical)

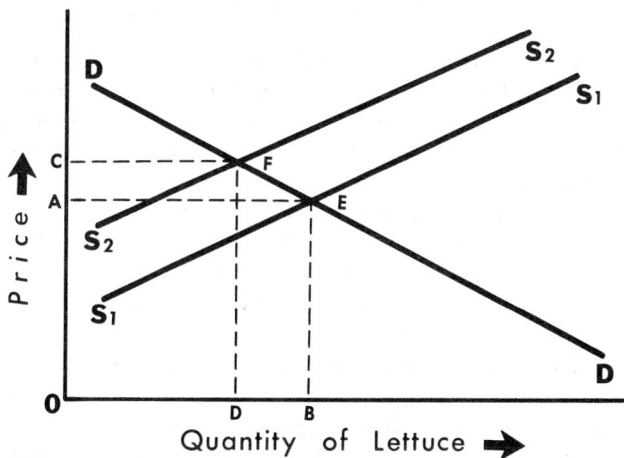

Figure 8. Lettuce Supply and Demand at the Farm Level (Hypothetical)

elastic a smaller quantity sold will always return a smaller gross revenue. Revenues may be increased only by increasing output.

What is the actual demand situation facing United States lettuce producers? Attempts to estimate statistically the price elasticities of demand for vegetables and lettuce in particular have not been completely successful. Still it may be useful to examine some of the estimates that are available.

Brandow (1961:40) gives the price elasticity of demand for lettuce as −0.35. This makes lettuce one of the most inelastic of any fruit or vegetable. It implies that a one percent change in the price of lettuce would cause only a 0.35 percent change in the quantity of lettuce demanded. Conversely, it also implies that a one percent change in quantity supplied would result in a 2.87 percent change in lettuce price (at the farm level).

The elasticity estimate for all vegetables taken as a whole is −.1047 (Brandow 1961:59). This value means that the relationship between price and quantity for vegetables is very inelastic. While the particular vegetable chosen may be importantly influenced by price, about the same amount of one vegetable or another is likely to be used unless extreme price variations occur. Lettuce, as a prime ingredient of salads, has a more fixed position than most vegetables. The price elasticity of lettuce is quite low, yet not as low as vegetables as a whole.

Thus, it is seen that the demand situation facing lettuce producers is similar to that illustrated in Figure 7 rather than as shown in Figure 8. The new equilibrium point implies a small cutback in quantity produced, a relatively larger increase in price received, and an increase in the producers' gross revenues.

IMPLICATIONS OF PRICE ELASTICITY
FOR LETTUCE AND LABOR

Before the bracero program ended, growers indicated that they might reduce lettuce acreage by as much as 50 percent if the bracero program was terminated as planned. Thus far, however, (for the crop immediately following termination) such acreage cuts have failed to materialize. This is not hard to understand. First, growers must actually prove that they cannot get enough domestic labor to harvest their crops if they expect to induce Congress to renew the program. But, perhaps more importantly, such a drastic reduction in quantity would cause a large price increase — by as much as 144 percent if the estimate of price elasticity is correct and applies over such a large range of output.[1] Growers would be willing to supply much more lettuce than this at these prices if labor is not in such short supply as to be actually unavailable at any price.

Thus, since any cut in lettuce acreage would cause rapidly rising lettuce prices, growers as individuals will make every attempt to maintain their acreage so as to take advantage of favorable prices. Switching to a shed pack will reduce their labor needs. Probably lettuce output will fall to 10 or 15 percent below present production while lettuce prices rise and remain some 25 to 40 percent above present levels.

Within two to three years, adaptation to machine harvest will take place and the supply function will drop to somewhere near its 1962-63 level, possibly even lower. Lower machine costs will be somewhat balanced out by higher packinghouse wages. Lettuce quantities and lettuce prices will be similar to those occurring before the program terminated.

The implications of these supply and demand relationships on the labor market are as follows. The inelastic demand for lettuce creates a pressure on producers to keep lettuce production up even in the face of rising costs. Therefore, if producers do not have an alternative labor saving method of production available, labor may push for higher wages without sacrificing a great number of jobs.

Unfortunately for labor, alternative labor saving techniques are being rapidly developed. While rising wages will not cause large production cutbacks, they will result in large cuts in the amount of labor required. Labor's power to raise wages without losing jobs will return only after the present mechanical revolution in the lettuce industry subsides. At that time, the few semi-skilled domestic workers who will be handling the lettuce harvest and pack will find union help in raising wages and improving working conditions beneficial to their cause. Until that time arrives, such pressures can only contribute to the reduction in the total number of available jobs.

---

[1]We would not expect the elasticity estimate to remain constant over this large an output change. Thus, while the actual price change would be considerable, it probably would not reach 144 percent.

Nevertheless, it is to the advantage of certain classes of labor to keep the wage pressures on. While field-hand jobs are being eliminated, shed type jobs will actually increase until the process of converting from the field-pack to the shed-pack is complete. Of course, since mechanization is already underway, this change will take place even without further wage pressures at this time. Continued pressures will hasten the process, but possibly by as little as a year.

10 Cotton Harvesting

THE PATTERN of adoption of the mechanical cotton harvester in Arizona and the United States well illustrates the capital-labor substitution problem. The harvester has been adopted on farms and in areas where it harvests cotton at a lower cost per dollar of return than with hand labor. In other areas, hand labor still predominates.

Hand labor has been available throughout the adoption period. The disappearance of cotton picker labor in Arizona has largely been in response to the absence of cotton picking jobs rather than the job disappearing from the lack of available labor.

WHEN IS MECHANIZATION ECONOMIC?

The major economic variables involved in the labor vs. capital choice in the cotton harvest are the price of labor, the percentage of field loss, the grade loss, the yield per acre, and the amount of cotton acreage in the farm.

A detailed economic analysis of these variables was published in 1954 by Vanvig and St. Clair. At that time about 40 percent of Arizona's cotton crop was being harvested by machine. They showed that if a hand picking rate of $3.00 per hundred weight was assumed, if grade losses, extra ginning costs and extra cultural practices (such as defoliation) were included, and if the farm had 100 acres or less of cotton yielding one bale or less per acre no matter how low the percentage of field loss, hand picking was the least-cost method of harvest. On one-bale yields machine harvest became least costly with 140 acres and six percent field loss or 180 acres with eight percent field loss. With one and one-half bale yields machine harvest was the least-cost method with 100 acres and ten percent field loss, or 180 acres and 14 percent field loss. If two bale yields were achieved machine harvest was cheapest with 100 acres and 14 percent field loss, 140 acres and 16 percent field loss, or 180 acres and 17 percent field loss.

The above figures considered all the costs of owning and operating a machine. This is the situation facing the farmer who is thinking of buying a machine. The decision to machine pick or hand pick is not the same for the farmer who already owns a machine as for the farmer who must buy a machine. The cost of ownership need not be considered by the machine owner since these costs are fixed and would occur whether the machine was used or not. These costs can be escaped only by selling the machine. With a field loss of ten percent these ownership costs vary from about $1.00 per hundredweight with 100 acres of bale and one-half cotton to $.50 with 140 acres of two-bale cotton. Thus we see that unless wage, yield, or acreage conditions later vary widely from conditions causing the original shift to machines, the shift between labor and machinery is a one-way process. Once the machine is purchased, it rarely pays to leave it idle or dispose of it at a loss. Of course the technological variables, percent of field loss, and loss of grade always will change in favor of the machine.

THE SITUATION IN ARIZONA

Since 1954, both amount of cotton acreage per farm and yield per acre have increased. Wages have remained relatively constant. Where average yields for the state varied from 1.35 to 1.65 bales per acre from 1949 through 1953 they have varied from 1.86 to 2.36 bales per acre from 1954 to 1963. Naturally to get an average of 2.36 bales per acre many farmers must be doing much better than that. Yields as high as six bales per acre are not now uncommon in certain areas of the state. As yields rose, so did pressures for mechanization.

Cotton acreage per farm has also risen steadily as the smaller farms have combined or been absorbed by the larger operators. Exact data for Arizona are not yet available. But, preliminary results from interviews with a random sample of all persons holding cotton allotments in Yuma and Maricopa Counties (the major producing areas of the State) show the smaller farms to be rapidly disappearing (University of Arizona 1964b).

The wage actually paid for hand cotton picking has not changed very much during the shift to machine harvest. Vanvig and St. Clair (1954) gave $3.00 per hundred as a typical rate in 1953. Of the farms studied by this report in 1963, Company K, who hand picked 14 percent of its cotton, was still paying $3.00 per hundredweight for hand pickers. Companies L and M who machine picked 100 percent and 98 percent of their cotton, respectively, quoted $3.30 and $3.35 as the wage rates facing them in their particular areas. These facts do not mean that wage rates have not been a causal factor in shifting to machines. The threat of rising wage rates has been enough to effect the shift and thus maintain wages for the remaining hand work constant over time. For example, the Arizona Cotton Growers Association did not contract braceros for hand picking cotton in 1950 because of the required 60 cents per hour guarantee. Thereafter, mechanization rose each year (except 1954-56) while the free market piece rate stayed at $3.00 or less per hundredweight. On December 6, 1962, the adverse effect rate for hand picking short staple cotton was set at $3.30 per hundredweight in Yuma County and $3.75 per hundredweight in Maricopa County. Mechanization was so far advanced at this time (see Figure 1, Chapter 5) that the free market rate remained at $3.00 (ASES 1964d).

MECHANIZATION THROUGHOUT THE UNITED STATES

Thus, machine technology, size of farm, yields per acre, and wage rates have all conspired to replace the hand cotton picker by the machine in Arizona. Yet most cotton states are still much less mechanized than Arizona. Since the technology is available throughout the United States, the wage, size, and yield variables must provide the answer to this discrepancy.

Table 4 provides rough data on these variables for the 16 cotton producing states. These data are plotted against the percent of cotton that is machine harvested in each state in Figures 9, 10 and 11. California, Arizona, and New Mexico all harvested above 91 percent of their cotton by machine. The states of the West South Central region harvested from 64 percent to 78 percent of their crop by machine. The East South Central and Southern Atlantic states all have less than a 60 percent machine harvest with Virginia still harvesting all cotton by hand.

In Figure 9 the composite wage rate per hour for farm labor in each state is plotted against the percent of machine harvest. The freehand trend

Table 4. Percent of Cotton that is Machine Harvested and Related Variables, by State

	Percent Machine Harvested 1962-63[a]	Wage Rate Per Hour Oct. 1962[b]	Average Size Cotton Farm in Acres 1959[c]	Average Yield Per Acre in Pounds 1962[d]
United States	70	—	—	—
Virginia	0	.86	36	363
North Carolina	27	.76	69	337
Alabama	29	.63	102	327
South Carolina	32	.54	86	337
Georgia	39	.68	147	354
Tennessee	41	.68	95	493
Florida	53	.81	123	279
Mississippi	58	.59	121	493
Louisiana	64	.71	116	429
Arkansas	68	.78	179	512
Oklahoma	73	1.02	334	274
Missouri	77	1.05	145	469
Texas	78	.84	381	350
New Mexico	91	.90	706	728
Arizona	92	1.01	868	1010
California	94	1.30	400	990

[a]USDA, 1963 b.
[b]USDA, 1963 d.
[c]USDC, 1959.
[d]USDA, 1963 c.

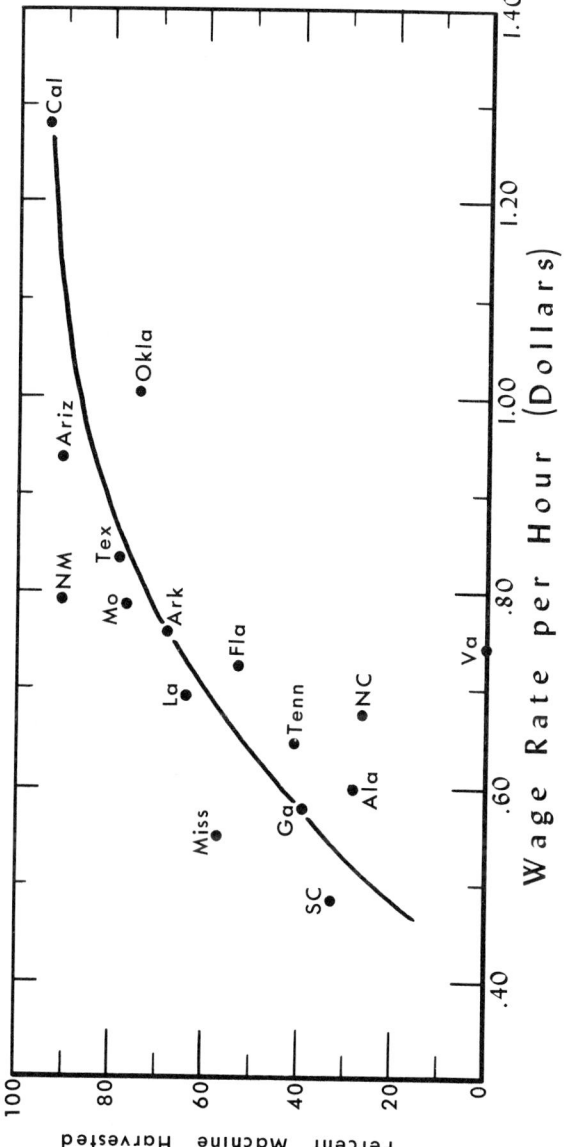

Figure 9. Percent of Cotton that is Machine Harvested Related to the Hourly Wage Rate, by State

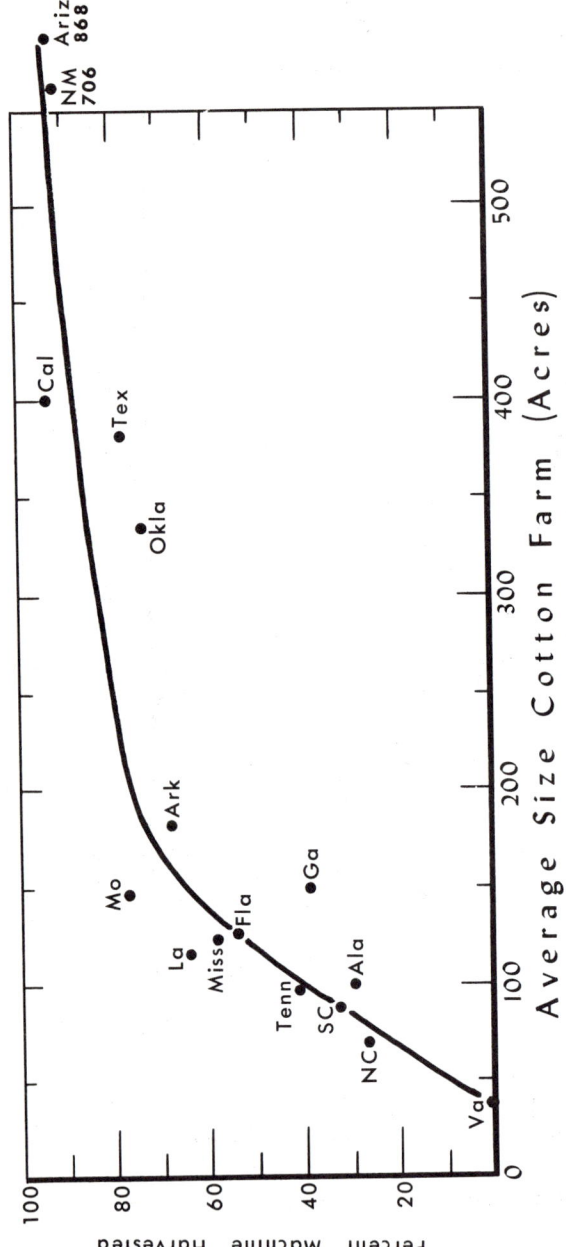

Figure 10. Percent of Cotton that is Machine Harvested Related to the Average Size of Cotton Farm, by State

line drawn through the points shows that where wages are relatively low the percentage of cotton that is machine harvested is low. California, with the highest wage rate, has the highest percent machine harvest. South Carolina, with the lowest wage rate, is fourth lowest in machine harvested cotton.

The points are scattered about the trend line rather than making a perfect fit since other variables than wages are also influencing the outcome. Figure 10 shows the average size of cotton farm within each state as a function of the percent of cotton machine harvested. Immediately the reason for much of the variation about the trend line in Figure 9 becomes obvious. Virginia had relatively high wages but very small farms. Machine harvest has been economically not feasible in Virginia simply because of the small fields. North Carolina has high wages compared to other southern states but has the second smallest farm size. Size again balances out the wage rate. South Carolina has the lowest wage rate but larger farms than North Carolina or Virginia. Thus, the percentage of machine harvest is higher than in these other two states. Similar relationships between wage rates and farm size may be discovered for most of the remaining states. Arizona, California, and Oklahoma all have very large farms in addition to high wage rates. Mechanization is very nearly complete in these states. New Mexico and Texas have such large farms that mechanization is occurring despite their relatively low wage rates.

Further variation from the trend lines may be explained by Figure 11. Average yields are plotted against the percent of cotton that was machine harvested. A continuous relationship is less obvious here. The very high yield states of New Mexico, California, and Arizona are almost completely mechanized. But, for states with yields of only 500 pounds or below, yield appears to have little effect on degree of mechanization. Evidently, yields of a bale and one-half or more are necessary before yield becomes a significant factor. Wages and farm size are apparently the overriding factors for the high rate of mechanization in such states as Oklahoma, Texas, Missouri, and Arkansas where yields are relatively low.

The variables, "percent of machine harvest," "wage rate," and "farm size," were subjected to multiple regression analysis in order to check statistically the relationships observable in Figures 9 and 10. The results showed that the two variables, "wage rates" and "farm size," explain 84 percent of the variation in percent of machine harvest between states. Wages alone explain 40 percent of the variation while farm size alone explains 81 percent of the variation. This does not imply that wages are not a potent explanatory variable. Instead, it infers something about the shape of the input possibility map on small and large farms. Small farms will begin to mechanize only at very high wage rates. Large farms will partially mechanize at relatively low wage rates and increase their degree of mechanization as wage rates rise.

A further reason for the relatively low explanatory value of wage rates

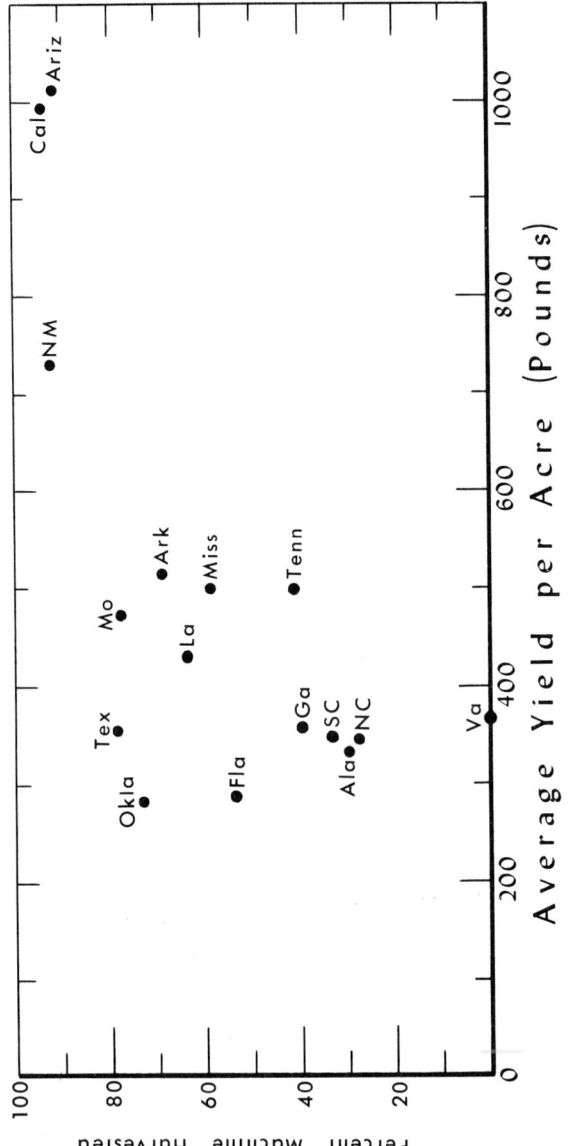

Figure 11. Percent of Cotton that is Machine Harvested Related to Average Yield per Acre, by State

is that large farm sizes may themselves produce higher wage rates. The intercorrelation between farm size and wage rate was .55. This is not a particularly strong relationship yet it may imply that the need for large gangs of labor creates wage pressures that do not occur where labor is hired on an individual or small group basis.

LESSONS LEARNED FROM COTTON

Since cotton harvest mechanization is essentially complete in Arizona, what are the implications of the discussion for Arizona farmers and farm labor?

Farm Size

The generally large size of farms in Arizona provides the base for efficient (low cost per unit of output) machinery use. This is so whether we are considering cotton harvesting or chopping, the lettuce or cantaloupe harvest, or the citrus harvest.

In lettuce, 63 packers control and harvest a total of 56,919 acres, an average of 903 acres apiece and a median of about 835 acres. The grower-packers above the median harvested 90.1 percent of the crop in 1962-1963 (Arizona Fruits and Vegetable Standardization Service 1962). With an average yield of 342 cartons per acre, the median farm would use approximately 714 hours of mechanical harvesting if an output of 400 cartons per hour were maintained. As previously shown, only 570 hours are necessary to make the mechanical harvester comparable to the 22 man crew shed-pack method at wages of $1.00 per hour. Since harvesters may be used both within and outside of the state the relevant average farm size is actually larger than shown.

The situation is similar in cantaloupes. The 25 Arizona shippers who control the harvest average 719 acres apiece with a median acreage of 755. The sixth smallest still had about 400 acres (Arizona Fruits and Vegetable Standardization Service 1962). Again, farm size is favorable for mechanization.

Although no mechanical breakthrough appears in prospect in the citrus harvest, the practice of packing shed operators harvesting the fruit rather than growers harvesting and delivering to the sheds again makes the farm size climate propitious for mechanization. At present only 17 non-grower packing sheds operate in Maricopa County and four such sheds operate in Yuma. These sheds control 86 percent and 97 percent of the fruit, respectively. Average acreage per packer-harvester is 642 acres in Maricopa County and 2,416 acres in Yuma County. The seven grower-packers average 306 acres each.

Such control overcomes the fact that many Arizona citrus groves are owned in very small blocks. For example, of the 404 groves in Maricopa County, 200 are less than ten acres in size. Of course, these 200 groves make up only nine percent of total Maricopa citrus acreage anyway — and could, for all practical purposes, be ignored in terms of labor needs. Another 132 growers have only 11 percent of the acreage with farms of 11 to 39 acres in size. Sixty growers, with farms of from 40 to 200 acres, make up the next 40 percent of the acreage. Only 12 growers have groves of 280 to 700 acres each making up the final 40 percent of Maricopa County citrus acreage (University of Arizona 1964b).

Wage Rates

In contrast to the situation in cotton, Arizona wage rates are lower than in most other lettuce producing states. California hourly wages average about $.40 higher; New York, New Jersey and Wisconsin are about $.10 higher. Wages in Colorado are comparable to those in Arizona. Texas and Florida are about $.11 lower.

But wage comparisons between states are not relevant to the central problem of whether Arizona mechanizes or not. The cost saving ability of the proposed lettuce harvester has already been illustrated using prevailing wage rates. Any increase in Arizona wage rates can only intensify the pressures toward mechanization. Even in citrus we see the pressures at work. The packing sheds studied are moving toward mechanization, although at present only the hauling activities have been affected.

Thus, in lettuce and citrus it is suggested, but in cotton it is history that, as far as labor is concerned, rising agricultural wage rates can only reduce the number of available agricultural jobs.

PART THREE

THE WORKERS

11 Method and Intent of Worker Interviews

GENERAL

THE SAMPLE of 13 farm companies and nine independent harvesting crews yielded a total of 603 workers. The 13 farm companies accounted for 503 workers; the nine independent crews accounted for 100 workers. The average number of workers interviewed per farm unit was slightly more than 38; the average independent crew yielded approximately 11 workers each. The greatest number of workers interviewed from any one employment unit was 140. These were obtained from the largest of the 13 farm companies, a lettuce corporation. The smallest number of workers interviewed from an employment unit was four, obtained from a small independent picking and chopping crew.

Of the total, 287 worker interviews or 48 percent were obtained from the four lettuce companies and one independent lettuce crew, 200 interviews or 33 percent from the six citrus companies, and 116 interviews or 19 percent from the three cotton farms and the eight independent picking-chopping crews.

Two hundred and fifty-four or 42 percent of the workers were working in Pinal County at the time that they were interviewed, 217 or 36 percent were working in Maricopa County, and 132 or 22 percent were working in Yuma County.

SAMPLING METHODS

Citrus, lettuce, and cotton harvest technologies as operating systems are the basic units of our investigation. The farm companies and independent harvesting crews studied were purposively selected to provide representation of the sources of uniformity and variation in the technical and organizational aspects of these crop technologies. Theoretically the farm workers who were actively employed by each company and crew during the time its operations were studied would comprise the universe of workers for that organization. It would follow methodologically that a given percentage of these workers taken at random would be interviewed. Problems arose in that these universes taken individually or collectively were not sufficiently uniform or stable to justify a random sample.

Perhaps the most outstanding feature of seasonal farm work is its instability. Any precise delimitation of a universe of such a work force for any one crop, area, farm, or even crew is an arbitrary fiction of the investigator. To proceed methodically as if such a universe were attainable is to perpetuate ignorance. There is no precise universe of seasonal workers. There is only a modal universe which fluctuates around a patterned norm of human comings and goings that varies, in many instances, by the hour.

Another factor contributing to the misrepresentation of a "precise" universe of workers is the fact that such a universe for one farm company would represent that company at a different phase of its harvest activity than the universe of workers for another company. For instance F Company in citrus was studied at the peak of their harvest season. C Company was studied after their peak period had passed, and D Company was studied after the 1963 freeze had all but shut them down. In the case of F Company, a universe of workers constructed around a given pay period would have represented, because of the high turnover and replacement factor, approximately 140 percent of their minimum daily required number of workers. In this case the universe would be technically in error because it was too large. In the case of C Company, a universe of workers would have represented approximately 50 percent of the workers they normally employ at a phase in their harvest activity comparable to the phase in which F Company was studied. In the case of D Company such a universe would bear almost no resemblance in size to their requirements during the peak season.

All three companies are complicated by the fact that they each rely in differing degrees at differing phases of their harvest activities upon Mexican Nationals. They therefore have two discrete universes of workers at a given moment. One consists solely of their domestic workers—United States citizens or those having immigration papers — who were the subject of our worker interviews. The other consists of their *total* work force consisting of domestics and Mexican Nationals.

To meet these peculiar demands, we used a sampling technique based upon a concept of a "modal universe." This means that rather than using an actual list of names of workers for each employment unit, we used a list of worker groupings and picked individual informants from these groups. Previous study had indicated the kinds of groups in seasonal farm work which have importance are ethnic groups, age groups, job groups, and wage groups. These clusterings of human sentiment and activity that operate as important determinants of worker behavior are, for the most part, revealed by the viewpoints of the participants in the farm and crew organizations.

Each unit's modal universe is represented in the Organizational Structure of Harvest Activities. For example, the sample of workers interviewed for the first company, A Company, represented first of all, each group of job tasks — foremen, drivers, swampers, and pickers. Secondly, it represented the natural worker groupings which characterized their field operations, viz. the "old fruit tramps" and the Texas Mexican-Americans. Likewise the age groups and the different wage levels were also represented. Sampling by a quota system was done in the field with the immediate help of the participants themselves.

The only bias might result from the fact that a constant percentage sampling of each grouping in each employment unit could only be approximated. The fundamental focus of the study is the sample farm company or crew caught in a particular phase of a highly seasonal activity. Furthermore, it was a field activity exposed to all the exigencies of the weather. Rarely could the time allotted to an organization be pre-determined. Moreover, the time at which the study of a company commenced could be controlled only to a limited degree.

This bias is offset by the fundamentally informal nature of farm field activities which defies anything other than an approximate delineation of a "grouping" and the relatively high percentage of sampling we were able to maintain. The over-all average for all farms and crews is 54 percent.

Therefore the sample is representative in all important respects of the universe of workers who were engaged in the crop activities conducted by the sample organizations. The modal universe method provided representation of the patterned human groupings peculiar to each organization in a way that, were their actual personnel different, findings would be essentially the same.

An exception to the quota sampling of a modal universe must be reported for cotton picking-chopping crews. This exception involved the conscious by-passing of many of the extremely young children encountered in the crews. This exception was deliberate because school had just let out and therefore, to a certain extent, the influx of school-age children could not be considered representative of our modal universe of chopping and picking crews except for weekends. Another reason was that we needed economic, household, migration, and work history data on workers that were not obtainable from school children. Field workers recorded each crew's makeup of personnel in terms of ethnicity and family relationships, interviewed a few children, and then aimed at an ethnic representation of adults. A bias therefore exists for this task group in terms of frequencies for age groups. The mean age will tend to be too high.

Listed below, arranged in percentage order, are the farm companies and independent crews. The percentages represent for each employment unit the percentage sample obtained from the approximate total number of *domestic* workers employed at the time its field operation was studied.

Company and Crop	Approximate Number of Domestics	Number in Sample	Percent
D Citrus	7	7	100
E Citrus	27	26	96
A Citrus	52	43	83
J Lettuce	25	19	76
C Citrus	68	50	74
B Citrus	26	19	73
F Citrus	84	55	66
H Lettuce	102	64	63
G Lettuce	225	140	62
L Cotton	15	8	53
K Cotton	27	12	44
I Lettuce	99	42	42
M Cotton	80	18	23
Independent Crews			
1 Lettuce crew	49	24	49
8 Cotton crews	225	76	34
Total	1,111	603	54

INTERVIEWING METHODS

By prior arrangement with each sample farm company, workers were interviewed on the spot. During the pretesting period, field interviewers tried differing methods. We found generally that after hours the workers became fatigued more easily with the sometimes tedious questioning necessary to establish reliable work sequences and economic data. Results were almost always more favorable in the field. Also, it was far more expensive for us to locate workers in their widely separated community clusters than it was to talk to them localized in the fields. Although this method of interviewing on the job tended to sacrifice physical comfort, it was offset by the rapport gained. Another benefit, of course, was that it allowed a closer integration of interviewing with field observations, working to the benefit of both phases of the research.

It was a simple matter to implement a reimbursement procedure. "Guide fees" were used to reimburse growers for workers' time lost in the case of hourly wages and to reimburse workers themselves in the case of piece-rate work. They were also used to hire translators for some of the Indians. All farm companies except one donated their time. All companies granted permission to reimburse their piece-rate workers.

Because the interview schedule was open ended, the length of time devoted to interviewing informants was a highly individual matter. Time required to complete all categories with a sophisticated Anglo informant, without further depth interviewing, was a little over 40 minutes. Other informants required up to two hours. Follow-up depth interviewing was generally carried out during off-hours.

Reliability of informant responses was insured by four devices. First, each ethnic group had its interviewing peculiarities. These peculiarities were patterned differently even within ethnic groups according to age and level of sophistication. For example, the old Filipinos do not regard any work as important except the work they identify themselves with — cutting and packing in truck garden crops. Likewise Indians tend to lump all work for Anglos off the reservation as simply "irrigating," "chopping," etc. without regard to time, place, or employer. With these unsophisticated groups it was necessary to employ a check list procedure. This consisted of starting with a date one year prior to the date of the interview and asking, "In January of 1962 what work were you doing?" Then the interviewer would ask, "Who was the work for? What did it consist of? Was your boss a private contractor or an owner?" etc. The interviewers accumulated a detailed list of questions which had to be asked point blank for every inquiry. All responses were recorded on the schedule so that judgements could be rechecked and definitions tightened.

A second method used was the standard technique of checking internal consistency. The questionnaire had numerous areas of overlap that functioned effectively for this purpose. For instance, job history and migration pattern; job history and income; residence description, personal property, and number of dependents; marital status and number of dependents; and number of dependents working and income. Added to specific inquiries was the depth interviewing at the end of the questionnaire when it was the general practice of the interviewers to put away the schedule and talk with the informant without the use of any recording device. An hour and a half of this kind of dialogue gave a fairly accurate picture of an informant's occupational experience and economic background.

A third method was to check the cross consistency of interviews of informants who were closely related by kinship ties or long association. A final method was a check of the integral consistency of worker interviews with data obtained from the other phases of the farm company study—technical, organizational, and economic. The senior author worked in the field full time. Two interviewers were employed half-time.

Only in the case of the Papago were interpreters needed. Every farm company on which they were found had bilingual Papagos available as interpreters. The senior author's Spanish proved adequate to interview monolingual Mexican-Americans.

THE QUESTIONNAIRE

The Format

The focus of this phase of data gathering was the relationships between changes in jobs or worker roles and changes in workers and worker populations. A questionnaire, to help provide data for an investigation of these relationships, must provide observations in both vocational and social categories. Moreover, time depth is needed.

On the occupational side are the first order observations such as the identification of the worker by crop-area, company, job group, wage group, how he obtained his present job, and the length of time on his present job. The second order of vocational information researches the informant's occupational past. This is done by compiling a list of his jobs prior (1962-63) to his present one, by establishing his prime vocation at a stable period in his past (10 to 15 years ago) and by recording the occupation of his father.

Social data pertinent to a worker's employment patterns are separated, for the sake of analysis, into three portions in the questionnaire: Skill Factors, Material and Economic Factors, and Value and Adaptive Factors. Skill factors include the standard categories such as formal schooling, vocational training, lingualism, and literacy. Also included as a skill factor is past vocational experience. Job history, of course, is a source of both vocational data and social data.

Material and economic factors represent a rather complicated inquiry into the worker's material status. All factors taken together provide an operational method of comparing one group of workers with another. Included are the following:

> access to transportation
> commuting and migration pattern
> personal property
> household facilities
> number of rooms
> ownership
> income
> indebtedness
> number of dependents

Value and adaptive factors are in essence the questionnaire portion of the depth interviewing. The aim of these questions is to give the researcher a picture of the social stability and occupation adjustment of the worker. Church affiliation, frequency of attendance, union membership, marital status, oscillation between old cultural patterns and new, and even age are important in this picture. In addition, attitudes from the informant about his job, past or present, are solicited, sometimes with the aid of standardized leading questions, sometimes not. Information on the latter was synthesized and abstracted into two general categories that were coded later under Attitude Toward Present Vocational Situation and General Value Orientation. The more involved statements by informants were entered as field notes. Most of this information was more typically ethnographic since it provided insights into human groupings on the job and off the job. More discussion of the ethnographic phase of the research is given in Part Four.

Pretesting and Revision

Two months were given to pretesting. A population of workers engaged in the cotton harvests in Pima County was used. The first version of the questionnaire consisted primarily of organized headings covering in general fashion the categories outlined. From this version standardized questions were formulated. The second version was tested among lettuce and cotton workers in Pinal County. From these tests we made final revision of the instrument and precoded it for IBM. We then ordered mimeograph reproduction in limited quantity to allow for still further minor revision after the first few days of intensive field work.

In spite of the fact that the final questionnaire underwent three revisions, clarification of definitions and minor revisions in the form of additional categories were required by the extreme diversity of the population. All definitions and clarifications were noted, dated and filed. This constantly expanding file was consulted daily throughout the interviewing period by all field researchers. All questions were open-ended with ample space provided in the schedule for each individual exception to be described. Responses to all but the simplest questions were recorded in writing. This procedure made it possible to add additional coded categories for unanticipated patterns. This was done when the schedules were readied for IBM punching. When a modification of response definitions or response groupings was made which affected complete interviews, the changes were made retroactively. All completed schedules were proofread twice; once at the end of each week in the field and again just prior to IBM punching.

A discussion of the questionnaire item by item would be too tedious and digressive. The final revised interview schedule is given in the Appendix with the additional definitions of questions required for clarification. Also included in the Appendix is the Specimen of Code Sheet used for coding quantifiable information obtained in open-ended inquiries.

The results of the questionnaires are given as follows. General results for the entire sample are discussed first in Chapter 12. This helps explain the questions in more detail. In addition it describes the Arizona farm worker population conceptualized as an entity in itself. The use and limitations of this concept are discussed at the beginning of Chapter 12, appropriately titled "Workers out of Context." Chapter 13 analyzes ethnic affiliation as sources of variation in all factors. Chapter 14 analyzes the effects of variation in education, vocational history, age, and family stability.

Standard deviations for all means and confidence intervals at the 95 percent level are indicated in parentheses and tables as "SD" and "CI" respectively.

12 Workers Out of Context

WHY OUT OF CONTEXT?

IF ETHNIC AFFILIATION, cultural background, and technological setting are necessary to understand farm workers, why discuss farm workers as a population entity? We begin our analysis of workers this way because the latter view is the lay view, because rightly or wrongly questions of economic and social interests are commonly framed in terms of *the* farm labor force, *the* farm labor population, *the* migrant worker, etc. Moreover, looking at the farm labor population as a whole gives us an opportunity to delineate and discuss elementary features, such as income, housing, and education, that are the proper concern of those agencies and firms dealing with the farm labor population as a whole. Setting aside these practical considerations, beginning with gross characteristics of the whole sample will show the tap roots of the main trunks of organization in later chapters. Finally, the paucity of information gained by viewing workers out of context will offer remarkable contrast to the wealth of information revealed by viewing workers in their settings — a contrast missed without this kind of beginning.

The chapter begins with the distribution of states of origin, age, ethnic membership, and sex. This is followed by a discussion of the sample in terms of Skill Factors, Material Factors, and Value Factors.

ORIGINS, AGE, ETHNICITY, AND SEX

Origins

The states of origin for the workers include 39 of the 50 states in addition to the territory of Puerto Rico and five foreign countries—Mexico, Philippines, Argentina, Canada, and El Salvador. All states or countries contributing ten percent or more of the 603 workers are listed below in the order of their frequencies:

State	Number	Percent
Arizona	146	24
Texas	115	19
Mexico	76	13
California	61	10

Oklahoma, Arkansas, Louisiana, Missouri, Alabama, Kentucky, Mississippi, and Tennessee, each contributing in the relative order they are arranged, accounted collectively for 81 workers or 13 percent of the sample.

Age

Age Group	Number	Percent
13 to 15	9	2
16 to 20	66	11
21 to 30	141	23
31 to 40	134	22
41 to 50	117	19
51 to 61	107	18
over 62	29	5
Total	603	100

Forty-two percent of the sample fell in the older age categories of 41 and older. Almost a quarter, 23 percent, were 51 and over.

Ethnicity

Ethnic Groups	Number	Percent
Anglo	213	35
Mexican-American	178	30
Negro	75	12
Mexican Immigrants ("green carders")	62	10
Indian	53	9
Filipino	15	3
Other	7	1
Total	603	100

The Mexican-Americans and Mexican immigrants combine to form the largest single ethnic group in our sample—240 or 40 percent. This gives some idea of the importance of the Mexican element in the Arizona domestic farm labor force.

Sex and Marital Status

The data on marital status proved to be almost useless in evaluating the actual social-familial situation of an informant because most of the single younger men and women were living with parents or siblings. This was especially true of Mexican-Americans. Moreover many of the divorced and separated were remarried or living with common-law wives. Therefore we sought other criteria that were more valid indicators. These criteria will be discussed under the headings of Residence Household and Subsistence Household. Seven percent of the sample are females.

SKILL FACTORS

Formal Schooling

Following is the distribution of frequencies for years of school completed (these figures exclude the number [6] not reporting):

Years Completed	Number	Percent
0 to 4	147	25
5 to 6	93	16
7 to 9	229	38
10 to 11	55	9
12 and over	73	12
Total	597	100

An interesting comparison can be made to data on the entire farm work force in the United States for 1961 (Cowhig 1963: 4). Cowhig reports that 17.3 percent fall in the 0 to 4 group, which he defines as "functional illiterates." Our figure of 24.6 percent in the 0 to 4 group is considerably higher than this. The group 5 to 11 is 67.2 nationally, for which we have a comparable figure of 63.2. In the grouping with 12 years of school and above, the national percentage is 17.4; our sample shows a percentage of 12.2. Thus our sample shows a greater percentage of functional illiterates with a lower percentage of high school graduates.

Mean years of schooling for our sample is 7.1 years (SD: 3.53; CI: ± .289 @ 95%).

Language

Ninety-three workers or 15 percent could not speak English, and 138 or 23 percent could not read English. These data suggest even more strongly that the sample represents a population of workers that differs from the national farm worker population in terms of higher frequencies of nonacculturated peoples.

Vocational Training

Following is a breakdown of frequencies for type of vocational training experience:

Type Training	Number	Percent
None or does not know	430	71
Skilled nonfarm	127	21
Other nonfarm	46	8
Farm skilled	12	2

(Frequencies total more than sample because of multiple response.)

The outstanding fact is that 71 percent had no vocational training of any kind and that only two percent had any formal vocational training in farm skills.

First Job Pattern 1962-63

An informant's (1962-63) job pattern was abstracted from his job history as reported during the interview. Because of job shifting, it was necessary to assign an order of importance to differing job patterns. This was done on the basis of time spent. Following is a breakdown of frequencies for the most important job patterns:

Type of Job	Number	Percent
Farm hand	299	50
Farm skilled	138	23
Small farmer	9	1
Total farm	446	74
Total nonfarm	73	12
Drifting and/or unemployed	84	14

"Farm hand" includes two categories on the code sheet (see Specimen of Code Sheet in the Appendix)—Harvest Hand Labor (strictly seasonal) and Farm Hand General (hand only, but year round). "Farm skilled" is inclusive of the following categories: Farm Supervisory I (managers and general foremen), Farm Supervisory II (row bosses and crew foremen), Farm Equipment Operator and/or Mechanic, Farm Services, and Farm Crew Leader Independent. "Small farmer" is inclusive of Farm Owner, Tenant Farmer, Sharecrop Farmer, and On-reservation Subsistence.

Significant is the fact that 12 percent of the workers interviewed on the farms had *nonfarm* job patterns for that year.

Length of Time Jobs Held

A measurement which gives some idea of the occupational flux of farm workers is the average length of time the worker held each job he had. The mean for the sample is 6.6 months (SD: 3.98; CI: $\pm$ .32 @ 95%).

Second Job Pattern 1962-63

We also recorded the second most important job pattern. Of the 603 workers interviewed, 213 or 35 percent did not show a second job pattern. Their job patterns were consistent. Although they may have shifted employers or have held each job they had only a few weeks, every job they had was in the same pattern. Of the 390 who did show a second type of job pattern the breakdown of frequencies is as follows:

Type of Job	Number	Percent
Farm hand	195	50
Farm skilled	55	14
Small farmer	7	2
Total farm	257	66
Total nonfarm	63	16
Drifting and/or unemployed	70	18

The ratios for the 390 who show a second job pattern are similar to the first job pattern ratios for the whole sample (see above). Frequencies for third job patterns are too low for analysis.

Harvest Hand for Any Length of Time

Four hundred and ninety-seven workers or 82 percent reported working as a harvest hand for some length of time in the past year. Listed below is the crop breakdown:

Crop worked in for any length time as a harvest hand	Number Responses	Percent Harvest Hands	Percent Whole Sample
Lettuce plus other crops	249	50	41
Cotton plus other crops	191	38	32
Citrus plus other crops	177	36	29
(Multiple response)			

The 32 percent figure in cotton is especially significant since only 19 percent of the sample had been drawn as cotton workers. This gives some indication of the amount of job and crop diversity which characterizes seasonal farm workers in general.

Pattern for Obtaining Jobs

The workers' patterns of obtaining jobs they reported show the following response frequencies:

How Job Obtained	Number	Percent
Used informal channels (word of mouth via friends)	510	85
Used a state employment office	133	22
Used formal channels (through personnel office, etc.)	40	7
(Multiple response)		

The outstanding feature of this pattern for the sample is the use of informal channels. The nature of farm work systems is informal compared to other industries; in addition, the unsophisticated nature of farm workers themselves make this pattern a logical expectation.

MATERIAL AND ECONOMIC FACTORS

Transportation

Ability to get to work is an important factor affecting an individual's opportunity for certain kinds of employment. Three hundred and twelve or 52 percent of the sample reported having automobiles which they could use to commute. The other 48 percent (294) either had no cars whatsoever or were not sure of their car's dependability. Following is a distribution of methods of getting to work:

Method	Number	Percent
Own or family car	227	38
Lives on place of work	161	27
Farm furnished	141	23
Friend's car	82	14
Walk	51	8
(Multiple response)		

Residence Household

Because of the need to follow crops, actual day to day residences of workers will vary. Before descriptions of residences have any meaning, it has to be determined just what residence it is we are talking about. To clarify this question the dichotomy of "residence household" and "subsistence household" was made. If a worker did not have a pattern of living with immediate family and integrating his income with immediate family, then he was an "isolate." Because of this pattern, his residence of the moment was as significant as any of a score of places he may have resided in the past year.

On the other hand, if an individual showed a strong tendency to live with, and help support a parent, brothers, sisters or his children at a stable location on weekends, or between crop harvests lasting only a few weeks, he was an "aggregate." In his case it was more important to describe the residence in which he was maintaining his family rather than the motel or trailer court he was occupying at the moment. (See item 34 of Questionnaire in the Appendix). Subsistence Household is discussed under separate heading below.

Three hundred and fifty or 58 percent of our sample are aggregates and 253 or 42 percent are isolates.

All observations concerning residence for isolates pertain to their immediate residences. For aggregates these data pertain to the residences of their families.

Ownership of Residence

Ownership	Number	Percent
Rent	291	48
Free	201	33
Own	108	18
Unknown	3	1
Total	603	100

Of the 201 free residences, 175 were farm furnished. This means that 29 percent of our worker sample lived in farm furnished housing at the time they were interviewed. Seventy-one percent therefore lived independent of the farm.

Household Facilities

Three hundred and sixteen or 52 percent reported having modern facilities—inside water, toilet, electricity, and refrigerator. The 87 or 14 percent who lived with Mexican Nationals had barracks type housing which met the qualifications set forth in Public Law 78, including lights, central kitchen, and central modern toilets.

In all, 31 percent were living in substandard housing. Sixty-three or ten percent had inside water, electricity, storage, but outside toilets. One hundred and eight or 18 percent lived in houses with outside community water as well as outside toilets, and 17 or three percent lived with no plumbing at all. Twelve or two percent did not report.

Number of People per Room in Residence

Forty-nine or eight percent averaged more than two rooms per occupant, whereas 62 or ten percent had four or more people per room. The mean ratio for the total is 1.8 people per room (SD: 1.4; CI: $\pm$ .263 @ 95%).

Commuting Patterns

Listed below is the distribution of frequencies for seven different commuting patterns. These patterns bear a significant relationship to job patterns which will be analyzed later. More detailed definitions are in the Appendix. The patterns are arranged in the order of degree of workers' migrancy—from least to most:

Pattern	Number	Percentage
Permanent residence on farm where working at time of interview	46	8
Permanent residence off farm where working at time of interview and commutes daily	148	25
Permanent residence off farm and double commutes (commutes daily to job and to permanent home periodically)	38	6
Dual residence (alternates between two places)	42	7
Circular migration (to the same places)	195	32
Immigration (to area now in)	50	8
Anomic (drifting) migration	80	13
Indefinite and unclear	4	1
Total	603	100

It is significant that only eight percent established a permanent residence pattern on the farm for which they were working. The highest percentage, almost a third, had a circular pattern. The second highest percentage, a quarter, live in a permanent off-farm residence and work within a daily commuting radius.

Except for the immigrants, drifters, and unknowns amounting to only 22 percent, all workers had occupied the same residence or residences through the year. This does not fit the stereotype picture of seasonal farm workers as being wandering gypsies. When the term "migrant" is used it must certainly be qualified, as the above frequencies of regularized residence patterns indicate.

Subsistence Household

A subsistence household consists of those who have a regular paycheck-by-paycheck subsistence relationship either by integrated incomes or by a provider-dependent relationship. Its members may or may not be otherwise related, and may have separate residences.

Subsistence Household must be distinguished from Residence Household, which emphasizes dwelling units. Subsistence Household frames an inquiry into the economic position that any individual occupies—this operates as a valid determinant of a different order than dwelling and resident determinants. The one are economic determinants, the latter are psychological and social.

Subsistence Household and Residence Household have an identical reality for probably 80 percent of our informants. For the other 20 percent it will range from a partially identical to a completely different reality. For instance, in a large Mexican-American family living in Eloy, Calexico, or Salinas, the father and mother stay in one location while two to five of their sons and daughters move to different locations. They will have partially differing resident and subsistence households because the children may be away from the parents for over six months at a time while they continue to send their money home. In the case of a divorced male who has been living alone for the last year or so but who must support one or more children, residence and subsistence households differ maximally. (For a complete definition see the Appendix).

The subsistence household concept is the basis of all the information having to do with income and indebtedness. For those informants interviewed who were members of the same subsistence household, this information was naturally duplicated. This included number of participants, income, indebtedness, personal property, and use of welfare. Before frequencies in these categories were tabulated, all duplications were sorted out. The number of discrete subsistence households was 578.

Number of Participants in the Subsistence Household

Following are the frequencies and percentages of grouped observations:

Size of Household by Number of Members	Number of Households in Each Size Range	Percent of Total Households
1	186	32
2 to 4	181	31
5 to 7	126	22
8 to 11	59	10
12 to 15	21	4
16 to 18	1	—
Not reporting	4	1
Total	578	100

These data will be more meaningful when compared across ethnic groups and class groups. Over 36 percent of the households had five or more members.

The mean is 4.0 members per household (SD: 3.2; CI: $\pm$ .27 @ 95%).

Income of Subsistence Household

Information on income was obtained by asking the informant to give his rate of pay for each job that he had held the year past and the length of time that he held it. He then was asked who else contributed income to the household. Then the rate of pay and length of time for all jobs of the other contributor or contributors were solicited. In this manner the total income of the household was estimated. The higher up the economic scale our informant was the less involved and more precise his reporting was. For instance, in the case of equipment operators and crew foremen, many of whom were the only working members of their households, an exact annual income figure was readily recalled. On the other hand, most harvest hands, many of whom do not file income tax returns, had no precise knowledge of their total annual income. However, they could recall rates of pay and length of time on the various jobs they had in the past year. In the cases of duplicated information from two members of the same household, estimates from the two sources generally agreed to within ten percent.

Given below are the income groups, the number of subsistence households that fall within each group, and the percentage of the total number of subsistence households:

Income Group	Number of Households	Percent
$ 600 and less	22	4
600 – 1,200	49	8
1,200 – 1,800	76	13
1,800 – 2,400	121	21
2,400 – 3,000	80	14
3,000 – 4,000	81	14
4,000 – 6,000	53	9
6,000 – 8,000	35	6
8,000 and above	21	4
Not reporting	40	7
Total	578	100

Almost half of these households (46 percent) took in less than $2,400. The mean income per household is $3,045 (SD: $2,143; CI: ± $185 @95%). This figure represents the entire income of the household. In order to assess the economic circumstances of these workers one must take into account the number of people that this income must support. This follows.

Per Capita Income

By dividing the mean income per subsistence household by the mean number of persons per subsistence household one obtains a mean per capita income of $761. As with other statistics pertaining to all 603 workers, a mean per capita figure will be more meaningful when compared across ethnic, educational, age, skill, and class groups. For instance, the per capita income among the Pima-Papago Indian group is $391. Anglos have a per capita figure almost four times this amount—$1,388. This will be discussed in more detail in the following chapter.

Indebtedness

Indebtedness includes all debts of all participants in the subsistence household, whether dependent, provider, co-provider, or simply partners. All forms of indebtedness were tabulated from home mortgages to grocery store bills and personal loans. Non-monetary forms of obligation such as gift exchange among the Papago are not included in these figures for obvious reasons. Indebtedness varies radically from one ethnic group to another and for this reason it is reserved for discussion across groupings in the following chapter.

Real and Personal Property

Using the discrete subsistence household concept further, 167 or 29 percent reported owning real property, and 257 or 44 percent included television among their possessions. Two hundred and twenty-five or 39 percent reported owning no property of any kind.

VALUE AND ADAPTIVE FACTORS

Church Affiliation

Church	Number	Percent
Roman Catholic	303	50
None	132	22
Baptist	74	12
Other	94	16
Total	603	100

The high frequency of Catholics is due to the great percentage of Mexican-Americans. Of the 303 Roman Catholics, 222 or 73 percent are of Mexican descent.

Union Membership

Status	Number	Percent
Never belonged	281	47
Belonged at one time	168	28
Presently active	135	22
Not reporting	19	3
Total	603	100

Vocational Attitude

The informant's attitude toward his present vocational situation was abstracted from all the statements he made about his job, his future plans, what kind of job he considered good, and whether or not he was generally satisfied with the kind of job he was now doing. We established five categories into which all except 46 or seven percent of the workers interviewed could be placed. The categories, the frequencies, and percentages are given below:

Attitude	Number	Percent
Generally positive	239	40
General rejection	179	30
No concept of "vocation"	52	9
Passive or resigned acceptance	47	7
Ambivalent or mixed	40	7
Unclassifiable	46	7
Total	603	100

Comparison of these observations is made across job lines in a later chapter. At the present level of analysis, it is sufficient to emphasize that 40 percent fell in the positive category. Another revealing frequency is the number of "no concept." The workers who fell in this category tended to be unsophisticated folk-oriented people, e.g. older Indians and Mexican-Americans. Also some of the very young fell in this category.

General Value Orientation

This concept, also abstracted from the depth interview material, is considered to be the focal point of the informant's ambitions or satisfaction-giving minimums by which he seems motivated. It sums up the general locus of meaning to his work-life (for detailed definitions see Specimen of Code Sheet in the Appendix). Each category is listed in percentage order:

Category	Number	Percent
Class or status (work has class or prestige connotations)	273	45
Folk-farm-rural (work inseparable from way of life)	121	20
Subsistence (work a means to the end of meeting minimal needs)	88	15
Independence and avoidance (work a means to the end of avoiding social commitment)	62	10
Unclassifiable	59	10
Total	603	100

It is interesting to note that only 20 percent of all workers could be classified as folk or farm. Also the low percentage (15) in the subsistence category does not support the stereotype picture of seasonal farm workers.

Vocational Pattern Through Time

The past occupational patterns (10-15 years ago) of workers are useful for measuring job shifts. This is done in analyses to come by comparing past occupational patterns to present patterns. Given below are the frequencies and percentages of their job patterns in the past:

Type of Job	Number	Percent
Farm hand	156	26
Farm skilled	37	6
Small farmer	42	7
Total farm	235	39
Total nonfarm	200	33
Total attending school	160	27
Drifting and/or unemployed	8	1

An interesting fact here is that 33 percent of the workers were actively employed in nonfarm occupations 10 to 15 years ago. Adding this percentage to those attending school brings to 60 percent the proportion who were *not* engaged in farm work 10 to 15 years ago.

Further analysis of those 200 workers who are from nonfarm vocational backgrounds reveals that over two-thirds of them are isolates, 56 percent of them are Anglos, 60 percent of them are older than 41, and 42 percent of them now have a job pattern at the bottom of the farm job scale — harvest hand labor. The significance of this is discussed more fully in the chapters to follow.

Vocation of Parents of Sample Workers

Farm background predominates in the ancestry of the sample. Below are the vocations, frequencies, and percentage of the sample:

Vocation of Parent	Number	Percent
Small farmer	218	36
Farm hand	121	20
Farm skilled	53	9
Total farm	392	65
Total nonfarm	194	32
Not reporting	17	3

It is significant that 218 or over one-third of the workers interviewed have parents who were farmers of one kind or another, and a combined total of 392 or 65 percent have parents who had either farmed or worked on farms. A special breakdown of the 200 workers who came from nonfarm vocations reveals that 91 of them, or almost half, have parents with nonfarm backgrounds as compared to only 29 percent of the workers who came from farm vocations (see Table 5 below — does not include 17 not reporting).

Table 5
Vocation of Parents of Workers by Farm and Nonfarm Occupational Past of Worker

	Workers with nonfarm past		Workers with farm past		All	
	No.	Pct.	No.	Pct.	No.	Pct.
Farm parents	103	53	289	71	392	66
Nonfarm parents	91	47	103	29	194	34
Total	194	100	409	100	603	100

13 Effects of Ethnic Affiliation

SKILL FACTORS

RAISING THE EDUCATIONAL level of the farm worker is one of the most frequently cited means of improving his condition. With this in mind the following analyses of skills are made. The hyphenated upper case letters "M-A" designate "Mexican-American." Both the letter designation "M-A" and the name "Mexican-American" are used here and in all subsequent chapters to include *both* citizens and green card immigrants of Mexican descent.

Table 6
Years Schooling by Ethnic Affiliation
(Does not include those not reporting)

Years Completed	Anglo No.	Anglo Pct.	Negro No.	Negro Pct.	Indian No.	Indian Pct.	M-A No.	M-A Pct.	All No.	All Pct.
0 – 4	19	9	17	23	12	23	86	37	147	25
5 – 11	144	67	46	61	39	75	141	61	377	63
12 & above	50	24	12	16	1	2	8	2	73	12
Total	213	100	75	100	52	100	235	100	597	100
Mean	8.9		7.6		6.2		5.6		7.0	
SD	3.1		3.6		3.0		3.0		3.5	
CI @ 95%	±.4		±.8		±.8		±.4		±.3	

Anglos rank highest with only nine percent falling in the functional illiterate group. Mexican-Americans are lowest with over one-third falling in the functional illiterate group. This is 14 percent higher than for any other ethnic group. Yet as will later be shown the M-A group shows the greatest farm success.

Table 7
The Use of English by Ethnic Affiliation

	Anglo No.	Anglo Pct.	Negro No.	Negro Pct.	Indian No.	Indian Pct.	M-A No.	M-A Pct.	All No.	All Pct.
Cannot speak English	0	0	0	0	10	19	81	34	93	15
Cannot read English	3	1	5	7	15	28	106	44	138	23

Mexican-Americans show the greatest proportion who cannot use English. Eighty-one or 34 percent cannot speak English and 106 or 44 percent cannot read English. To comment further, the M-A group has a literacy breakdown as follows: 26 or 11 percent are illiterate, 80 or 33 percent read Spanish only, 79 or 33 percent are bi-literate, and 55 or 23 percent read English only.

Differences among these subgroupings seem to indicate that literacy patterns are good indices of social, economic, and occupational traits with respect to the M-A farm element. Because Spanish is the common language of Southwestern farm systems, bi-literates and bi-linguals are in a strategic position. Fluency in Spanish *only* is less of a detriment than fluency in English *only*.

Table 8
Vocational Pattern in Stable Past (10-15 Years Ago) by Ethnic Affiliation

	Anglo No.	Anglo Pct.	Negro No.	Negro Pct.	Indian No.	Indian Pct.	M-A No.	M-A Pct.	All No.	All Pct.
Farm										
Farm skilled	13	6	1	1	0	0	22	9	37	6
Farm hand	39	18	16	22	9	17	76	32	156	26
Small farmer	15	7	1	1	19	36	7	3	42	7
Total farm	67	31	18	24	28	53	105	44	235	39
Nonfarm										
Skilled & semi-skilled	57	27	16	21	1	—	23	10	98	16
Unskilled & service occupations	22	10	19	25	1	—	16	7	59	10
Military	17	8	5	7	1	—	4	1	28	5
Other nonfarm	21	10	6	8	0	0	6	2	33	5
Total nonfarm	117	55	46	61	3	6	49	20	218	36
School										
School & preschool	29	14	11	15	22	41	86	36	150	25
Grand total	213	100	75	100	53	100	240	100	603	100

Notable is the almost complete absence of Negro and Indian backgrounds in farm skilled, the high percentage (32) of M-A's engaged in farm hand labor, and the high preponderance of Indians engaged in reservation farming.

The relatively high ranking of M-A's and Indians in school tends to indicate that both of these subgroups are relatively young.

One other significant cross-group comparison is that both Anglo and Negro show comparatively high percentages in the nonfarm category — 55 and 61 percent respectively—but 27 percent of the Anglos are from skilled and semi-skilled occupations, whereas the largest percentage of nonfarm Negroes are from unskilled and service occupations.

Table 9

Vocational Pattern of Parent by Ethnic Affiliation
(Does not include those not reporting)

	Anglo		Negro		Indian		M-A		All	
	No.	Pct.	No.	Pct.	No.	Pct.	No.	Pct.	No.	Pct.
Farm										
Farm skilled	16	8	2	3	1	—	33	14	53	9
Farm hand	9	4	12	16	12	23	84	37	121	21
Small farmer	91	43	32	44	35	66	47	21	218	37
Total farm	116	55	46	63	48	91	164	72	392	67
Nonfarm										
Skilled & semi-skilled	55	26	16	22	1	—	35	15	108	18
Other nonfarm	39	19	11	15	4	—	30	13	86	15
Total nonfarm	94	45	27	37	5	9	65	28	194	33
Grand total	210	100	73	100	53	100	229	100	586	100

An important characteristic shared by all four ethnic groups is the relatively large percentage of parents classed as small farmers. For Anglos this means small, family farms or tenant farms. For M-A's it means subsistence farms mostly in Mexico. For Negroes it means tenant or sharecrop farms. And for Indians it refers to reservation farming in the traditional flood-plain pattern.

Anglos with parents in skilled or semi-skilled non-farm occupations comprise 26 percent as compared to 15 percent for M-A's and none for Indians.

SUMMARY OF ETHNIC PATTERNS IN SKILL FACTORS

Using degree of formal schooling, literacy, and degree of experience in skilled job categories, Anglos rank consistently highest. In schooling and literacy Negroes rank second with M-A's lowest. In job pattern 10 to 15 years ago and parent vocational background, M-A's rank second with Indians last. Negroes have the unique pattern of neither being highest nor lowest in any category. They range from second place for schooling and literacy to third place for job past and job parent. Illustrated below are the rank orders with the initial letter of each ethnic grouping corresponding to that group:

Schooling:	A N I M
Literacy:	A N I M
Job past:	A M N I
Job parent:	A M N I

VALUE AND ADAPTIVE FACTORS

Table 10
Age Groupings by Ethnic Affiliation

Age Groups	M-A No.	Pct.	Indian No.	Pct.	Negro No.	Pct.	Anglo No.	Pct.	All No.	Pct.
Below 40	187	78	39	74	34	45	85	40	350	58
Above 40	53	22	14	26	41	55	128	60	253	42
Total	240	100	53	100	75	100	213	100	603	100
Mean	32.2		33.6		42.0		43.0		38.0	
SD	12.1		14.7		12.1		13.4		14.0	
CI @ 95%	±1.6		±4.0		±2.8		±1.8		±1.1	

Mexican-Americans and Indians have about the same distribution and average ages, showing a ratio of three below 40 to every one above. The Anglo and Negro farm workers are older populations.

Table 11
Isolate and Aggregate Residence by Ethnic Affiliation

	M-A No.	Pct.	Indian No.	Pct.	Negro No.	Pct.	Anglo No.	Pct.	All No.	Pct.
Aggregate	201	84	40	75	28	37	72	34	350	58
Isolate	39	16	13	25	47	63	141	66	253	42
Total	240	100	53	100	75	100	213	100	603	100

Mexican-Americans and Indians again exhibit a common pattern with three-fourths or more of them falling in the aggregate category. Negroes and Anglos share the opposite feature. Whereas the Mexican-American and Indian populations are predominately family units, the Negro and Anglo populations show dysfunctional patterns since although older, two-thirds of them (Table 10), are social isolates.

Table 12
Average Length of Time Jobs Reported Were Held
by Ethnic Affiliation
"Job" is defined as with the same employer regardless of the task.

	M-A	Indian	Negro	Anglo	All
Average months	7.9	6.8	5.6	5.5	6.6
SD	4.0	4.0	3.8	3.6	4.0
CI @ 95%	± .5	±1.1	± .9	± .5	± .3

Mexican-Americans and Indians again both show much higher job stability than Anglos and Negroes. The averages of the former are brought up because of the high number who have worked for the same company for the entire year.

Table 13

Attitude Toward Present Vocational Situation by Ethnic Affiliation

	M-A No.	M-A Pct.	Indian No.	Indian Pct.	Negro No.	Negro Pct.	Anglo No.	Anglo Pct.	All No.	All Pct.
Generally positive	103	43	12	23	26	35	80	38	239	40
General rejection	67	28	9	17	36	48	113	53	226	37
No concept	31	13	18	34	0	0	3	1	52	9
Ambivalent & not reporting	39	16	14	26	13	17	17	8	86	14
Total	240	100	53	100	75	100	213	100	603	100

Mexican-Americans rank highest in positive attitude toward their job situations. Indians rank a close second with the smallest percentage (17) in the rejection category. Indians, however, are more distinguished by having the highest percentage (34) in the no-concept category. Again Anglo and Negro patterns are almost the same with both showing approximately half of their frequencies in the rejection category.

Table 14

Presence or Absence of Church Identification by Ethnic Affiliation

	Indian No.	Indian Pct.	M-A No.	M-A Pct.	Negro No.	Negro Pct.	Anglo No.	Anglo Pct.	All No.	All Pct.
Church	53	100	234	98	44	59	115	54	467	77
No church	0	0	4	2	31	41	96	45	132	22
Not reporting	0	0	2	—	0	0	2	1	4	1
Total	53	100	240	100	75	100	213	100	603	100

All Indians reported church affiliation as did 98 percent of the Mexicans. The paired grouping dichotomy continues to link Negroes and Anglos, both groups having just over half with church affiliation.

Corroborating these patterns are the relative frequencies of active participation in church. Mexican-Americans show 78 percent active, Indians 72 percent, Negroes 39 percent, and Anglos a low 20 percent.

Table 15
General Value Orientation by Ethnic Affiliation

	M-A No.	M-A Pct.	Anglo No.	Anglo Pct.	Negro No.	Negro Pct.	Indian No.	Indian Pct.	All No.	All Pct.
Class or status	142	59	85	40	26	35	14	26	273	46
Folk-farm-rural	50	21	21	10	13	17	23	44	121	20
Independence & avoidance	4	2	46	21	8	11	2	4	62	10
Subsistence	20	8	42	20	21	28	5	9	88	14
Unclassifiable	24	10	19	9	7	9	9	17	59	10
Total	240	100	213	100	75	100	53	100	603	100

The M-A group ranks highest in status orientation which by definition most closely resembles Anglo middle class values.

Anglo workers are distinguished by having a significantly larger percentage than any of the other groups in independence and avoidance.

Negroes have almost a third in the subsistence category. Indians are distinguished by a high percentage in the folk-farm-rural category.

Table 16
Union Membership by Ethnic Affiliation

	M-A No.	M-A Pct.	Anglo No.	Anglo Pct.	Negro No.	Negro Pct.	Indian No.	Indian Pct.	All No.	All Pct.
Current	81	34	47	22	6	8	0	0	135	22
Inactive	23	9	105	49	28	37	4	7	168	28
Never	122	51	61	29	40	54	46	87	281	47
Not reporting	14	6	0	0	1	1	3	6	19	3
Total	240	100	213	100	75	100	53	100	603	100

Mexican-Americans show the highest percentage having current membership and are 12 percentage points higher than Anglos. Indians have no current members with 87 percent reporting they never had had union affiliation.

A very significant comparison between M-A and Anglo is that half of M-A's never belonged to a union, whereas almost precisely that same percentage of Anglos reported once belonging to a union. This seems to indicate along with other data, that the Anglo group has seen better days. They are in direct contrast to an M-A population who are working their way up.

Table 17
Arizona and Out-of-State Origins by Ethnic Affiliation

	Indian No.	Indian Pct.	M-A No.	M-A Pct.	Anglo No.	Anglo Pct.	Negro No.	Negro Pct.	All No.	All Pct.
Arizona	45	85	74	31	19	9	4	5	146	24
Out-of-State	8	15	166	69	194	91	71	95	457	76
Total	53	100	240	100	213	100	75	100	603	100

Anglos and Negroes show almost no Arizona origins. Indians by contrast are almost all from Arizona. The M-A group is about equally divided among Arizona, Texas and Mexico, with only 19 from California.

The largest percentage of Negros cite Texas. Counting Texas, a total of 42 or 56 percent are from the South. Anglos do not have especially high frequencies in any one place.

Table 18
Identification with Mexico by Workers of Mexican Descent

	Number	Percent
Green card holders or immigrants	62	26
U. S. citizens but spent part of their childhood in Mexico (viz. born and raised preschool in Mexico; born and schooled in Mexico; born U.S. but schooled in Mexico)	38	16
Born and raised all of life in U.S.	136	57
Not reporting	4	1
Total	240	100

One hundred or 42 percent of the farm workers of Mexican descent in the sample spent at least part of their childhood in Mexico.

Table 19
Reservation Identification of Indians

	Number	Percent
Lived on reservation all or part of last year	24	45
No longer lives on reservation but visits regularly	9	17
No regular contact of any kind with reservation	18	34
Not reporting	2	4
Total	53	100
Participated in a Saint's day celebration or a native Indian ceremonial on reservation last year	27	51
No ceremonial participation last year	26	49
Total	53	100

A total of 33 or 62 percent of the Indians still maintain active physical contact with the reservation (this does not count health services), and over half of them participated in some religious event on the reservation last year.

SUMMARY OF ETHNIC PATTERNS IN VALUE AND ADAPTIVE FACTORS

Mexican-Americans rank consistently highest in all categories for which a hierarchy can be postulated. More M-A's are at the optimum age for work, almost all are members of a family social unit and show the highest job stability. They have the greatest frequency of positive attitudes, almost a hundred percent in church affiliation, the highest frequency in value orientation compatible with Anglo middle class culture, and the greatest percentage of active membership in a union.

Anglos rank consistently lowest in age desirability, stable family patterns, job stability, attitude, and church affiliation. Also, although Anglos do not rank lowest in status orientation and active membership in unions, they do rank below M-A's.

Negroes rank consistently third in all value and adaptive factors.

Indians are characteristically paired with M-A's to form the familiar Mexican-Indian and Negro-Anglo dichotomy in age, family residence, job stability, attitude, and church activity. In value orientation and union membership, however, Indians show a much lower incidence of class sophistication than M-A's, the latter at the top and Indians at the bottom. It is significant that the M-A group includes many who show a very low level of sophistication resembling more the Indian pattern; e.g., Table 15 shows 50 or 21 percent in the folk category and Table 16 shows 51 percent with no history of union membership.

The fact that the Mexican-American group has so few in the having-once-belonged-to-a-union category, only nine percent, indicates that the 81 or 34 percent who now belong find themselves involved in union activities connected with their present employment. On the whole these and other data seem to indicate a more continuous cultural transition on the part of the Mexican-American element, e.g. the pattern of union membership (Table 16); the fairly even distribution of literacy along a continuum of illiterate, Spanish only, biliterate, and English only (Table 7); and their even distribution of origins among Mexico, Texas, and Arizona (Table 17). A very important factor in this transition is the preponderance of Mexican-American workers in Arizona agriculture. When one includes the Mexican Nationals, the Mexican cultural element is enormous. This native Mexican element tends to eliminate the language handicap of the 80 percent who read Spanish only and the 34 percent monolinguals.

In contrast to this are the Indians, none of whom can ever hope to find their language a generally valuable asset in industrial farm work. If anything, their ties with their native culture and the reservation tend to be incompatible with tenure in permanent farm work. Thus the *Mexican* Mexican-American has a relative advantage over the *Papago* Papago-American. This does not mean that Indians are not making a vocational transition. There are unmistakable indications they are becoming more permanently involved in farm work through the years, as will be discussed later.

Encapsulated below are the rank orders for Value and Adaptive Factors:

Age:	M	I	N	A
Aggregate residence household:	M	I	N	A
Job stability:	M	I	N	A
Attitude:	M	I	N	A
Church:	I	M	N	A
Value orientation:	M	A	N	I
Union:	M	A	N	I

MATERIAL AND ECONOMIC FACTORS

Table 20

Mean Income Per Subsistence Household by Ethnic Affiliation

	M-A	Anglo	Negro	Indian	All
Mean	$3,446	$3,192	$2,147	$2,021	$3,045
SD	2,248	2,277	993	1,500	2,144
CI @ 95%	± 308	± 328	± 241	± 438	± 185

Table 21

Mean Indebtedness and Percent Indebtedness of Mean Annual Income by Ethnic Affiliation

	M-A Amount	Pct.	Anglo Amount	Pct.	Indian Amount	Pct.	Negro Amount	Pct.	All Amount	Pct.
Mean	$839	24	$508	16	$194	10	$193	9	$593	19
SD	153		129		325		457		1,331	
CI @ 95%	± 207		± 183		± 95		± 105		± 112	

A different picture begins to emerge from the data depicting the relative economic positions of the four main ethnic groups. Although the above averages pertain to *family* incomes and indebtedness, Anglo ranks close to the top. Degree of indebtedness is considered in hierarchical order from most to least because it is considered as giving access to material goods.

Ownership of a dependable car follows the pattern of indebtedness with M-A's having 166 or 69 percent owners, Anglos 102 or 48 percent owners, Indians with 15 or 28 percent owners, and Negroes with 17 or 23 percent. The ratio of car ownership among the four ethnic groups is almost exactly the same ratio of percentage of indebtedness—12-8-5-5.

Table 22
Number of Persons Per Subsistence Household by Ethnic Affiliation

Number	Anglo No.	Anglo Pct.	Negro No.	Negro Pct.	Indian No.	Indian Pct.	M-A No.	M-A Pct.	All No.	All Pct.
1 only	122	59	32	43	6	12	14	6	186	32
2-4	58	28	26	35	20	40	71	32	181	31
5-7	23	11	12	16	12	24	75	34	126	22
8 or more	5	2	5	6	11	22	60	27	80	14
Not reporting	0	0	0	0	1	2	3	1	5	1
Total	208	100	75	100	50	100	223	100	578	100
Mean		2.3		3.1		5.0		5.9		4.0
SD		2.0		2.7		3.3		3.2		3.2
CI @ 95%		±.3		±.6		±.9		±.4		±.3

The above order of arrangement does not necessarily reflect an over-all economic advantage of small subsistence units. This is a complicated matter that would have to be considered in terms of the kinds of work the family members are engaged in, the commissary patterns of large household units as opposed to smaller, etc.

As illustrated above almost 60 percent of the Anglos are economically independent. Compared to only six percent for the M-A's, it is a percentage figure ten times greater. The Mexican-American figures re-emphasize the importance of family ties.

The averages reveal the familiar Anglo-Negro and Mexican-Indian dichotomy.

Table 23
Mean Per Capita Income by Ethnic Affiliation

	Anglo	Negro	M-A	Indian	All
Mean	$1,388	$693	$584	$404	$761

Anglo per capita income is more than double any other group. Because of many other social and cultural factors, however, this figure is not valid as a direct indicator of relative material welfare.

Table 24
Mean Ratios of People Per Room in Residence by Ethnic Affiliation

	Anglo	Negro	M-A	Indian	All
Mean	1.2	1.5	2.1	2.7	1.8
SD	1.0	1.2	1.4	1.7	1.4
CI @ 95%	± .2	± .4	± .2	± .5	± .1

Table 25

Residence Household Facilities by Ethnic Affiliation
(Does not include those living in housing for Mexican Nationals, or not reporting)

	Anglo No.	Pct.	M-A No.	Pct.	Negro No.	Pct.	Indian No.	Pct.	All No.	Pct.
Modern	131	79	147	66	20	44	3	6	316	63
Lacking plumbing, electricity and/or cold storage	35	21	77	34	25	56	47	94	188	37
Total	166	100	224	100	45	100	50	100	504	100

Ratio of people to rooms in residence as an economic indicator of another sort supports the relative positioning of the per capita income averages. The degree of differences between the ratios is not nearly so great, however, as the degree of differences between the per capita income figures—especially with respect to Anglos.

Lack of modern household facilities shows significant percentage differences between each of the four ethnic groups. Especially notable is that 94 percent of the Indians are in non-modern housing. Since 45 percent of the Indians interviewed show reservation residence patterns (Table 19), some of the lack of modern facilities can be attributed to traditional house designs. This does not necessarily indicate as poor a living condition for them as it indicated for those living in obsolete cotton camps.

Table 26

Regular and Irregular Migration Pattern by Ethnic Affiliation

	Indian No.	Pct.	M-A No.	Pct.	Negro No.	Pct.	Anglo No.	Pct.	All No.	Pct.
Regular	49	92	215	90	52	69	132	62	469	78
Irregular	4	8	23	10	21	28	81	38	130	21
Not reporting	0	0	2	—	2	3	0	0	4	1
Total	53	100	240	100	75	100	213	100	603	100

Regularity of migration pattern is an economic indicator since it reflects, in part, regularity of access to subsistence sources. Thus it is a rough indicator of an efficiency factor that would tend to offset the disadvantage of an income differential. Note that the order of per capita income (Table 23) is exactly reversed in this table.

SUMMARY OF ETHNIC PATTERNS IN
MATERIAL AND ECONOMIC FACTORS

Ethnic variations in material and economic factors are not entirely uniform. There is only one consistent pattern: Anglo-Negro-Mexican-Indian for per capita income, ratio of people to rooms, and household facilities. This tends to be offset by other economically relevant factors. For instance, Mexican-Americans rank next to the lowest and much lower than Anglos with respect to the above variables (Tables 23, 25). But in terms of family income, indebtedness, car ownership, and regularity of migration (Tables 20, 21, and 26), M-A's rank at the top.

The material advantage of a larger total family income is that more resources are available at any one time. More credit gives greater access to material goods which may contribute to a more efficient commissary—e.g. refrigerators, freezers, bulk buying, etc. The economic advantages of an automobile to seasonal farm workers are obvious. Regularity of household movements has already been discussed.

In the light of all the information available on the sample, including depth interview material and observations which will be fully developed in Part Four, we would class material circumstances of the average Anglo and Mexican-American very close together at the top. Anglo would show a sharp split with an upper group much above M-A and a bottom group below the M-A average.

Indian and Negro would fall at the bottom with Negroes showing a superficial advantage in their higher frequencies in the modern household facilities. This could be offset easily by the higher stability of the Indian residences. The higher average per capita income of the Negro group could be offset by the Indians' greater access to a wider variety of material resources —e.g. hospital and medical care, Bureau of Indian Affairs welfare, traditional gift and food exchange, and tillable farm plots. Although off-reservation Indians do not benefit from the latter three with any regularity, all Indians reported that they used reservation medical care.

Encapsulated rank orders appear below:

Family income:	M	A	N	I
Debts:	M	A	I	N
Car ownership:	M	A	I	N
Per capita income:	A	N	M	I
People per room:	A	N	M	I
House facilities:	A	N	M	I
Regular migration:	I	M	N	A

JOB PATTERN NOW

Table 27
Predominant 1962-63 Job Pattern by Ethnic Affiliation

	M-A No.	M-A Pct.	Anglo No.	Anglo Pct.	Indian No.	Indian Pct.	Negro No.	Negro Pct.	All No.	All Pct.
Farm skilled	75	31	46	22	10	19	6	8	138	23
Farm hand	135	57	85	40	29	55	31	42	299	50
Small farmer	0	0	3	1	6	11	0	0	9	1
Nonfarm	20	8	34	16	2	4	16	21	74	12
Drifting and unemployed	10	4	45	21	6	11	22	29	83	14
Total	240	100	213	100	53	100	75	100	603	100

The M-A group ranks highest in farm skilled. Two other patterns of general importance stand out. First is the familiar Anglo-Negro sharing of traits, this time in the relatively high percentages in the drifting and unemployed category. Second is the unusually high percentage of Negroes with employment experience for last year in nonfarm categories. It is highly significant that one-half of all Negroes drawn in the act of working on a farm reported most of their time was spent the year preceding their interview in nonfarm employment or unemployed.

Significant ethnic differences emerge from a comparison of present job pattern to job pattern 10 to 15 years ago (Table 8). First, a percentage of farm workers in all categories reported being engaged in nonfarm work in the stable past. That is, as far as this population is concerned, there has been a shift from nonfarm to farm employment in all categories, with the exception of the "small farmer" group.

The Mexican-American group shows a shift primarily from school and preschool to farm. They show a 20 percent increase in farm skilled and a 25 percent increase in farm hand.

The Indian group, like the M-A, shows a shift from school as well as from reservation farming to farm hand primarily—a 38 percent increase. Another significant shift is indicated for this group: 25 percent ceased reservation farming. It is also important that not one Indian reported being employed as a skilled farm worker 10 to 15 years ago. Now 19 percent of this group are working as skilled farm workers.

Unlike the Indian and M-A groups, the Anglo group shows a shift from nonfarm employment. Most of those in nonfarm were engaged in skilled or semi-skilled occupations. A 16 percent increase is shown in farm skilled and a 22 percent increase in farm hand. A significant number, 45 or 21 percent, have become drifters.

The Negro group, like the Anglo, shows a large shift from nonfarm, with very few coming from school. The majority who made this shift were employed in skilled, semi-skilled, unskilled, and service occupations. Twenty percent went to farm hand and only seven percent to farm skilled. Almost a third went to a drifting and unemployed pattern.

Although differing occupation patterns emerge with respect to each ethnic group, the variance is obviously due to more than ethnic affiliation. In an attempt to get at some of the underlying factors which seem to be associated with ethnic affiliation, the present job pattern is compared to ethnic patterns in Skill Factors and Value and Adaptive Factors. Material and Economic Factors are not compared to present job pattern because they can be considered to be functions of present job experiences.

Factors Considered	Ethnic Ranking	Table Cited
Skill factors		
Schooling:	A N I M	6
Use of English:	A N I M	7
Job pattern past:	A M N I	8
Job pattern parent:	A M N I	9
Value and adaptive factors		
Age:	M I N A	10
Aggregate residence household:	M I N A	11
Job stability:	M I N A	12
Attitude:	M I N A	13
Church:	M I N A	14
Value orientation:	M A N I	15
Union:	M A N I	16
Job pattern now	M A_1 I N A_2	27

In terms of greatest percentage in the farm skilled category, Mexican-Americans rank at the top, Anglos are split between a significant frequency of farm skilled ranking second in percentages, and a significantly high percentage in drifting and unemployed which would tend to put them at the bottom. Indians rank third, with Negroes at the bottom on two counts — the lowest percentage of farm skilled and the highest percentage in drifting and unemployed.

Three important similarities indicate value and adaptive factors are more important than skill factors in explaining job success in farm work, at least insofar as they are expressed through ethnicity. First, the M-A group ranks consistently highest in value factors. In skill factors it never ranks highest and in two important categories ranks at the bottom by wide margins—schooling and use of English. Second, the Anglo split-group pattern shows up to a certain extent in value factors. There is no indication of this in skill factors. Third, the Negro group is consistently low in value factors, but in skill factors ranks very close to highest. Their actual ranking in job pattern past and job pattern of parent is not clear-cut. If anything Negroes should rank higher than M-A's on the basis of their high percentages in the nonfarm skilled and semi-skilled categories. This all the more disproves correlation between skill factors and success in farm work.

This indication of a low degree of correlation between skill factors and success in farm work and high correlation for value and adaptive factors and success in farm work, will be tested further by attempting to isolate several of these variables.

14 Schooling Versus Cultural Background

YEARS OF FORMAL EDUCATION

Table 28

Predominant 1962-63 Job Pattern by Years School Completed
(0-2 includes six not reporting)

	0-2 No.	0-2 Pct.	3-6 No.	3-6 Pct.	7-9 No.	7-9 Pct.	10 and above No.	10 and above Pct.	All No.	All Pct.
Farm skilled	16	22	42	25	47	21	33	26	138	23
Farm hand	48	64	100	58	111	48	39	30	299	50
Small farmer	1	1	1	1	6	3	1	1	9	1
Nonfarm	4	5	12	7	31	13	28	22	74	12
Drifting and unemployed	6	8	16	9	34	15	27	21	83	14
Total	75	100	171	100	229	100	128	100	603	100

ALL EDUCATIONAL levels show almost the same percentage in the farm skilled category. There is only a five percent difference between the highest group (10 and above) and the lowest group (7-9) which is not statistically significant at the 5% level.

The pattern of a steady rise in the percentage of drifting and unemployed with the level of education is suggestive of a negative correlation.

Table 29

Predominant 1962-63 Job Pattern of Functional Illiterates, Mexicans with 3-6 Years School, and Anglos with 7-9 Years of School

	Functional Illiterates (Having 0-4 Years of Schooling) No.	Functional Illiterates (Having 0-4 Years of Schooling) Pct.	Mexican, Grades 3-6 No.	Mexican, Grades 3-6 Pct.	Anglo, Grades 7-9 No.	Anglo, Grades 7-9 Pct.
Farm skilled	33	22	33	32	18	19
Farm hand	93	61	63	60	43	45
Small farmer	1	—	0	0	2	2
Nonfarm	12	8	5	5	11	11
Drifting & unemployed	14	9	3	3	22	23
Total	153	100	104	100	96	100

Although this arrangement of cross groupings for job categories is not amenable to statistical inference, it does tend to indicate that ethnic affiliation or non-educational factors associated with ethnicity are more important than schooling. This is also indicated by the table below.

Table 30
Attitude Toward Present Vocational Situation by Years School Completed

	0-2		3-6		7-9		10 and above		All	
	No.	Pct.	No.	Pct.	No.	Pct.	No.	Pct.	No.	Pct.
Generally positive	40	54	81	47	78	34	40	31	239	40
General rejection	12	16	47	28	98	43	68	53	226	37
No concept	16	21	15	9	17	7	4	3	52	9
Ambivalent and not reporting	7	9	28	16	36	16	16	13	86	14
Total	75	100	171	100	229	100	128	100	603	100

A negative correlation is indicated between positive attitude and years of formal education. This supports the correlation between level of education and drifting-unemployed suggested in Table 28. Also, a negative correlation is indicated between no concept and years of schooling; viz. the higher the level of schooling, the lower the incidence of no concept of vocational identity.

Table 31
Mean Ages by Years School Completed

	0-2	3-6	7-9	10 and above	All
Mean age	46.5	38.7	36.1	35.3	30.5
SD	12.8	13.2	14.0	11.7	21.4
CI @ 95%	±2.96	±2.0	±2.0	±2.0	±1.9

This table indicates a general rise in level of education of the farm worker population through time.

JOB SKILLS IN STABLE PAST
Table 32
Predominant 1962-63 Job Pattern by Job Pattern in Past

Present Job	Skilled and semi-skilled		Farm Hand		All	
	No.	Pct.	No.	Pct.	No.	Pct.
Farm skilled	25	26	35	23	138	23
Farm hand	43	44	97	62	299	50
Small farmer	0	0	0	0	9	1
Nonfarm	14	14	8	5	74	12
Drifting & unemployed	16	16	16	10	83	14
Total	98	100	156	100	603	100

There is no significant difference between the present job patterns of either of these skill groups except in farm hand. Farm hands of 10 to 15 years ago show a significantly higher percentage in the farm hand category for present job. However neither of these past skills groups shows an advantage over the other for farm skilled jobs today.

AGE

Table 33

Predominant 1962-63 Job Pattern by Age Groups
(Below 21 not included)

| | 21-30 | | 31-40 | | 41-50 | | 51 and above | | All | |
	No.	Pct.	No.	Pct.	No.	Pct.	No.	Pct.	No.	Pct.
Farm skilled	37	26	57	43	19	16	17	12	138	23
Farm hand	68	48	47	35	54	46	86	63	299	50
Small farmer	4	3	3	2	1	1	1	1	9	1
Nonfarm	18	13	11	8	18	16	12	9	74	12
Drifting and unemployed	14	10	16	12	25	21	20	15	83	14
Total	141	100	134	100	117	100	136	100	603	100

Age seems to have a pronounced effect on farm job success. Two frequencies loom large in percentage differences. The 31 to 40 group shows a high percentage (43) in farm skilled. This is 17 percentage points higher than the closest group. The 51 and above group shows the highest percentage (63) in farm hand.

Table 34

Average Length of Time Jobs Reported Were Held by Age Groups
(Below 21 not included)

	21-30	31-40	41-50	51 and above	All
Mean months	7.8	7.5	5.6	5.4	6.6
SD	3.9	4.1	3.8	3.4	4.0
CI @ 95%	± .7	± .7	± .7	± .6	± .3

A steady decline in job stability with age is indicated. This supports the indication of Table 33 that youth is one of the conditions for farm work success.

AGGREGATE AND ISOLATE HOUSEHOLDS

Table 35

Predominant 1962-63 Job Pattern by
Aggregate and Isolate Households

	Aggregate		Isolate		All	
	No.	Pct.	No.	Pct.	No.	Pct.
Farm skilled	117	33	21	8	138	23
Farm hand	166	48	133	53	299	50
Small farmer	4	1	5	2	9	1
Nonfarm	41	12	33	13	74	12
Drifting and unemployed	22	6	61	24	83	14
Total	350	100	253	100	603	100

Extreme percentage differences here indicate a high degree of correlation between family social stability in terms of living in family (aggregate) units and farm work success. Especially noteworthy is that 117 or 33 percent of the aggregates fall in farm skilled as opposed to 21 or eight percent of the isolates. This is a ratio of over four to one. Almost the same ratio in reverse order appears in drifting and unemployed.

Also, job stability and family social stability go hand in hand as indicated by the table below.

Table 36

Job Stability by Aggregate and Isolate Household

	Aggregate	Isolate	All
Mean months	7.6	5.2	6.6
SD	4.0	3.6	4.0
CI @ 95%	± .43	± .45	± .30

Table 37

Predominant 1962-63 Job Pattern by Anglo-Aggregate
and Anglo-Isolate Households

	Anglo-aggregate		Anglo-isolate		All Anglo	
	No.	Pct.	No.	Pct.	No.	Pct.
Farm skilled	34	47	12	9	46	22
Farm hand	17	24	68	48	85	40
Small farmer	1	1	2	1	3	1
Nonfarm	13	18	21	15	34	16
Drifting and unemployed	7	10	38	27	45	21
Total	72	100	141	100	213	100

Table 37 was constructed to separate the family factor from ethnicity. Anglos were selected because they are the only group who have enough frequencies in both isolate and aggregate to analyze.

Again a dichotomy is strongly indicated. A difference of 38 percentage points in favor of aggregates exists between the two in farm skilled. Also significant is the 17 percentage point difference in the drifting and unemployed category, again in favor of aggregates.

Table 38
Predominant 1962-63 Job Pattern of All Aggregate Workers by Years School Completed

	0-2 No.	0-2 Pct.	3-6 No.	3-6 Pct.	7-9 No.	7-9 Pct.	10 and above No.	10 and above Pct.	All No.	All Pct.
Farm skilled	14	27	38	36	40	29	25	46	117	33
Farm hand	33	63	56	53	63	46	14	26	166	48
Small farmer	0	0	1	—	3	2	0	0	4	1
Nonfarm	3	6	6	6	20	14	12	22	41	12
Drifting and unemployed	2	4	5	5	12	9	3	6	22	6
Total	52	100	106	100	138	100	54	100	350	100

In the light of the high degree of correlation between the family factor and farm job skills, the above table was constructed to re-examine the effects of formal education holding the family factor constant.

Percentage differences between grade levels appear greater than in the undifferentiated analysis in Table 28. However only one category (10 and above) is significantly higher and this is partially vitiated by the second highest percentage of farm skilled falling in the 3 to 6 group. Certainly no real correlation is indicated.

SUMMARY

Skill factors as reflected in formal schooling and past job experiences must be rejected as having any discernible correlation with the incidence of farm skilled job patterns among our sample. On the other hand the importance of value and adaptive factors is corroborated. Aggregate social residence patterns correlate with farm skilled job patterns. Another important factor in farm skilled job patterns is youth.

A high incidence of aged and isolate workers are two of the important characteristics of the Anglo and Negro groups (Tables 10 and 11). The reader can see some of the factors which accompany ethnicity among farm workers that explain the effects of ethnic affiliation upon job pattern. The inference is that it is not ethnicity which explains the variation in farm job patterns but the traits which accompany *farm worker* ethnic groups. Of these traits, youth and social stability as expressed by aggregate residence patterns are among the most important.

The questions as to why certain traits characterize particular farm ethnic groups and why these groups are in farm work will require analysis of a different sort. The ethnographic description of major ethnic groups as sub-cultures and a functional analysis of the nature of their participation in the farm production system is one method of answering some of these questions. A study of the major farm subcultures follows.

PART FOUR

THE PARTICIPANTS IN THEIR
DISTINCTIVE CULTURAL
and
INSTITUTIONAL SETTINGS

15 From Ethnic Group to Cultural Background to Institutions

CONCEPTS AND DEFINITIONS

DATA ON FARM WORKERS consistently revolve around ethnic groupings. This should not surprise us because these groups to a great extent define the limits of social intercourse and form the natural bases of associational and institutional participation. Moreover because all groups are immigrant or migrant populations, staying together as a group is a necessity in work location and community settlement. It is most natural that this cohesiveness should form along ethnic lines. Ethnic group solidarity manifests itself in all phases of their lives. It governs work, religious, and recreational associations. Papagos associate with Papagos, Mexican-Americans wiith Mexican-Americans, Negroes with Negroes, and White alcoholics with other White alcoholics. To be sure there are profound social differences that operate within these ethnic boundaries, but these do not obviate the fundamental core of commonality that must come as the primary consideration and the beginning of analysis of the Arizona farm labor force.

For the most part workers from each of the major ethnic groups represented by Arizona farm workers have a common geographic origin and a common history. Many of the important characteristics exhibited by these groups are attributable to this fact. Because of a common history they will share a common language, common beliefs, common institutions, and common ways of evaluating and behaving. A common history means a common experience. Because of this, each group will see the work world in a peculiar way, and each will react upon it in a distinctive fashion. Recognizing this fact is important in gaining insight into the agricultural systems of the Southwest.

In the following chapters each distinctive group is described first by its peculiar background. Background history will be interspersed with the personal accounts of members which typify this or that aspect of their group. These studies will go far in explaining the nature of the group's participation in industrial agriculture, the effects of its participation upon the technologies, and the reciprocal effects that its participation has upon its ongoing history. This applies no less to management than to workers. For these reasons, the analysis will commence with what can be termed the *cultural* view.

We do not try to speak of an ethnic culture in the same sense that we speak of the culture of an isolated aboriginal band or a small peasant village. In this sense there is not *the* culture of Mexican-Americans any more than there is *the* culture of farm management or *the* culture of the United States.

[179]

Social experience, particularly on the cultural frontiers of industrial society, is a ceaseless and infinitely discriminating process. For this reason, Anglo-Americans, Mexican-Americans, Negro-Americans, and even reservation Indians, depending upon the purposes of the investigator, can be segmented into culturally distinct subgroups and sub-subgroups. Nevertheless, the several subgroups of Mexican, Negro, or Anglo revolve around a common axis. Just as the term *ethnic* denotes, there are distinctions between peoples based upon core differences in language, beliefs, customs, and institutions that are analytically useful. These core features are especially significant when they can be traced back in a one or two generation time span to a geographic focus. A more appropriate term which distinguishes the behavior of these groups is *subculture*.

There are many accepted usages of the term subculture. Some investigators regard social classes as subcultures (Dollard 1937; Davis and Dollard 1940; Davis, Gardner, and Gardner 1941; and Warner 1949). Redfield sees the community as a type of subculture (1960). Others (see Wagley and Harris 1955) regard subcultures as the different ways of life found in a national culture. Most agree that subcultures are variations of a larger cultural tradition. Goldschmidt (1955: 1211) refers to them as "watersheds of social interaction." For our purposes the most meaningful usage of the subculture concept is employed by Evon Vogt in his study of Mormon and Texas subcultures. He considers a subculture as an historically derived continuum – that is group behavior that has a common origin and a common history. ". . . the most important facts about the unit (subculture) are that it was derived from a chain of historical circumstances and that it tends to maintain special patterns and values that cut across the other axes of differentiation in American culture" (Vogt 1955: 1163-1164). The historical emphasis is the important ingredient in the application of this concept to the major participant groups in Arizona agriculture. The behavior patterns and institutions of Mexican-American, Negro, and Indian farm workers go back in history and have geographic connotations just as Vogt's Mormon and Texas subcultures.

The following subculture types identify the most important participant groups in Arizona agriculture: *Anglo-Aggregate Farm, Mexican-American Farm, Anglo-Isolate Farm, Negro Farm, Indian Farm,* and *Farm Management.*

Anglo-Aggregate Farm represents the skilled Anglo-American family workers. Its participants occupy the top supervisory positions. They operate the most expensive and complicated machinery. They are the most highly paid of all farm workers. For all intents and purposes they are industrial workers. Farm background has little to do with their participation in farm work. For the most part they correspond to Lloyd Warner's (1949: 13-14) *lower-middle* and *upper-lower* social classes in the United States. Because they constitute the best known group from the point of view of the dominant segments of our society, we do not deal with them in this portion of the study.

Mexican-American Farm are those farm workers of Mexican descent who are American citizens or who have immigration papers to become citizens (green carders). They comprise the largest single subculture in Arizona agriculture.

The *Anglo-Isolate Farm* group differs sharply from Anglo-Aggregate in that they generally occupy the lowest positions. They are social isolates, whereas the latter are aggregates. They are old and middle-aged men who are social and vocational rejects. Alcoholism is part of their pattern.

The *Negro Farm* group, for the most part, are ex-sharecroppers or first generation descendents of sharecroppers from the cotton belt.

Indian Farm corresponds primarily to Indians who oscillate between reservation society and off-reservation society. The farm plays a key role in this experience.

Farm Management cannot be called a subculture in the same sense as the worker groups. Those who make up this group are the owners or general managers of farm companies or corporations. Their ideologies, institutions, and logics are not *vis-a-vis* the group structures of their workers. They confront opposing institutions that, from their point of view, vie for power and control of vital aspects of the production process — viz. government, management, and organized labor. Their sentiments and the logics and ideologies which underlie them will be examined.

These analyses of subcultures make no pretense of presenting a comprehensive picture of each type. We will stress those institutions of each subculture which are instrumental in their participation in Arizona farm technologies. An additional theoretical note is important in this connection — the use of Malinowski's concept of *institution*. Quoting from his Sigma Xi Lectures:

> . . . man never has to seek for the satisfaction of any of his needs, bodily, instrumental or spiritual; they are awaiting him, stored and prepared. . . . Man finds his food (or income), his shelter, the remedies for ill health, the redress of injuries, and spiritual comforts in definite places and within organized groups. Those are the home, the workshop (including work groups and instruments of production), the hostelry, the school, the hospital, or the church. We shall describe such standardized systems of cooperation, as well as their material embodiment and the groups running them, by the term *institution*.
>
> . . . At a much higher level, we can see that no individual initiative is ever culturally relevant unless incorporated into an institution. The man who conceives a new scientific idea has to present it before an academy, publish it, teach it at a school, and compel its recognition by the organized profession before it becomes an accepted part of science. The inventor has to take out a patent, and thus obtain a charter. He has to organize the group of engineers and workmen, to finance them, and thus to implement the production of his practice device. He then has to find the market of con-

sumers by creating new wants or redirecting old ones, and make the productive activity of his organization perform a function in satisfying a need (Malinowski 1942: 73-74).

A membership with equipment and norms by which behavior is standardized are essential qualities of institutions. Also, a common purpose is recognized explicitly or implicitly by the institutional membership. This is referred to as the "charter." All of these factors work co-effectively to satisfy their real needs which Malinowski refers to as the "function" of the institution. These factors are summarized as follows:

CHARTER

PERSONNEL

NORMS

MATERIAL APPARATUS

ACTIVITIES

FUNCTION

. . . human beings organize under a *charter* that defines their common aims and that also determines the *personnel* and the norms of conduct of the group. Applying these *norms* and with the use of the *material apparatus*, the members engage in *activities*, through which they contribute towards the integral *function* of the institution (pp. 74-75; italics ours).

For example, Mexican-American Farm subculture is made up of many institutions. The Mexican-American family work-group is one which is most important in their participation in farm work. It has a definite *membership, equipment*—automobile, mobile household, tools, etc.—and a *common objective*. It engages in activities in the fields and at home; it is regulated by *norms* or standards; and it *functions* to serve the real needs — social, psychological, and economic — of its members collectively and individually.

The analyses which follow will stress institutions — institutions which, in addition to having important functions groupward, are instrumental in the participation of these subcultural groups in Arizona agricultural technologies. Moreover it is our view that the historical continuity of these institutions plays as important a part in their existence as any other single feature, functional or otherwise. Hopefully the better part of the institutional and the historical emphases will provide insights otherwise obscured in the application of either alone.

METHOD

Ethnographic data emerged in the open-end portions of the worker interviews. These inquiries were followed up by more intensive depth interviewing both on the job and in the home. Ethnographic data were also obtained in the course of field observations. All data were supplemented by family histories obtained by both depth interviewing and case study methods. Members of the informant's family were interviewed in the home. Public and community agencies were consulted in these family histories.

We were assisted in worker interviewing by a full time male interviewer and in the family studies by a woman who had years of experience in social case work with migrant and rural families. The senior author worked full time gathering both questionnaire and ethnographic data by interview and participant observation. Also, he was born and raised in the farm area of West Chandler and Guadalupe, Arizona and has conducted studies among farm workers of Pima, Pinal, and Maricopa Counties over the past five years.

16 Mexican-American Farm Subculture

THE INFLUENCE OF RURAL MEXICO

MANY DATA from our Mexican-American group point to a population who are recent immigrants from the old country. A summation of stated origins of the 240 Mexican-Americans interviewed (Table 17) shows that 166 or 69 percent of them are relative newcomers to Arizona. Of these 240 only 27 or 11 percent are known to be second generation United States citizens. The generation of 67 or 28 percent was not reported but the remaining *61 percent* are either:

(1) Green carders
(2) Born and raised in Mexico but naturalized
(3) Born in Mexico but raised in the United States
(4) Born in the United States but raised in Mexico
(5) Born and raised in the United States but first generation.

Language facility also indicates close cultural ties with Mexico (Table 7). Thirty-four percent reported that they could not speak English and 44 percent reported that they could not read English.

Vocational histories of these people point to a strong rural Mexican and peasant background. Forty-four percent reported farm labor or subsistence farming 10 to 15 years ago (Table 8). However, 86 of the 240 interviewed were too young to work 10 or 15 years ago. Subtracting these 86 leaves 154. This then raises to 68 the percentage showing rural vocations in the past. Parents' vocations (Table 9) show an even higher percentage with a rural background. Seventy-two percent reported parents who were either farm laborers or subsistence farmers.

Finally there is the evidence of institutional patterns. Eighty-four percent of all M-A's interviewed (Table 11) were integral parts of family units. An even higher percentage would exist except for the fact that many of the green carders had families in the interior of Mexico. Although they were sending money home, they were technically isolates because they could not visit them. Size of family is an even stronger indication (Table 22). Mexican-American families averaged over five members and almost a third of them reported eight or more members.

In addition to family, the church (Table 14) is a prevailing theme in the lives of almost all M-A informants. Ninety-eight percent reported church affiliation (93 percent Roman Catholic) and 78 percent could be classed as active. As will be developed later, family and church institutions are vital in the lives of rural Mexicans.

Studies of Mexican immigration strongly support the indications from these data that the culture of the immigrant is essentially a rural one. John Burma in his study of *Spanish Speaking Groups in the United States* writes:

> The largest numbers of immigrants have come from the central and northern plateaus in the states of Michoacan, Jalisco, and Guana-juato. There most of the population is agricultural, the birth rate is high, and the peon farm laborers have long been exploited on large, monopolistic land holdings. . . . Although the immigrants were of all varieties of culture, literacy, religion, language, racial stock, and experience, they most typically were peons and mestizos, poorly educated, Catholic, without any special skills. Folklore, tradition, and custom played large roles in their lives, particularly since many of the elders were illiterate (1954: 39).

Oscar Lewis, writing of the bracero movement in *Social Change in Latin America Today,* also indicates the central region as the chief source of this kind of immigration (frequently the forerunner of permanent immigration) where ". . . traditional (village) agricultural practices prevail and government efforts at irrigation, mechanization, and the distribution of land to the landless have been at a minimum" (1960: 293).

Manuel Gamio in *Mexican Immigration to the United States* stresses the mixed profusion of cultural elements — partly due to diversity of origins, partly to differences in adaptation to the new land — among the immigrant groups in the early nineteen hundreds (1930: 63). Nevertheless, he does not hesitate to class all immigrants as generally unsophisticated folk peoples who relied upon "folk-lorisms," superstitions, magical beliefs, and medicinal herbs despite rather rapid adoption of the more material aspects of American culture (1930: 71-83, 138).

SOME PERTINENT CULTURAL CHARACTERISTICS OF RURAL MEXICANS

An excellent summary of the ". . . deeprooted and common characteristics of Mexican and Mexican-American society and culture . . ." is presented in an article by Edward P. Dozier, *Folk Culture to Urbanism: The Case of the Mexicans and Mexican-Americans in the Southwest* (1964). Dozier, drawing on an extensive bibliography, stresses the importance of the village as the social unit. This tendency to settle in villages is carried over in the immigrant communities of the Southwest. Institutional patterns which are an integral part of the village complex are the patron system, the church, the family, and the *compadrazgo* (godparent) system.

The patron system is a form of institutionalized paternalism. The most prominent landowning family in a village receives work from the villagers and in return the family provides the village lands and helps direct and assist the lives of the villagers in dealing with the outer world. In its most exploitative form it was identical to the hacienda system except that in the hacienda system the landowner was usually absentee and his foreman or *mayordomo* was lord and the villagers peons. In the United States, the patron is usually a large rancher, farmer, or factory owner. In early Arizona territorial days he was usually the owner or superintendent of a mine (Park 1960: 46-95). The significant factor here is that historically the rural or peasant Mexican had been conditioned through centuries to a dependency relationship which he sought automatically when he settled in a new land. However, the patron system was only one institution which conditioned a dependency mentality in the rural Mexican.

Mexican Catholicism, through the colonial system of reducing all settlements to villages, had long conditioned the rural Mexican to its own brand of paternalism and exploitation (Gamino 1930: 113). By means of this the village priest assumed the role of the authoritarian intercessor in both secular and ritual matters. Oftentimes, as Dozier points out (1964: 17), the role of the *padre* complemented the role of the patron. Often the *padre* functioned in both roles. Still another institution, also an outgrowth of Mexican Catholicism and also centered in village life, is the patron saint. The villager uses the village saint in a patron-client relationship as an intercessor, guide, and counselor. The marks of this institution are the individual home altar with its votive candles, the vow, penance, and the village Saints'-day celebration. As Dozier points out, all three — the patron, priest, and patron saint — have conditioned the rural Mexican to interact in a dependency relationship with the outside world. This is pertinent background for the Mexican-American.

Dozier also summarizes (1964: 25-29) two other very important institutions which are of central importance in regulating inner-village or interpersonal life. The most important of the two is the family. Male dominance is the pattern with the tendency for newly married son to settle in his father's household. Descent and inheritance is traced from both sides of the family with authority passing to the eldest son. Deference, ideally, is shown to parents even after the children are grown, married, and have children of their own.

An institution complementary to the family is the godparent system. This is a fictional kinship system whereby children have ceremonial fathers and mothers. The latter have special duties and obligations to them — mostly religious. The child, the initiate, is called *ahijado* (male) or *ahijada* (female). The godfather is called *padrino,* and the godmother *madrina.* Collectively they are referred to as *padrinos.* The actual parents and godparents who are thus integrated in this institution refer collectively to one another as *compadres,* or specifically *compadre* for the male relationship and *comadre* for the female. "In its simplest form, the *compadrazgo* provides for the selection of sponsors on the following occasions: two sponsors, one of each sex, for the rite of baptism; one of the same sex as the initiate for confirmation; and two, one of each sex, for marriage" (Dozier 1964: 31). The network of relationships goes much farther than this, however, in that the *compadres* are second only to blood relations in the mutual help – social, material, and ritual – that their reciprocal obligations call for.

Dozier goes on to say that the *compadrazgo* system seems to vary among Mexican-Americans in inverse extensity to the family. Where the family unit expands to the extended family unit of three generations as among the more isolated New Mexico groups, the *compadrazgo* is relatively weak or in its simplest form; where the *compadrazgo* is elaborate as among the rural villagers of central Mexico, the family unit is relatively simple.

Social values that originate in these basic institutional patterns stress dependency and submission to the inevitable. Similarly the roles of the male and female as provided for in the Mexican family vary about central themes. Value upon male dominance can take the extreme form of *Machismo* in which the Mexican male must compensate for frustrations encountered in an urban society by abusing his wife and children and compulsively seeking sexual reassurance outside marriage. Oscar Lewis describes this in the "Gomez Family" in *Five Families* (1962). Also, in the delicately balanced male-female roles in the Mexican family, the woman is considered weak and prone to evil and must be carefully cloistered. The double standard for sexual conduct prevails. Nevertheless the wife-mother occupies a powerful position in the Mexican household. She exercises this through her influence on the children. She is their confidant, their ally and their intercessor with the father.

In summary, the patron system, the church, the patron saint, the family, and the compadrazgo are all deeply ingrained institutional complexes in the lives of the rural Mexican stock from which the largest part of the American immigrants have come. The stress placed upon the specific institution will vary according to the needs of peculiar circumstances of the immigrant group. Nevertheless, they are the basic mechanisms by which the social, economic, religious, and psychological needs of non-industrial Mexican village populations are met (Dozier 1964: 38).

CULTURAL VARIATIONS OF THE ARIZONA FARM MEXICAN-AMERICANS

Generalizations about *the* culture of any group are, at best, tenuous. Generalizations about this or that group of farm workers tend to be hazardous. People who are steady harvest workers generally must move over great distances which subject them to highly variable communal experiences. People who are not steady harvest workers are generally subject to highly variable occupational experiences. The fact that most Mexican-American farm workers have had, at some point, in their cultural past, rural influences as summarized does not mean that these influences continue to operate in a uniform manner. Mexicans have been immigrating and reimmigrating to the Southwest since the Mexican war. Before that, the Southwest was part of Mexico. Moreover, different regions of the United States have had significantly different influences upon the immigrant settlers. Finally, many of the new generation of Mexican immigrants, the green carders, are coming from cities. Although working in agriculture, they, like the higher status Anglo-American farm workers, are distinctly urban.

Taking these factors into account, the generalized Mexican-American farm subculture in Arizona exhibits three variations: the *Old Arizona,* the *Texas,* and the *Green Card* Mexican-American farm workers. This typology is complicated however by the fact that all three types are beginning to develop an urbanized overlay. The urbanized segment of the Old Arizona and the Texas group are the younger generations (the teen to 25 group) whereas the urbanized green carder is one who has undergone the urbanizing process in Mexico or as a result of peculiar vocational experience. Therefore we will add to these three types a fourth variant which we call the *Urbanized* Mexican-American farm worker. The group is not discussed as such because they cannot be considered a cohesive group in the same sense as the other sub-groups. This is an element or a tendency which is developed in the course of the over-all discussion of the Mexican-American farm worker.

The Old Arizona Mexican-American Farm Worker

Roughly one-third of the Mexican-Americans interviewed considered themselves from Arizona. These people immigrated during the revolutions of the early nineteen hundreds and the wars of presidential succession in the twenties. Although some may have immigrated via other Southwestern border states, by and large, Arizona was the state of their first permanent residency. Early Mexican immigration prior to large scale agriculture in Arizona was stimulated by the demand for cheap labor brought on by the great copper and railroad boom at the close of the nineteenth century (Park 1961: 203). Early Mexican settlements took the form of labor camps. Around these camps sprang up mining towns. The Mexican element was an important part of these towns. Some towns in territorial days were almost entirely Mexican at one time or another — e.g. Tucson, Yuma, Florence, and Morenci. According to Park (1961: 230) the major inflow of Mexican workers originated in the border states of Sonora and Chihuahua but by the turn of the century, with the completion of the Mexican railway systems in the interior, an influx of workers from the agricultural states of the Central Mesa began. This coincided roughly with the development of the Salt River irrigation system and the expansion of the agricultural industries. As the labor demand of agriculture grew, Mexican immigrants settled in farm camps, some of them coming from other industries and some directly from Mexico.

Today the Old Arizona Mexican-American farm workers have largely forsaken the farm-owned settlement pattern in favor of autonomous and semi-autonomous villages or squatter communities such as Guadalupe, Sende Vista, Pueblo Alto, Sal Se Puede, San Francisco, etc. Other settlements have taken the form of fringe appendages to agricultural towns such as Glendale, Chandler, Casa Grande, Eloy and Yuma. Some agricultural towns, Somerton for example, are predominantly Mexican-American. Although the nuclei of some of these rural Mexican-American settlements were formed by immigrant groups directly from Mexico, and date back several generations, for the most part they have grown as a result of a unique combination of rural and urban influences upon the Mexican-American after he had settled originally in mining, railroad, and farm labor camps. Usually a village nucleus was formed where land was cheap or unused, with ownership established eventually by squatters' rights. Sometimes a speculator bought up the land dirt cheap after it became apparent that a community was forming and rented or sold it to the squatters.

Once a village nucleus was formed it was fed by a constant trickle of of friends and relations who could see more economic opportunity in independent settlement. Many of the workers would oscillate between these squatter communities and farm labor camps, moving from one to the other according to the fluctuation in demand for labor. Although there was an overall tendency to move *into* more than *away* from these villages, the Second World War greatly accelerated the trend. The M-A's who moved soon saw the economic advantage of independent housing in that they could sell their labor to the highest bidder, whether it was farm, construction, or civil service. This pattern of occupational diversity is the hallmark of these independent residents, and persists today.

Although economic motives could be said to be the prime factor in the formation and growth of these communities, once formed they began to function as centers of social and cultural integration. Whether the community took the form of a rural village as Guadalupe, a barrio as in sections of South Tucson and South Phoenix, or a settlement surrounding the cult of a Saint, as San Francisco, an integrated network of kinship and godparent ties served to hold families in place and to draw others there. The strong dependency of the rural unsophisticated Mexican was transferred from the patron relationship of farmer or superintendent and worker, to relationships with the local priest and the cults of the supernatural. Pictures, likenesses, and images of Christ and popular saints adorn the houses of the farm workers who lived in these communities. Expressions such as ". . . with God's help," ". . . if it is God's will," "If Jesus gives me work, I'm happy!" are common. The authority and leadership of the local priest extends not only to personal matters but to community and civic affairs. One such community has a strong Catholic lay association promoting a community health clinic and administering a kind of local welfare program.

These dependency ties to nucleated community settlement have a powerful hold upon the workers even in a depressed local labor market. Many of the younger workers, newly married and settled adjacent to father's or a widowed mother's household, say that they could make higher wages in another locality or state, but that they cannot bring themselves to leave the community.

Another characteristic of the Old Arizona M-A farm worker is the absence of working wives. In the older pre-World War II days when these families lived on farms, wives worked along with husband and children in the fields. Now either the wives stay at home entirely or work in non-farm jobs more in line with the Anglo pattern. Also there is a tendency for wives to be active in civic and church-oriented associations. This has altered the traditional husband-wife relationship of the rural Mexican. This is also in contrast to the pattern of the *Texas* Mexican-American, which more typifies the traditional.

Generally the sample of Old Arizona M-A farm workers ranks higher than either the Texas or green carder in schooling, literacy, job skills, per capita income, and indebtedness. After a brief discussion of the Texas and Green Card Mexican-American farm workers, we will analyze work institutions which serve to contrast each group and are useful in explaining some of the effects of changes in farm technologies.

The Texas Mexican-American Farm Worker

From Odessa, Alamo, Rio Hondo, Pecos, Donner, Eagle Pass, Brownsville, Big Spring, Corpus Christi, and other Texas towns a steady trickle of Mexican-American farm workers is feeding the farm labor pools of Arizona. Migrating as large family units on regular seasonal routes during the 1950's, they looped through Arizona for the cotton harvest. During these migrations some families would leave the migrant stream and settle in farm camps as year-round workers (for a more detailed discussion of the migratory patterns of the Texas M-A's see Burma 1954: 35-71). Migratory patterns of our sample varied considerably. A typical past migratory pattern of a Texas M-A family who had now settled in Pinal County was as follows: Arizona, August through January in cotton; Texas, January through May in onions; and Wyoming, May through August in sugar beets. Another family used to harvest cotton in Texas and Arizona, and sugar beets in Colorado in the spring and summer. Still another had essentially the same route except for harvesting beets in Montana. One family went regularly to Ohio for the tomato harvest.

Many of the Texas M-A families interviewed in the citrus harvest in Maricopa County were still in the migratory stream; although they were tending to settle for increasingly longer periods of time in Arizona. One family picked citrus in Arizona in the winter, moved to Oregon in the spring and summer for the prune and beet harvests, and returned to Arizona for fall cotton picking. Another family picked citrus in Arizona in the winter, cut onions in California in the spring, chopped cotton in Arizona in late spring, picked potatoes in Arizona in the summer, picked summer grapes in Fresno, and some fall cotton in Arizona before again joining the Arizona citrus harvest.

More recently Texas M-A's, rather than settling in Arizona out of a migrant stream, are immigrating directly to this state looking for higher wages in year-round farm work. Most of the Texas M-A's interviewed had come to Arizona within the last decade. Most came as harvest hands, but some had come as equipment operators looking for better wages. The latter immigrated because, as they put it, they had been underbid in Texas, or New Mexico, or even Willcox, Arizona by other Texas M-A's who were willing to work for

50 to 60 cents an hour. Still other Texas M-A's, in Pinal County especially, complained of the Texas M-A's who were emigrating from the 50 and 60 cent areas to underbid them.

Whether immigrating to or migrating through Arizona, the Texas M-A's are undergoing a general stabilizing process accelerated in the last decade by cotton mechanization, and depressed farm wage conditions in Texas. This stabilizing process assumes four general patterns among the Texas group. Many of these families are achieving a crop-centered stability. With a kind of central residence hub, e.g. Eloy, Salinas, Calexico, etc., the family moves with the harvests in *one* crop, such as lettuce, and works year round for *one* employer. Many of the workers for G Company, Inc., growers and shippers of lettuce, are in this category. Throughout the annual crop cycle in California and Arizona, these families will set up temporary residences in Salinas, Watsonville, Eloy, Firebaugh, El Centro, or Calexico.

Another pattern is an area-centered stability. This involves a family settling in one locality, usually the fringe of an agricultural town (e.g. Chandler, Eloy, Casa Grande, etc.), living there the year through and working in the thinning and harvests of several crops. A broad wage base of crop diversity is further strengthened by the occasional migration of one or two of the older boys of the family to California harvest areas to augment unusually slack months. Money is sent home, and when harvests are complete the departed members return quickly to the family's "permanent" residence.

A third pattern is that of a farm-centered stability. The family head obtains a permanent job on one farm, usually operating equipment. This he sometimes does by underbidding other contenders for the job, which the Texas M-A can more easily do because of his generally lower standard of living. The family head's income is supplemented throughout the year by his wife and children taking up the hoe or the cotton sack whenever they can.

A fourth pattern is the stability of reduced migration. The family reduces its farflung migration routes to an oscillation between two principal crop-labor demand areas, e.g. Central Arizona and Central California. Although legal residence in one area is not established, the area visited and revisited is familiar, and more likely than not inlaws and distant relations occupy permanent residences in one or the other areas. These ties sooner or later tend to cause the migrating family to settle in one area.

Because of the vastly different vocational and communal experiences that differentiate the Texas from the Old Arizona M-A, deep social differences set them apart. Dependency behavior manifests itself through diffuse channels such as interaction with paternalistic growers or crew leaders rather than a village priest-civic leader. Because of the economic importance of the harvest work unit, family solidarity receives supreme emphasis. In many cases, it extends lineally several generations, and laterally to include the wives of the sons. Unlike the families of the Older M-A village and town residents, the Texas family is essentially an isolated unit. Of necessity it is the integrative core of their social and vocational organization. The social and economic ramifications of this require deeper study than this investigation provides. One ramification is evident, however. The role of the family head has a dual function which, unlike the emerging middle class Old Arizona M-A, serves to reinforce the value of male dominance. In addition to being the prime provider, the male head of the Texas M-A farm worker family is a work leader. In many instances he is the crew leader or row boss of a crew made up exclusively of his children. Moreover, any crew leader in the sample who was a Texas M-A invariably had members of his family among his crew. The implications of this pattern will be developed more completely in the discussion of the work institutions.

In summary, the Texas M-A farm workers rank the lowest in schooling, job skills, and per capita income. The size of their nuclear (immediate) family averages about that of the Old Arizona group and larger than the Green Card group. However, its *effective* size, its organization, and its function vary radically from either the Old Arizona or Green Card groups. Data also show tentatively that Pinal County is becoming the county of residence for more of this group than any other Mexican-American farm worker group.

The Green Card Mexican-American Farm Worker[1]

Timed almost identically with the influx of Texas M-A's is the inflow of a different breed of Mexican immigrant — the green carder. A green carder should not be confused with a Mexican National, better known as a *bracero*. Braceros are admitted entry to the United States under Public Law 78, 82nd Congress, 1951, which amends the Agricultural Act of 1949. It is set up specifically to provide agricultural workers in areas in which it is determined that a shortage of domestic agricultural workers exists. It is administered by the Secretary of Labor who delegates authority to State Employment Security offices. Through these offices workers are certified, transported, housed, and employed. They are not immigrants in any sense of the word. They are admitted for a specified purpose to a specified employer in a specified area for a specified length of time. At the end of this time they are returned to staging areas in Mexico where they leave for their homes or are readmitted for another term under another contract.

The green carder is a Mexican alien admitted as an immigrant for permanent residence in the United States under Public Law 414. He receives his name from his green alien registration card (Form I-151). While he may or may not become a naturalized citizen of the United States, he is accorded all rights, privileges, and duties of United States citizens. His status differs from other Mexican immigrant stock only by the recency of his entry and the immigration and naturalization act by which his residency and citizenship is established.

---

[1]Public Law 78 terminated after the first draft of this book was written. After due deliberation, the authors decided to let this passage stand as is. The *present tense,* although technically incorrect, will serve to emphasize the enduring effects of the bracero program in contrast to the *past tense* of its legal status.

Public Law 414, unlike Public Law 78, is administered by the Immigration and Naturalization Service of the Department of State. Only under certain specified conditions does its administration involve the Department of Labor. Public Law 414 requires first that a United States consul in Mexico investigate sufficiently the applicant's background to indicate that he will not become a public charge. Second, the applicant must submit with his application to the consul a documented letter of intent-to-hire from a dependable employer-sponsor who is a United States citizen. The United States Department of Labor assumes a responsibility in the granting of visas under 414 when an "employer" attempts to sponsor a given number of immigrants. In these cases the United States Consul holds the application in abeyance while he seeks a ruling from the Department of Labor. The Department, by means of its employment office serving the locality of the sponsor, determines first whether the sponsor is a bona fide employer offering steady, year-round work for this worker or workers; second, whether there are enough domestics to do the work; and third, whether the employment of aliens will adversely affect the wages and working conditions of domestic labor.

For more complete information on the green carder, the reader is referred to an article in the January 1963 issue of *Employment Security Review* by Lloyd L. Gallardo entitled "The 'green carder'." To summarize the points that have the most pertinence to this discussion, Professor Gallardo stresses the increasing magnitude of the green card immigrant stream. Although the *Annual Report of the Immigration and Naturalization Service 1961* reports a total of 299,811 Mexican immigrants in the ten-year period from 1951 to 1960, Gallardo cites the fact that this is a 395 percent increase over the previous decade; that the rate of increase from July 1, 1952 to June 30, 1961 has averaged better than 25 percent per annum; and that more immigrants have come from Mexico than any other country in every year beginning with 1954, except 1958 and 1959. The number admitted in 1961 alone (41,632) was over two-thirds the figure (60,589) for the entire preceding *decade*.

Gallardo, citing naturalization statistics and original data, maintains that the agricultural industries are the prime consumer of Mexican immigrant labor, and that they are finding the 414 method of obtaining workers increasingly efficient as opposed to the increased expense and complexity incurred in the contracting of braceros. Gallardo also discloses that a rising class of sophisticated middlemen called "visa consultants" are soliciting labor demand as well as supply. This is accomplished by partnership arrangements between consultants, one of whom operates at the sponsor's (United States) end while the other operates at the immigrant's (Mexico) end. Gallardo concludes his assessment of the quantitative impact of the green carder by the statement that, left alone, these factors will continue to accelerate this form of immigration. However, new programs of administration providing for a greater degree of review and denial of visa applicants than practiced at the time of Gallardo's study may tend to mitigate his prediction.

Irrespective of this, Gallardo's study also suggests that the green carders' role in agricultural labor is as important as the quantitative dimension of their immigration. Being used primarily in highly seasonal tasks means that they tend to return to residences in Mexico during slack seasons. This, combined with proximity of large agricultural areas to the border which permits green carders to live in Mexico and commute to work, has created a vast international migratory labor force.

Our data support this suggestion. During peak season for agricultural work, the Calexico port of entry estimates that between 8,000 and 10,000 commuters pass through their gates daily. Moreover, officials there reported that their office as of early 1963 was processing on the average 20 *new* green card applications per day. On some days they were processing as many as 50. They said that the majority of the sponsors were growers. Calexico is but one of eight major ports of entry on the Mexican border. The San Luis, Arizona border station, not listed as one of the eight major ports of entry in the Annual Reports of the Immigration and Naturalization Service, made available an official count report dated March 8, 1963 which certified a total of 1,387 green card commuters within a 24-hour period.

Arizona's share of green carders, though small compared to California and Texas, is nevertheless significant. Of the 577,895 Mexican Aliens processed by the alien address program during 1963, 29,484 resided in Arizona (USDJ 1963: 84). Arizona, as the state of intended residence, also accounted for better than six percent (3,548) of the 55,253 green carders admitted in the fiscal year 1962-63 (USDJ 1963: 41). More revealing and more pertinent are the figures from recent Arizona Farm Placement Office surveys of green card M-A's being used in agricultural work. An annual high of 2,613 is reported for March 1964 (ASES 1964c). This amounts to almost eight percent of the total number of agricultural workers employed in the state during the same month in the year previous (ASES 1964a).

Although green carders resemble the older Mexican-American groups, there are important differences. These differences arise out of refinements of fundamentally similar forces operating for decades to push and pull the Mexican peasant to the North. The pull force—chiefly labor demand—operating on the present generation of Mexican immigrant does not differ essentially from that on the earlier generation from the standpoint of the type or size. The rapid inter-stimulating expansion of the railway and mining industries in the early 1900's rivaled the agricultural industries of today in their need for enormous quantities of cheap labor. As the rail systems were completed and new copper rich areas were opened to exploitation, massive recruitment programs were extended south of the border. Peons eager to escape the forced labor of the haciendas and mines of Diaz' regime streamed northward over the newly completed Mexican railways that tapped the regions of the interior. El Paso became the clearing house for Mexican labor, and Arizona alone, by United States Department of Commerce estimates in 1908, was the destination of 60,000 to 100,000 immigrants annually. The outflow of Mexican labor resources was so great during this period that according to Park in *The History of Mexican*

Labor in Arizona During the Territorial Period, "Mexican papers were filled with dispatches telling of crops unharvested and railroad and construction work delayed due to the impossibility of securing workers" (1961: 203-228).

In other respects as well, Mexican population pressures function today as they did in previous generations. The push factor that operates perennially in the form of the depressed economic position of the Mexican laborer has been heightened periodically by social and political upheavals (Gamio 1930: 40-41). The seasonal aspect of immigration and reimmigration characterized these movements even in territorial days (Park 1961: 228). Gamio refers repeatedly to this phenomenon in his study of Mexican immigration (1930: 3, 43). Moreover the stimulation of border traffic caused by the labor recruiter has been, lawfully or unlawfully, an important factor throughout the history of Mexican immigration (Gamio 1930: 11; Park 1961: 220).

In summary, continuous demand of Southwestern industries for Mexican labor, chronic social and economic restlessness of a depressed *mestizo* population, and the international labor recruiter have been the fundamental dynamics of Mexican immigration since territorial days. Nevertheless, in its most recent form, Mexican immigration is responding to an intensification of a very specialized demand. It differs today in its industrial specificity. For ten years agricultural demand for Mexican labor and Mexican labor supply have been synchronized through international cooperation of specialized agencies. Unique in the history of Mexican labor, this—the bracero program— has permitted the rapid industrial expansion of Mexican-dependent crop systems. At the same time ceaseless pressure has been exerted by other segments of the economy to restrict and repeal the bracro program. As restrictions and talk of repeal gradually increased so did the incentive to try other methods of obtaining Mexican labor. From the point of view of farm management, the use of Public Law 414 for this purpose is a logical alternative. A comparison of the number of Mexican Nationals admitted to the United States under Public Law 78 and the number of visas granted for permanent residency under Public Law 414 from 1959 to 1963 reflect this trend (USDJ 1963):

Year	1959	1960	1961	1962	1963
Braceros	447,535	427,240	294,149	292,556	195,450
Immigrants	23,061	32,864	41,632	55,805	55,986

As agricultural industries turned to immigration as a solution, the bracero system itself became one important mechanism of recruitment. Braceros are logical candidates for sponsorship. The most successful, by Anglo management's standards, are selected for sponsorship. Inasmuch as success has a relationship to experience, those braceros who have the most experience in the fields and the greatest familiarity *vis-a-vis* grower management are the most successful.

Conversations with scores of braceros in different localities bear this out. They readily recognize the salient features of this system and its method of operation. The following is a consensus of how braceros view the system:

1. It is much better to be a green card Mexican than a bracero.
2. A green carder can get more than $1 an hour which is the limit for braceros.
3. A green carder can work for more than one employer.
4. A green carder can even get out of farm work altogether.
5. If Nationals are discontinued there will be more green card people than ever.
6. The going *mordida* ("under the table" money) rate presently to get green card papers in Mexico is $300.
7. Sponsors are hard to find and they are interested only if the worker will become valuable to them.

That many green carders have immigrated via this system explains the features many of them exhibit. The ex-bracero green carder is a product of years of interaction with Americans. He is accustomed to dealing with Anglo supervisors, labor recruiters, and the ever-present *mordida*. Because of the experiences upon which this process places a premium, the ex-bracero green carder is an atypical bracero. He is the most sophisticated of the lot. Whereas the Texas M-A immigrant has committed himself, family and all, the ex-bracero green carder, conditioned by the bracero system, has made a different vocational adaptation. He is a loner. More likely than not, his family is in Mexico and he, already in a relatively highly-paid position, is the sole wage earner. In addition, the urbanizing process is intensified by the fact that, either in anticipation of becoming a green carder or as a result of becoming one, he moves his family to a Mexican border city. We suggest that this difference in work institutions, developed more fully later, is important in the acculturating process of the Mexican-American farm workers.

The impression must not be given that the bracero system is the only system or the predominant system of recruiting green card workers. Too little is known about the whole picture of the green carder phenomenon to make definitive statements. It is known that other systems, such as the time honored method of the international recruiter, serve to channel significant numbers of rural villagers into the United States. Precisely how many have immigrated by means of this or that system is not known. It is known that a great many of these recent immigrants are filtering through the Texas milieu and that, like Texas M-A's described above, they migrate and work as family units, returning seasonally to home bases in Mexico. To what extent this type of worker reaches Arizona farms is not known. Few of the green card workers in our sample (not more than 13 out of 62) had this pattern. The majority had the individual-worker/family-in-Mexico pattern. Furthermore, most of them (77 percent) had immigrated since 1950.

The profile of these 62 green carders is pertinent. They ranked with the Texas group, among the lowest, in average years of formal schooling — 4.6 years. A graduation of time-distance from homeland is illustrated by the relative percentages of parents who were subsistence farmers. Thirty-seven percent of the green carders' parents were subsistence farmers as compared to 21 percent for the Texas group and eight percent for the Arizona group. This is also reflected in the comparative percentages of each group who can read Spanish. Green carders show 87 percent, Texas M-A's 60 percent, and the Arizona group 43 percent. The reverse ranking hierarchy according to ability to read English also confirms cultural distance from homeland. It is Arizona, 89 percent; Texas, 55 percent; and green carders, 19 percent.

The suggestion that the Texas group is suffering from an awkward between-two-cultures stage is shown by the fact that their percentage of those unable to read any language (20 percent) is the highest of the three and is more than double that of the green carder, more of whom can read Spanish. The Texas group also shows the lowest per capita income of the three groups, with the green carder between the two. If the economic factor of the green carder's living in Mexico is considered, differences in per capita income are even more pronounced.

The sophisticated character of the work institutions of the green carder as characterized by our sample appears in their tendency to have smaller families than either of the Old Arizona or the Texas groups. Moreover, they rank highest in status orientation. They have 71 percent in this category as compared to 62 percent among the Arizona group and 41 percent among the Texas group. These and other data discussed above suggest that a large segment of the most recent immigrants are leap-frogging some of the traditional stages of assimilation through which earlier groups of Mexican immigrant farm workers have passed.

The general cultural characteristics accompanying the green carders were not well documented. Generally they appear to have less integrative ties along traditionally rural lines. They share the general M-A pattern of deference to authority but the nature and the extent of their religious life is not known. Interview data indicate a strong family orientation in terms of materialistic aspirations. Family units that green carders are supporting tend to be extended as is typical of the Texas group. They differ in that residence separation is common. Although a worker may be supporting a large group of close relatives, it is common to find a double residence separation. The worker's wife and children will be in one place — e.g. Mexicali — and his father, mother, and siblings will be living in another Mexican town. Most of the commuters, however, have their families located in the border town closest to their jobs.

The theme of male dominance in the circumstances of family separation lends itself to the *casa chica* or mistress pattern. This is evident in the night life some carry on in the border towns where free women are profuse. Some have mistresses they visit during the week. Others limit themselves to brothels on weekends. Accounts of these experiences are the subject of much lusty and colorful banter in the fields and the barracks.

WORK INSTITUTIONS, VALUES, AND ATTITUDES

We suggest that an important, frequently neglected integrative organization among Mexican-Americans is the work institution. For most M-A farm workers, presently and historically, the work unit is the family unit. Values underlying one underlie the other. Attitudes toward work and vocational experiences, past and future, are the expressions of these values. At the same time the work-family unit is not static. As with other M-A institutions it is both reflective of and instrumental in the adaptive process.

Mexican-American farm workers show three basically different work institutions: the *migratory family,* which most characterizes the Texas group; the *multi-vocational family,* which most typifies the Old Arizona; and the *one-vocational family,* toward which many Old Arizona have moved and many green carders have attained by working in the United States and living in Mexico. Two other types must be added to these in order to provide a complete transitional continuum. One, the *peasant family,* is inferred by the cultural past of the Mexican immigrant. The other, *bi-vocational family,* is inferred by the aspirations and attitudes of the younger, more highly educated M-A farm worker. Listed in the hypothetical order of their transitional stages, they are:

> I.   Peasant Family
> II. Migratory Family
> III. Multi-Vocational Family
> IV. One-Vocational Family
> V.   Bi-Vocational Family

Family profiles, anecdotes, and interviews will be used to illustrate each type except peasant. All names are fictitious. All material which might serve to identify the individual family has been altered in a manner that will not bias the conclusions to be drawn from it.

The Peasant Family

For a penetrating description of the Mexican peasant see Oscar Lewis' *Pedro Martinez: A Mexican Peasant and His Family* (1964). Also a much briefer version of the Martinez family can be found in Lewis' *Five Families* (1962). The work institution of the peasant family follows strict lines of sex delineated responsibilities. Men—father and sons—work the fields; slash and clear land; plant, cultivate, and harvest their crops. To meet their needs for supplemental cash income, the sons occasionally hire out as farm field hands, but not the women. The work of the mother and daughters is confined to housekeeping, mending, sewing, food buying, grinding, cooking, and cleaning.

The Migratory Family

In this pattern, family membership most nearly coincides with membership in the work unit. Generally, only the disabled or the very young and old are omitted — the mother only if she has babies to watch and frequently not then. The family is basically nuclear but large. It may extend lineally to include the father's parents and laterally to include the sons' wives. This unit moves, works, and lives together. Its members work in the same crop, the same field and the same crew. It may, in fact, comprise a crew. All income is pooled. Frequently the father receives all wages earned in one undifferentiated sum. Occasionally aged or disabled members will be left in a kind of hub residence location to which the unit returns seasonally. The support of these members is nevertheless maintained by sending money. The father is the head of the work unit and the household. The mother generally has a key role in the handling of the common purse. Children have little opportunity to remain in school beyond the legal age limit, if that long. The influence of education during the time they are in school is seriously hampered by a conflict of values. The Anglo middle-class-oriented school system stresses the value of self development as opposed to the value that an individual's prime responsibility is to help support his parents and brothers and sisters. The only responsibility which takes precedent over this obligation is an individual son or daughter's responsibility to her own spouse and children — still family.

JOSÉ LOPEZ — José Lopez was born in 1925 in Nuevo Laredo, Tamaulipas, a Mexican border town at the southern tip of Texas. At the age of two months he was brought to the American side, Laredo, where he was raised. His mother was a United States citizen by birth, his father was an alien. His father worked as a cowboy on Texas cattle ranches until his death.

José went to school in Texas for four years before quitting. At barely 16 he began working in the tomato and onion harvests in Texas, also doing irrigating and some tractor driving. In 1946 he began contracting crews on interstate harvest routes which took him to Wyoming for sugar beets, Arizona for cotton, and back to Texas for onions. His activity in Arizona was confined principally to one farm, the Norman farm in Pinal County, to which he returned every cotton season, first with picking crews and later chopping crews. As he began to spend more time working for Norman, he started operating tractors and cats.

Now, with a wife and ten children, he has not returned to Texas for over a year. He works off and on for a thousand acre cotton farm near Stanfield where he does equipment operating and independent contracting which is now limited almost entirely to chopping. He lives in a three room, wood frame house with his family. The house does not have an indoor toilet but it does have inside water and electricity.

Although Lopez is a Roman Catholic, not all of his children have *padrinos* (godparents) because his wife is a Jehovah's Witness.

Three of Lopez' children are old enough now to work in the fields. José estimates that his contracting in chopping, five days a week all summer, grosses him $30 a day ($2400). His children chopping all summer will earn collectively approximately $900. The rest of the year, Lopez does general farm work, including operating picking machines, Roods and cats, for an hourly wage of 90 cents or $1. This brings in $800. The total is $4,100. For a family of 12, the average is $342 per member.

The Lopez family has begun to settle down in one locality and gradually rely more upon diverse occupations. However, José said that he may be forced to go on the move again or to look for permanent work in another state:

> Everybody says next year no chopping. (Asked why he did not drive machinery the year round) — For just nine dollars a day, I work myself and put all my kids in school and then we need some clothes, some food, and that's not enough money to cover my bills. I make more by children chopping and running a crew. In summer time I can save a little money and buy clothes for my kids. Now that money has gone pretty quick. I have a kid in high school, maybe this year I take him out because we need his help. (Asked if this might not be bad for the boy) — Oh yeah, but I've got a big family, I don't know what you want me to do!

The account of another Texas M-A family man with a similar background is pertinent. This man, now chopping with his wife and three children in Lopez' crew, had operated farm equipment year round for the same farm that Lopez had worked for in Pinal County. When asked why he had quit this work to chop cotton he gave this account:

> I started working for 90 cents an hour and was willing to work at the low wages thinking that after I worked for a year or so Norman would appreciate my work and raise me. I stayed several years and asked for a raise. Norman told me, 'You wanta work or you wanta quit?' He said he could get a man cheaper.

This man was especially bitter because, as he put it,

> I trained Mexican immigrants to operate equipment, and they took my job cheaper. After that I got a job in Casa Grande for $2.50 an hour and didn't start to work yet before some guy came in and offered to do this job cheaper and got it. I like driving tractor better, but at the wages they pay, I can do better looking for work and chopping with my family.

In summary, these values, which are most characteristic of the Texas M-A farm worker, underlie the migratory family work institution:

1. Family solidarity and family responsibility laterally and vertically — parent to children and children to siblings and parents as each member comes of working age.
2. A strong, pervading, unpretentious emphasis on self reliance localized in and expressed by means of the family-work institutions. This is sometimes given expression in the statement: *no hay trabajo no hay comer!* — no work no eat!

In conflict with these are the following:

3. A desire to settle in one place and stop moving.
4. A subordinate but nevertheless conflicting value recognition of the importance of formal schooling.

The Multi-Vocational Family

The *multi-vocational family* most typifies the Old Arizona group. The unit most generally includes the father, mother, and unmarried or divorced children. The membership of this unit can be physically delimited by those who live under one roof and share living expenses and incomes. The members live together in one or adjoining houses in a permanent location, usually within the structure of some recognized community, whether barrio, village, or camp. The unit differs from the *migratory family* since it does not migrate, and its members generally do not work together. The father may be an irrigator for a local cotton farm, one son may work for a cattle feeding operation, another may be a loader for a lettuce company, while a school-aged daughter or son may chop cotton in the summer. Vocational patterns of its members tend to be highly diverse and unstable both with regard to length of duration and type.

The father is the head of the household and the mother is the book-keeper. She receives the money, buys the food, and makes installment payments. Her sons will often register their automobiles in her name. As with the migratory unit, this institution places a value on all the children helping out. Because of the numerous sources of subsistence, ranging from Aid to Dependent Children to *compadrazgo* (godparent system) obligations, this value is not so compelling as it is to the Texas migratory family. Although in interviews with the younger sons of these families this was a frequent reason given for dropping out of school, followup studies suggested in many instances that this was more of an excuse than a real cause.

MARTIN GARCIA — Martin Garcia was born in 1904 in Atil, a small town in Sonora, Mexico. His father had 30 acres and raised corn, tobacco, and wheat. In 1913, shortly after his father died, his mother, two sisters, himself, and a brother immigrated to Mobile, a small railroad town west of Maricopa. Soon after they moved to the minorities section of Phoenix, in the vicinity of south 16th Street, where his mother took a common-law husband. Martin went to Washington School at 3rd and Lincoln and then to Grant School from 1914 to 1918. Martin said, "I didn't learn much, because when a kid is sick and cold and hungry, he is not going to be very fast in school. What I learned, I learned outside."

His mother died in 1918. Now 14 years old, Martin had to work. He moved to the Harrison Ranch near Tempe, where he and his brother and sisters lived in a two-room board house with a wood floor. They had a bed, a wood stove, a few plates, and used tortillas for spoons. Their water came from the irrigation canal. "I used to see hogs and chickens in the canal. I would close my eyes and throw myself down and drink and we used to bring this water to the house. Thanks be to God we never got sick!"

However, sickness was almost a daily part of their lives. Martin could recall this, sometimes vaguely, sometimes vividly. A 1924 illness was recalled in detail:

I slept overnight in the winter on the floor of a cabin in Glendale. I was with another man, and I gave the other man the place on the bed. The floor had open cracks in it where the wind came through. When I woke up the next morning, I was paralyzed, I couldn't walk. For twelve years I was rheumatic, my eyes were as hard as a board. I couldn't sleep at night, pains all over my body! I went to four doctors, but they couldn't help. Finally in 1936 I saw some pills advertised in the paper. I sent off five dollars for a hundred tablets. But before I took them I prayed to God to be cured. I said, 'God, you're first, they're second!' And I said if I was cured, it would be because of God, and he would get the thanks. I took all of the pills and got well. Today I'm better than ever.

Martin recalls that in 1942 he had a head operation to relieve an infection which had occurred from hitting his head on a rail car while working on the railroad in California. His memory had been very bad and he had terrible headaches. These symptoms improved since then but his vision has been bad since this operation. He says it is getting steadily worse. He uses a dime-store pair of magnifying glasses to read by.

In 1928 Martin married Elena Macias. Elena was born in 1909 in Aguascalientes, Mexico. Her memory is very vague about her early life. She remembers one-room shacks. There were many and so alike she had forgotten. She remembered carrying wood for stoves and water from canals to drink. She remembers being very cold sometimes. She doesn't remember playing and having fun as a child, only working in the fields and in the house. Elena's sister remembers their father telling that a man came to him in Juarez, Chihuahua to offer him a job on his farm in Alamogordo, New Mexico. The father didn't know about farming but the man said he would teach him all about horses, cows, raising things, and give him a house to live in if he would come and work. He would feed him too. That is when the family left everything behind in Juarez, even their papers, and moved to the United States. "That was when you needed no papers to cross the line. You just paid one penny and crossed." Elena was a child and her sister a baby.

From then on the family moved a lot, the father doing both farm work and working a few times in the city. Their two brothers were born near Denver, Colorado. Elena remembers going to school there. The family also lived at one time in Kansas City. The family were living and working on a ranch near Phoenix when Elena met Martin working on the same farm. She was nineteen when they were married.

Martin and Elena Garcia continued to live and work on farms in the Salt River Valley, Martin driving teams, irrigating, chopping, and picking cotton until 1932. Then they moved to Santa Teresa, a small rural Mexican-American settlement in the valley. When they moved there it consisted of a very few houses. They bought their plot and built a one-room house with a ramada kitchen, later adding two bedrooms. Elena's mother died that same year, and her father lived with her sister in Santa Teresa until he died.

The Garcia's home now has four rooms, a linoleum floor throughout, no sink but an inside water tap to a porcelain basin in the kitchen. They still have an outside toilet, but inside there is no lack of adequate furniture. They have a divan set in the style of the forties, a TV that needs repair, a radio that runs constantly, chairs, tables, and several beds in fair shape, one of which is in the living room. Although the Garcias ". . . don't go to Mass very often," their house is adorned with devotional artifacts. There is a miniature family shrine with candles and two pictures of Christ. One is a picture of a Crucifix and the other is a picture of His ascent to Heaven. Placed among the religious motifs are pictures of their children and grandchildren. Crocheted doilies embellish every conceivable flat surface. Where any space remains un-occupied by any of these above things, a knick knack appears. The house is kept spotless.

Outside the Garcias have a vegetable garden and a flower garden. Martin plants the vegetables — onions, radishes, chili peppers, etc., and Elena cultivates the flowers. Although Santa Teresa has three grocery stores, Elena shops in Phoenix, claiming the local markets are too expensive. Every Saturday is shopping day. She spends $25 to $30 for a week's supply for six — herself, Martin, a son, Doña, their divorced daughter, and Doña's two children, aged four and five. Their gas and light bill runs a little over $5. Electricity powers the cooler, iron, lights, radio, and TV. Gas is needed only for one small heater in the living room and the stove. The family use medical doctors in the closest city, paying "regular prices."

Martin and Elena have six children and ten grandchildren. All have *padrinos* and *madrinas*. The oldest, Doña, was born in 1932, Juana in 1934, Panchita in 1938, Martin, Jr., the first boy, in 1940, followed by Luz in 1943, and Alex, the youngest, in 1945. Luz, Panchita, and Juana are married and living in separate residences with their husbands and children. Doña, divorced, lives with her two children in the Garcia household. She receives Aid to Dependent Children. This goes in the central purse. Alex, unmarried, has just returned from the Army. During his six months hitch he sent them money. Now he is out of work. Martin, Jr. works at the Waco Cattle Company. While living at home he gave money to his mother and made car payments on a 1956 Chevrolet sedan which is in both his and his father's names. Now as Martin Sr. says, "I don't count on him anymore because he took a girl last Saturday." Elena in her own version, proudly says, "Martin has just eloped. We think he will get married soon."

All conversation among the Garcias, children and grandchildren included, is in Spanish. No women in the family work. When Elena was asked why, she said, "The women have children to take care of and cooking to do."

The mainstay of the income still rests on old Garcia's shoulders. Now sixty, he picks citrus for a valley company seven to eight months out of the year. His wages, due to fluctuations in weather and time lost moving from grove to grove, will vary from $25 to $50 a week. In June and July, after citrus is through, he works in watermelons. In early cotton season he will pick when hand picking is available.

Although the old man has failing eyes and occasional sicknesses he labors in the fields, glad for the work that he can get. He proudly insists that he likes farm work "better than any other thing." Moving between groves and on the bus home, when the young pickers whistle at the girls and insult one another in Yaqui-ized Spanish, Old Garcia dozes, and when he walks up the path from the plaza where the bus stops, his head slumps a little. In the house he pulls out a half empty bottle of tequila from behind the cushion of the couch, pours out a third of a glass. Sometimes this is followed by another, maybe two, maybe three, but *el viejo* is too proud to feel sorry for himself.

As long as Jesus gives me my piece of bread and others then I'm happy. I'm not satisfied to have a great big belly and know that someone is hungry in the world — all the world! You may go to some houses where people cry (complain) too much. That isn't good. If you say I'm going to live one week on a glass of water, you can do it! I'm going to tell you how we live — if we have eggs and butter and the next day we don't have anything, we're going to get by with tortillas and potatoes — whatever we have — we won't die.

While pointing out that —

If these braceros make five dollars a day they make a lot, but if I make five dollars a day, I don't get as much. They get free house, electricity, and doctors.

He adds —

. . . I wouldn't begrudge them. If a millionaire came to work then I would be mad, but these men need it, they don't take my job. If Jesus lets me work I'm proud. I'd rather work for three dollars a day than go on welfare—I can't wait for better wages. Maybe someone else can get fat by living on welfare, because they don't like 85 cents an hour, but I can't. These fellows (braceros) never hurt me. If I was a farmer, I wouldn't like to see my crops without workers. I wouldn't like to wait for one man to come one day and not the other.

Although Doña has received ADC (Aid to Dependent Children) since her divorce, Martin and Elena insist they have never received welfare. This applies to them and their unmarried children. Moreover, Martin is very active in the local Santa Teresa Catholic civic club which helps *needy* families in the village. That same week a boy had been killed in a car crash. Martin was proud that his dues and volunteer labor had helped send the bereaved family a $25 bouquet. "If I live to be a hundred and pay my dollar every week to the club and never need help from them, I have no complaint. Money is to help people with. I may never need help myself, but I am glad to help other people."

In summary, some of the values that underlie the Garcia (multi-vocational) family are:

1. Less father domination in favor of more individualistic expression.
2. Dependence on supernatural sanction.
3. Children's responsibility to work for the family is present but not as compelling as to the migratory family.
4. A wife's place is in the home rather than in the fields.

5. A strong sense of community responsibility expressed by cross family *compadrazgo* (godparent) ties and volunteer associations in the form of civic, church, and clique groups. This makes desirable seasonal and local farm work, and any other kind of work which allows the individual to remain in his community.

6. Value on schooling as a kind of abstract principle but still not an integral part of their value system.

The One-Vocational Family

This family-work unit consists of a working father in a higher paying position in farm work, usually operating more expensive farm equipment or supervising. The wife raises the children and keeps house. Children go to school and are not expected to go to work for their parents. Although this is the ideal, and is not always attainable, it functions as a dominant incentive for the working father who has ambitiously worked his way up to higher paying jobs.

This stage of economic transition is the most critical for the Mexican-American. This is the stress stage in his transition to the Anglo value system. Although extreme poverty has its peculiar miseries, the conflicts and anxieties of the transitional Mexican are not part of them. The frustrations he experienced in his father's house were not the deprivations of basic needs. They were deprivations of the spirit, the frustrated ambitions for a material world that he thought he could gain by marketing his labor. Now swamped by an avalanche of debts, with seven or eight mouths to feed and physical labor becoming more competitive, he is fired with single minded ambition to project his offspring through the class barriers that he could not transcend. The one-vocational family, in its fixed objective to achieve this transition, has made education an integral part of their value system. However, other requisite values are not automatic by-products of this experience. He desires the glittering symbols of an unobtainable class which were too remote, even, for his father to covet. These things a multitude of peddlers, promoters, and Madison Avenue hawkers through a host of media are all too willing to provide. The *rural*-urban fringe settlements have their peculiar versions — the blanket salesman going from door to door selling a three dollar item for a dollar down and a dollar a month for a year, or the door-to-door photographer selling pictures and gaudy frames for 50 cents down and 25 cents a week. Then there is the everpresent television.

Another value lags to frustrate his ambition for his children — family. The family continues to make its demands in many forms, all of which are antithetical to class mobility. Children, the source of joy and family solidarity, continue to arrive in pre-urban profusion. Obligations toward needy, aged, or disabled in-laws and parents are still keenly felt. Finally godparent obligations appear on regular prescribed occasions. To be sure these are reciprocal obligations. But because need is a frequent incentive for invoking these obligations, they result among other things as a leveler, a brake on the higher income groups. The Ramirez family provides a case study of stress in the transitional Mexican-American farm worker.

AUGUSTO RAMIREZ — Augusto was born in Miami, Arizona, June 24th, 1924. He was the third child in a family of 11 children. Augusto's father immigrated to Arizona from San Bernardo, Durango. He came over in the twenties when he was young and started right to work in the mines of Superior and Miami. Augusto's mother was born in Miami to a mining family. The senior Ramirezes lived most of their married lives in Superior, though there was a period when they lived in San Manuel. Mr. Ramirez began to develop lung trouble. During the war, while living in Superior, the family made a few trips to the Salt River Valley to work in cotton. On these trips they lived temporarily in Santa Teresa. It was during the time of intermittent cotton picking that Ramirez Senior scratched an eye on a cotton branch. He thought nothing of it at first, but an infection developed and six months later he lost the eye entirely. They went back to Superior but, because of his eye, he could no longer work in the mines. This was in the early fifties. It was then that the senior Ramirezes moved permanently to Santa Teresa. They were the vanguard of the family, most of whom eventually followed. Two years later, Augusto's father died, "killed by the mines," his mother said.

Augusto's youth was spent in the mining atmosphere of Miami and Superior. He went to the Lower Miami School to the fifth grade. His house was close to school and he played on the school grounds in most of his free time. He didn't learn much that he recalls, more math than English. Classes were made up of about half Whites and half Mexicans. The fifth grade was as far as Augusto progressed, ". . . because there were too many in the family and my father had hard times." Although 16 and in only the fifth grade, Augusto thinks that he could have graduated if he had stayed. He says that he learns very easily but that he has to be shown: "I don't think I'm too slow to learn things. I learn things when I see them. When I go to a job, they ask me if I can do that, I say, 'let me see you do it.' I learned everything in the mine from the bottom up."

After leaving school he went to work washing windows in a local grocery. Stocky, powerful, and robust, Augusto wanted to become a boxer like his mother's brother but his mother wouldn't let him. At 18 he went to work for the mine on the surface as a laborer. He commenced underground work at 21, starting as a mucker. He was a blaster at 22 and got half way to the "top" in one year. In 1950 he married a woman from Superior. Although he and his bride lived in Miami with Augusto's parents, he commuted to Superior where he had just begun work for a different mine. He started as motorman, but he didn't like it because it was too hot and there was no contract. He returned to the mines in Miami where he worked until 1956. That year he hired on at San Manuel and worked up to timberman, "the highest paying job."

In 1959 his father died. His mother and wife, Margaret, wanted him to quit the mines because they felt that mining had killed his father.

We talked it over, and I decided that maybe they were right. I knew that there was work in the fields so that same year I moved my wife and children to Santa Teresa. I started picking cotton right away because I had to have two or three dollars for my family to live. I picked cotton for four weeks, and went on unemployment for two weeks. The third week I got a job loading crop dusting planes for Elliot Aviation in Mesa.

I worked a few seasons and asked the boss for more money but he wouldn't give it so I quit. There was no future there because it was not steady work — only from June to December. I would pick cotton sometimes, do garden work, pick potatoes, and irrigated. It was all right when working. But I can't stay that way and work six months and look for work the other six months. If a man wants to take care of his family — not an expensive life, but take good care of his family — he has to work every day!

Augusto borrowed $200 from a friend in Superior and bought a second-hand 2-ton truck in his brother's name. Hauling farm produce, he made expenses and groceries. While he was in the hauling business he met the Martinez boys who were in the trucking business. Through them he got word that a produce company was looking for dependable drivers. Augusto went to work for them in the 1961-62 season as a harvest hand. He kept after the foreman to give him a driving job. Before the season was over he got one. He is now driving trucks for this company for the second season. He still hauls hay in the spring. He traded in his old truck to the Martinez boys and has since bought another.

My wife wanted me to buy a new truck but I refused. If I buy a new truck I have to make payments every month. That's what I want to get away from. I work on it a little bit, I buy a few parts and I save that payment for my family. I know a guy who bought a new truck and he might make 20 to 30 dollars more than me, but he has to make 60 to 70 dollar payments.

I'm going to give my older truck to my kid brother. If he wants to give me a few dollars for payment, ok. If he needs it that's ok—that's the way we were raised, to help one another. I try to tell my brother that he will do better working for himself than working for someone else.

Augusto and Margaret have six children ranging in age from ten months to ten years. The family of eight live in a wood frame, three room house with an outside toilet. The house has electricity and cold water tapped to the inside. The house, relative to others in the same village, is poorly furnished. With only the necessities, it looks almost bare in comparison to the knick knack filled rooms of other villagers. A large TV console with a finger-smeared screen occupies a central position in the combination bedroom and living room. It runs day and night but the picture is so dim that daylight almost obscures it. When the TV is low enough, the din of a radio can be heard in one of the back rooms. Two undersized windows with faded cotton curtains admit what light there is into the dull, dark green sitting room. The wooden floors are completely bare. The walls are bare except for the one colored picture of a Madonna hung almost to the ceiling. Below the picture is a very worn daybed with protruding springs. This is flanked by one wooden straight-back chair. On the other end is a heavy wooden chair with upholstered back and seat. The kitchen in contrast to the sitting room is cluttered with laundry, utensils, remnants of food, toys, and two babies playing with pots and pans.

Margaret has been poor as far back as she can remember. Now only 37, weariness dulls her delicate features. She is pretty and sad. She shows none of the robust spontaneity characteristic of Garcia's daughters. Both her mother and father were born in the old country. They came through Juarez in 1920 to New Mexico where Margaret was born. She remembers almost nothing about her father because he died when she was a baby. Her mother told her he used to cut wood and carry it door to door. She told her, "He worked very hard and died." The family, mother and five children, moved to the mine country where Margaret finished the sixth grade. Still a girl, she went to work as a house girl in private homes, floor scrubbing, washing, and ironing. At 16 she got a permanent job in a laundry in Florence where she worked for the next eight years until she married Augusto in 1950 at the age of 25.

They met at a dance in Miami. She stopped working after that, ". . . babies came too fast." She doesn't like living in Santa Teresa, but it's cheaper to live there than in the mining towns. After living five years in Santa Teresa she knows no other people than the closest four families. She doesn't visit often. She has no time for that because it's all she can do to cook and wash and iron for her children. Dorothy was the first. Born a little over a year after they were married, in a Miami hospital, she was "paid for" by mining insurance. After Dorothy came Josephine, now nine, born in a Tempe hospital. Margaret had to pay $20 to be admitted. Augusto paid $80 more later. Frank, age seven, was born in a Globe hospital and was paid for by mining insurance. Helen, five, was born in Mammoth. Her birth was also paid for by mining insurance. The last two — Victorio, two, and Michael, ten months — were born in Tempe. They've paid the doctor $75 for the first but still owe the hospital for Victorio. They haven't started to pay for Michael yet.

Although the Ramirezes live next door to Augusto's mother, Margaret's own mother comes down from Superior to help her when she has her babies. Her mother keeps urging her to have no more babies because, "They're too expensive!" Margaret's oldest sister lives in Phoenix and has only two daughters. They are both married now. Margaret's own children seem healthy, with only colds and once in a while "fevers." The three older children go to the local school where they get a hot lunch for 25 cents and if they are out of money they can charge. The babies look undernourished. Margaret does her own doctoring, but if they are very sick she takes them to a doctor's clinic in Tempe. Margaret complains constantly about how much it costs to keep six children in clothes, but she never goes to second-hand sales. Augusto's mother buys things for them sometimes, and Margaret's sister in Superior sends her hand-me-downs. Margaret buys groceries in Phoenix but once in a while buys at the local village market, ". . . which is very expensive." Sometimes in the summer when there are no hauling jobs, they have to get surplus foods.

The three children in school are doing very well. Dorothy and Josephine are in the upper part of their classes. Dorothy had rated 85 on the IQ tests when they were administered the first time. Two years later she rated 115. Little Frank, big and husky and good natured like his father, brings home good report cards. The two oldest girls are learning to help with the cooking but they don't like to make tortillas. They prefer to make cakes and cookies. Margaret wishes she had more schooling so she could speak better English.

Before the intricate web of finances and family can be understood, the central character of the drama must be viewed in her proper role — father's mother. All pervading in her dominance, she is the alter ego of her son. Her place in the household of her eldest son is authoritative. Although the intensity of this role varies from family to family, it is a basic tendency in the family culture of the Old Arizona Mexican-American. The institution is self-perpetuative since the wife, in accepting a subordinate role in her own household, tends to project herself into her children. Her eldest son, especially, is made to feel his responsibility toward his mother. Their bond is a singularly close one, and it is quite natural and logical that she in turn will take her place in her son's house. After becoming widowed she will move into the eldest son's home. In the case of the Ramirez family where Mother Ramirez has four unmarried sons capable of supporting her, she simply lives next door to her eldest son, Augusto. Despite the fact that Augusto and Margaret have been married 14 years, the mother still plays a dominant role in their household. She is there on any occasion of the slightest significance. She lends her advice in all important matters.

Mother Ramirez, in contrast to Margaret, is heavy featured and strong. Down to earth and straight forward, she recounts her life, her experience and difficulties in a matter-of-fact manner. She shows the older generation pattern of deference to the supernatural by repeatedly interjecting the comment, ". . . with God's help" or ". . . with God's will." She goes to mass at the village church three times a week taking her youngest son with her when she can.

Having borne 11 children, Mrs. Ramirez is not wanting for sons. Of her six sons, only one lives away, in Superior. He is married. Besides Augusto living next door, there are Emilio, Ramon, Rudolpho, and Alejandro, all single, all living with her. Of the two remaining children living, both married daughters, one lives in Phoenix and the other lives across the street. Thus out of her eight living children, she has succeeded in keeping six at her side. Her emphasis seems always on her boys: "I can never complain about my family. My children have never given me any trouble. They are all fine *boys*. I have 24 grandchildren now. Some grandmothers complain about how their grandchildren act and what they do but I like my grandchildren. They are all good children." Her oldest single son, Emilio, is 24. He served in the Army in Europe and was offered a job away from home but Mother Ramirez says, "He chose to come home and take care of me because of my health."

In spite of Emilio's full-time job, "taking care" of his mother's household has led them deeper and deeper in debt. One by one his younger brothers have dropped their schooling. Ramon left high school at the age of 18 to work in a supermarket. Recently, when payments on the house fell far behind, they were threatened with foreclosure. Then Rudolpho, 16, the car-crazy member of the family, left high school. So far he has been unable to get anything except yard work. Alejandro, 14, is the last of Mother Ramirez' sons still in school. She makes it clear that she doesn't like the fact that her sons are leaving school, ". . . but," she gestures, "there was no choice."

The material goods that surround Mother Ramirez' household tell something of the story. They have a late model car with a $2,000 lien. Inside, a new 21-inch TV console and a new bookcase with a new set of World Book Encyclopedias is prominently displayed in the small sitting room. There are individual portraits of family, one very large and elaborately framed. Over Emilio's portrait is hung his army discharge, framed. Over the bookcase is an American Legion award given to Emilio, also framed. A used phonograph and matched divan and chair are new by Santa Teresa standards.

Augusto tries to project his own ambition into his kid brothers. He said the only reason he let Rudolpho quit school was to go to barber's school. Augusto says, "I can't get ahead much more because of my education, but my children are going to get it!" Nevertheless, like his brothers, Augusto also has a strong desire to ". . . live better, to give better things to my kids, better house, better furniture, better car." Although he seems more realistic than his brothers about debts, he spends to the limit of his income on his children. He feels that to be proud his children must have new things. Last Christmas he saved three checks to get them new clothes and new toys. At Christmas he is also obligated to give clothes and presents to his *ahijados* (godchildren).

It would be a mistake to read in Augusto's character the dependency attitudes of the older generation Mexican-American. This is evident in his attitudes toward his job. They are in obvious contrast to old Garcia's.

> The farmers should not hire braceros. They should look for people here for jobs first. I won't say these people (braceros) don't need a job, they do. But there is this thing. Local people don't want to work like slaves. Braceros work day and night if they have to. We can't compare a working man here with them. If you put me with one of them, I can do it — but they are desperate! Braceros work for five or six dollars a day. This is not enough for a local.
>
> A while back there was an old man and he couldn't keep up with the young men and they fired him. That's not right. An old man has to make a living too. I worked for a lot of companies, I know. The company won't say, 'Let's keep this old man on because he has to have a job, he's been a good worker all his life.' This will not happen. The company wants to make a profit. They say, 'For

every day you worked, we paid you.' That's not right! But a lot of things are wrong and we have to live with them.

I say we should blame the pickers a little too. If you want something better, you have to ask for it — you have to try. The pickers work harder than the drivers do and get less — why? That isn't right. When I started, I was picking. The first day I made $7.50, by five days I was top man — but I had to work! I saw the drivers and they made the same thing without working. I said to myself, 'If I can do that, I'm going to do it!'—so I kept asking the foreman. If the workers want something better, they have to push for it. When I first came to Santa Teresa, I didn't know anybody there. Now I know everybody. You have to be friendly with everybody so they can help you. The worker has to push for something for himself!

ROBERT FELIX — The differences between the Felix family and the Ramirez family — both one-vocational families — are primarily differences of degree. Both Augusto and Robert are in their mid-thirties. Both married first generation Mexican-American women with grade school educations. Both are themselves first generation Mexican-American. Both have six children of almost exactly the same ages and spacing. Although they live in different communities, the communities are basically similar in size, composition, and structure. Yet in spite of their socio-economic similarities, the Felixes' experience and the Ramirezes' experience are different. Whereas the Ramirez family are struggling to maintain their socio-economic position, the Felix family are secure in it.

Robert, born of Sonoran stock, is part Yaqui. He lived in Phoenix as a boy and his father did his share of being Jack-of-all-trades, eventually becoming a skilled tradesman in housebuilding. His family had only three children. This made it easier. They settled in Santiago, a Mexican village in the Chandler area, where he went to a rural elementary school and later to Chandler Union High School. Robert's brother dropped out of high school against his father's objections but Robert got his diploma. The same year (1950) he married a Santiago girl in the community church there.

Maria Luis was born in Chandler in 1931. Her family immigrated to the United States in the twenties. Before settling in one place, they worked in the crops. The whole family helped, Maria included. She had one brother and three sisters. Her parents divorced and her father moved to Santiago, where he remarried and still lives. She now has three more half-brothers. Her natural mother lives in California but most of the rest of her family live in Santiago. Maria progressed as far as the seventh grade in the local elementary school. It was in the Santiago School that she met Robert. They married in Santiago and have lived there ever since.

After they were married Robert worked in the harvests. For three years, when harvest season slacked off in the Salt River Valley, they migrated to California to work in tree crops — prunes and citrus, etc. In 1951 he got on as a driver for a local citrus house. This job lasted about seven months out of the year. He and Maria continued to work the summer months in California until the babies came. After five years driving for the same company, he was promoted to foreman and was given extra work in the summer to tide him over. After five years as foreman, he was made assistant field superintendent and for the last two years has been on a steady, monthly salary all year long.

Their first house in Santiago was a rented one. After three years Robert bought a two-room block house. Since then they have added two rooms and a bath. They now own their house, lot, and an extra lot free and clear. They have the standard appliances — TV, gas range, automatic washer. The living room is over-furnished with a divan and two large overstuffed chairs. Small pillows brighten the divan. There are several occasional chairs, a coffee table, and an end table with a lamp. Vases and doilies adorn the tables. The cement slab floor is covered with a large rug covered with children's toys. The family car is a 1956 sedan, well kept and paid for. Maria does all her shopping in city supermarkets, and spends all her time "keeping house and raising children." They go to city doctors and pay regular prices.

Robert Felix occupies an enviable position in his community. Unlike most of the other residents of Santiago, he has an annual income from a salaried position. Also unlike others in his community, he has the power of hiring people to fill skilled, permanent jobs coveted by most farm workers. His status is reflected in the house he lives in and the new company pickup he drives. Although his income may not average as high as the income of some of the family trucking enterprises in Santiago, it is secure. However, this security that Robert recently enjoys is linked unavoidably with a specific role that he must assume. This is a new thing for most M-A farm workers. To be sure every M-A farm worker knows he must work well, that he must follow directions, and that behavior which interferes with the performance of his duties — insubordination, rowdiness, goldbricking, or drinking, etc. — is not sanctioned. But this has little to do with his identity. Work is work, and being a father, grandfather, *padrino, compadre,* a friend, or a Mexican has little to do with it. If he is a good trimmer, a good packer, a good truck driver, a good cat-man, a liked and admired crew boss, he is proud of this. The social content of this work experience will enhance his relationships with his barracks community, his family, or his village. Nevertheless, work experience is most meaningful in a work world. A person's identity and the qualitative aspect of his personal relationships remain fundamentally separate from his job.

For Robert, this dichotomy is beginning to blur. His status in the work world is beginning to affect his participation in his community. In his role as a personnel man, he has a responsibility to the corporation that takes precedence over friend, family, and ceremonial relationships. Corporation management logic, impersonal by nature, must be practiced by him to keep his position with the company. These are antithetical to values of the rural structure of Mexican-American Santiago. This puts him on the spot. In the structure of community relationships he tries to fulfill the expectations of his friends. These take the form of requests for employment in coveted positions such as foreman and equipment operators. In the fields he is called upon to carry their grievances to the office, many of them reasonable. On the other hand, in the management structure of the corporation, being young, newly appointed, and a Mexican, with a conditioned deference to authority, he is unable to function as effectively as he might in the interests of the tightly integrated community in which he was brought up. He resolves this conflict by going out of his way to be the "good guy."

Robert says that by being friendly he will do the most good. As he says, "It is better to work with people than against them. That's one thing I learned from the boss. If I get along with the ranch foreman, then he will tell me if one of my boys slips up before he will take it to the head office."

Decisions which he has the authority to make, especially those involving his friends, he defers to higher authority. In this manner his responsibility and hence possible resentment is minimized. In addition to these, he repeatedly verbalizes his aspirations for the workers in Santiago by saying that he wants to see decent wages and ". . . take care of these boys and treat them right."

Robert's new position intrudes in the world of non-work in another sphere. As with the white collar vocational class in general, he is conscious of his behavior from the standpoint of how it will reflect upon his job. His children, down to the two-year-old toddler, are uncommonly obedient and polite. They attend church every Sunday. Robert himself is extremely active in church and civic activities. Unlike the unsophisticated Mexican-Americans, Robert articulates his aspirations in middle class terms. He wants to build a house large enough to give his boys and girls separate rooms. He expresses the determination of limiting the size of his family. He expresses the desire to move out of Santiago into a more modern community ". . . where his children will have more opportunities." At the same time he speaks of his desire to help his community. He says the priest keeps urging him to stay, saying, "If all the educated people of Santiago move out as soon as they get better jobs, how can it become any more than a slum?"

In summary, some of the values that underlie the one-vocational family are:

1. The father's responsibility is to bring a better life — material and social — to his children.
2. School is a key mechanism in this achievement.
3. A wife's place is in the home taking care of the children and stressing to the children the importance of education by reading English and paying attention to report cards.

In conflict with these are the following:

4. Traditional Mexican-American family values in terms of having many children and honoring claims of the extended family and community.
5. Class symbols without class membership — e.g. fancy automobiles and other material objects.

The Urbanized (Bi-Vocational) Family

The bi-vocational family-work institution fits the Anglo "joint income" pattern. Both husband and wife work, each in his individually suited vocation.

Children are cared for by school, nursery, or a paid baby sitter. In its application to the Mexican-American farm worker the bi-vocational family is a hypothetical institution. Generally, their norms, an essential ingredient in an institutional structure, do not stress this pattern. The coincidental pattern of a young husband and wife working in farm jobs, their young children watched by the grandmother or some other older female relative, is not the same institution. The Mexican-American value upon the mother staying in the home is too strong. Even the migratory family tends toward the wife-at-home pattern as soon as the children become old enough to work. In a sense, the M-A migratory pattern of a woman's moving to the fields and back to the home is the transition of the female from daughter of father's family to mother of her own. Also, if a M-A farm wife works in the fields, as many will do in the summer, her children will be there too if they are old enough. Nevertheless, there are indications the household role of the wife-mother is changing.

In spite of the fact that the Mexican-American plays a very important role in the farm labor systems of Arizona, the younger generation by and large want out. This is indicated by their attitudes toward their work, their experiences in nonfarm jobs, their schooling, and their aspirations. Quantitatively, this is demonstrated by a comparison of 49 M-A farm workers aged 20 and below with 191 who are 21 or older. Of 42 youths classifiable with respect to general attitude toward their vocational situation (see Chapter 12 for previous discussion of this concept), eight or 19 percent had no concept, 19 percent were positive, and 26 or *62 percent were generally negative*. Of the 173 in the older group who were classifiable, 23 or 13 percent had no concept, 95 or 55 percent were positive, and 55 or *32 percent were generally negative*. The younger M-A's show almost double the percentage in the negative category. Perhaps the most impressive fact is that only eight pre-adult workers out of 49 conveyed unambiguous approval of farm work as a vocation. This impression is supported by the job histories of the two groups. Work histories of the younger group disclose that 14 percent had worked at nonfarm jobs in the past year as compared to 27 percent of the older group. An even stronger tendency toward nonfarm work is indicated by the fact that 20 percent of the younger group had accumulated *more* time in nonfarm work than farm work in the past year, whereas only ten percent of the older M-A's showed this type of work history.

The expression of negative sentiments comes from people who, for the most part, are successful, reliable workers. The following case is an example.

Louis, 25, has worked as a harvest hand for the same company for ten years. He says that he would prefer anything to what he is doing. Because he is a member of a large family who have lived in the same community for two generations, he doesn't want to move. This, plus only an eighth grade education, limits his opportunity. He is trying to get a job working in a warehouse or a stockroom. He stresses, more than any other single factor, the unpredictability of his earnings. One week on a straight piece rate basis he may earn $24, the next week $48. Most of the loss in earnings occurs as a result of moving from field to field and having his crew used as a clean-up crew ". . . more than their share."

Pete, 19, has been working as part of a family work unit for the same company for over a year. He graduated from the eighth grade and attended high school two months before dropping out. He says that he had no choice because he had nine brothers and sisters. He is resentful about quitting school. "My teachers said I was smart. I still read a lot. I wanted to be a lawyer, but that seemed impossible, so I planned to become a barber. My family had a thousand dollars saved and I was going to use it to start, but we had to use it up last winter in El Centro when work was cut down. I have no choice. I'm probably stuck with this kind of life." Pete concedes, however, "This is the best job I've ever had because it is steady." Pete gives the following reasons for wanting something besides farm work: too unpredictable, wages not high enough, and ". . . you're liable to be fired."

Antonio, 17, had to leave school at the age of 14 to help his father support a family of 12. He and his father have worked steadily for two years for the same company. Antonio isn't mature enough to know exactly what kind of job he wants. He does know that he doesn't like farm work. He says he wants a city job, ". . . maybe a bellboy job."

Ignacio, 20 years old with a wife and two babies, progressed as far as the sixth grade. He was the oldest child in a family of 13. He was ten when he worked at his first job as a caddy. He first worked in cotton when he was 12. His father, mother, and brothers moved to Eloy from Texas three years ago. He and his bride came six months later. He and two brothers are working to support the others. He and his wife plan to return this summer to Corpus Christi where their grandparents live. Ignacio says that he is saving money for a diesel mechanic's course. He says, ". . . a man came to my house and tested me. I passed and the man said I needed $395." Ignacio likes farm work but says it doesn't pay enough. He hopes to limit his family to the two that he has now so ". . . they can finish school and have something better than I have."

Another says he likes farm work ". . . because it is all I know," but adds, "I want my kids to do something besides farm work." He cites job security and wages in that order.

Not all youngsters reject the farm industry as a place to work, but those who did cited one or more of the following aspects of agricultural labor motivating them to seek nonagricultural vocations. They are listed in the order of their frequency.

1. Irregularity:
   Irregularity of job availability and job security
   Irregularity of hours
   Irregularity of residence
2. Wages inadequate
3. Status of farm vocations inferior to other vocations
4. Physically hard

The benefit of schooling to the average farm worker is dubious. This was discussed more at length in Chapter 14 (Tables 28-31 and Table 38). Higher schooling apparently does little to enhance a worker's chances of getting a higher skilled, higher paying farm job. On the other hand, a negative relationship is indicated (Table 30) between the amount of formal education a worker has and his attitude toward his work situation. A comparison of the preadult M-A workers with the adult is one more indication of this. The preadults average 7.6 years of formal schooling as compared to 5.1 years for the latter. The fact that education is invariably offered as the *sine qua non* of social and individual improvements tends to blind us to its disorganizing aspects. As discussed in the preceding pages, the family-work unit, *compadrazgo,* community, and institutionalized dependency behavior have interdeveloped with the farm labor systems of the Southwest. Education, as it becomes more and more an integral value of the Mexican-American farm worker, acts dissolvingly upon the institutions that commit him to the rural milieu.

The impact of education upon the M-A farm worker is, if nothing else, an economic one. Required attendance has substantially reduced the potential productivity of the family-work unit. Moreover, aided by other agencies and mass media, it has weakened the traditional values which underlie the Mexican family and other communal institutions by its emphasis, implicitly and explicitly upon individualistic development. No inference is made that these processes are good or bad, only that they must be recognized before the traditional role and the shifting role of the Mexican-American in the farm labor system can be understood. Moreover, no attempt is made to imply they are unique. These are familiar and well documented processes that operate generally in the acculturation and assimilation of folk peoples by industrial society. What is not understood as well is that the farm also plays a transitional role in these processes. This will be developed in the concluding chapters. At this point we wish to stress that emerging values of today's younger generation M-A farm workers are generally in conflict with the values of their rural institutions.

Interviews with the younger women working in the fields also show changing attitudes toward their role. Although members of family work units, they show no hesitancy about showing a preference for typically urban vocations. Secretarial work, sales, nursing, and simply "working in the city" were cited. One unmarried girl working in a family unit said that she and her sister ". . . would like to get a job in town, but our parents are strict. They won't let us."

Attitudes stressing security, status, material possessions, and women working in city jobs are indications of a tendency toward new institutions. It must be kept in mind that in almost every case these youth are members of, and are still subject to, the old institutions—viz. migratory or multi-vocational families. Their attitudes toward the farm as well as their vocational experiences, their vocational aspirations, and their experiences in Anglo middle class educational institutions stress values that are at variance with these institutions. But this does not mean unequivocably that they and their children will develop institutions that are carbon copies of the urban Anglo's. More study is needed to establish this. At the same time it is argued that change in this direction is a strong possibility. Hence the bi-vocational urbanized family is hypothesized as the end result of the participation of the Mexican immigrant family in industrial agriculture.

17 Anglo-Isolate Farm Subculture

PERHAPS THE MOST colorful group to be found in the orchards and fields of Arizona's farms are the solitary oldtimers. A contradiction in concepts is suggested by such terms as *group* and *subculture* on the one hand and the terms *isolate* and *solitary* on the other. It should be emphasized at the outset that these people, as humans everywhere, interact within an identifiable framework of social organization. They are participants in a system that has its peculiar code of ethics, its norms for behavior, and its mutually recognized symbols of membership. True, they are outcasts from the more common institutions that make up American society. In this sense they are *isolates,* hence the term. But the loner, fruit tramp, wino, alcoholic, hobo, bum, or whatever he may be called, in his isolation forms his peculiar organization. It may be a society that is unrecognized by so-called respectable society. It may be largely clandestine in its operation. Nevertheless, it provides for its membership the essential services that a social being requires. Therefore, the term isolate refers to their being isolated, voluntarily or involuntarily, from more integrated institutions in their past lives. But it does not mean they do not belong to any institution at all.

Another misconception is that only Anglos fit this pattern. There are Negroes, Indians, Filipinos, and even Mexican-Americans who fall in this pattern. Nevertheless, our data show the majority of isolates in Arizona farm work are Anglo. One hundred forty-one or 56 percent of the 253 isolates in our sample were Anglo. This is more than all other ethnic groups combined. Numerically the Anglo-isolate group is second only to the Mexican-American group in size. The Anglo-isolates are analyzed as a distinct group for two reasons. They comprise quantitatively a major segment of the work force. Also, isolates of other ethnic groups interact first as Negroes, Filipinos, etc., and second as isolates. Another generalization that must be qualified is that all who make up this work segment are alcoholics. It is not possible within the framework of this study to determine precisely the number of workers who are or have been alcoholics. It is clearly recognizable as a tendency among many Anglo-isolates, however. With others it is simply not known. Many single, middle-aged White males who perform agricultural harvest labor undoubtedly have never had this problem. Moreover, with or without a drinking problem, the Anglo-isolate continues to play an economically important role in industrial agriculture.

THE CHARACTERISTICS OF THE ANGLO-ISOLATE

Unlike Mexican-Americans, Negroes, Indians, and Filipinos, this group does not have a well defined geographical-cultural locus. On the contrary, reported states of origin covered 36 different states. The southern states, including Oklahoma, Arkansas and Texas, are represented in greater proportion than any other region, however. Sixty-two or 44 percent reported home states that fall in this area. Oklahoma was cited more frequently than any other single state with 18 or 13 percent reporting. Arizona was cited as the home state of only five A-I workers.

The A-I worker tends to be older and more highly educated than the other groups. One hundred and one, or 72 percent, are above the age of 40, and 40 percent are above the age of 50. Their mean years of school completed is 8.8, with 26 percent reporting a high school or college education.

Sixty, or 43 percent, almost half, although working at the time of their interview, reported spending a major segment of the previous year drifting or unemployed. Seventy-four percent had a harvest hand pattern either as most or second most time spent. Past vocational histories of these men, however, disclose that less than a third of them had farm vocations. Forty-seven, or 33 percent of them, had been engaged in skilled or semiskilled occupations.

The industries represented by 29 skilled workers are as follows:

Mining	6
Petroleum production	6
Construction	5
Machine shop	4
Miscellaneous	8

The occupations of parents for these 141 men showed that a majority, 68 or 48 percent, were farmers. The next largest group, 33 or 23 percent, had (nonfarm) skilled occupations.

Finally, 54 percent of them were ex-servicemen, 58 percent were ex-union members, 84 percent claimed no church affiliation whatever or were inactive, and 54 percent rejected their present job situations. Most of the latter maintained that they were in harvest work only temporarily and were planning to take up their old or similar vocation as soon as they could. Significantly 45 percent accepted or were resigned to the type of work they were doing.

THE SOCIETY OF THE ANGLO-ISOLATE

"Everyone here has something wrong with their past." This statement by a fruit picker foreman underscores the basic premise of those who deal with the A-I. No doubt an overgeneralization, it nevertheless serves as the proper prerequisite for successful relations between a foreman and Anglo-isolates. Actually many foremen who deal with them have similar social backgrounds and are considered by the A-I's to be one of them.

One foreman, T. C., who has been using essentially the same crew for over seven years knows every individual member of his crew:

> These guys work year after year, just show up when the season starts at Thompson's corner. Some draw Social Security. They ain't able to work all the time. When these old guys go we are going to have trouble getting pickers. The younger guys don't want to work in it.

According to T. C.:

> All these guys are running away from their wives. There's old Jake. He gets drunk every night on one or two fifths of wine but he'll always come to work the next day. Sometimes he will go two or three weeks without drinking and then he'll drink every night.
>
> His wife up and divorced him, told the judge he was an alcoholic. The judge threw him in the jug for thirty days and said, 'We'll see!' Old Jake said, 'I just had me a good rest.' At the end of thirty days the judge said, 'Hell, he ain't no alcoholic.' Jake said, 'I went on down to the corner and got drunker 'n hell!'

T. C. tells about another picker called Wild Bill. T. C. says the welfare people are after him because his children are supposed to be left in the care of his brother and sister, but his father, 70 years old, came and picked them up. T. C. says that Wild Bill's wife died in 1954, ". . . he liked to went off his rocker."

T. C. pointed to an old man and said:

> I've been trying to get old Harry there to apply for Social Security. Hell, he can't pick more than one of those boxes (bins) in a day. If he carries a ladder a city block he'd have to sit down and get his breath for 30 minutes. I don't see how he makes it. Hell, he only makes 17 dollars a week, his rent costs him 20 to 30 dollars a month — he's got asthma and arthritis. He finally went down to apply for Social Security the other day and they told him it would take six months and he would have to go get a doctor's exam and fill out papers and all that ___. He picks all day on one set. We may leave him behind a half a mile and I'll go back and see how he's getting along — if he needs any boxes or anything like that. I wouldn't keep him on if he was a wine-head or something like that. He don't make me nor the company no money, but ___, a fella hates to put a poor old sonofabitch like that on the mercy of the world.

T. C. talks about their information network:

> We have a starting date on the grapefruit around the first of October. About one out of a hundred will call me and then word goes from one to the other and they will start coming in out of Washington. About half will be here when we start and half come in later. They've got a grapevine system out of this world — there ain't a dozen guys will call all over this valley but everyone of them knows almost to the day when we are starting. Some years there ain't one call but they will drive or ride right on down to Thompson's corner the day I start. I had 11 the first day I went to work this season. I didn't have a single call. Some came in early. Some came in the day I started, and some a few days after I started.

Turner Jones is a foreman who, his pickers say, has a past. Turner, who runs a 35-man crew for a large citrus operation, prides himself on being a sharp recruiter. Turner claims he never uses state employment offices because the real pro fruit picker knows where the jobs are by the grapevine, which operates around the skid row areas of the big agricultural centers:

> . . . all of the transients come there. Any fruit or vegetable city has this. In Stockton they have their area where the professional fruit tramps come in — onion toppers, broccoli cutters. There it isn't all spread out like in Phoenix. In Chelan the same deal. These guys know where to go in each town.

Turner says that people who can't get work use the employment offices and adds:

> . . . There's about as much difference between a man looking for a job and a real picker as there is between an accountant and a farmer. It would be like bringing a bunch of school kids out here and trying to learn them a man's job — this ain't no college!
> In order for me to hire a new man, if I do have a seat open for him, he'd have to look like a fruit picker and I'd have to get somebody's OK. These guys on the bus will say, 'There's so-and-so; he's from Stockton.' I go by what my men say. These guys are professional, they're transients. If I don't know a guy or none of my men knows him, then he has to look like a picker, then I'd try him.

Turner says that he can tell a picker in the following manner:

> If a man walks up to you in working clothes and talks about the trade — just as soon as he picks up his ladder I can tell if he is a picker or not. Last Sunday I hired a couple of cowboys. They wanted me to give them a chance. I said, 'You won't last.' The first thing I know he is butting his head through the ladder and carrying it like a yoke. Well, it might be easier for him, but it's stupid! —A picker knows what he is doing and how to handle the ladder, take care of the trees, and keep from getting hurt, and he stays with the job.

Although the consensus among those foremen and employers who use strictly the grapevine-skid-row system is that "professionals" *never* use the state employment offices, this in fact is not true. One large company which relies heavily upon the employment office reports that although there is this tendency of the professionals to avoid the employment office, about a third of their men who come through the office would fall in this category. Furthermore, out of the 141 A-I's, almost two-thirds reported using a state employment office in the past year. Had employment histories gone further back than one year, undoubtedly a still higher proportion would have shown such a pattern. What this consensus reflects more than anything is a stable relationship between individual workers and employers. Secondly, owing to the social pasts of this type of worker, he will naturally tend to use informal systems so long as they are effective in maintaining an equilibrium between him and his employers. If they are not, he more than likely will turn to employment offices, if not in one time and place, then in another.

One difficulty in making generalizations about fruit tramps or Anglo-isolates is that the ephemeral and informal nature of their organizations defy delimitation. Its boundaries for investigator and participant alike rely unavoidably upon individual experience. Most A-I's interviewed had worked at some time in fruit crops. Ninety or 64 percent had worked in fruit harvests within the previous year alone. Because of the changes taking place in fruit industries and fruit pickers themselves, many of them are working in crops they have never worked in before, such as cotton. Of the 90 who had worked in fruit crops the year previous, 64 percent were employed in other activities also.

Be this as it may, Anglo-isolates have certain common traits: their social past, the tendency to migrate on regular routes year after year, the habit of picking up a buddy, living and moving in trios, and interacting in a wider network of standardized relationships in their migration. The migratory routes of these workers generally tend toward the Northwest in the hotter months and the desert areas of California and Arizona in the winter months. Ordinarily they return to the same towns, the same skid row areas, and the same residences. Many work for the same employers year after year. A surprising regularity of interaction is achieved in this fashion. If a buddy does not meet another in their old rendezvous — a certain bar, cafe, or street corner — an account of his whereabouts and latest experiences will most likely be carried by a mutual acquaintance. Dramatic episodes of another's exploits, especially those with which the social outcast can identify, are repeated by word of mouth from bar to cot-hut. They metamorphose in time into a kind of oral tradition. In this manner contact of a personal nature is maintained over a period of years. The inner workings of Anglo-isolate social and value systems are more specifically detailed in the following biographical sketch.

THE WORLD OF CHARLEY TATUM

The Setting

Thompson's Corner is the hub of Charley's world. The intersection of two main southside streets inadvertently serves to divide the locality into four distinct areas. The center of the most intense activity is the Jobber's Cafe on the southwest corner. A continuous stream of humanity enters, leaves, and re-enters the swinging doors. The aroma of steaming coffees lining a thirty-foot counter, the hill-billy rhythm of "Beautiful Brown Eyes," the pretty waitress in skin-tight cowboy pants, the constant "hi's" of familiarity, the hawk-eyed cashier-bouncer looking down from his elevated podium mingle in an atmosphere of raw friendliness. The cemented ramp in front of the cafe is the pickup area for the fruit harvest foremen. Crews, foremen, and hopefuls exchange scuttlebutt in the predawn hours. This is the territory of the elite of the harvest stream.

Surrounding and directly across from the Jobber's Cafe is the fresh foods market where the dime-begging down-and-outer can usually get a half-hour job unloading refrigerated vans, enough to get another fifth of Tokay. Diagonal from the Cafe is a dimly lit hotel advertising rooms for $2.50. Directly across from the cafe on the north side of the street is the Gospel Rescue Mission where revivals, soup, and cots are provided the desperate, the bottom of the bottom. Across the street from the mission, west of the Jobber's Cafe, is the pit of the jungle. Here in almost complete darkness is situated the Worker's Liquor Store. Inside, stacked in two piles as high as a man can reach are cartons of wine, all one brand of California Tokay. Outside, in the darkened wings of the sidewalk, standing, slumped, and prone are the winos. In front of it, bumper to bumper nine or ten deep, are the broken-down buses of the cotton picking and onion topping contractors who, unlike the fruit foremen, openly solicit drunks.

In the early morning hours the action begins at Thompson's Corner:

Workers are lined up twenty to thirty deep in a line that extends from the liquor store cash register backward through the door to a spot somewhere in the dark sidewalk. The register is ringing as rapidly as the clerk can take 50 cents and a nickel from the bearer, ring it up, close the drawer, and hold his hand out for the next. A stream of traffic pours out the door, on to the buses, some workers wrapping fifths inside their dirty, tattered cotton sack; others stuffing them inside the pockets of their dirty, tattered jackets. Outside crew leaders are pacing up and down the walk competing for members. One keeps shouting, 'Straight pullin' boys, two and a quarter, pay you every sack, free coffee in the field! You might as well ride a new bus!'

Almost all the workers in the vicinity of the liquor store are in various stages of drunkenness. In two's and three's they mingle, unmix and remingle, some grabbing cigarette butts that others discard, some trying to get someone to listen to a story, not noticing when a listener meanders away. One fellow keeps a half coherent outpouring going, half to himself, half to a glazed-eyed Indian: 'There I was frozen right on the trigger, goddam — I shot a lot of guys — I only had a machine gun, what did they want me to do? —only a corporal — you know the 25th lost its stripes — we couldn't even run those North Koreans out. I was a POW — while I was in camp a little old lady came in on her knees right in front of me and prayed for me — you can't close yourself to anything! ____ gi' me a drag!'

Not far from these two is a man in his late twenties wearing a long black overcoat with a blood-spattered shirt. Half doped, but chuckling and grinning, he keeps telling two of his buddies about some guy trying to roll him, and that he got the better of him and rolled him for his shoes and overcoat. He keeps saying over and over 'That ____ wanted to jack roll me—I jack rolled him!'

Farther up toward the cafe, the drunks thin out. There a tall, skinny man in plaster-bleached denim overalls is trying to sell a shiny new can opener to everyone that he can stop. A little old man turns to another and starts complaining about all the bums walking up and down trying to beg from 'us working guys'. And he doesn't see why, if a guy was going to beg, that he wouldn't go to the other side of town. The skinny man walks into the cafe finally, to try pawning his can opener there. He no sooner gets into the door than the cashier-bouncer hurls himself off his podium, and in two bounds reaches the skinny man, seizes him by the nape of the neck, bodily propels him out the door, all the while clubbing him with a black jack and saying, 'You son-of-a-bitch, when I tell you to get out of here that's what I mean!' As the bouncer turns back into the door another man, also begging outside, walks in the door. The bouncer, still in a state of excitement, starts clubbing him yelling the same thing. Outside, the skinny man picks himself up with his hat cocked and hair disheveled, starts shaking his fist at the cashier through the window, and cursing him. He walks over to the curb, spits, walks back, shakes his fist at the bouncer and curses him some more, all the while explaining to everyone that if the cafe man would come on the other side of the street that he would '. . . beat the ___ out of him!' The second man who had stumbled inadvertently into the middle of a black jack clubbing, now in a state of manic excitement, is running around blurting out to everyone, 'Did ya see that! Did ya see that! He came after me with a club!'

Several crews by now have already been loaded, the fruit crews from the cafe end of the block and the cotton and onion crews from the dark end of the block. Turner Jones, one of the last foremen to finish his coffee in the cafe, walks out to his bus, carries on an informal interviewing session with several hopefuls. An old citrus picker vouches for one. Turner tells him he'll put him on tomorrow, and turns the others away. Turner, missing two of his regulars, asks the pickers where old Harry and Charley are. One of the pickers says they are sick. Turner starts his motor, closes his door, and heads for the groves.

No sooner is he out of sight, than Charley pokes his head out of a darkened doorway and says, 'Has he left yet?' meaning Turner. Charley explains that he didn't want to go to work today and that he was going to take the day off.

Home

Less than a mile from Thompson's Corner, in a section of town that has block after block of skid row housing, Charley lives in a place called Julia's Court. The cabins are a jerry-built mixture of stucco and wood. Most are the one-room variety in various stages of dilapidation. Most of them are out of square somewhere — either where one wall meets another or where the walls meet the cement slabs on which they are built. The owner-manager lives in a large house off to the edge of the court and runs her court from a heavily padlocked and chain-guarded door with a peep hole about the size of a small orange.

Two signs are prominently displayed close to the central toilets and shower. One reads:

> Mrs. Nary said if you use
> dirty swear words and talk
> loud so as to disturb the
> other tenants you will have
> to move.

The second sign reads:

> Warning, no women in these
> rooms at night or else you
> will have to move out, if
> caught. Orders from the
> owner of the court.

Charley's cabin, number 32, sits just off to the east of the shower rooms. It is just wide enough to accommodate the length of a cot. Its length is about equal to two cots placed end to end. Inside is a narrow cot with a bare mattress covered by a dirty, ragged chenille spread. There is a slipless pillow black with dirt. The floor is covered with worn-out linoleum showing the cement in places. In the corner, to the right of the door, is a tiny sink with one cold water tap, a tiny linoleum-covered counter, and two small shelves overhead. On the counter is an open flame cooking top that doubles for heating and cooking. There is also one very small refrigerator. On the counter are several blackened pots, one with congealed corn meal mush. Overhead are opened cans and dried-out food packages. On the floor is a scattering of soiled clothing, a cardboard trash box filled to the top with empty pint California Tokay wine bottles, and an old tomato can that Charley uses for a spittoon.

The Past

Charley picked his first apples when he was 15 years old. He was born in Franklin, North Carolina, and came from a family of nine children. His father was a farmer and had 127 acres of corn and wheat and 250 acres of mountain land. The first experience he can remember was being sent over to his Uncle Edward's place where they were boiling syrup. After he had been there a while his Uncle said, "You have a (new) pretty baby brother."

He said that his dad gave each of the kids a piece of ground to farm on his own. He got 90 acres and farmed wheat, and before his wheat was harvested he was offered $3 a bushel "from some guy that was buying up crops." He turned it down. At this time he was 13 years old. He said right after that the bottom dropped out and he had to take it down to the mill where he got $1.75. His dad always thought this taught him a lesson.

He went to school to the ninth grade and had to walk four miles to school. In school they did not allow boys and girls to sit together. Charley went back to work on a problem with a girl and the teacher went back and brought 15 of them up to the stage and whipped them in front of the whole class. Charley said:

> I walked right back to the girl's seat and said, 'I'm going to finish this problem' and she said, 'I'm going to keep you after school.' After school she took me to the library and I said, 'This is one time you are not going to whip me.' She said she would expel me and went home with me. My father said, 'I'll spank him when you do.' She never spanked me. She said, 'I'll expel him,' and father said, 'You can't, he's under age.' Next year she was elected prin-

cipal again and I quit. Dad didn't like it and said I'd always be sorry. I have been.

After school Charley went to work for a farmer at a dollar a day. Shortly after his brother and sister-in-law came from Atlanta and Charley told his father he wanted to live with them. His father responded, "Don't send for no money. I'll give you two days to come home." Recalling this Charley said, "I told him, 'I'll take two years.' — I did. I came home two years later in a car."

Charley served an apprenticeship in machinist school for $18.55 a week and did this for four years. He said he became a journeyman machinist. This was in 1925. In 1928 he took up carpentry work. Between the time he got out of apprentice school and started carpentry he married. That was in 1926. He remained married for 17 years. He had three children, two boys and one daughter who died recently. His oldest boy has worked in the post office for 19 years. His other boy is a garage mechanic in Cincinnati. Charley's wife divorced him in 1942. She has since remarried.

When asked why the divorce, he pointed to the half-empty wine bottle in his hand and said:

> . . . same as this. She kept telling me, 'When the kids get through school I'm leaving you.' When my daughter graduated from high school my wife said, 'This is it.' Jimmy, my oldest boy, once asked her if she made a mistake, and she said, 'No, I stuck by my word.' But one thing she will admit, I always supported her. She had a father who was an alcoholic — I never saw him drunk, but he'd drink it every day. She hated it. That's what got my wife's goat— her people thought so much of me she always hated it.

Charley worked 11 years for the Tennesse Valley Authority as a master mechanic and had at one time averaged $400 a month. His family stayed at Elizabeth, Tennessee. He was still working for TVA when his wife divorced him. Because Charley contested it, it took her two years to get it. Her grounds were mental cruelty. She got $40 a month. She didn't get more because the children took his side and threatened to live with their father. Charley added:

> When my daughter died and we went to the funeral, my wife told her mother at the funeral, 'You can't beat Charles; he's beat me out of everything.' Her mother said, 'You should never have left him,' right in front of her husband. I ain't braggin'; I used to be up in the money. I ain't got ___ now! I will say this — I've always got a place to go home to — that's Atlanta, Georgia. My sis owns her own home, and works in Georgia Tech School as a telephone operator. She's working until she's sixty-seven so she can get a full pension. I've got a room there that I've got suits hangin' in, but I'm not goin' back for three years. I'm just like her, I just want to be as stubborn as she is. She's stubborn trying to get me to come and stay with her at her home. She thinks the world of me but I want to stay independent. To tell you the truth, I don't want her to know I _____ up. You won't believe this but I can walk into a bank in Atlanta and borrow a hundred dollars just on my name. In Spokane last year I was sick and called her and she sent me a bus ticket, but I have never used it.

Although Charley had obliquely admitted that his drinking had been the cause of his wife's leaving him, he implied that it never interfered with his work until *after* the divorce. He insisted that the divorce was the cause of its becoming a problem. It began to interfere while he was still at TVA. By 1947 he was all washed up at TVA. He moved to Detroit where he worked for a big van line as a furniture loader for $2.10 an hour. This job lasted two years. He went back to Atlanta where he bought a truck and started hauling produce. He hauled a little over a year and returned to the van line in Detroit where, by this time, he was reduced to working odd jobs only, part time. After this, in the fifties, he started the fruit harvest route and has been in it ever since. He said he started eight years ago in Chelan, Washington in apples. He has hit Chelan every season since.

From Chelan or Okanagan picking fall apples, he goes to Indio topping carrots or Phoenix for citrus in the winter. In early spring he hits Portland for strawberries, Washington for thinning apples, and sometimes Stockton. In July and August he moves to Eugene, picking beans and cherries, and in the fall, Chelan or Okanagan for apple picking again. He generally hops a freight. Some years Charley goes to Florida and he added, "Generally, where I wind up is according to how drunk I get."

Charley lives in Julia's Courts with Harry and Joe. Three days ago, Turner had fired Joe because he caught him with a bottle in the field. The three of them had been on a lost weekend since the day Joe had been fired. Harry, who had been friends with Joe for years, was especially upset about Joe's being fired.

He kept repeating, "Turner wouldn't hire Joe back again — once he fires a guy he'll never take him back." Half belligerently Harry continually referred to Joe as ". . . the best goddam mechanic in the whole _____' state! His arthritis keeps him from working — that's how he got started drinkin'."

Charley said, referring to Turner, "He's _____ up too, ya know, that's what I understand from the guys who know him in Stockton. He's a damn good foreman, but he'll show up drunk one of these days."

Harry jerked his elbow back, and slammed it into Charley's chest, "Whada ya mean one of these days! He was drunk last Sunday, and I know goddam good and well he was drunk Monday!"

GENERAL ATTITUDES AND VALUES

With or without the alcoholic pattern, Anglo-isolates share certain basic features in common. One general theme which invariably runs through their conversation and dialogues, both with strangers and friends, is the issue of failure. This might be termed *the demise focus*. It is the basis of their acceptance of consorts, leveling their enemies, and their compulsion to defend. Among friends this is the badge of recognition and identity. One of the most significant things to be known about another is that he fouled up somewhere along the line. Interpersonal understanding often begins with this premise.

The knowledge of failure in another's past is an important means of feeling adequate to deal with him, especially if he is in a status position. In conflict situations — as in the case of Charley, Joe, and Harry vs. Turner, the foreman — it is used to get even, if not actually, at least psychologically.

The demise focus plays an important role in their patterns of compensation. These compensations take a number of forms. A-I's have a tendency to stress the high status they may have enjoyed in the past and to disassociate themselves from their present occupational situation. This is a constant theme. Statements such as "I was the best damn overhead crane operator in the business!" or "I laid more goddam pipe for El Paso than anybody!" are common. In connection with this before-the-fall emphasis, many are quick to point out that it was an accident, an industrial injury, or wife desertion that led to their demise. A lettuce worker from Texas said he was a roughneck in Odessa for years, but that his wife died in 1949, ". . . and I came out and began drinking." He said that he broke his arm while roughnecking and had to be laid off. He feels that the company would take him back but ". . . I've just never done it." An ex-body and fender man, 50 but a very alert and youthful looking man, now spreading boxes on a lettuce crew, said that he had a throat tumor removed by surgery. He emphasized that his doctor told him to stay away from auto painting for 18 months to prevent irritation. He commented:

> . . . I'm just about ready to go back — I'd rather die in a body shop (chuckle). I miss that eight hours and a coffee break — I guess I'm lazy (chuckle). Body work is the only thing I know. If I hadn't gone into this I probably would have gone to college. My father set me up in a body shop — Once in a while I go looking for a dish-washing job — this (spreading boxes) I consider scraping the bottom of the barrel, but it's better than nothing — (But adding later) — It isn't a living, it's an existence! This way you have to live the way they want you to live, not the way you want to live — there is no protection at all in this work, no pay for waiting-around time for harvest. Sometimes the crews may wait as long as five hours total, waiting for the lettuce to thaw and things like that. This is a national disgrace! They should pay a living wage. The only thing that ever ruined farm work is greed!

Compensation is often achieved by stressing their association with well-known and successful people or the esteem in which they are held by an organization which is the epitome of social respectability, such as a bank, or a well-known firm. One A-I speaks of bygone days and his association with a millionaire:

> Old Johnson — there's a guy for you. ___, worth seventy million dollars, a Mexican drivin' his Cadillac, rentin' a suite of rooms in the Westward Ho for twenty-five dollars a night — a hundred and fifty dollar suit, a seventy-five dollar silk hat, and a goddam sack of Bull Durham hangin' out of his pocket! His old lady drove her own car — she'd drive right up on the construction job and sit down at board with us men — truck drivers, jackhammer

men, and blasters — and eat pork chops and steak right along with the rest of us!

Another form of compensation is the tendency to make a cult of themselves, to express the attitude that others who have not experienced their peculiar kind of social failure are just babes in the woods. This was evidenced in statements some of the foremen make about fruit tramps. One such foreman compares braceros and fruit tramps:

> A National isn't a fruit picker. It's all right if you're stripping —when you have to grade they're no good. Take a bunch of fruit pickers and a bunch of Nationals and that's it — they (Nationals) just can't cut her! As far as hard work is concerned, they are able to do equivalent if not more than locals — locals have more goddam sense!

Another expression of the old-timer's kind of independence is expressed by a 57-year-old cotton chopper who, working by the row, was just standing around with a belligerent look on his face puffing on a pipe, "If I job (hoe) one round and if I don't git back in an hour, I quit. The hell with it!" This old man estimated that at 25 cents a row, which he was getting paid, he was making about 45 cents an hour.

Finally there is the compensation in the form of a hope based on the long shot. This is shown by references to "I'm just waiting to hear from (such and such) company to start back to work." Or "I'm just going to make one more season around, then I'm going to go into business with a buddy of mine." Another manifestation of this is apparent in the stories of tramps who make the long shot. Informants who give such accounts enjoy telling of them almost as much as stories about clever tramps who outfoxed the local cops. One informant tells of a fellow who got his big break in the fruit business by hauling a load of watermelons to Alaska by boat during the forties. When he got there he sold them for a dollar to a dollar and a half a pound. Others make statements such as, "You know old (well-to-do grower)? Hell, I knew him when he was packin' lettuce right along with the Mexicans!"

SUMMARY OF VALUES

In summary some of the values which underlie Anglo-isolate institutions are as follows:

1. The value of self respect. This is a very tender spot with the A-I. It plays a decisive role in his occupational and interpersonal relations.
2. The value of independence. The privilege of withdrawal is an important adaptive practice. In its more extreme form it is a regressive tendency whereby self respect can be salvaged.
3. The value of anonymity. This is relative. It is sought after more in some social situations than others.

The Anglo-isolate farm worker tends to stress informal institutions as described earlier — the grapevine, street corner, back-of-the-barracks kind of society. Interaction with formal structures, whether church, welfare agencies, employment offices, or management tends to be superficial and utilitarian. His attitudes toward Mexican Nationals, wages, and working conditions are outgrowths of these values. Generally they feel that wages are too low, the use of Nationals is unfair, and they favor informally organized technologies that rely upon face-to-face relationships.

How Anglo-isolate systems interact with specific kinds of farm systems will be discussed in more detail in the concluding chapters.

18 Negro Farm Subculture

THE NEGRO SAMPLE (75) is smaller and correspondingly fewer generalizations can be made. Nevertheless, drawing upon data of the senior author accumulated over a five-year period pertaining to these groups (see Padfield 1961), much can be said that could not otherwise be substantiated.

GENERAL CHARACTERISTICS

The Isolate/Aggregate Dichotomy

Negro farm workers show a dichotomy similar to that of Anglo farm workers. Forty-seven of the 75 are isolates. A brief examination of some characteristics of the Negro-isolate, however, discloses fundamental differences between Negro and Anglo isolates. First the Negro-isolates are a younger group with a mean age of 42.6 years as compared to 46 years for the A-I. The former show 55 percent above the age of 40 and only 25 percent above the age of 50. This is opposed to the A-I's 72 percent and 40 percent respectively.

In addition, differences in levels of formal schooling appear between the two groups. A-I's have a mean a year higher—showing 8.8 to the N-I's 7.8. This difference in skill factors is further illustrated by the occupational backgrounds of the two groups. Both the N-I and the A-I show a singular lack of farm success in their 1962-1963 job patterns—N-I show four percent and A-I nine percent in skilled farm jobs; N-I show 34 percent and A-I 27 percent with a drifting and unemployed pattern. However, past occupational patterns of the Negro-isolate cluster in the semiskilled and unskilled categories whereas the A-I group shows the highest concentration in the skilled and semiskilled categories. In addition, general observation, depth interview, and impressionistic data indicate a much higher incidence of alcoholism among the A-I farm workers than among the Negro group.

The strongest evidence that the two groups are different comes from the fact that the isolate/aggregate dichotomy is a meaningful social differentiation among the Anglos. Among the Negro farm workers it is, for the most part, meaningless. Just a few comparisons will serve to illustrate:

Characteristic	Anglo Isolate	Anglo Aggregate	Negro Isolate	Negro Aggregate
Mean Age	46	36.4	42.6	40.6
Farm skilled	9%	47%	9%	7%
Drifting and unemployed	27%	8%	34%	21%
Attitude job situation neg.	69%	44%	60%	68%
Number of cases	128	85	47	28

Lack of farm success, the high degree of job diversity in their occupational histories, and attitude toward their present vocational situations—indices which serve to differentiate the isolate from the aggregate among the Anglo group—serve as points of similarity between the Negro-isolate and Negro-aggregate farm worker. Actually, owing to the characteristic of family instability generally applicable to Negro farm workers as a whole, isolate and aggregate are categories within which an individual falls as much by the accident of circumstance as by social-psychological differences. This will be developed more fully in the discussions to follow.

Occupational Diversity

The overriding question with the Negro farm worker, isolate or aggregate, is not so much a question of his desire to become integrated into the urban-industrial segment of Anglo society as it is the question of *how* he is going about it. Forty-seven or 64 percent of 73 classifiable informants expressed a decided preference for urban occupations (see Table 13). These sentiments are substantiated by the extreme occupational diversity of the sample. Fifty or two-thirds reported nonfarm jobs of one sort or another in their 1962-1963 work histories. Moreover, past occupational histories disclose 18 workers in farm occupations, 45 workers engaged in nonfarm occupations, one unemployed, and 11 in school. Of the 64 employable workers (leaving out the 11 pupils), 70 percent had relatively stable nonfarm occupational histories.

Further support for this view is furnished by a study conducted in 1959-1960 (Padfield 1961) involving occupational studies of 50 Negro farm worker families and 53 Anglo farm worker families. Findings indicated (p. 6) that 75 percent of the male heads of Negro families had a year or more of continuous work experience in nonfarm jobs. Also, 64 percent (p. 7) indicated aspirations for urban jobs.

Working Wives and Family Organization

Peculiar features of the Negro family lend themselves to this pattern of occupational diversity and mobility. One feature suggested by our data is that Negro wives show quite the opposite tendency found among rural Mexican-Americans. Of 29 heads of families interviewed, 21 either were working mothers or male heads who reported having working wives. Interview schedules from Padfield's 1959-1960 survey show that 33 or 66 percent of 50 female heads of household worked.

Another characteristic which stands out among the Negro sample is the loosely integrated family. Not counting the isolates, most of whom reported being divorced or separated, over half of the 29 heads of families reported being divorced, separated, or living in free union. This pattern which makes for large, informal, and casually related families is further substantiated by data collected by Padfield among Arizona Negro farm workers over a period of years.

None of the outstanding characteristics indicated by these data are new. All are long established in the historical-cultural context of the rural South, of which the Arizona Negro farm worker is a part.

CULTURAL INFLUENCES OF THE RURAL SOUTH

Fifty-two or almost 70 percent of the 75 Negro informants declared themselves emigrants from Southern states. Forty-six or 63 percent had parents who were farm wage workers, tenant farmers, or sharecroppers in the South (see Table 9). Padfield's 1959-60 survey revealed an even higher incidence of Southern rural ties among Arizona Negro farm workers. Out of 100 adult male and female heads of households, 87 percent reported themselves from Mississippi, Arkansas, Oklahoma, and Texas in that order. In addition 73 percent of these 100 household heads had strong rural backgrounds in terms of sharecropping parents (Padfield 1961: 5-6).

Arnold Rose in *The Negro in America* with data from 1944, documents Negro population and migration trends through World War II (1961: 55-67). He cites two peak periods. The first substantial movements began with what he refers to as "The Great Migration" starting in 1915. The proportion of all Negroes living in the North and West rose from 10.4 percent in 1910 to 23.8 percent in 1940. This amounted to a net emigration of approximately 1,750,000 from the South. A second impetus came during World War II. Negroes did not begin to migrate to the West until the late twenties and early thirties. This coincided with the ravages of the Boll Weevil which swept across the Cotton Belt from 1910 through the 1920's (Rose 1961: 84). Commenting further on the possibility of an increase in Negro migration to the West, Rose says,

> There has now been established a new pattern — migration to the West. While this is strictly in the realm of prophecy, it may be that the growth of Negro settlements in the large Western cities may mean the establishment of a new path of migration — from the South to the West (p. 67).

Arizona shows an increase in its Negro population of 8,005 in 1920 to 43,403 in 1960. More significant is the recent rate of increase. Whereas increments from 1920 to 1930 and 1930 to 1940 were 34 percent and 39 percent respectively, percentage increases from 1940 to 1950 and 1950 to 1960 were in the seventies (USDC 1960: 4-17). As brought out in Chapter 5, the Boll Weevil catastrophe helped the spread of cotton farming in Arizona and other states of the Southwest. This catastrophe may have operated in double fashion to increase Negro migration to Arizona—first, by the severe depression in cotton labor demand in the Cotton Belt; and second, by the sharp increase in cotton labor demand in Arizona as cotton acreage rose.

Victor Perlo, in a more recent study (1953), cites the trend among the the young rural Negro of the South to emigrate. Citing South Carolina as a case in point, he says that three-fifths of the Anglos and two-thirds of the Negroes left the farm, but of those leaving, only 20 percent of the Anglos emigrated from the state as compared to 90 percent of the Negroes (p. 19).

Not all of the Negro population movements have been emigrant movements. Much population shifting occurs from farm to city. This, however, has not benefited the Negro economically and occupationally as much as Anglos. Caught between farm mechanization on the one hand, and occupational discrimination in the cities and towns on the other, Negro movement between farm and city degenerates into a form of unstable oscillation (Rose 1961: 64; Perlo 1953; 18-19).

Although Perlo's data were compiled in the early fifties, they indicated even at that time that an increasing percentage of farm Negroes were acquiring nonfarm occupational experiences. Some of these, termed "worker-farmers," are small independent (as opposed to sharecrop) farmers who augment their meager farm incomes by city wage work. This group accounted for about one-seventh of the rural Negroes in the Carolinas, Georgia, Alabama, Louisiana, and Mississippi (1953: 62). Perlo provides a further breakdown of this group showing 22 percent working as industrial craftsmen, three percent as white collar, and 73 percent as unskilled workers—viz. road construction, lumbering, and domestic service (p. 105). In addition to the worker-farmers, a larger group which Perlo refers to as "farm wage laborers" made up about a third of the rural Negro population (pp. 60-62). The migratory pattern of this segment (p. 78) undoubtedly exposed many to nonfarm (albeit unskilled) wage labor experience. Our purpose here is not to discuss the plight of the Southern rural Negro. It is to establish precedent for the pattern of occupational instability and oscillation between farm and nonfarm industries exhibited by the rural Southern Negroes who have migrated to Arizona.

Historical continuities appear in other characteristics. Family-work institutions of the Arizona Farm Negro resemble slave and cropper institutions. Rose, discussing the rural Southern Negro family, has this to say:

> The uniqueness of the Negro family is a product of slavery. Most slave owners either did not care about the marital state of their slaves or were interested in seeing to it that they did not form

strong marital bonds. Certain practices grew up in slavery which retain their influence today in rural Southern areas: marriages sometimes occur by simple public declaration or with a ceremony conducted by a minister but without a marriage license. Coupled with this was the popular belief that divorce could occur by public declaration or simply by crossing state or county lines. At the close of the Civil War the slave states legalized existing common-law marriages and, with the disappearance of the master's interests and of forced sale, there was a great increase in family stability. But the starting point was so low that Negroes never caught up. Isolation, poverty, and ignorance were again the obstacles to raising standards (1961: 294-295).

While hastening to add that upper and middle-class Negroes probably have fewer extramarital relations and less divorce than upper-class Whites, Rose, citing 1944 figures, says that for the United States as a whole, the number of illegitimate births among Negroes is eight and one-half times the number among Whites. Lodgers and "one person" families (isolates) made up about ten percent of the Negro population as opposed to five percent among Whites. Broken families were 28 percent and 12 percent respectively (pp. 295–296).

In reality cross-ethnic comparisons of this sort are misleading. Whereas among middle-class Whites, rates of illegitimacy and divorce are valid indices of institutional disintegration, among the rural Negro they are indicators of institutional norms. They are cited here not for the purpose of measuring the extent to which Negroes measure up to standards of middle-class White morality, but to contrast the rural Negro family institution, at least in its historical context, with family institutions of other rural populations. Norms cannot be lifted out of their institutional context, nor can participants in one institution be evaluated by standards for behavior of participants in another. The rural Negro family as an institution differs from the middle-class Anglo family, the rural Mexican-American family, and the Indian family. These differences help to understand the peculiar character of the Negro experience in Arizona farm industries.

Rose, emphasizing the counter-balancing integrative (normative) aspects of the Negro family, says:

> While the Negro masses undoubtedly have more of all those characteristics which define family disorganization in the traditional American sense, they have certain other cultural traits which tend to reduce the disorganizing effect of those characteristics. One is marriage for almost all, and a high rate of remarriage for divorcees and widowed persons. Futher, common-law marriage and illegitimacy are not seriously condemned within the Negro community—except among the upper classes — and they have, therefore, fewer disorganizing effects on the individual. The Negro community also has the healthy social custom of attaching no stigma to the illegitimate child and of freely adopting illegitimate children and orphans into established families. A high value is placed on children generally, and those who mate outside of marriage do not usually

prevent the coming of children. There are few unwanted children (1961: 296).

John Dollard, in *Caste and Class in a Southern Town*, provides a comprehensive analysis of the adaptive features of Negro family behavior (1937: 390–433). Although he does not discuss the family as an institution *per se*, he stresses the interrelationships of its norms with the caste institutions of the rural South. He concludes the chapter, "Gains of the Lower-Class Negroes," with this statement which has pertinence to the Negro farm worker in Arizona:

> Of course, the behavior patterns of lower-class Negroes could not be standardized as an independent culture; it is very doubtful if any culture could survive when its members were permitted so much direct and dependent gratification. A reader of these pages has suggested that the American Negro has much more personal freedom than is possible in a primitive society and that at the same time he gets some benefit from our modern technology. It is in this sense that one may speak of the lower-class Negro culture as parasitic; the Negro is able to indulge extraordinary impulse freedom at the expense of the nervous energy and moral renunciation of the White upper classes. Negro habits of life could not survive in an independent competing society.
>
> It remains to be stressed that the dominant aim of our (U.S.) society seems to be to middle-class-ify all of its members. Negroes, including lower-class Negroes, are no exceptions. Eventually they must all enter the competition for higher status which is so basic and compulsive an element in our way of life. This will mean giving up their "gains" and approximating more nearly the ideal of restraint, independence, and personal maturity which is implicitly attached to our demands for individual competition and mobility (pp. 432-433).

Although we do not agree with Dollard's suggestion that an independent culture could not survive with such patterns of sexual freedom (Oceania and Africa itself furnish us with many examples), his focus upon the interdependent aspect of this behavior is a meaningful vantage point from which to view the rural Negro family. This loosely integrated institution interlocks with a way of life that is passing. It bespeaks a role which the emerging Negro himself rejects. Nevertheless, its norms linger with the Negro in farm occupations and along with its disadvantages continues to provide certain advantages that Arizona farm Negroes by and large are putting to use.

The working wife is another common trait among the Southern rural Negro. A Mississippi State College Agricultural Experiment Station survey of 292 farm families consisting of 728 members aged 14 years or older states that 53 percent of the Negro labor supply were females. In fact, 50 or 17 percent of the 292 family heads were women. Among the 226 "homemakers" (wives) included in the sample, only 13 or less than nine percent did not report working. Of 111 female offspring 14 years and older, only 15 or 14 percent fell in the no-work category (1949: 9–10).

Rose extends this characteristic beyond simply the rural Negro and points out that in the nonfarm areas as well the employment of Negro women exceeds that of Whites. Commenting on the "race" (cultural) differences he says:

> These race differences in employment are the result of two opposing factors. One is that the extreme poverty of most Negro families forces Negro women as well as Negro boys and aged Negro men on the labor market to a much greater extent than among Whites. On the other hand, among both men and women who 'are in the labor market' the proportion of those who fail to get any jobs is much higher for Negroes than for Whites. There is often a causal relation between these two factors. A Negro woman may take a job because her husband is without one. On the other hand, if the employment situation is discouraging, some of the workers, particularly if they have secured public assistance, and especially if they are getting old, will tend to leave the labor market permanently (1961: 105-106).

These two characteristics which the rural Southern Negro family and the Arizona Farm Negro family tend to share in common—working homemakers or wife-mothers and a loosely integrated structure — contribute to the farm Negro's occupational mobility. This will be further developed in the case profiles to follow.

ARIZONA FARM NEGRO PROFILES

MARY FOSTER — Mary Foster was born in Jackson, Mississippi in 1905. Her father was a worker in a rural sawmill. Her parents separated soon after she was born and Mary was raised in her mother's house. She was still a child when her mother died. At 16, in the seventh grade, she quit school to help her grandmother support the family. Her grandmother worked as a domestic servant in private homes. She sent Mary to work on an uncle's tenant farm where she picked and chopped cotton.

Mary had two illegitimate children before her first marriage in 1933. In 1942 she took a steady job as a maid in a private home in Memphis. This job lasted until 1956. In 1944 her first husband died and with eight children—two illegitimate and six by her first husband—she married again in 1952. She and her second husband, William Foster, migrated to Eloy in 1957 where they have lived and worked since, principally in cotton chopping and picking. They had originally intended to pick only one season in Eloy, but their car broke down, they both got sick, and they have been "stranded" there ever since. For the last two years they have occupied a one-room shack in an obsolete farm camp. They work for the owner chopping and picking less than six months out of the year. A married daughter and her husband chop and pick for the same company.

Mary, now 58, knows that next season, except for ends and corners, the company plans to pick all acreage by machine. When asked what preparations she and her husband are making she answered, "It looks like we're stuck here." She added, "My husband is getting too old to work — he's suffering from a foot injury — I guess we'll try soon to get some help (welfare)."

ELMA WILKINS — Elma Wilkins illustrates another type of occupational adaptation. Elma was born in Tulsa, Oklahoma in 1936. At 11 her family moved to New Mexico where she began chopping and picking with her family at the age of 12. She graduated from high school but continued to work as a seasonal cotton hand. The same year she graduated, 1953, she married. In 1955 she and her husband migrated to work in the cotton harvests in the Casa Grande Valley. Later her husband obtained a mechanic's job in Coolidge. This job, in combination with her job house cleaning and ironing in private homes and chopping and picking cotton in season, enabled them to rent a five-room house with plumbing and electricity in the Coolidge area.

Now, however, according to Elma, her husband is not working. With four children, they receive surplus foods regularly, but no welfare payments. Her husband is trying to find another mechanic's job but she says, ". . . these jobs are hard to find." He refuses to chop in the fields meanwhile because he has a "disability."

LOUELLA WIRTZ — Louella Wirtz, now 40, has 15 living children, 11 still dependent. All were born since 1939, the year of her first and only marriage. She was born on her father's sharecrop farm in Houston County, Texas. She first went to work at the age of eight helping in the chopping and picking. At 16 and in the ninth grade she quit school to help her parents support the family of nine children. In 1939 she married a sharecropper. Her chopping and picking continued on her husband's farm. In 1946 they moved to New Mexico where her husband worked in the stockyards. In 1947 her husband hired on as a section hand for Southern Pacific. He has been working for Southern Pacific ever since. They moved to Eloy in 1956, her husband still with the railroad. In 1957 Louella started chopping and picking in the fields around Eloy. Alternating seasonally with housecleaning jobs she has continued to augment their income in this fashion ever since. This she has done in spite of having 15 babies in 24 years. They now own a six-room house with modern facilities in the Negro section of Eloy.

Although Mr. Wirtz has worked his way up to a track line machine operator, Louella wishes he could find a job that would keep him more at home. She feels that he should be paid more. With his $350 a month plus the money that she, a daughter, and a son make chopping and picking, she estimates they earn a combined total of $5400. Divided among 13 this comes to a per capita income of $415. Louella proudly states that her husband has two sisters who graduated from college. She wants to send her children through college.

ALVIN TURNER — Alvin Turner was born in a farm wage laborer's family in Trinidad, Texas. Now 45, Alvin has been through four marriages, and is presently "living" with a common-law wife. His first marriage lasted a little over seven years. He has two grown children from this marriage. The second marriage lasted three to four months, the third seven years, and the fourth three months. He has been living with his present companion, who has eight children of her own, for three years. Although he refers to this woman as his common-law wife, they do not actually keep house together. Alvin rents a two-room apartment in Yuma and she and her eight children live separately in their own house. She "visits" him regularly and he "helps support" her, although she also has a job and a meager but independent income.

Alvin's occupational history is as diverse as his marital experiences. He has no formal vocational training and only three years of schooling. At the present time he is working as a windrower for a lettuce company. This job he obtained through the local state employment office. During the cotton season he drives a bus for a local contractor and works for the same employer as a cement finisher and general construction hand other times of the year. He has worked for this contractor in the Yuma area for the last three years. Prior to this he worked in the sawmills in Northern Arizona for 22 years. He operated a lift truck. During the slack months he worked as a laborer in yard cleanup. His early years in lumber work were interrupted by military service in the Army from 1942 to 1945.

Alvin is one of the few Negro workers who expressed a desire to remain in farm work. He said that he would like to establish himself as a machine operator.

THOMAS HOLMES — An altogether different situation is that of Thomas Holmes. Tom, 57, illiterate, wizened, and gray-haired, looks seventy. He was born in Galveston, Texas. He has a wife and three children in New Orleans, where he had a laborer's job in a rice mill for six years from 1949 to 1955. Tom's father worked at a variety of laboring jobs on the docks of Galveston and alternated with door-to-door wood and ice peddling. In similar fashion Tom has worked all his life at anything and everything he can get. His last year's employment history runs as follows. Prior to spray-padding for a Yuma lettuce company, he picked cotton six weeks for a local contractor. This was preceded by four months of employment for a carnival show in Fontana, California as a general handyman. Prior to this he worked for three months as a "hide shaker" in a Fresno slaughter house. He also worked in cotton chopping and peach picking in Fresno. With the exception of his present job, which he obtained through the employment office, he obtained all his jobs ". . . just standing on corners and getting picked up."

Tom, although technically employed at the time of his interview, was not working because he had broken his leg the week before and was partially immobilized with a plaster cast up to his knee. He said—and others in the barracks with him agreed—that he had tried for four days after his leg was broken to get the foreman of the lettuce company to take him to the doctor. Each day when the foreman drove the company bus in to pick up his crew he would tell him "tomorrow." This continued for four days without any attention. Finally Holmes got to the doctor on his own.

When asked what kind of work he thought he had the best chance of keeping, he said the one job he liked the best was hide shaking in a meat packing plant. He said he would keep trying to get work there because it's hard to keep people on that job. It is because this is one of the least desirable jobs that Tom felt that he stood a chance of getting it — ". . . because no one else wants it."

STANLEY BROWN — At the age of 38, with a Bachelor of Science Degree from Wayne University in Detroit, Stanley Brown is folding boxes on a stitcher truck. His father was a machinist for a railroad. When Stanley graduated in 1952, he began as a public relations man for a razor manufacturing company. This job lasted nine months. His next job was that of an auto mechanic. This lasted for five years. Since 1959 he has been in seasonal farm work. He has had his present job, obtained through the state employment office, one week. Although divorced, Brown insists that he helps support his ex-wife and two children. He offers no explanation for his past but when pressed vents a bitter shotgun blast of general protest:

> . . . You're a hero today and a tramp tomorrow! This country is a _____' mess — when you're in the service and drink wine, you're a hero — and get out and drink it and you're a tramp! They let their own people starve and then bring in these people (braceros)! — Hell, what else can you do? They run you out of town — they run you off the rails — hell, what can you do except hit the bread line! That's it!

SUMMARY OF VALUES

In summary some of the values which underlie the Arizona Farm Negro are:

1. The value of a loosely integrated and highly mobile family-work institution.
2. The value of social and occupational versatility and mobility.
3. The value of working homemakers or female heads of households. This is partly a concomitant of the loosely integrated family, partly a concomitant of social and occupational versatility and mobility resulting from economic necessity and occupational prejudice.
4. The value of rural life is largely negative. The industrial farm is an occupational episode, albeit a recurring one, in the rural Negro's emigration from the South.

19 Indian Farm Subculture

THE SAMPLE of 53 Indian farm workers breaks down as follows:

> 38 Pima-Papagos
> 7 Yaquis
> 3 Apaches
> 5 Miscellaneous

Eight tribal cultures are represented. Owing to this fact and the small size of the sample, it is not appropriate or pertinent to discuss differences and similarities in the cultural backgrounds of these eight tribes. In the course of the quantitative descriptions in Part Three, certain characteristics emerged which were generally applicable to all Indian farm workers in the sample. They rank lowest in skills in past occupational histories (Tables 8 and 9), per capita income, and other material indices (Tables 23, 24, and 25). Also, as with Mexican-American farm workers, the Indian family is an important work institution. Three-fourths of them (Table 11) had a family residence pattern and two-thirds of them work as families. Dominating Indian interaction with farm employment, however, is one structural feature that is entirely absent among the Mexican-American or any group — the reservation.

THE PULL OF THE RESERVATION

Considering all forms of interaction with reservation society, ties of one form or another emerge in the case histories of nearly every Indian (Yaquis are excepted because they do not have a reservation). This is to be expected. The reservation is his ancestral home. It is the scene of activities that reinforce tribal identity. It is the residence of family relations. It is the administrative channel whereby he receives health and welfare assistance. It is a buffer between him and the Anglo world. Moreover, for many the reservation is the location of small-scale commercial agriculture or stock raising. For others, communal fields serve as a last-ditch source for household staples. Reservation geography and society are a *known* factor. The non-reservation world is an unknown factor.

Opposed to this are the economic entanglements of the Indian in the Anglo world which create in him an increasing demand for its material goods, and therefore an increasing demand for money (see Dobyns 1950: 76-78). Claude Smith, a 23-year-old Papago, illustrates the conflict that in some degree confronts every reservation Indian.

CLAUDE SMITH — Claude was born in the village of San Miguel in Chukut Kuk, the southernmost district of the Papago Reservation. His father raised corn, wheat, beans, and melons on their small flood plain farm. He also participated in communal cattle raising. During the early forties, after Claude was born, his father moved "permanently" off the reservation to live on a large farm in the Sahuarita-Continental area where he worked as a general laborer. Now Claude's father is too old to work. He has moved back to the reservation where he lives with his daughter in a village close to Topawa in the Baboquivari District.

In 1949 Claude's father and mother separated. Claude moved to Tucson to live with a sister. He attended a Catholic elementary school. In 1953 his sister and her husband, José, moved to Eloy to be nearer the cotton harvests. José's home village was Santa Rosa. His family lived alternately in the Eloy area during the cotton season and in the village during the winter and spring. Claude graduated from the eighth grade in Eloy, but his sister's family could not afford to keep him in high school in Eloy. At this point Claude made an important decision to move to Phoenix Indian School. With his academic courses, Claude received training in auto mechanics and the operation of farm equipment. He credits two jobs he has held since to this vocational training. One is a past job in a Los Angeles canning factory. The second, which he had at the time of his interview, is a tractor-driving job on an Eloy farm.

Claude graduated from the Phoenix Indian School in 1960, and immediately joined the Indian Service's relocation program. He reported to the agency headquarters in Los Angeles where he was boarded in a hotel until he got a job. He soon got on at a canning factory where his job ". . . was to keep the machines running." He worked for this factory for two years during which time he had five layoffs. The first four layoffs lasted only a few weeks or a month at the most. The last layoff lasted seven months. Claude was eventually forced in January 1962 to return to live with his sister's family in Santa Rosa and the Jackson farm south of Eloy. Jackson gave Claude a cabin and started him on equipment operation. Claude has been working continuously for Jackson ever since. Claude said that he was able to start immediately operating power equipment because he had learned all the essential operations at the Phoenix Indian School.

During his participation in the relocation program, Claude met his wife, a full-blooded Hopi girl, also a relocatee. Although Mary had graduated from the Phoenix Indian School the same year as he, Claude did not know her until he met her in an Indian Agency office in Los Angeles. They were married in 1961 by a Justice of the Peace in a small town out of Los Angeles. Mary worked in an appliance factory in Los Angeles and was laid off at about the same time as Claude. Since returning to the Jackson farm, they have had a marriage blessing by a visiting Catholic priest at Friendly Corners, a tiny community 11 miles south of Eloy.

Mary had a baby after their return to Eloy. At the age of 13 months the baby died. Claude had no idea as to the cause. It was born Caesarean, but it was healthy. Claude said:

> One day it started shaking. The doctor in Eloy gave it a shot. Then we came home and bathed it in cold water and alcohol — then it just had convulsions and died. We buried it on the reservation at Komolik with its grandmother because the godfather wanted it. My wife wanted this, too. Jackson gave me a pickup to take it and bought a coffin to take, so I think a great deal about him. My wife didn't get over it for six months. She still cries once in a while. We are afraid to have another baby because of Caesarean birth. She misses her reservation badly — especially her mother. Her mother wants her to come back for a visit.

Claude still visits his (Papago) reservation. Just three weeks ago he went to the Cinco de Mayo festival. Although his sentiments toward his present job are obviously positive, Claude doesn't think that he will stay in farm work—"I think I'd rather work in a factory. I don't like life in the city better but that's where the money comes from—even though your expenses are more, granted. There's nothing anyone can do on the reservation—all the people are moving away to the farms." When asked why he preferred factory work to farm work, he mentioned the ten-hour working day, working Saturday and Sunday, and the pay as factors. He added:

> . . . you live better with a city job — much better. My wife wants a factory job, too. She doesn't want to work in the cotton fields. Last year she tried to chop but said it hurt her feet to walk the rows. Indian boys in Los Angeles say its too far and they get lonely, but I went to the YMCA and got me a card and played basketball and I didn't even get lonely or anything — that's what kept me from getting in trouble.

Asked about training and qualifications for factory work, Claude answered:

> I'm not worried because you get special training courses at these factories — and even if I can't I'm not worried because I know I can get additional training through relocation or on my own. Over there at the employment office in L.A. they ask if you want to go to school for training — and even if I can't, I know enough to get a job — I can always get something — even an usher job.

Among many tribes including the Papago, seasonal oscillation between reservation and off-reservation labor is not recent. This pattern in itself does not indicate the degree of conflict Claude and Mary experienced. Papagos working for hire in harvest activities is recorded as long ago as 1740 and by the middle 1800's the pattern of dual seasonal residence was firmly established:

> In lean years among the desert Papago the bulk of the harvesting on Pima farms was done by the Papago, and the custom of such labor for hire was continued until quite recent times. However, desert Papagos almost invariably returned to their homes later as it was very rarely that these Indians lived outside their own village except by intermarriage. In ancient times the Pima usually

had a rather large and dependable crop, but Pima agriculture was given a strong stimulus beginning with gold rush days in the fifties and by the eighties the increased penetration of Whites created a demand for crop production on a commercial basis. Thus the Papago almost abandoned the Northern part of their desert territory to work for the Pima during wheat harvest on the Gila. This was always a great boon to the Papago for whom this time was the leanest part of the year. Here they remained for about a month, a fourth of which was spent trading and cutting willow for making baskets. For their labor the Papagos were given daily food and a share of the crop. Although May and June, the time of wheat harvest, constituted the period of greatest Papago movement to the Gila, some of these Indians returned in late fall to assist in planting, and to pick cotton (Castetter and Bell 1942: 46-47).

Of ten Indians 50 years or older, five of them remember their fathers' working part of the time off the reservation, three reported that their fathers did not work, and two could not recall.

Pablo Antone, a 50-year-old Papago with a 20-year history of oscillating between the same village and the same cotton farm, illustrates the traditionalism of this pattern.

PABLO ANTONE — Pablo was born in 1913 in one of the more traditional northern Papago villages. His father raised cattle and horses on village range land and corn, beans, and melons on the family plot. Pablo never attended school except for one brief period when, as a boy, he was sent away by the Indian Service to a boarding school at Fort Mohave. He ran away one month later. He was never taken away again after that. He continued to help his father farm on the reservation. To this day he neither speaks nor reads English.

As far back as Pablo can remember drouth was a constant problem. In the thirties, after his father died, he obtained some relief working as a construction laborer on government-sponsored flood-control and road-building projects on the Papago Reservation. During World War II, after these projects ceased and when labor shortages among farmers began to be felt, a grower by the name of Wheeler who had a cotton farm adjacent to the reservation came to his village in an effort to recruit workers. Pablo went to work for him and has worked for him every season since. Pablo has never desired to operate equipment and is therefore limited to general hand labor—chopping, picking, irrigating, fence mending, ditching, and hand planting. He works about nine months for Wheeler during which time he lives on the farm. The remaining three months he lives in his home village on the reservation.

Pablo's participation in village society is not limited to the three months he resides there. Wheeler, having worked Papagos for over 20 years, has grown accustomed to their periodic departures to fulfill family and ceremonial obligations. Pablo occupies the ceremonial role of runner or messenger for his village. One of his prescribed duties, among others not discussed here, is to inform the village of certain ritual events that are about to take place during their traditional August Rain (Sahuaro Wine) ceremony. During the past year, in addition to the Rain ceremony, he participated in the San Juan's Day celebration, the Cinco de Mayo festival, the annual pilgrimage to Magdalena (Mexico), the Christmas feast, and two marriage feasts. Most recently, just a few days prior to his interview, he interrupted his work on Wheeler's farm to "help bury" his village's ceremonial leader, "the Keeper of the Smoke." Pablo, commenting on this event, said maybe this year they would not have their August Rain ceremony because the Keeper of the Smoke is dead. Pablo is also a Roman Catholic and attends weekly mass while on the reservation.

Pablo is single. He lives with his sister and brother-in-law and her two sons. This sister, her two boys, and another sister work for Wheeler during chopping and picking season. His brother-in-law works for a farm neighboring Wheeler's. He also has a brother who works and lives in Casa Grande. Pablo helps support one of his nephews. Commenting on his 20 years of working on the Wheeler farm, he says he likes this work ". . . because this is the only work I know how to do. I can't go (work) home because there is nothing to do — except when I am old enough to get old age money."

JOSÉ — A number of older Indians show similar patterns. José, a 64-year-old Papago from the same village as Pablo and also working for Wheeler, reports that his first recollection of working off the reservation for wages goes back to the early thirties when he and his father worked on farms in the Chandler area cleaning ditches and picking cotton. Picking cotton was the first off-reservation farm job he or his father had done. Up to this time his family subsisted entirely on reservation flood-farming, hunting, and gathering. In the later thirties he worked on reservation construction projects and during the war came to work for Wheeler a year or two before the Antone family. José, also maintaining a farm/reservation residence pattern, limits his work for Wheeler to chopping and picking. This occupies him, his wife, and one daughter from the latter part of May to January. In January they return to their village where they remain until cotton-chopping time again in May.

José has had no schooling and does not speak or read English. His two children have received schooling. One daughter is still going to school and his son, a graduate of Phoenix Indian School, is now on a relocation program. José says he doesn't like his boy to go away—he wants him to have a job close.

RESERVATION RESIDENCE AND OCCUPATIONAL ADJUSTMENT

Approximately 18 of the Indian farm workers interviewed had this dual or reservation-hub residence pattern. This is not the only method of staying on the reservation, however. Some reservations and some villages on reservations are close enough to farms to permit daily commuting.

Approximately ten Indian farm workers, mostly Pimas, could be classed in this category. This makes a total of 28 or a little better than half who were maintaining reservation residences either by commuting, oscillating, or migrating and returning to their home villages at least once a year.

In spite of the general desire among these Indians to stay on their reservations, the basic limitations of reservation economics combined with technological changes in their traditional "helper" occupations are putting them in an ever tightening squeeze. Alternatives are limited. In order to remain within the sphere of reservation society, its demands must necessarily come first. This is hardly compatible with occupational mobility. The more specialized a worker becomes — which is necessary for him to maintain a role in mechanized and automated industries — the more formalized and rigid are the demands placed upon him. Those Indian farm workers who are unable or unwilling to respond to this must necessarily find themselves farther and farther on the periphery of labor-reducing technologies. Given these conditions, the worker must seek a wider range of tasks that can supply him his needed supplemental income while still permitting him participational flexibility. Another alternative is to commit himself more deeply to those industries that lie closest to his reservation — farming, mining, etc. — and achieve a certain degree of occupational mobility in this manner.

Of course, if an Indian *is* willing to leave the reservation, he can make himself available for occupational specialization regardless of the geographic location — a more extreme form of occupational mobility.

Thus reservation Indians can seek more and more diverse marginal and obsolete occupations, become occupationally mobile in industries that exist on or close to their reservations, or relocate.

Occupational Diversity

This term applies to the following work patterns:
1. Working at very different jobs for the same employer—e.g. hand harvest, irrigating, and equipment operation.
2. Moving from employer to employer without regularity.
3. Working for a few months at a time off the reservation for wages, then working at some form of subsistence activity on the reservation for a few months.

At least 35 or about two-thirds of the Indian farm workers in our sample could be determined as having this pattern.

A good example of occupational and subsistence diversity is the case of a 21-year-old Pima living in Casa Blanca village. As of June 1963 he was hired as an irrigator for a thousand-acre cotton farm adjacent to the Pima Reservation. In May of that year he harvested his family's 20 acres of barley which they farm on a government allotment program. During April and part of May he also did some cotton chopping with an independent chopping crew. Between February and March he broke wild horses at $15 a head. Between October, 1962 and January, 1963 he picked cotton for an independent contractor. Between June and September, 1962 he broke horses. In May of that year he chopped cotton and worked his family's 20-acre allotment. He was able to live at home during all of these jobs.

He has received no vocational training of any kind and has only an eighth grade education. He likes what he is doing and has no plans to change. When asked why he liked to irrigate he answered, "Just because I learned it when I got out of school." He had never heard of relocation and when asked why he thought it was ". . . more better in the country" he thought a long time and answered, "I don't know how to work in town."

Occupational Mobility in Farm Industry

As indicated in Tables 8 and 27, no Indians in the sample of 53 were engaged in skilled farm occupations 10 to 15 years ago. Now ten occupy this category. An example of occupational mobility in the farm industry is provided by Pancho Listo, a 52-year-old Papago. Pancho was born in the village of Kom Vo in the Pisinimo district. His father subsistence-farmed and raised cattle. He never worked off the reservation that Pancho can remember. Fifteen years ago, Pancho picked his first sack of cotton. For six years he continued to live on the reservation in late winter and spring and to pick cotton in Stanfield during the harvest season. He worked on the same farm each season—the Bob Williams farm, a large cotton company in the Stanfield area. After the first season Pancho, in addition to picking cotton, started irrigating. Time spent on the reservation began to decrease as the degree of involvement in farm jobs began to increase. When the irrigating season passed, he began operating power equipment. Six years later (nine years ago) he was hired as irrigator foreman. At this time Pancho said he moved "permanently" off the reservation. Nevertheless he still occasionally visits his brothers who live in the family house. Last year he spent one month at his family's reservation home.

Pancho has a wife and nine children. He receives a salary of $100 a week, and the use of a company pickup and a three-room house with modern facilities.

Relocation

Relocation training was a subject with which most of the Indian farm workers were not familiar. The question in most instances had to be posed in general descriptive terms rather than using simply the name relocation. The informant's sentiments were then judged in terms of being favorable or unfavorable toward relocation. Of the 46 Indians to whom relocation programs would pertain, barely half found the concept of vocation or specialized training remotely meaningful. Of these 23 Indian farm workers 12 could be classed (on the basis of verbal behavior alone, of course) as favorable. One notable example is Claude Smith discussed earlier. Another 22-year-old Pima Indian said that he had been accepted for relocation training but was unable to report because he was serving a 30-day jail sentence for drinking and disturbing the peace. Since getting out he has not re-applied. He is tired of irrigating because ". . . it is too hard and does not pay enough."

A 56-year-old Papago cannot find a better job now than chopping, although he worked six years for one large farm in the Marana area operating machine pickers and cultivators. He and his wife, nearly 60, tramp the rows together. He has been living in an obsolete farm camp for a year but plans to go back to Pisinimo this year. He said, "I've been looking for machine work, but I can't find it anymore. My feet are kind of hard this year." He was familiar with relocation and said that he was too old, ". . . but I might send my boy down."

A 31-year-old Apache now working as a hand laborer in the lettuce harvests said that he had tried to get into the relocation program but they turned him down. He seems bewildered about this as well as his dealings with his present employer. He had his hand chewed up on an automatic carton stapler and was supposed to get $98 in compensation, but so far has received only $48. He has no idea how to go about looking into the matter. His father and mother died when he was a child. He had to drop out of school after the third grade to help his grandmother support him. The only other type of work he has done is handyman on a ranch on the San Carlos reservation. He is single, alone, and confused.

Another young Apache, also a lettuce harvest hand, had a relocation job in Chicago, but his wife got sick from continually eating potato chips with soft drinks and wanted to move back to the reservation at San Carlos. He is working in Yuma alone and his wife is living with her mother and father on the reservation. She does not want to leave her home again. He is trying now to save his money to give relocation another try in Los Angeles. He has a tenth grade education, vocational training in carpentry, and relocation training and experience working in an electronics factory.

Among the negative sentiments expressed about relocation were remarks that living expenses are too high. One 28-year-old Pima, a Korean War veteran commuting from his reservation home to work as an irrigator said, "A lotta guys say it's OK until they give you a job then drop you and you have to look for another job — you're better off at home. I never have tried relocation — I don't want to try. Even though I have no job, I'm home. I'd have to give up the job I've got, to go, then lose that job — then where am I?" One young Indian insisted that he didn't want relocation because a tribal judge advised him against it. Another, a 20-year-old Papago, now irrigating, had spent four years in a relocation program in Riverside, California. He had been assigned a job as a painter's helper while he attended night school. One day he turned up at home in Sells. He seemed at a loss to explain why. His only answer was, "I just came back to see my parents and I didn't go back again."

The Incomprehensibility of the Non-Reservation World

More significant than the enumeration of sentiments for or against relocation is the fact that to most Indians in the sample the concept was entirely foreign. To a lesser degree this was true even of those who could articulate the appropriate verbal symbols *vis-a-vis* the question. No frame of social reality is available to the reservation-reared and reservation-oriented Indian for the relocation experience. The parroting of generalized statements communicated by word of mouth cannot be taken as a reliable or valid indication of his preparedness to undertake or to assimilate the relocation experience. To a White protestant middle-class Arizona farm boy, accommodation to an industrial metropolis is hardly simple. To a dark-skinned Indian boy with an accent, whose parents still on occasion dance around in pagan paraphernalia, the road from his mud hut and ocotillo ramada to the roaring freeways of Los Angeles is not as direct as it seems — the friendly boys at the YMCA, as Claude says, notwithstanding.

The incomprehensibility of the non-reservation world to the Indian farm worker is evident by his inappropriate response. A 38-year-old Pima had this to say about his irrigating job and his future plans:

> I don't think I'm goin' stay here (irrigating) — I'm goin' quit. I like it here but there's work to be done at home. I think I'm goin' put in maize and build me another home. (Asked how he was going to make a living) — when I quit? Haaa — the same — chop wood. But I think I might come back when I finish over there (reservation). I'm goin' ask Alex (the farm foreman) if I can do that.

The informant had the expression of being forced to think about very profound things which he had never really thought about before. When asked why he liked the reservation he looked in utter disbelief, broke into a great toothy laugh and said, "That's my place!"

A 43-year-old cotton chopper said he would want a city job, ". . . but I don't know it." Another chopper, 38, said that he wanted relocation but when asked why he didn't go said, ". . . because I am doing everything at my home." Pressed further, he responded, "I don't want to leave reservation exactly—once in a while I want to come back."

By no means is this type of response limited to the older or illiterate Indian. Typical are the following: A 21-year-old Pima, an eighth grade graduate with a wife and two children, has had a steady tractor driving job on a farm just off the Pima Reservation for over a year. He said he was having trouble living on his wages alone. He reasoned further and said, ". . . but I don't know what to do—sometimes I think about leaving and going to live in the city." When asked what he would do there he answered, "I don't know — look for a job somewhere."

A 19-year-old Papago, an eighth grade graduate operating a caterpillar tractor, said he had applied for relocation training but had backed out at the last minute. The best explanation he could give was, "I just think I couldn't do it or something."

Perhaps it would be more truthful to say that to these Indians the matter of relocation is an inappropriate question.

In the final analysis, given the strongest of motivations to make the urban adjustment, the Indian farm worker, as the rural Negro, finds himself compelled to fall back at unpredictable intervals to the baseboard of farm wage work.

SUMMARY OF VALUES

In summary some of the values which underlie the work institutions of the Arizona Indian farm worker are:

1. The value of tribal membership.
2. Lacking this, the value of staying in contact with reservation society.

In conflict with these are the following:

3. The value of survival.
4. The value placed on the material goods of the Anglo world.

The conflict is partially resolved by occupational and subsistence diversity or by limited occupational mobility — limited in the sense of confining his vocational aspirations to those industries adjacent to or on his reservation, or by entering and withdrawing periodically from industries in more distant areas.

20 The Viewpoints of Management

THE INSTITUTION OF PRIVATE OWNERSHIP

PERHAPS THE HARDEST THINGS to see are the institutions to which we have become accustomed. We can more easily abstract the elements of exotic institutions or those which we contact infrequently. The familiar, geared by our own unanalytical participation, insulated by a shroud of rationalizations, tends to blind us to its workings. One of the commonest institutions in which middle and upper class Anglo-Americans are enmeshed is the institution of private property. We are at a disadvantage here because it is romanticized on every hand. But we must disenchant ourselves in order to see how it operates. As with the other institutions we have discussed, it is necessary to analyze the institution of private ownership to see the values which determine farm management's behavior toward farm labor groups and government agencies. As in the analysis of Anglo-Isolate, Mexican-American, Negro, and Indian farm work groups, recurring values will be found to be fundamental in the attitudes and behavior of Farm Management. Let us look at the "firm" as an institution.

Profit Maximization

The Theory of the Firm as outlined in Chapter 6, is an adaptation to the particular institution we have to work with—the privately owned farm. This is a type of institution. Profit maximization is its norm. Chapter 6 gives a model analysis of the application of this norm. It is a system of logic, a formula which takes as its base the norm, the necessity, or need for profit maximization. It is necessary to maximize profits in order to maintain ownership. To *own* competitively *is* to maximize profits. Beginning here with the particular firm we have to work with − the farm − the theory of the firm projects the economic behavior of the institutional membership which will result first by altering one set of variables and then another. Remaining constant throughout is the norm of profit maximization and the institution it perpetuates—private property.

For the purposes of sociological analysis and economic projection, our institution could just as well be state ownership or cooperative ownership. If it were, then other norms would apply and our model of the theory of the firm would not fit.

Control of Access to the Instruments of Production

As fundamental to ownership as profit maximization is *control*. In order to own, it is necessary to maximize profits; in order to maximize profits, it is necessary to control. James Burnham furnishes a vivid concise development of this principle in *The Managerial Revolution:*

> . . . The truth is that, whatever its legal merits, the concept of 'the separation of ownership and control' has no sociological or historical meaning. Ownership means *control;* if there is no control, then there is no ownership. The central aspects of the control which is ownership, are, as we have seen, control over access to the object in question and preferential treatment in the distribution of its products. If ownership and control are in reality separated, then ownership has changed hands to the 'control,' and the separated ownership is a meaningless fiction. . . .
>
> This is perfectly obvious as soon as we think about it. If I own a house, let us say, that means that — at least under normal circumstances — I can prevent others from entering it. In developed societies with political institutions, it means also that the state (the police in this instance, backed by the courts) will if necessary enforce this control of mine over access to the house. If I cannot, when I wish to, prevent others from entering the house, if anyone else or everyone has the same rights of entry as I, then neither I nor anyone would say that I am the "owner" of the house. . . . Moreover, insofar as there are products of the house (warmth, shelter, privacy might be so considered, as well as rent) I, as owner, am, by the very fact of control over access in this case, entitled to preferential treatment in receiving these products.
>
> Where the object owned takes the form of instruments of production (factories, machines, mines, railroads . . .) the situation is the same, only more complicated. For sociological and practical purposes, the owner (or owners) of the instruments of production is the one (or group) that in *fact* — whether or not in theory and words — controls access to those instruments and controls preferential treatment in the distribution of their products (Burnham 1941: 92-93).

Of the two conditions necessary to the ownership of property, Burnham maintains that control of access to the instruments of production is a prerequisite of the second and is therefore the critical element:

> Control over access is decisive, and, when consolidated, will carry control over preferential treatment distribution with it: that is, will shift ownership unambiguously to the new controlling, a new dominant, class. Here we see, from a new viewpoint, the mechanism of the managerial (bureaucratic) revolution (p. 95).

Our purpose is not to dispute the accuracies of or to speculate on the full implications of Burnham's predictions — that control, and thus ownership, will pass from the hands of the investors (capitalists) into the hands of the managerial (bureaucratic) class. He is cited to bring into focus the central element in the institution of private ownership. To proceed further with the focus that Burnham has provided, it would seem that the control of access to the instruments of production depends also upon the control of manpower and manpower resources. This being the case, it is incorrect to attribute the only threat to private ownership to bureaucratic or social management. The top echelons of organized labor, itself a type of managerial class, have accrued enormous power in the control of manpower resources. This automatically places organized labor in the position of competing for control of access to production, the most decisive element in property ownership.

Perhaps to the extent that Burnham's predictions have not materialized is the extent to which capital ownership has made massive technological breakthroughs in the field of labor substitution. In this context, automation, the step-child of the conflict between capital, labor, and government for control of access to the instruments of production, functions to preserve capital ownership.

This digression into general industrial economics provides contrasts to the agricultural industry, especially as it exists in Arizona. The arena of agricultural production is marked by the conspicuous absence of organized labor. This then reduces the competition for control of access to one protagonist — government. Agricultural industries have other unusual advantages. Publicly subsidized research in technical development is provided the industry on the part of the Agricultural Extension Service and Agricultural Experiment Stations. Moreover, the industry has been given access to labor resources closed to other industries. The over-all benefits of these "advantages" can be debated. It is the effects of the labor advantage, however, which we wish to pursue further.

Although Arizona agriculture has never depended upon monopolistic institutions such as slavery, sharecropping, or peonage, it has historically relied upon noncompetitive labor either in the form of labor surplus, or highly mobile, unsophisticated immigrant populations. The whole cost structure of Southwestern agriculture in general is based upon this condition. When a labor shortage is said to exist in agriculture, only a specific kind of labor shortage is meant — noncompetitive labor. When such shortages exist government has intervened on behalf of agricultural industries to give it access to other noncompetitive labor resources — e.g. prisoners of war, Puerto Ricans, Mexican immigrants, and most recently Mexican Nationals. This peculiar system has contributed immeasurably to a cost-efficient agriculture, the benefits of which are discussed in Chapter 6. On the other hand, having continuous access to labor resources of this kind has created artificial conditions. It has rendered the law of supply and demand with respect to domestic labor inoperative. This has arrested technological processes normally operative in industries who must function under the stress of intensive labor competition. If this has favored the industry on the one hand, on the other it has amplified its vulnerability to variations and fluctuations in labor supply to which other industries have long since been immune.

Agriculture's disproportionate dependence upon control of access to labor is compounded by still another feature which is largely peculiar to agriculture. Climatic factors are critical in product formation and maturation. This means that agriculture cannot control the market to the degree other industries can because market control means product control. This is, at best, tenuous with climatic and organic processes involved in maturation and preservation. Relative to all other industries involved in the processing, distribution, retailing, and preparation of foods, the grower is the most vulnerable to these critical variables. This type of production structure places even greater emphasis upon control of instruments of production — in this case labor, already a sore point in a cost efficient, labor-bound industry.

From this complex of structural and historical factors has emerged a labor-obsessed industry which, in the midst of labor surpluses created by automation in other industries, fears a shortage of labor amenable to the peculiar controls upon which their present economics are based.

THE SOCIAL LOGICS OF A LABOR-DEPENDENT AGRICULTURE

In the dialogue between agricultural research and agricultural management the impression is frequently given that the social content of management behavior is simply a function of the economic. To be sure the principles of economics in contrast to other principles of behavior tend to be more operational and reliable. Also, given the present limitations of the social sciences, it is methodologically appropriate to certain problems to treat economics as an independent system. Nevertheless, economic behavior, however well defined it may be, belongs in the total spectrum of social behavior, and it is necessary to remind ourselves from time to time that its separation is more convenient than real. Every firm, though guided by the laws of economics, must deal in all crucial matters with human beings. To do this, management must operate explicitly or implicitly from a set of standardized concepts about the individuals or groups with whom they deal. These ideas, whether a formalized theory or simply a configuration of notions, are called social logics. The social logics of labor is an important element in the understanding of management. As discussed in previous pages, this is especially true of the labor-intensive industries of agriculture.

The Right to Noncompetitive Labor

Given the premises of private ownership and profit maximization and the economic base of vast populations of immigrant workers upon which Arizona's agricultural industries grew, it is logical from the viewpoint of farm management to regard noncompetitive labor as legitimate a resource as water. Thus they argue that minimum wage laws should not apply to farm workers and that lacking an "adequate" domestic labor supply, alien workers should be allowed to fill in the gap. These sentiments are evident in such phraseologies as, "They (the local labor commission) recognize that Nationals must do an important job." or, "We've always had Mexicans, wet or dry!" Regarding the Congressional repeal of Public Law 78, the view is one of the government taking away something which is rightfully theirs. As one irate grower expresses it, ". . . if they take them (braceros) away, let them! I hope the farmers would refuse to feed the people—let them eat horse ___! You can't do it without them!"

Growers generally feel that this kind of labor is essential to remain competitive. Stressing this point one large grower said, "I'll pay my cutters $5 an hour as long as every other grower does the same!" The general manager of another large firm emphasizes:

> . . . foreign labor has always supported the lettuce. I don't agree that we are better to go back to the sheds although it would put it in the hands of the strong and the economic consequences would be pretty tough and the product would go up. Arizona lettuce is not localized around a shed operation investment. We farm Aguila and Harquahala. This scares me — if this goes to shed then outlying districts are cooked geese — *our* cooked geese. There's no domestic labor force — the investment for such a short shipping season in these outlying areas would be fabulous. Aguila, Harquahala, and Willcox came about because of the shift from the Salt River gravity irrigation system to pumping. These are field packing areas. They would collapse or become one central cooperative. There would be tremendous changes!

Continuing he adds:

> We don't get the big bite. The big larceny is at the chain store level — whether one dollar or two dollars a carton, they sell lettuce 29¢ a head. They really throw their weight around. A guy that buys 100 cars a day has more power and control than a guy that buys two.
>
> When we go into a real glut it would sure make sense if a chain store would sell two for 19¢ and then they could move 500 cars of lettuce to help us out — a few do. The housewife is the worst enemy — 29¢ or 19¢ she will buy the same — 29¢ is the magic figure. Advertising studies indicate that she will buy 90 percent as much lettuce at 29¢ as she will buy at 19¢, but she will buy only 50 percent of the 19¢ lettuce at 33¢ a head. Advertising research shows that even the locations a product is put in has everything to do whether it sells. Therefore our industry is dependent to a great extent upon impulse buying.

The manager of a large citrus house also cites the chain stores and the return to the grower as the big factor in wages paid to harvest help. He says that the co-op generally receives at the shed 27 cents for a bag of grapefruit. The haulers charge 3 cents a bag and the same bag of fruit after a week to two weeks will retail in a store at 69 cents—

> . . . over a hundred percent mark-up with no middleman. The grower gets ½¢ a pound and the retail stores get 7 to 12¢ a pound. Occasionally big chains buy carloads of grapefruit and sell them at 29¢ a bag and freeze out the small merchant, then raise

their prices right back to 59¢ or 69¢ a bag. The grocer says, 'Why should I sell two bags for 29¢ when I can sell one for 69¢?' — There is less grapefruit being consumed in California now than ten years ago!

The Principle of the Unknown (Stereotype) Worker

In order for an organization to maintain equilibrium, interaction among its participants must be regularized and stable. In certain kinds of contacts with large numbers of people and shifting relationships, interpersonal interaction tends to be difficult and inefficient. As a result interaction under these circumstances or within these kinds of organizations is more image interaction than it is personal interaction. Regularity rather than being achieved by particular knowledge, is achieved by doctrinaire knowledge. Participants interact in terms of a stereotype. A mask is substituted in place of a face. The mask is the stereotyped image existing in the mind of the person who projects it. It is theoretical. Its user behaves toward people who fit the type not as they *are* but as he *believes* them to be. The cashier, the manager, or the butcher of a supermarket deals with a theoretical customer; the loan manager of a large bank deals with a theoretical borrower; the university registrar deals with a theoretical student; just as a farm manager deals with a theoretical harvest hand. All of them are using stereotypes.

The validity of a stereotype is irrelevant. Its purpose is not to mirror the *true* person. Its function is to enable its user to predict within tolerances, key behavior patterns of decisive importance in stock situations. Farm management's stereotype of seasonal workers is no more nor less valid than a Papago's or a union organizer's stereotyped view of the farmer. The only requirement in either instance is that it be reliable. It is a guide to slot behavior or standardized inter-role relations. All such relations, regardless of the participants, must of necessity be based upon the stereotype mechanism. Although stereotype interaction functions as a stabilizing mechanism, it is, of course, never static. It is subject to constant and, to a certain extent, unconscious revision in the direction of more personalized knowledge. In the opposite direction stereotype interaction in postulating behavior tends to *determine* it, and to this extent is self validating and self intensifying.

Farm management's stereotyped view of seasonal workers is reflective of the peculiar structure and history of its technologies. Extreme dependence upon great quantities of disciplined and reliable workers is matched by a domestic labor supply which is anything but reliable. As discussed previously this is partly due to geographic mobility and partly due to the trait shared by grower and worker alike—an inclination to sell to the highest bidder. A non-competitive wage market under normal conditions can only attract the least successful or least acculturated workers. Being at the bottom of the wage scale in the United States economy, domestic seasonal workers will necessarily be unsophisticated and frequently linguistically isolated peoples with whom growers and managers do not ordinarily interact except through intermediaries. Individually they are unknown. They are transient strangers with erratic comings and goings whose association with the firm is accounted for by little more than a name on a time sheet. In the case of independent crews not even names appear. From the point of view of management, chronic instability can best describe the domestic seasonal farm labor supply.

Two processes have responded to this—mechanization and special access (the bracero program). This has only partially stabilized the situation, however, because the bracero program has retarded mechanization, and the route of special access has had its own peculiar pitfalls. Due to the broad ramifications and implications of importing alien workers by the hundreds of thousands, the program is subject to pressures beyond agriculture's sphere of influence. Agencies responsible for its administration have a responsibility to all segments of the economy. Methods of determining domestic labor shortages therefore must be accountable to interests that are not necessarily compatible with the interests of simply one regional variant of one industry. For this reason responses to growers' labor demands are unavoidably involved. Moreover the program itself never ceases to be under attack. Although the chronic instability of the domestic migratory labor supply is alleviated by the bracero program, farm management is anything but secure in its implementation. Thus instability of one sort is replaced by instability of another sort caused by restrictions that are not in their interests and by the constant threat of repeal. The result is a defensive attitude conditioned by chronic anxiety about labor shortages actual or projected.

Farm management's stereotyped view of the domestic seasonal farm worker therefore has two functions. One is to interpret the occupational behavior of strange people with seemingly nonwork centered values, and the other is to justify the need for supplemental workers. The former is basic to the latter. Fundamental in the grower's view is the general worthlessness of domestic help. "Bums and winos" is the stock phrase used to categorize seasonal workers. When pressed to defend such a broad categorical generalization, most will admit that some domestic help is good. Permanent workers are not generally included in this view. The seasonal, the *unknown* workers are its chief focus. By the time a worker has obtained a permanent working relationship with a farm, a certain degree of face-to-face relationship has been established, and the stereotype ceases to apply.

In their own way growers tend to recognize the structural aspects of the characteristics of seasonal labor supply. Some refer to them as rejects from other vocations, which is the same as saying that low wages tend to attract the least able workers. One manager put it this way, "Anybody with anything on the ball is not going to pick fruit except those that don't give a damn and unemployables!" "Adverse Effect" rulings of the Department of Labor (discussed more fully in the following section) intensify the image of the vocational reject. A manager describes a placement through the Involuntary Day Haul:

> We had a crew foreman hooking to us on a labor card. He worked right up (to foreman). We put him on a truck and then

on a crew, moving right up. Then one day he fell off the wagon. Wow! Was he blasted! Hell, he was a periodic drunk. We didn't know it until it happened — he was a real nice guy.

A field superintendent savors the following incident:

> One of the local growers got in dutch with the compliance people and couldn't use Nationals in their fields. They argued and finally got permission to use half locals and half Nationals. The grower couldn't get enough locals through the employment office, so they got a Yuma Indian to go round up a bunch of other Yumans and they used them three weeks before they finally got rid of them. They were the sorriest help we've (the citrus house) ever had. I found one of them lying flat on his back on the ground catching the grapefruit while another one at the top of the ladder was picking them and dropping them down to him one at a time.

The superintendent went on to say that the Indian crew if paid by the piece rate would have earned 31 cents an hour; although they received the adverse effect wage of 95 cents. The National crew picking in the same fruit earned $1.20 an hour piece rate.

Although races or ethnic groups are frequently cited in specific complaints, in actuality the stereotype is seldom, if ever, applied to any single group. The stereotyped view is simply that locals "can't do it." This view is rationalized by the growers' insistence that there is some peculiar quality about seasonal harvest work in a given area or a given crop that is inherently repugnant to domestic help. Most frequently mentioned is the "stoop labor" aspect. Some arguments along this line of reasoning become quite sophisticated. A district manager cites the Asiatic sitting position and centuries-old tradition of stoop work in the rice cultures of the Orient as a factor in making the Chinese and Filipino more amenable to vegetable work. He cites the fact that Europeans have never adopted these patterns and goes on to say that the farm technical systems that are the bases of the large industrial farms of California and the Southwest are actually technical systems imported from the Orient along with Oriental labor. He says that the Mexican National is inferior to the Oriental in this respect.

Citrus growers, especially those in the Yuma area, cite the heat and the insects:

> In early fall we need 500 workers (this is for one house)— you may get five locals. It's 135 degrees in those groves and no movement of air at all. The gnats are unbearable. This Yuma lemon grows 24 hours a day. When it gets to size you had better harvest it or it is out of size for commercial value. By November you would get a few snow birds (locals who winter over in the Southwest) but there is very little fruit left for commercial picking. All lemons in the Yuma area have to be off the tree by December first, even for by-product acid.
>
> Discontinuation of Nationals would hurt this area worst because you couldn't get domestics regardless of what you would pay— the same thing in cantaloupes, those guys would die! If the price of labor did go up, it could go up only to a point, then we would have to quit picking.

Other growers stress the fact that certain classes have become identified with this kind of work, and that other groups simply will not do it. Just as the stereotype local cannot or will not work reliably in seasonal tasks, the stereotyped view of the Mexican National is the opposite. He is pictured as inherently hard working, happy-go-lucky, and cooperative. Inconsistencies appear in growers' rationale on this subject, however. Already mentioned is the inconsistent view that the fact of working as a harvest hand automatically makes a local a failure, yet at the same time he is regarded as a failure if he draws unemployment compensation rather than do stoop work. On the other side of the coin is the inconsistency in the stereotyped view of the bracero as opposed to the bracero who becomes a green carder. Typical are the following five comments, each from a different manager:

> These guys get that green card in their hand and their loyalty to you, if they ever did have any, ceases and they take to the four winds!
>
> The first thing a green card Mexican wants as soon as he gets his papers is the good things — a car, an apartment, to marry a white woman, and then he has to have more money. They become more aggressive. They get hard to work with. They want the easiest jobs in the group — they want to be pushers or lidders — they don't want to do stoop work!
>
> Green card men pick up the undesirable characteristics of our locals.
>
> We do not sponsor green card Mexicans, but we have occasion to be quite close to some ranchers who have used green carders and the minute they get their cards they immediately want a high rate of pay or move — generally to Los Angeles.
>
> They're the ___! They're just like the locals — too goddamned independent!

THE ROLE OF GOVERNMENT

(The discussions which follow apply chiefly to companies who use Mexican Nationals.)

An integral part of the ideological system of industrial farm management is the mixed attitudes they have toward the role of government agencies. On the one hand they feel that these agencies should provide them special access to labor resources outside the domestic market system. On the other hand they resent bitterly the hand of these same agencies in their employment practices. These attitudes are especially apparent since the 1962 adverse effect rulings which require the users of braceros to pay all workers, domestic and National, employed in the same crop activities an adverse effect guaranteed wage. In addition users of Nationals are required to hire at this wage rate *all* domestic workers who desire employment.

General Complaints

Complaints fall into two categories that can be termed General and Procedural. Generally growers feel that they are being penalized for using

Nationals. They refer to being treated as "second class citizens." General complaints center around the costs of hiring workers who are not qualified by temperament or experience. These costs are both direct and indirect. The direct costs which growers are quick to cite are those caused by below-average production in combination with an hourly guaranteed wage. One large citrus house estimates a loss of $150,000 in 1963 paid in guaranteed wages in excess of actual production in terms of the piece rate. The manager of another company insists that a crew of 16 Nationals during the first week of picking will seldom miss their piece rate wages by more than $12, but that a crew of 16 Involuntary Day Haul locals will generally miss theirs by $100. Accounts from other growers are similar.

Indirect costs result from the high rate of turnover of the Involuntary Day Haul worker. One corporation displayed time sheets for 1963 to prove its point. Out of a total of 1,900 locals hired for the year, 1,288 made less than $150. Accounts of weekly rates of turnover of 70 and 80 percent are almost too numerous to mention. Another indirect cost is the daily fluctuation in the numbers of domestic workers a company may be called upon to absorb. The ruling being what it is, neither the state employment office nor the company involved has much control over this factor. During the months of November to December, especially in the Phoenix area, the number of locals a company is asked to take may double from one day to the next. An entry in the authors' field notes dated December 20, 1962 is pertinent:

> The crews were very large today, 35-40. This was obviously too big. As one informant pointed out to me — a bin held only 27 boxes or sacks, and one whole truck held only 9 bins or 243 boxes in all. This means that by the time each man has picked only 6 sacks the truck is filled. A good picker can pick 6 sacks in less than 30 minutes. An average picker picks 4 to 5 sacks in 30 minutes. This means that the truck is filled in 30 to 45 minutes. From grove to shed, 20 miles round trip, would take at least an hour. Considering even a record 15 minutes for the truck's unloading and loading, this means 1 hour and 15 minutes per truck from grove back to grove again. Now only 2 trucks are allotted to a crew. In this case the arithmetic is clear — a 30 to 45 minute wait between each truck. This means that the guaranteed minimum wage would not be made by the workers because they cannot pick when there is no truck present.

Procedural Complaints

Procedural complaints are more individual and complicated. It is not possible to go into the specific instances and details of these complaints. Following the ramifications of disagreements becomes hopelessly involved in the complexities of locating and investigating first hand participants and witnesses. Moreover, this entails methods more appropriate to the concept and theory of criminal and civil law than to the sciences of human behavior. For this reason the following discussion makes no attempt to disclose facts in the legal sense. It presents attitudes which originate primarily from *one* participant group (farm management) in a contentious situation. These attitudes are not important so much for their detail or accuracy as they are for the issues around which contention most frequently revolves in the implementation of the bracero program. Considering the responsibilities of state employment offices and compliance people (Foreign Labor Service Representatives) in this matter, sentiment toward them was generally favorable.

Yuma growers felt generally that procedures there had been developed in Maricopa County and were therefore not entirely suited to their peculiar needs. Among the specifics cited are wage rates and production ratios. Also cited was the time required for a company to move their Nationals from a farm in one county to a farm in another. According to one Yuma grower referring to the Aguila area in Maricopa County, the normal time period required for a certificate of authorization did not allow for the unusually short maturation period of lettuce.

> Aguila is a trap! In 24 to 48 hours the growth is phenomenal. You will look at it today and say it will be OK Monday and then Saturday morning you will find that your crop is overripe. I defy anyone to predict within 48 hours the date of maturation of lettuce in Aguila!

In the Phoenix area growers' complaints centered around the fact that Phoenix was the destination of a much larger population of drifters (applicants for the Involuntary Day Haul placement) than other cities. Their reasoning was that the hiring of this type of person was an expense (see above), and that the accident of their being in the Phoenix area penalized them disproportionately.

Area complaints, however, could be considered by the board when it comes to the central issue which growers in *all* areas focused upon—the complicated machinery involved in the administration of the Involuntary Day Haul program. Referred to as IDH, it guarantees access of employment to *all* domestic workers as a compensation for any adverse effects Public Law 78 may have upon the domestic labor market. The IDH program requires growers using Mexican Nationals to hire *all* domestic applicants. At first glance, perhaps this kind of program appears simple enough. To be sure its motives are admirable. But carrying out this task, both from the standpoint of the employer and the employment people, is anything but simple.

First there is the problem of qualifications. Is a worker qualified by the mere act of his presence and the presence of a Mexican National on a farm? If a worker has been delinquent on one farm, should he be sent to another? When is a grower supposed to hire the worker—at the moment he completes his application in the employment office or on the following day? If the worker applied on a Friday and the grower does not harvest on the weekend, is the worker entitled to housing if he wants it? Once it has been decided who is to hire him and when he is supposed to begin work or move into grower housing, who is to pick him up? Where? When? When the worker begins work (e.g. at the 95¢ hourly wage and with furnished housing) what if he does not make an honest effort to do a job? Who is to determine what an "honest effort" is? How is it to be determined? If the worker quits or is fired (after the employer shows "just cause") when is he entitled to his pay check, at the moment he walks off the job, 24 hours later, or at the end of the normal pay period? If the worker receives an amount less than he thinks he is entitled to, who is to be contacted at the grower's office, the bookkeeper or the foreman, who by now is in the middle of a field 30 miles on the other side of town? Suppose the worker quit just before lunch, yet the meal was ordered by the grower in anticipation of his being there. Should the worker pay his normal fee for the meal he didn't eat or should the grower absorb the expense? Actually who can verify that he did or did not eat the meal? Who can verify that he left at 11:55 instead of 12:35?

Multiply these considerations by a factor potential of 13,311 IDH mandays per month during peak season in Maricopa County alone (ASES 1964b: 34). Add to this the high strung, defensive temperaments that characterize many of the drifter personality types. Compound this with the frustrated manager of a citrus company facing a forecast of freezing weather, or a field superintendent of a lettuce harvest with 900 acres of lettuce and a mass of warm air hanging on for the third straight day. What could be expected to happen does in fact. Despite "working agreements" between local growers, grower associations, and their farm labor office the pressures generated by the unpredictable inflow and outflow of large populations of domestics occasionally taxes good relations to the limit. One firm whose total work force in peak season rarely exceeds 150 men received 97 IDH men in the space of four days. This was in addition to the hundred or so locals they already had. Two and a half months prior to this (in October), according to the manager, the company could not obtain half the labor they required from the local market. During peak season—peak for harvest and peak for the influx of winter workers—regulatory interaction between specific growers and/ or growers' associations and farm office personnel occurs daily. These contacts range from arranging the next day's quota of IDH workers to complaints about pay shortages or meal deductions made by quitting workers. One company office reported on the average five meal charge complaints alone to be researched per two-week period. We have witnessed deliberation —some heated, some restrained—over almost all of the minutiae of personnel management enumerated above. Resentment of the state and federal agencies who must assume the supervision of this program should come as no surprise.

Dilemma

On the other side of the coin are the attitudes of domestic workers, many of whom claim that foremen and pushers try to get rid of them by riding them until they quit. Apropos are the remarks of a United Packing House Workers Union official who criticizes state employment offices in both California and Arizona for being too *lax* in the administration of the adverse effect rulings in Public Law 78. Just as the agricultural interests have subjected government agencies to enormous pressures, the union movement has applied pressures equally compelling:

> Braceroism is another form of subsidy — maybe lettuce does need help, but if it does let's do it as a subsidy, not at the expense of the American worker. Go around El Centro and ask merchants about the economic state of the small business in El Centro and they will all say it is low. Why? Because the sheds are closed. Yet check the amount of crops and crop value and the Imperial Valley area ranks fifth in the country by crop value. This kind of wealth, where is it going? The merchants aren't getting it — the merchants aren't getting it — Mexico? I don't think so!

> These people here live in a dream world, they don't want anybody telling them what to do — the government, the union, nobody. These businesses are hurting and yet they all went out and got themselves deputized and a gun during the strikes of sixty and sixty-one and they were going to help the braceros and now they are going broke. —The contract agreements existing in the sheds in 1951 are rudimentary contracts, the kind which have been in other industries for decades.

The official went on to detail some of the pressures exerted by the unions:

> The strike in 1960 and 1961 (Imperial Valley) won minimum wage and piece rates. The union lost the strike but won the point. The government acted a year later and required the users of braceros to pay a minimum wage and a minimum piece rate. The role of government as an arbiter in the California farm union disputes is vital. Sometimes it took them months in a dispute to determine if it was a strike. Then it would take months to determine if it involved a farm — a series of strikes, hearings, determinations — all have gone to make up Public Law 78 in its present form.

The dilemma of the agricultural industry in Arizona as elsewhere is, government in or government out? There is not unanimity on this question just as there is not unanimity on the question of dealing with unions. Some growers, out of frustration of coping with the intricacies of the bracero program, seem ready to accept unions. The general manager of a large corporate farm states emphatically, "As far as union and the choice between union and government, I'd take the union, at least you can be heard!"

On the other hand are opinions like the following:

> I would never be in the shed because I detest a man telling me what to do — some union bosses telling me I'm going to put a man here or there!

SUMMARY

In summary are listed some of the ideologies and logics of Arizona farm management as they pertain to the labor problem:

1. The norm of private ownership and its economic expression—profit maximization — with a history of labor-intensive technical systems based upon reservoirs of noncompetitive labor.

2. Lacking reliable noncompetitive labor domestically, the right of special access to alien labor.

3. Government should grant this access but not interfere in their personnel practices.

4. Although labor surpluses in the United States are in excess of the demand for agricultural labor, they are either unreliable or not temperamentally or culturally suited to seasonal harvest work.

5. Higher wages may alter this condition, but higher wages require more output, and more output requires increased mechanization, which would have far reaching effects upon present technologies and businesses.

6. Conflict and confusion over the solution to an increasingly intricate and controlled foreign labor program and its repeal, over the role of government agencies, the role of organized labor, and capital-labor substitution.

PART FIVE

THE PARTICIPANTS
in their
COMMON
TECHNOLOGICAL SETTING

21 | The Harvest Organization as a Composite Institution

INTRODUCTION

IN ORDER TO VIEW a farm harvest system, specific or generalized, we must shift our focus from the institutions of the participant groups to the farm system itself. This system can be thought of as an institution in its own right with its peculiar dynamics. Precisely how it is conceptualized is important in the conclusions we are led to. We can view it internally, de-emphasizing the cultural backgrounds and institutions of the workers, and look for the forces which motivate their behavior in the interaction between management (formal organization) and workers (informal organization), who will group and cluster according to their jobs, their grievances, and how they are being treated. Much is lost in this view, particularly in those industrial systems manned by unassimilated and unsophisticated immigrant populations (see Chapter 1). Two important concepts in this regard (Malinowski 1961: 65-72) will be used in this synthesis. The first concept is that all sociologically relevant interaction occurs between *institutions*. To be sure, people, not institutions, work together, make rules, react to rules, work efficiently or inefficiently, and curse and swear at one another. The theoretician is simply telling us that interaction behavior of people from divergent cultural backgrounds depends upon the *institutions* which have conditioned them and which continue to bind them together. This means that an individual worker — picking oranges, driving a mechanical cotton picker, or trimming lettuce — must be understood first as a member of an institution or institutions *outside* the work organization which he happens to be a member of.

We have seen five core institutions in the analyses of four farm-oriented subcultures and farm management. Mexican-American subculture revolves around a tightly integrated family. This varies, according to its subsistence or occupational pattern, along a continuum from the peasant family with its division of labor by sex to the hypothetical bi-vocational family. In contrast to this is the loosely integrated family of the Negro farm worker which provides maximum occupational mobility in a caste-structured society. Indian subculture revolves around a reservation organizational system which is actually a network of institutions. This tends to immobilize the reservation Indian occupationally and socially. The abnormally mobile Anglo-isolate achieves a degree of social and occupational integrity in semi-clandestine subsistence-oriented institutions which are informally organized around a common experience and a common status. Farm management institutions are

[265]

proprietary in nature with the norms of profit maximization and control of labor. We might say these institutions interact in the harvest systems of the crop industries studied. More precisely these institutions are instrumental in the participation of their members in the harvest systems or generalized farm harvest system in question. As stated in the introductory chapter, we refer to them as *participant institutions.* Used interchangeably with this term are the terms "participant organization" and "participant group."[1]

The second equally useful concept is that whenever institutions come together two important things happen: mutual exploitation (in the broader social sense) occurs and a new social organization (institution) is formed. This coming together of the participant institutions is the result of a *"Common Factor* of interests and intentions" frequently referred to as "joint interests" (Malinowski 1961: 66).

Both the company and the workers have different needs. The organization of each has formed to meet these needs. Meeting these needs is the *function* of the organization or institution. To the extent that each can utilize the other to meet its needs is the extent to which they have joint interests. In a sense the term joint interest is a misnomer since it implies identical needs. The needs of the company and its worker groups are anything but identical. This is amply demonstrated in the analyses of the participant groups. But the fact that the act of cooperating or interacting in a certain activity reciprocally fulfills those needs is the key thought in the whole matter. A simple example will illustrate. A food store's basic need is to sell food. A basic need of a family commissary is providing food for its members. The needs in either case are not identical. They are compatible, reciprocal, even complementary, but they are not identical. The needs are common in the sense that each can be met in a common meeting ground. The meeting ground is the market place where both the store and the consumer interact to serve their individual interests. These interests are joint in the sense that each is structured with the other in mind. Thus mutual benefit or exploitation takes place in the act of the store's selling and the consumer's buying food.

The view that a third organization or institution forms in this act can be illustrated by further use of the same example. The organization of the local supermarket has all of the essential elements of an institution. It has its personnel, prescribed activities, its rules (norms) of behavior, its equipment, etc. Likewise the family commissary has its personnel, roles, appropriate tastes, and appropriate behavior in food preparation, consumption and disposal. Each of these institutions can be viewed independently of the other. Now let

---

[1]Although the terms are used interchangeably, the use of one or the other for certain purposes seems to offer some conceptual advantage. For instance it seems more meaningful to speak of the interaction of organizations than of institutions. When discussing the occupational class affiliations of workers across institutional lines, it seems more meaningful to speak of groups. Be that as it may, for the purposes of this study, whether using participant institution, organization, or group, the basic concept applies as developed in all discussions of the *institution* as *the* fundamental unit of human organization.

us view the two brought together in the hustle and bustle of "double stamp day." What we see is neither the supermarket organization as such nor the family commissary as such. It is a unique institution having different personnel and different behavior patterns. The role of the butcher is one thing within the supermarket corporation structure and quite another during the eight hours he is interacting with customers. The same is true of the housewife. The market society of the supermarket's floor personnel and hundreds of shoppers representing hundreds of family commissaries is a third institution referred to as a *composite institution*.

In the farm harvest systems a commercial citrus company may hire Anglo-isolates because they are the most efficient labor for its technical system. The Anglo-isolate works for the company because all of his buddies are there and the company does not require his name. Thus his group remains intact and his anonymity is preserved. In spite of the fact that a certain amount of conflict arises between management and labor, both the worker and the company *cooperate* in the fields to meet their respective needs. This cooperation is implemented by one activity — harvesting citrus. In the meeting to effect their respective interests, a unique institution is formed — the harvest organization. Specific or generalized, the farm harvest system is a composite institution interrelated with, but differing from the participant institutions.

An analysis of the generalized farm harvest system of Arizona agricultural industries follows. Then the participation of Mexican-Americans, Anglo-isolates, Negroes, and Indians' in this system will be examined.

THE GENERALIZED FARM HARVEST SYSTEM— A COMPOSITE INSTITUTION

A detailed description of each harvesting system of each farm company and each crop was given in Part One. The *generalized* farm harvest system is conceived as a system of occupational status groups. Each status group has its symbols, its prescribed duties, its function in the production system, and its appropriate behavior (norms). Status indicators are such things as wage level, type of farm-furnished housing, type of equipment (if any) given over for personal use, type of equipment the worker operates — how new, how expensive, how intricate, etc. — and finally, behavior itself. For the most part, norms center around work behavior appropriate to job tasks. There is a correct behavior toward the product being harvested, toward the equipment used in the harvest, toward personnel in the same status group, and toward personnel in different status groups. These occupational status groups will be termed *occupational classes*.

It is difficult to think of social change and technological change and not think of class phenomena in the broader sense. To avoid confusion on this, *occupational class* as we use it should not be used to infer a worker's social class — e.g. lower-lower, upper-lower, lower-middle, etc. Lloyd Warner in his classic study of *Social Class in America* lists a person's general occupation as one of four indicators of his social class (1960:41). However, Warner does not go into ranking systems which exist *within* production systems among the members themselves of occupational groups. He establishes the class related-ness of general occupational categories by criteria *outside* the factory in the community at large (1960: 131-142). *Occupational class* as used in this analy-sis refers to the status which a particular class of jobs has *within* the technol-ogy. To be sure there are correlations between a worker's occupational class and his social class but they are not germane to our discussion. Our focus is upon occupational structure and experience as an instrumental factor, a kind of catalytic agent between technological change and institutional change.

Six occupational classes — five integral and one artificial — are described. They rank in order from top to bottom: Technical Elite, Supervisory, Machine and Semi-Machine, Marginal, Obsolete, and IDH (referring to workers placed through the Involuntary Day Haul system). These occupational classes cut across the subcultural groups as analyzed in Part Four. Members of each subcultural group can be found in all occupational classes and vice versa (although in reality our sample of workers discloses no Indians in either the top or bottom classes). Occupational classes are not subcultural or ethnic groupings but class groupings based upon a worker's position in the status system on the job.

This ranking system was generalized from the actual hierarchies of jobs in the harvest organizations of each of the 13 companies and nine crews studied. Stated simply, these hierarchies were made from rankings of jobs according to the degree they were sought after by the workers. These rankings follow wage rankings generally but not precisely. The sample of 603 workers was broken down into these six occupational classes:

Class	No.	Percent
Technical Elite	64	11
Supervisory	47	8
Machine and Semi-Machine	88	14
Marginal	225	37
Obsolete	72	12
IDH	107	18
Total	603	100

Each occupational class will be discussed separately in somewhat the same format. The jobs or assigned activities of the class will be listed with a discussion of its characteristics. This will be followed by an analysis of its function in the harvest system.

Because the jobs have been discussed in detail in Part One (Crop His-tories and Harvest Organizations), only their titles will be given. The main emphasis here is on the functional aspect of the classes — viz. how they serve the human needs of the workers in the system. An example will offer a contrast between "job activity" and "function." A crew foreman's job activity is described in terms of his formal duties and responsibilities — e.g. to record the production of each worker, to regulate the quality of the worker's product, etc. The same foreman, however, has much more to accomplish than his list of formal duties. One of his most important functions is to understand and interpret the behavior of a culturally different people to management and to communicate the aims of an efficiency-oriented management to the workers.

Technical Elite Occupational Class

This occupational class includes assistant field superintendents, assistant general foremen, lettuce-machine and stitcher-machine operators, citrus and lettuce truck operators, and specialist mechanics.

They rank the highest in socio-economic indicators. Eighty-eight percent own cars and 92 percent live in homes with modern facilities. The class averages slightly more than one occupant per room and a per capita annual income of $1,250. They have the highest level of schooling, averaging 8.6 years. They rank the highest in active union membership with 60 percent. This class also has the highest percentage (78) who like their jobs.

These are the technicians of the agricultural industry. Job behavior varies from company to company, but, by and large, they exhibit their status by disdaining to assist in manual operations. Loaders or swampers are hired for that purpose. They do not relate with the harvest workers. They do not have to deal with them except indirectly. While they relate to supervisory people, their most frequent area of social interaction is their own class. They congregate together during free time, visit from truck to truck on the road, and take pride in assisting one another in diagnosing mechanical difficulties. Operators are identified with the equipment they run. These are the instruments of production. The importance of one enhances the importance of the other. As machines are valued over men, they are valued over laborers.

Assistant field supervisors occupy a rank slightly higher than operators and mechanics. Their function is an alternate of the other. Whereas equipment men derive their special status from a specialized knowledge of machinery, field men derive theirs from a specialized knowledge of personnel. This has two facets — understanding workers and understanding management. They are the links between the world of the worker and the firm. They are articulate in the divergent participant institutions. They have a split cultural personality so to speak. Their symbols of status are pressed pants, field boots, and late model pickups furnished by the company.

Supervisory Occupational Class

Foremen, row bosses, and independent crew leaders make up this occupational class. Eighty-seven percent own automobiles and 77 percent live in homes with modern facilities averaging slightly less than two occupants per room. Their per capita annual income is $820. In these four indices they rank second highest. They also have the highest percentage of aggregate households represented (94 percent).

Three characteristics distinguish the supervisory class and serve to indicate their role in the harvest system. Approximately half of them were harvest *hands* ten years ago. They have the lowest mean number years of formal schooling — 5.8 years — ranking equivalent to the obsolete class, but they have the highest ratio who speak both English and Spanish—almost two-thirds.

The supervisory class are a necessary link between the mass of *unknown* harvest hands and the field supervisors. They are acquainted with the hands' devious ways, participate in their institutions, and identify with their interests. The latter however is a two-way street. In order for a row boss or crew foreman to play ball with his crew, the worker must not leave him exposed to censure from above. To do this is the real crime in foremen-worker relations. On the other hand it is a simple matter for a crew to get rid of a row boss or foreman who rides them too hard.

These men are the pressure points in the production system. In the best crews they are the pets. A foreman or pusher who is deft with his men has a team. They show it in their production rate and in the quality of their product. Such crews are high spirited, relaxed, and proud. Literally they sing while they work and brag in their barracks at night. Foremen and pushers (row bosses) in such crews are indulged by the managers and owners and admired to the point of adulation by the hands.

There is a tendency for the best supervisors to become spoiled and undisciplined. Sometimes they are fired abruptly when they least expect it. Coming from humble beginnings, as many of them do, the power and adulation is more than some can handle. They tend to build miniature empires of corruption playing both ends against the middle. These indulgences usually center around women and money. One foreman, making about $12,000 a year, had an investment in a duplex or two in Salinas. He had a wife in Salinas looking after the apartments, another wife in Mexicali, and a 17-year-old sweetheart working for his company. This didn't catch up with him until his pusher, one of the best, began "beating his time" with the girl. The foreman fired the pusher. It got back to the field superintendent right away, and the situation was immediately reversed. The superintendent claimed he could see his work dropping off for some time before it came to a head, but he had been their top foreman for so many years they let it go until they had no choice but to fire him.

A story was making the rounds in one company of two foremen who were running a drug business on the side — smuggling Benzedrine across the border and peddling it at two or three times the cost. Another story tells about a row boss smuggling prostitutes out of Mexicali in the trunk of his fancy car and running a mobile "cat house" outside the Mexican National camp.

Lettuce foremen and row bosses tend to be conspicuously conscious of their prestige. They congregate as company commanders with their lieutenants gathered around them, as a star football team with its hangers-on — secure in a status system which obviously excludes "farm office boys" (IDH workers). They banter about their latest escapades, the excitement of the day's work, the tensions and the competition of the production line, putting up with locals, etc. They have a certain *esprit de corps,* a peculiar kind of cockiness exhibited in their dress — white levis, American-made field boots, and flamboyant pork pie hats. Above all, a good crew foreman or row boss has style. Years of practice in trimming and packing have taught him a tradition. He doesn't cut lettuce, he sculpts it with a few clean, deft strokes of a razor-sharp instrument. In less than three minutes he molds it, three heads at a time, into a pack that's clean, heavy, and springy. It takes fifteen minutes for a novice to transform 24 crisp heads and a new carton into a bag of squashed salad.

The supervisory class in the citrus and cotton systems tend to be more stable and less colorful. Still they have the same function—of understanding the ethnic and institutional traits of the workers and interacting between grower and worker.

Machine and Semi-Machine Occupational Class

This occupational class is made up of workers who work on conventional row-crop machinery or work interdependently with more complex machinery. The former include tractor and cotton machine drivers, fork-lift operators, and less specialized equipment mechanics. The latter include wrappers, fillers, gluers on lettuce packing machines, folder-stackers on stitching machines, and truck loaders. They rank next in order of socio-economic indices. Fifty-eight percent own cars, 68 percent occupy homes with modern facilities. They average two occupants per room, and earn $730 per capita annual income. Their educational level is also intermediate, averaging 7.4 years, approximately one grade level lower than the technical elite and one grade level higher than the marginal class (see Table 39).

The status of this class is equivalent to the degree of specialized knowledge required to do their jobs. They are midway between hand laborers and technical specialists. They do not command a high wage on the labor market because their skills have ceased to be scarce. But their importance must also be represented by the fact that a machine or tractor operator's time is gauged by the costs of his misusing or immobilizing a costly machine as well as by the plentiful supply of his fellow tradesmen. Because of this, machine workers' traits must include stability and reliability in addition to the skill appropriate to the equipment. The class functions as the backbone of the cotton industry, having gradually replaced the centuries-old hand picker. This class has undergone ethnic transition in the process. It has played and continues to play a key role in the transition in the family-work institution of the Mexican-American farm worker.

On the cotton farms their status is marked by intermediate-quality permanent, farm-furnished housing. Foremen's and technicians' farm-furnished housing is equipped with modern facilities. But machine workers housing varies; some is completely modern and some has indoor plumbing and electricity but outdoor toilets. Status among the machine class workers in lettuce and citrus is evidenced by longevity with the company, a wage higher than the harvest hands, and automobiles. These workers are not generally status conscious. Their social relations at work cut across all class lines. They are the most occupationally mobile and versatile of all classes.

Marginal Occupational Class

This class includes general farm hands in cotton, most of whom supplement their income with some picking and chopping. In lettuce it includes the job tasks in the ground crew system — cutters, packers, closers, spray-pad, spreader, and windrower. In citrus harvest systems it includes the hand pickers. They rank next to the bottom in car ownership, modern home facilities, and annual per capita income—45 percent, 63 percent, and $620 respectively. They are distinguished by two other characteristics. They are the oldest class, having a mean age slightly higher than 41 years, and they have the highest percentage of illiterates—21 percent. They have a mean educational level of 6.7 years.

Marginal class workers are engaged in economically marginal positions within a production system. The type of tasks which they are engaged in have already been supplanted in cotton harvesting. These workers do not exhibit status awareness as the higher occupational classes do. As a whole they take pride in work. In this respect they are critical of undependable and inefficient workmen. They derive prestige satisfaction from the quality of their work and their production rates. They also take pride in knowing the subtleties of what the old-time harvest hands consider to be an art. Younger workers covet the higher positions and try to move into better jobs. Many, of course, work in the harvests to supplement other income or until they can find higher paying nonfarm work.

Interaction among marginal workers tends to be along ethnic or subcultural lines. Cotton companies furnish housing for their marginal workers. This housing is the poorest quality housing available that is farm owned and farm *maintained*. It is still one step higher than farm owned cotton camps turned over to crew leaders. The steady citrus pickers and lettuce harvesters, in contrast to the IDH workers, do not generally occupy company furnished housing. The status of their housing varies with the circumstances of the individual worker and the purpose of his participation in harvest work — e.g. Mexican-Americans tend to live in villages and Anglo-isolates in cabin courts.

Obsolete Occupational Class

Cotton chopper-pickers are an obsolete occupational class. Picking machines have been substituted for hand picking. Mechanical blockers, spaced planting, and weed control techniques are efficient alternatives for chopping.

While rising wage levels among the marginal class will accelerate their obsolescence, the services of the obsolete class can be sold *only* as a depressed commodity. Varying slightly with the area, size of farm, and local growing conditions, fixed wage limits are operative. If the limits are exceeded the workers will be eliminated altogether. These workers are a technologically by-passed class. They rank lowest in all socio-economic categories, showing only 43 percent with cars, 18 percent with modern living facilities, and a per capita annual income of $470. By-passed technologically, they are by-passed economically and socially in so far as they must depend upon this work. Differentiating the many who pick and chop cotton to augment earnings from other skills or supplement family income derived from a variety of sources, the term obsolete is applied only to those workers who must depend upon this work as their *chief* source of subsistence.

The most noticeable material charactertistic of this class is their housing. This comes in three principal variations: *rural*-urban fringe slums, urban or town slums, and farm slums. They vary in the intensity of their poverty in that order. *Rural*-urban fringe slums exist outside the city limits of incorporated cities and towns in the rural areas. Because *rural*-urban fringe communities (see Padfield 1961) vary in size and socio-economic characteristics, the title of slum is reserved for squatter communities that have never developed beyond the cardboard and tin-shack stage. The second type are the low income slum-type rentals *inside* the limits of incorporated towns and cities. These settlements are characterized by one-room cabins, community toilets, and no heating facilities except an unvented gas cooking stove. The third type is more accurately called obsolete farm housing. These communities are the remnants of the vast cotton camps formerly kept by cotton growers to house as many as a thousand people upon whom they would depend to hand pick thousands of acres of cotton. At this point in the technological and social processes taking place in the cotton industry, they are either abandoned entirely, or, as in many instances, turned over to entrepreneur labor contractors who use them to house the families making up their cotton chopping and picking crews. The camps are no longer considered the responsibility of the grower and are left entirely to the unlicensed contractor to operate as he sees fit. As a rule growers furnish power to these camps. In return the contractor and his crew give the owner-grower first choice on any seasonal hand labor he may yet need. The houses are one room, uninsulated cabins, oftentimes without doors or windows, and with both water and ground toilets outside. No rent is required.

This class are descended overwhelmingly (98 percent) from farm backgrounds. They rank equal to the supervisory class with the lowest average schooling. Social behavior is structured almost entirely along ethnic group lines. Participation in this class of work is casual and based on the most rudimentary requirements. This is its chief compensation. It poses the least threat to the institutional norms of the participant groups. It is not surprising that interaction across ethnic lines is minimal among this occupational class.

Interaction with management is nonexistent or filtered through crew foremen. They are no longer an integral part of the farm labor system. Even during the days of peak labor demand for Arizona cotton, integration of this class tended to be indirect — viz. through contractors and foremen.

IDH Occupational Class

This occupational class is a direct effect of USDL regulations that a domestic worker has "prior right of referral." They are placed in a separate occupational class because, by and large, they occupy the status of an outsider group in the farm harvest systems where they are found. They are nonexistent in cotton. In lettuce they are relegated to certain tasks — e.g. spray-padding, box spreading, windrowing, and set-up — which have taken on the connotations of their class. In citrus, while there are no special tasks as such for IDH men, they tend to be segregated because they are strangers.

A cluster of traits serves to identify this class and at the same time indicates to some extent the artificiality of their role in the technologies in which they are placed. They have the highest annual per capita income, next to the class of technical elite—$900. This is because they receive the guaranteed adverse effect wage and few of them have any dependents. They rank high in housing indices because so many of them occupy housing furnished for Nationals which is required to have modern facilities. Although few own automobiles, they do not need them as transportation is furnished from either the barracks or the employment office. They rank next to the technical class in mean years school completed (8). Sixty-three percent, the highest of all classes, are negative toward their job situation. They show the lowest index of job stability in terms of the average length of time spent per employer during the last year.

The interaction of IDH men with other occupational classes must be analyzed within the context of the conflict surrounding the bracero program (see the preceding chapter). There is no doubt that a significant percentage of these men are inefficient workmen in comparison to those who have had to make it on their own in their jobs. On the other hand there is no doubt that, hard-working or not, there is a tendency in many of the harvest organizations to ostracize them occupationally and socially. How many reliable relationships are eventually established in spite of this by workers who got their start through the IDH program is not known. Many of them do move from this "limbo" class to become an integral part of the organization. When they do, they are no longer identified as farm office boys but as folders, pickers, closers, etc.

Below is a cross-class listing of the more outstanding characteristics of the six occupational classes:

Table 39
Socio-Economic Traits by Occupational Class

	Technical Elite	Supervisory	Machine and Semi	Marginal	Obsolete	IDH
Percentage own car	88	87	58	45	43	29
Percentage in modern house	92	77	68	63	18	—
Per capita income	$1,250	$820	$730	$620	$470	$900
Mean number per room	1.2	1.6	2.1	1.8	2.2	—
CI @ 95%	(±.2)	(±.4)	(±.3)	(±.2)	(±.4)	—
Mean years schooling	8.6	5.8	7.4	6.7	5.8	8.0
CI @ 95%	(±.7)	(±.8)	(±.7)	(±.5)	(±.8)	(±.7)

22 Technological Systems as Mechanisms Whereby Management and Labor Groups Effect their Joint Interests

EACH PARTICIPANT GROUP has a different pattern of participation in the farm harvest system. This pattern has two aspects. First is the role it plays in the technological system. This will be referred to as its *technological role.* Each participant group has a peculiar *technological role,* i.e. it is exploited in a manner appropriate to its unique social and cultural characteristics.

However, as previously discussed, exploitation is not a one-way process. The work experience is a social experience. This experience meets certain social needs unique to each participant group. The reciprocal function, the function the technological system performs for the participant group, is fundamental to the view of the farm system as a composite institution. This function can be termed the *social role* of the technological system.

The *technological role* of the Anglo-isolate group (the function it performs for the farm harvest system) is quite different than the *technological role* of the Mexican-American group. Similarly the *social role* (the function) performed by the farm harvest system for the Anglo-isolate is quite different than the *social role* it performs for the Mexican-American. The occupational class scheme provides a means of analyzing these reciprocal roles.

THE TECHNOLOGICAL ROLES OF THE PARTICIPANT GROUPS

The participant groups analyzed are the familiar four Arizona farm worker subcultures — Mexican-American, Anglo-isolate, Negro, and Indian — plus Anglo-aggregate. Owing to their Anglo middle class affiliations mentioned earlier, the Anglo-aggregate group were not given an institutional analysis. But, because they comprise a major segment of the highest occupational class, they are included in the following analysis. Although the major analysis has been and continues to be devoted to the rank-and-file farm worker, the inclusion of the A-A's at this point will provide a more complete picture of the social and technological dynamics involved.

The *IDH occupational class* relies heavily upon the A-I (Figure 12).

[276]

Table 40

Patterns of Participation in the Occupational Classes by the Major Participant Groups

	IDH No.	IDH Pct.	Obsolete No.	Obsolete Pct.	Marginal No.	Marginal Pct.	Machine and Semi No.	Machine and Semi Pct.	Supervisory No.	Supervisory Pct.	Technical Elite No.	Technical Elite Pct.
Anglo-Aggregate	3	3	7	10	25	11	6	7	7	15	24	38
Mexican-American	20	19	18	25	84	37	54	61	33	70	31	48
Anglo-Isolate	51	48	6	8	71	32	7	8	0	9	6	9
Negro	27	25	19	26	11	5	11	13	4	0	3	5
Indian	5	4	22	31	16	7	9	10	1	2	0	0
Other	1	1	0	0	18	8	1	1	2	4	0	0
Total	107	100	72	100	225	100	88	100	47	100	64	100

The *obsolete occupational class* relies almost equally upon Mexican-Americans, Negroes, and Indians. The *marginal class* is made up about equally and exclusively by Mexican-Americans and Anglo-isolates. The Anglo-isolates are the traditional fruit tramps who identify themselves with tree crops. They tend to have contempt for harvest work in vegetable and other non-tree crops. The *machine and semi-machine class* depends to a far greater degree upon M-A than any other group. *Supervisory* is almost synonymous with M-A. The *technical elite class* depends heavily upon the Anglo-aggregate group and the M-A group as well.

Viewing the distribution of participant groups or institutions within the occupational class (technological) system as a whole, a line drawn (across class lines) from bar to bar of the same participant group should be visualized. This kind of visualization reveals striking differences in the class integration patterns from group to group. The line of participation for the Mexican-American group approximates a curve which rises steadily to a peak in the supervisory class and then drops down to a lesser but still relatively high point in the technical elite class. This confirms what other data indicate—that Mexican-Americans are an integral part of the Arizona farm technological system. The *technological role* of the M-A group is that of workhorse of the Arizona farm technological system. They are the backbone of the farm labor supply at all occupational levels.

The *technological role* of the Anglo-aggregate group contrasts sharply with this. Here is a group with one chief function — that of the technicians of the industry. The regular rise from the machine class through supervisory to technical elite suggests that the crest of their "curve of participation" has passed through the technological system, their participation in the obsolete and marginal classes notwithstanding. Another striking contrast is offered by the Anglo-isolate who functions primarily in two classes — IDH and marginal. Inasmuch as the IDH class can be regarded as an artificial class, the A-I group then has really only one significant *technological role* — that of fruit picker for tree crops.

The Indian sample is really too small to offer a reliable picture. Their *role* in the obsolete technologies of cotton is unmistakable, however. Disregarding the obsolete technology, their curve of participation, beginning in the marginal class, peaks in the machine (tractor driver) class and drops to almost nothing in the supervisory class. This suggests the beginnings of their integration in the higher occupational classes.

The Negro group function primarily in the IDH and obsolete classes. The obsolete occupational class is, of course, identified with obsolete cotton technologies, the historic industry of the rural Negro. Again regarding the

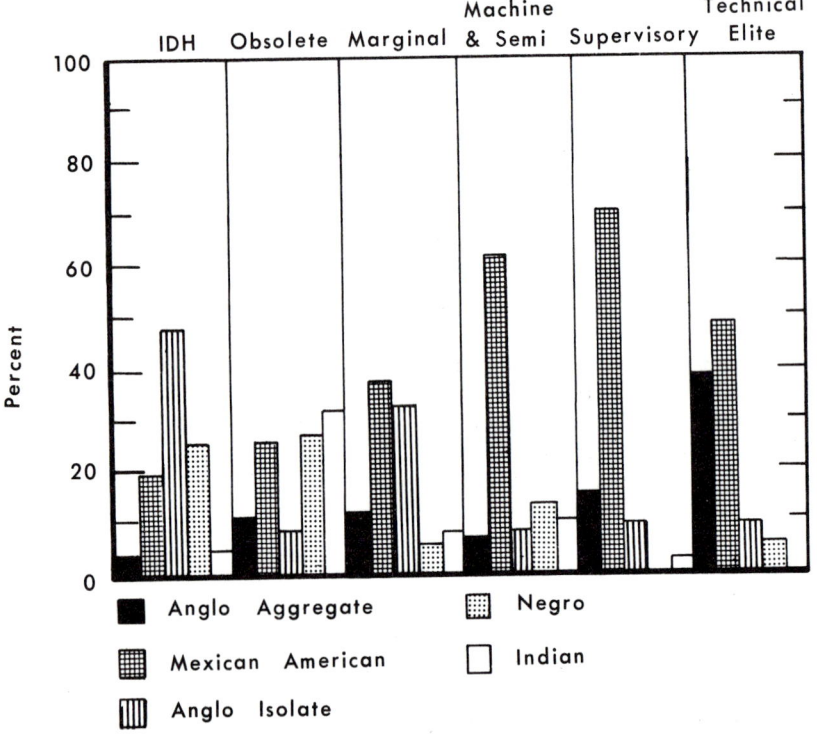

Figure 12
Percentage Frequency of Each Occupational Class
Made Up by Each Participant Group
(Bar graph from Table 40 — "Other" omitted)

IDH class as an artificial class, the Negro's *technological role* could be regarded chiefly as that of the cotton harvest hand. Also suggested in this case is the beginning of his integration in the higher occupational classes—viz. machine operators and supervisory.

THE SOCIAL ROLE OF FARM TECHNOLOGIES OR OCCUPATIONAL CLASSES

Table 41

Patterns of Occupational Class Distribution Among the Major Farm Subcultures

	Anglo-Aggregate No.	Anglo-Aggregate Pct.	Mexican-American No.	Mexican-American Pct.	Anglo-Isolate No.	Anglo-Isolate Pct.	Negro No.	Negro Pct.	Indian No.	Indian Pct.
IDH	3	4	20	8	51	37	27	36	5	9
Obsolete	7	10	18	7	6	4	19	25	22	42
Marginal	25	35	84	35	71	50	11	15	16	30
Machine and semi	6	8	54	23	7	5	11	15	9	17
Supervisory	7	10	33	14	0	0	4	5	1	2
Technical elite	24	33	31	13	6	4	3	4	0	0
Totals	72	100	240	100	141	100	75	100	53	100

The technological system of the generalized farm harvest system is conceptualized in terms of the occupational class scheme described in Chapter 21. Thus we speak of IDH, obsolete, marginal, machine, supervisory, and technical *technologies;* and IDH, obsolete, marginal, machine, supervisory, and technical *classes*. Each term has the complementary connotations of a *style* of work and the *status* of the workers performing this work.

The *Anglo-aggregate group* are using chiefly two occupational classes—marginal and technical elite. The marginal class functions for the Anglo-aggregate fruit pickers as it functions for the Anglo-isolate fruit pickers. The *Mexican-American group* show the heaviest reliance upon the marginal technologies with a significant reliance in decreasing amounts upon machine, supervisory, and technical elite. The *Anglo-isolate group* rely almost exclusively upon IDH placement and marginal (chiefly fruit picking) technologies. The *Negro group* rely most heavily upon IDH and obsolete. The *Indian group* rely upon obsolete, marginal, and machine technologies in that order.

In order to obtain a dynamic picture of the *social role* of the various technologies, a line connecting the peaks of each occupational class in each participant group (Figure 13) should be visualized. This can be referred to as the class distribution line. One can then speak of the function or *role* of the obsolete technologies or that of the machine technologies, for example.

The technical elite line begins at a high point in the Anglo-aggregate group, descends gradually through the M-A group, and disappears altogether

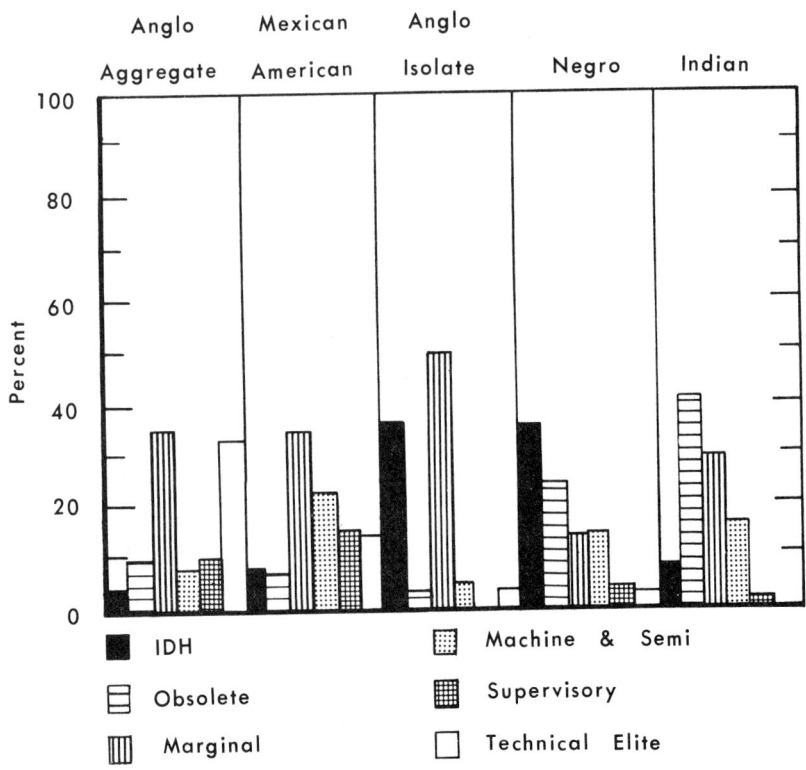

Figure 13
Percentage Frequency of Each Participant Group
Found in Each Occupational Class
(Bar graph from Table 41)

in the Indian group. The technical elite positions or technologies can therefore be said to function as status indicators or an index of status with the A-A ranking highest, the M-A next, the A-I and Negro close to the bottom, and the Indian group out altogether. This status position functions also as a good source of income for its members—e.g. over a third of the Anglo-aggregate farm workers are using the farm as a highly rewarding source of income.

The slope of the obsolete class line is almost the exact reverse of the technical elite line. Inasmuch as the obsolete class has the lowest status in the farm harvest system, the shape of the line corroborates the inferences to be drawn from the technical elite line. The obsolete class, too, can be said to function socially as a status indicator.

Marginal technologies play an important economic role for all groups except the Negro. The reason for its identification (fruit picking) with the Anglo-isolate is demonstrated by the fact that half of all Anglo-isolates fall in this class. Machine technologies function for the M-A, Negro, and Indian groups as an important source of income as well as an initiator into the higher status positions on the farm. The supervisory class plays an important role for the Mexican-American. It is a very high status position into which the M-A has been integrated as a result of the Mexican National program. This status (social) experience would not have come to many hundreds of Mexican-American farm workers except for the technological systems built around the bracero.

The IDH class serves primarily the Anglo-isolate and the Negro groups. In so doing it tends to reinforce their already low status. Economically this class functions as a stop-gap source of income for its members. Moreover, it may function socially to rehabilitate workers who might have never had another opportunity to get back into the production system. How effective it has been in this respect would require a separate study. We do know, however, that many workers in our sample who had been introduced into a harvest system by this method have since been integrated into higher status positions.

The social traits or institutional variations among the several participant groups which accompany their experiences in and their movements through the occupational classes of the farm harvest system will be analyzed in the following chapter.

23 Principles of Social Equilibrium and Change

OCCUPATIONAL CLASSES
AND MATCHING INSTITUTIONS

A Summary of Concepts and Terms Used So Far

THE SEPARATION of outer human organizations called *participant institutions* and inner (technological) organizations called *composite institutions* has been the over-all framework for the problem. In the beginning the scene opened on actual field activities. These preliminary descriptions of harvest organizations conveyed the first rudimentary idea of the composite organization. For the sake of convenience the mechanical operations and the organizational structure were described separately. The importance of outer human groupings emerged in rudimentary form in the descriptions of the harvest organizations. There the warp of culture was distinguishable in the whole cloth of the harvest organization.

Ethnic affiliation emerged as the most significant variable in the quantitative analyses of workers in Part Three. This was followed up in Part Four by analyzing these groups in depth as subcultures. The cultural concept was introduced because geographical and historical backgrounds were a meaningful and appropriate context within which to examine the participant groups. The institutions playing an important part in their participation in the farm system originate in the historic social milieu of these ethnic groups. Those institutions most relevant to farm labor became the main focus of analyses.

Part Five, up to this point, has sharpened and delineated the concepts of the *participant* institutions and the *composite* institution. The terms "participant organization" and "participant group" are used synonymously and have been substituted sparingly for the term "participant institution." Used also interchangeably with the term "composite institution" are the terms "technology," "technological system," and "farm harvest system." The farm harvest system is made up of six occupational classes. These six classes became the grid within which the distribution of the participant groups was plotted. The occupational class system is the mechanism of integration of the participant groups into the farm harvest system.

Two further concepts were derived from the participant and composite dichotomy. Each participant group is peculiarly exploited by its technology. By the same token the role in the production system of each group serves a peculiar function for that group. Technology is the instrument of this reciprocal exploitation. How the participant groups fit into this technology is termed

[282]

the *technological role* of that group. How the technology functions for the participant groups is termed the *social role* of the technological system. The technological role of a participant group is expressed in terms of where it fits in the *occupational class* system. The social role of a technology or farm harvest system is expressed in terms of the part it plays in the *institutions* of the participants.

Institutional Fit

We now have a model, or more accurately an institutional equation, whereby we can infer relationships between the characteristics and makeup of the farm labor supply and farm technologies. Specific or generalized, a farm harvest system or technology is viewed in terms of its occupational class structure. Conversely, a farm labor force can be spoken of in terms of its social structure—or *institutional* makeup. The units of relationship are *occupational class* and *participant institution*. As seen in the analysis in the previous chapter, specific institutions relate more frequently to some occupational classes than others. This might be called the principle of "institutional fit."

Anglo-isolate institutions coincide with the marginal occupational class in those companies informally organized, such as A and E Citrus Companies. Also, these same two companies generally do not use Nationals. In more rigidly organized systems Anglo-isolates are identified with the IDH class.

Mexican-American institutional patterns are dominated by the family unit. The migratory family institution represents a specialized adaptation to specific technologies—marginal and obsolete. The multi-vocational family institution is unspecialized. The key to this pattern is occupational diversity. Therefore, multi-vocational family workers are found in many crops and many occupational classes. The occupational classes they are identified with range from obsolete to machine. Frequently multi-vocational families have members working in obsolete technologies only to augment more stable income sources from marginal or machine occupations. One-vocational family institutions tend to be occupationally specialized, but at a higher level. The one-vocational family head is identified with the supervisory and technical elite classes. In addition to these two classes, an important variation of the one-vocational family is found among the green card workers who keep their families in Mexico. In this case the family head can be found in marginal occupations in addition to supervisory and technical elite. Moreover, in cotton the one-vocational family head, especially recent emigrants from Texas, can be found working in machine occupations, with an occasional lapse into multi-vocational patterns. His children often do summer work in cotton chopping.

As developed in the chapter dealing with the Mexican-American, these institutional-occupational adaptations have complex social ramifications.

Family size, educational background and orientation, residence pattern, and kinship organization are interrelated with the family-work institution.

The Negro family, occupationally diverse and loosely organized, is identified most frequently with IDH and obsolete occupational classes.

Indian occupational class identification is related to the degree of their participation in reservation institutions. Those most integrated in reservation society tend to be identified with obsolete technologies. Those who are least integrated in reservation society are generally found in the machine occupational classes.

Institutional and occupational class relationships infer that the social structure of the labor supply is interlocking and interdependent with the technological systems in which it takes part. A more thorough examination of this inference is provided by an analysis of changes that have taken place in recent years in Arizona farm technologies and the Arizona farm labor force.

LOOKING BACK OVER CHANGES AMONG THE FARM LABOR GROUPS AND THE FARM HARVEST SYSTEMS

The Lettuce Case

The lettuce case is unique in that control over the harvesting process was achieved through working agreements between management and *organized* labor. Because unsophisticated groups of workers such as Mexican-American migrant family workers, Filipinos, rural Negroes, and Indians do not revolve around institutions compatible with union institutions, it was inevitable that the union movement would tend to be ethnically selective in its membership. The more sophisticated classes of Anglos and Mexican-Americans built a labor monopoly out of a technological role. A labor group succeeded, in effect, in elevating their occupational status as a unified group. As they continued to raise themselves through the occupational status system to an elite class, costs also rose. Meanwhile, a factor not taken into account by the shed workers was that a potentially unlimited supply of unsophisticated, unorganizable peasant labor was at the disposal of the industry. Neither did the shed class realize that these workers were gaining skills that were technologically competitive with them.

While an exclusive and tightly knit labor organization was of enormous benefit to certain groups of lettuce workers, it also served to keep rights to production, shipment, and marketing in the hands of certain ice companies and certain lumber and labeling companies. The shed technology became a monopoly of congeries of organized, cooperative interest groups. Thus the incentive for a technological breakthrough that would allow outsiders to sidestep the tremendous investments and costs of the shed complex became stronger and stronger. Simple labor-saving machinery was not the answer. It had to be something which would throw production completely outside the tightly integrated network of control of the shed system. The unsophisticated groups of outsider workers were part of the answer. Only the refrigeration problem stood in the way of a complete break. The portable vacuum cooling process in combination with the half-size cardboard carton was the missing technological link. Thus all control groups – the union, ice companies, crate interests, and grower monopolies – were outflanked with one simple technological key. The result was a technological revolution.

Social and economic ramifications unfolded in inseparable order. The Mexicanization of a predominately Anglo occupation, a rapid acceleration of importation of Mexican workers (both bracero and green carders), a boost to the bracero economy of Mexico, the rise of border commuter communities, the rapid decline of Anglo communities centered around the shed economies, such as El Centro and Yuma, are some of these ramifications. Moreover, the industry was opened to unlimited acreages and production. Vast areas of desert and range land, previously locked out by a shed-centered technology, were opened up for lettuce cultivation. And finally, unforeseen by the innovators themselves, was the inevitable rise of government as a first party representative in labor grievances and negotiations.

Especially important from a sociological standpoint is the fact that, on the whole, the shed workers, a technical elite class in the old technology, did not step down in the occupational status system of the new technology. They were *displaced*. A completely new occupational status system grew up in which their institutions had no place.

The Cotton Case

Whereas the technological shift in lettuce, from the shed pack to the field pack, was in the direction of more labor-intensive systems, the change in cotton was in the opposite direction – one more common in industrial change. Moreover, the cotton case contrasts with lettuce because two familiar dynamics are generally lacking–labor unions and actual wage increases. Another contrast lies in the slower rate of mechanization in cotton.

As discussed more fully in Part One, incentives for machine investment received periodic motivation during times of labor shortages. Labor shortages in World War I boosted the development of the mechanical stripper and in World War II the development of both the stripper and picker. In Arizona, the Korean War coincided with some of the highest annual rates of increase in mechanical picking.

The result has been what might be called a technological and social *evolution*. There are important comparisons in this respect. In lettuce the top occupational classes were displaced abruptly by the lower occupational classes. In cotton the top class, in this case a new elite class of machine operators made up primarily of Anglos, began slowly to displace the bottom class–the hand pickers–made up of unsophisticated groups. The displaced groups in lettuce were out permanently. In cotton the groups gradually being displaced by machines – Indians, Negroes, and Mexican-Americans – began moving up in the occupational class systems to eventually take over machine operators' jobs. To be sure, many thousands of individual seasonal workers have been put out of work in cotton altogether. But the sociologically important point is that today it is common to see non-Anglo machine operators. In the late forties, when picking machines were introduced, this sight was rare.

The Citrus Case

Citrus is in contrast to both cotton and lettuce. Technological changes have been minor. Efficiency is gained primarily from loading, transporting, and warehouse labor and space-saving systems and from more formalized organization of picking crews. An attrition of their traditional type of worker, the Anglo fruit tramp, is evident. This is heightened by the use of Mexican Nationals and the formalization of their crews around mechanical transporting systems. Increased use of green carders, especially in the Yuma area, indicates the coming of new institutions into the occupational class system. Mexican-Americans are also evident in the harvest system of a major co-op in the Phoenix area.

A more thorough analysis of institutional changes among the workers caught up in the technological changes of the differing crop industries follows.

OCCUPATIONAL-CLASS MOBILITY
OF LETTUCE, COTTON, AND CITRUS WORKERS

Two criteria serve as indices of occupational-class mobility: the occupational class of the worker's job pattern 10 to 15 years prior to his present job and the occupational class of his parent or guardian. Both are compared

Table 42

Workers Now in Technical Elite, Supervisory, and Machine Occupational Classes by Occupational Class to Which They Belonged 10 to 15 Years Ago by Crop

Former Occupation	Cotton No.	Cotton Pct.	Lettuce No.	Lettuce Pct.	Citrus No.	Citrus Pct.	All Crops No.	All Crops Pct.
In farm work but lower occupational class	18	64	46	33	7	23	71	36
In farm work but equivalent class	3	11	0	—	7	23	10	5
In nonfarm occupation	3	11	43	31	11	35	57	28
In school	3	14	51	36	6	19	61	31
Totals	28	100	140	100	31	100	199	100

to the occupational class of the worker at the time of his interview. Upward mobility in terms of the occupational backgrounds of skilled workers is considered first. The tables are self explanatory except for the terms "lower" and "equivalent." Lower (farm) occupational classes include general hand, harvest hand, and small farmer—viz. subsistence, reservation farm, and sharecrop. All other farm occupational classes are considered equivalent classes except in the case of "technical elite" who have been promoted from equipment operating or foremen. The IDH class is omitted from all analyses because it is not an integral part of the occupational class system.

The cotton skilled classes have the greatest upward mobility, showing 18 out of 28 or 64 percent in this category. Lettuce skilled workers have come *new* to the industry with 94 out of 140 or 67 percent in this category.

The contrast between cotton and lettuce could be stated another way. The skilled classes among cotton workers have been recruited from within their own lower ranks, whereas today's skilled lettuce workers have been recruited from outside the farm industry as a whole.

Table 43
Workers in Technical Elite, Supervisory, and Machine Occupational Classes by Occupational Class of Parent by Crop

Parents' Occupation	Cotton No.	Cotton Pct.	Lettuce No.	Lettuce Pct.	Citrus No.	Citrus Pct.	All Crops No.	All Crops Pct.
Parents in lower farm occupational class	20	71	54	39	14	45	88	44
Parents in farm work but equivalent classes	1	4	19	13	7	23	27	14
Parents in nonfarm occupations	7	25	67	48	10	32	84	42
Totals	28	100	140	100	31	100	199	100

Occupational class of parents shows the same pattern. Cotton skilled workers show the greatest upward mobility *within* their own ranks, with the parents of 20 out of 28 or 71 percent of the skilled workers having been cotton pickers. Lettuce shows the greatest entrance from nonfarm occupations with the parents of 67 or almost half of the 140 skilled workers being from outside. Citrus frequencies in both tables are too small to support inferences.

In the two tables to follow (Tables 44 and 45) downward mobility and occupational continuity is analyzed by comparing the past occupational classes and the parents' occupational classes of marginal and obsolete workers. All categories of nonfarm occupation except "school" are considered "higher" occupational classes.

"Other" includes housewives, unemployed, jail, and drifting.

For farm occupations, supervisors, equipment operators, farm services, and independent crew leaders are considered "higher" occupational classes.

Also, for farm occupations, all categories of small farmers—reservation, subsistence, sharecrop, etc. — general hand and harvest hand are considered "same" occupational classes.

Table 44
Workers Now in Marginal or Obsolete Occupational Classes by Occupational Class to Which They Belonged 10 to 15 Years Ago by Crop

Former Occupation	Cotton No.	Cotton Pct.	Lettuce No.	Lettuce Pct.	Citrus No.	Citrus Pct.	All Crops No.	All Crops Pct.
In farm work but higher occupational class	3	3	2	3	10	8	15	5
In nonfarm occupation (equivalent to higher class)	12	14	14	18	57	43	83	28
In farm work but same occupational class	42	48	34	45	42	31	118	40
School	27	31	26	34	19	14	72	24
Other	4	4	0	—	6	4	10	3
Totals	88	100	76	100	134	100	298	100

Especially noteworthy are cotton and citrus. Cotton shows the greatest occupational continuity with 42 or 48 percent of their unskilled workers coming from the same occupational class in the same crop. Actually most of those workers of school age ten years ago chopped and picked during the summer months. Thus 79 percent show occupational continuity.

Citrus discloses the least occupational continuity. Its marginal class reveals that 51 percent have moved *downward* in the occupational scale. Lettuce matches cotton in its occupational continuity.

Table 45
Workers Now in Marginal or Obsolete Occupational Classes by Occupational Class of Parent

Parents' Occupation	Cotton No.	Cotton Pct.	Lettuce No.	Lettuce Pct.	Citrus No.	Citrus Pct.	All Crops No.	All Crops Pct.
Parents in farm work but higher occupational class	5	6	6	8	11	8	22	7
Parents in nonfarm occupation (equivalent to higher class)	7	8	20	26	54	40	81	27
Parents in farm work but same occupational class	76	86	50	66	69	52	195	66
Totals	88	100	76	100	134	100	298	100

Parent occupations reinforce the indications of the past occupations (Table 44) of the marginal and obsolete classes. Of the 88 cotton workers, 76 or 86 percent had parents in the same occupational class in the same crop. Citrus shows that half of their pickers had parents in higher occupational classes.

SUMMARY COMPARISONS

From their beginnings Arizona and Southwestern agricultural technologies have been generally the economic battleground of the classic struggle between assimilated (Anglo or Anglicized) groups and unassimilated immigrant or enclave populations of cheap labor. Assimilated groups have prevailed against the unassimilated only when they could render some technological advantage to offset their higher cost. Machines have played a strategic role in this struggle. As *dei ex machina* astride metal and fire, the Anglo elite spearheaded technological innovation offsetting the labor of twenty Mexicans, Chinese, or Filipinos, only to be displaced in time by members of the institutions they displaced. This social-technological struggle has persisted for decades. It characterized the birth and development of every major industry (including mining and railroads) in territorial days. It was an emotional issue in the struggle for statehood (Park 1961). What has taken place in the cotton and lettuce industries in recent years uniquely represents in the same time period, two opposing phases of the same old conflict. In cotton Anglo machine operators replaced non-Anglo pickers. In lettuce cheap peasant laborers were introduced into the production system to displace abruptly and completely a long established technologically and institutionally specialized elite class. This class then found themselves institutionally locked out of the new systems. In both cases occupational displacement and occupational mobility occurred. But the effects of occupational replacement by capital substitution (in the case of cotton) and displacement by cheap labor (in the case of lettuce) are radically different. Replacement by capital-intensive technologies reduces jobs and stimulates occupational class mobility (and social change) of industrially integrated groups. Displacement by labor-intensive technologies increases jobs as well as opportunities for occupational class mobility of nonintegrated groups. Table 46 encapsulates the essential steps in the sequence of changes that occurred and are taking place in each industry.

SUMMARY CONCLUSIONS

1. Arizona agriculture as a variant of Southwestern agriculture is an instrument of exploitation of unsophisticated, culturally unassimilated peoples.

2. Arizona agriculture as a variant of Southwestern agriculture functions also as an assimilative mechanism, an instrument of social change working in the direction of upward occupational mobility.

3. In the process of performing these two reciprocal functions, Arizona agriculture depletes itself of its own labor supply.

Table 46

Summary of the Sequence of Changes Occurring in the
Cotton, Lettuce, and Citrus Industries

COTTON	LETTUCE	CITRUS
1. Size acreage and institutional changes of migrant labor causing occasional shortages are prime incentives for technological change — little control of labor.	1. Technological (occupational class) change by occupational class monopoly — good control of labor through management/union contract.	1. Somewhat the same as cotton labor situation.
2. Technological change in the direction of capital substitution. — Institutional replacement of bottom occupational classes by top occupational classes.	2. The opposite of cotton. Institutional displacement of top occupational classes by bottom occupational classes.	2. Little technological change in harvest systems. — Institutional (fruit tramp) attrition accelerated by more formalized systems which favor braceros.
3. Technological and social change slow—evolution.	3. Change rapid — revolution.	3. Technology basically stable with fringe experimentation — little fundamental change.
4. Greatest occupational class mobility upward of groups (institutions) integral to the industry, but new institutions result from upward mobility.	4. Greatest occupational class mobility of alien groups inducted into the industry. Displaced groups institutionally locked out.	4. Institutions of participant groups — Anglo-isolate and Anglo-aggregate fruit tramps — not suited to occupational mobility.
5. Least induction of new institutions — decreased employment.	5. Greatest induction of new institutions—increased employment.	5. Gradual induction of new institutions to replace old institutions.
6. Least downward mobility and the most occupational class continuity.	6. Lower occupational classes rival cotton in occupational class continuity.	6. Lower occupational classes show greatest downward mobility. The traditional "fallback" industry for occupational rejects from nonfarm industries.

4. The occupational status system within a technology is the reflector in the relationship between social and technological change. This status system reflects change from either direction.

Thus in lettuce the net effect of union control of the shed-pack technology was a rise of a technical elite occupational class. The net effect of the vacuum cooling revolution was a sudden displacement of this technical elite class by a marginal (lower) occupational class.

In cotton, a marginal class was initially replaced by a technical elite (machine) class, but the pressure of unemployed marginal class workers became too great on the technical elite and the lower occupational classes began to move upward, gradually displacing the original membership of the elite.

5. Institutions at any given time fit certain occupational classes. Human beings are not individually isolable and exchangeable parts. They come always as a part of a social unit. These social units or institutions with their norms, values, and attitudes are the raw material of a technological system. These institutional groupings cannot be altered, entered, or withdrawn without affecting the technological system. Nor can the technological or occupational class system be altered without affecting the social structure of the labor supply which depends upon the technology in question. Thus a multi-vocational Mexican-American family participating in the farm harvest system will tend to utilize this experience to become one-vocational. At the same time, a Mexican-American population becoming one-vocational tends to react upon the farm labor system. More highly skilled jobs will be in demand by such a population and wage rates will tend to become lower. In response the farm system tends to rearrange its organization and its occupational class structure, hence its technology changes.

6. Technological and social change in farm harvest systems have occurred in three ways:

a. The induction of primitive (peasant) institutions into the industry with the displacement of institutions identified with the higher occupational classes. In the process the institutions of the incoming groups will undergo change.
b. Capital substitution for hand labor with increased competition for these newer, higher status jobs by the groups being replaced. In the process the institutions of the lower groups will undergo change.
c. Occupational class solidarity by union monopoly and elevation of its members in the occupational class system (technology). In the process the institutions of the organized group will undergo change.

7. Technological change means alteration of roles (jobs) in occupational status system—always tending toward the direction of the greatest output per unit of expenditure.

8. Social change means the adjustment of institutions to new occupational class roles—always tending to move up economically and socially.

9. Displacement of the higher occupational classes tends to be permanent because the institutions of its members do not fit the lower occupational classes. Its members become institutionally locked out. The incompatibility originates from both the members of the upper occupational classes and members of the lower occupational classes. (The fall-back phenomenon of the occupational rejects—e.g. Anglo-isolates—are an exception to this. But even in these cases, new institutions accompany their entrance into lower positions. They do not participate in bracero or Indian institutions with whom they compete, for instance.)

10. In contrast, when members of the lower occupational classes are replaced by higher class workers (technicians) the members of the lower classes tend to remain in the industry and compete for the new, incoming higher-status jobs. (The speed of the replacement and the degree of technical advance the incoming positions have over the lower positions are modifying factors, however.)

24 Implications for Farm Employment and Manpower Policies

THE FOLLOWING short summary statements represent the more important policy implications of this research. They are brief in the interests of clarity. Previous chapters have presented the data and analyses leading us to these conclusions.

RETRAINING, REHABILITATION, AND RELOCATION

1. If an unemployed worker is to be retrained, he should be retrained in the direction of what for him would be a higher occupational class.

2. If possible, he should be retrained for a job one or two steps higher in the same industry in which he has been previously employed.

3. As workers are displaced by the upward mobility of those from lower status positions, competition for the fewer upper-status positions will become severe. If a worker is displaced from the highest occupational status in the industry or if no jobs of higher occupational status are available to him he should be retrained for another industry.

4. As a whole, Anglo-isolates cannot be rehabilitated by training programs. Such programs propose vocational solutions for social and emotional problems. Short of an expansive, comprehensive rehabilitation program, the best solution is to keep these men employed in the informally organized tasks to which they have already adjusted.

5. Labor demand and labor supply is a dynamic process. Industries ordinarily do not greatly expand or develop job opportunities unless this development is predicated upon a continuing and increasing competent labor supply fed by colleges, trade schools, high schools, etc. This supply in turn was stimulated by the incentive of labor demand. Therefore, to retrain the unemployed who have been replaced by labor reducing technologies without at the same time *adding* more jobs to the total market, tends to aggravate the condition retraining seeks to alleviate by increasing competition for the available jobs.

6. The introduction of occupationally displaced workers from other industries on a wholesale basis will likely succeed only in jobs approximating or higher than their former occupational status. The degree of their poverty and destitution will have little to do with their willingness and ability to adapt. For instance, a Virginia coal miner family introduced into a migratory labor pattern (stoop work) would require enormous institutional adjustments.

Such an adjustment would be a step backward for both the parents and the children. To attach the necessary conditions for his participation in the lower occupational classes of the farm industry (such as higher wages, year-round employment and benefits, or wage subsidies) would cause the farm technology to alter in the direction of reducing jobs or eliminating them altogether. To introduce these displaced workers to higher status farm jobs would only increase the already severe competition which exists within the ranks of the traditional domestic farm workers and would tend to depress already low wages.

7. Generally, if it is to have validity, the concept of training for occupational adjustment must be broadened to deal effectively with institutional and cultural factors. It makes little sense to implement massive programs aimed specifically at imparting new motor skills to reservation Indians, Cotton Belt Negroes, Appalachian coal miners, or high school dropouts, when the social context of these skills is ignored. Valid training and rehabilitation programs must comprehend the institutional adjustments implicit in their training objectives — taking into account the social units the trainee must enter on his "new job" and the effect of his "new job" upon his primary institutions. This of course requires workers and administrators who understand the social groups they are dealing with. It also implies that these groups have a role in the determination of policy.

PUBLIC LAW 78 AND ITS ADMINISTRATION

1. Public Law 78 should be extended or some similar law enacted. However, no increases in the total foreign farm labor supply should be allowed.

Even with an extension of this law, the use of Mexican National workers would decrease rapidly without the aid of restrictive legislation under technological and economic pressures already set in motion. The only restriction should be on greatly increasing the importation of Mexican Nationals, thus avoiding formation of some new capital-saving, labor-using technology. Ending the program now will cause chaotic conditions within some crops and regions as adoption of new methods and technologies will be forced at too rapid a rate. During this period, consumer prices may rise precipitously.

The removal of the braceros simply implies the elimination of jobs they were performing. At the same time, the lower occupational classes, now complementary to the braceros' tasks, will be also eliminated. New but fewer jobs will be created for a different (and higher) occupational class. Continuation of the bracero program would cause these changes to occur more gradually while economic, social and technological processes eliminate the program within the next few years in a smooth and relatively nondisruptive manner.

2. If Public Law 78 should be extended or a similar law enacted, adverse effects rulings should be implemented in such a way as to establish stable relations btween IDH labor and employers. This would work two ways. The

driving out of workers on the whim of foremen who do not want "farm office boys" should not be allowed. But, if domestic workers do not exist at the start of a season, then allowances should be made in the interest of growers for having to absorb domestic workers in mid-season and lose them again as the season declines.

3. The employment service should recognize the worker's social unit. It should incorporate into the structure of policies a place for legitimate, legally constituted (bonded) independent harvest crews. Breaking up the traditional work unit in order to handle workers as individuals on the IDH program tends to reduce stability. Legitimate crews should be handled on the IDH program *as crews,* with the same grower/worker protection that was practiced in the *individual* placement IDH program.

OTHER FORMS OF ALIEN LABOR

To attempt to alleviate farm labor shortages by a naturalization process, such as under Public Law 414, is most undesirable. The green card worker cannot be regulated precisely in accordance with labor demand. Once admitted to the United States, he is free to move to any area and any industry. If he encounters social or economic difficulty he becomes a problem to society as a whole rather than being only a farm labor cost. He is a year-round problem imported to answer a seasonal labor demand.

SHARING THE RESPONSIBILITY FOR THE HANDLING OF LABOR RESOURCES

Although we have thus far discussed only farm labor, we believe that solutions of the farm labor problem are inseparable from solutions to the general labor problem. Solutions must be aimed at the fundamental difficulties involved in automation and unemployment.

In the past, in the conflict for control of the production process, neither Capital nor Labor has had to concern itself with the obsolete worker. Technological change was relatively slow and the growth of our economy usually absorbed the castoffs. Generally the castoffs' skills were still needed elsewhere in the economy.

But now Capital is moving toward production by capital alone and the obsolete worker is often finding himself obsolete throughout the economy. Capital is making this change for two reasons. First, the relative prices of capital and labor are such that it is more economical to do so; and under our economic system each individual firm must bow to economic pressures if it is to remain competitive with other firms in the industry, competing industries, and competing nations. Secondly, as less, higher-quality labor is used in the production process, labor is easier to obtain and control. This, too, is a cost reducing mechanism.

On its side, Labor is maintaining relentless pressure to elevate its membership on the socio-economic scale. Toward this objective Labor is adopting the same value system as is often attributed to Capital—viz., that power means money and money in turn means power. So long as unions can accrue greater capital as the process of automation continues, they are often content to pare off their membership in favor of an ever decreasing but upwardly mobile elite class. In doing so they are cooperating with management to shunt off greater numbers of technologically obsolete workers to become the responsibility of some other segment of the economy.

Whose responsibility are these technologically obsolete workers? To use a specific example, whose responsibility are the Anglo-isolates described in Chapter 17 or the Indians described in Chapter 19? Certainly we cannot blame their impoverished condition on the farmers for whom they usually work. The farm provides them a job where no other sector of our economy can. The Anglo-isolates are on the farm because they have been rejected elsewhere. The Indians are on the farm because the farm allows them to continue to participate in reservation life.

When viewed in this light the farm actually becomes a kind of nongovernmental social agency instead of the demonic exploiter of the poor as it is sometimes pictured. This is not to argue that farmers perform this function intentionally or that some do not take advantage of the poor if they have the chance. Farmers simply perform this function because farm technologies have been uncomplicated, because the work is often seasonal and because more sophisticated laborers are not needed. Farm wages are low because the equilibrium position of demand for and supply of farm labor dictates it so. It is a function of the entire economic system.

The system could be changed. But simple changes like minimum wage rates and regulated working conditions are not the answer—at least not the whole answer. Rising labor costs as compared to capital costs are what are making these workers obsolete in the first place. Further cost pressures will only hasten the process of passing these people on to become the responsibility of governmental agencies.

We believe that we should look upon labor as a natural resource just as water, or land, or petroleum. It would seem silly to most of us not to use our water resource to its greatest long-run advantage and it seems silly to us to allow stagnation of our labor resource. Prolonged unemployment of a labor resource as a result of technological obsolescence is analogous to permanent disruption of a resource ecology. Where this occurs, secondary ecologies tend to replace those which have been exhausted or disrupted. Once established they tend to become stable and self-perpetuating. Likewise, the disruption of occupational institutions, without replacing them with new ones in which the displaced worker has a productive role, tends to institutionalize the impoverishment of talent and technical skills which the worker experiences.

Just as there is no such thing as the complete absence of a biological ecology, so no one exists in the complete absence of institutions. Family culture, in the absence of participation in or preparation for work institutions, tends to lose its capacity to perpetuate and reinforce values, attitudes and patterned behaviors that adequately prepare its progeny for participation in the production system. Occupational institutions become replaced by dependency institutions. Thus is established permanent nonproductivity that becomes more firmly established in each passing year. Hence arises the term, quite correctly applied in this case, the "culture of poverty."

In summary, there is no "*farm* labor problem." There is a general problem of people who end up doing farm labor because of their culture or their circumstance. There is a general problem of people who end up unemployed after being displaced in their primary occupation because their institutions and the institutions of the apparently available occupations are not mutually adaptable.

These human problems are the problems of society rather than of simply the farm sector or the mining sector in particular. This is so not just for humanitarian reasons, but because the permanent displacement of workers on a wholesale basis, as the permanent loss of a resource ecology, adversely affects the whole economy.

Any solutions that attempt to solve their problems while accepting without question the objectives and methods of either management or organized labor can only be stop-gap measures, shifting the burden of the human by-products of automation from class to class and area to area. This process seems to lead ultimately to social and economic management by government as the only apparent alternative. Just as the responsibility for the proper use of other natural resources is often accepted by their users, it is frequently accepted only under some form of public management or regulation.

Perhaps governmental management is the only answer to the full utilization of our country's labor resources—perhaps not. We hope not. But if any policy measures are to be more than stop-gap measures, Capital, Labor and Government must all face the basic problem of mechanization and automation rather than striving separately to solve the problem while maintaining their own institutionalized values. We hope this study gives some insight into the dynamics that make these conflicts inevitable.

APPENDIX

SPECIMEN OF QUESTIONNAIRE

Farm Worker Interview Schedule — *Confidential*

Interviewer

BUREAU OF BUSINESS AND PUBLIC RESEARCH
THE UNIVERSITY OF ARIZONA

— —

Name: (surname first)_____

Date_____

IBM Cols. (All IBM Nos. in Cols. 1 thru 12 to be centrally assigned and *written* in spaces provided. Write responses in during interview.)

1-4.	Schedule No. (same as IBM No.)	IBM No.____
5-6.	Present residence: (specify settlement)	IBM No.____
7-8.	Place considers self from:	IBM No.____
9-10.	Farm or company now working for:	IBM No.____
11-12.	Job or job task now doing:	IBM No.____

(Check *one* item (number) only in each of the questions (columns) below *unless* otherwise directed. Write comments in space provided below each question.)

IBM Schedule No._____

13. County and Crop:	Maricopa	13.1____
(check one county *and* one crop)	Yuma	13.2____
	Pinal	13.3____
	Citrus	13.4____
	Lettuce	13.5____
	Cotton	13.6____
14. Age:	13-15	14.1____
(precisely according to birthday)	16-20	14.2____
	21-30	14.3____
	31-40	14.4____
	41-50	14.5____
	51-61	14.6____
	62+	14.7____

[298]

15. Sex and Marital Status:
    (check one item in *each* category)

Male vet	15.1_____
Male non vet	15.2_____
Female	15.3_____
Single	15.4_____
Married	15.5_____
Divorced	15.6_____
Separated	15.7_____
Widowed	15.8_____

16-17. Ethnic or racial background:
    (Check one only. In the case of more than one element, write the proportion in but check the one element which accounts for the higher or highest fraction. In cases where the fractions are equal, check the *one* element with which the informant identifies himself.)

Anglo	16.1_____
Anglo-Mexican	16.2_____
Mexican	16.3_____
Negro	16.4_____
Pima	16.5_____
Papago	16.6_____
Yaqui	16.7_____
Navajo	16.8_____
Apache	16.9_____
Hopi	16.0_____
Maricopa	17.1_____
Chemehuevi	17.2_____
Mohave	17.3_____
Cocopa	17.4_____
Yuma	17.5_____
Filipino	17.6_____
Other	17.7_____

18. Type of work presently doing:

Hand labor, individual production, piece rate, no min wage	18.1_____
Hand labor, individual production, piece rate, min wage	18.2_____
Hand labor, interdependent production (paid as a crew)	18.3_____
Equipment operator and/or supervisory	18.4_____
Hand labor, individual production, time rate	18.5_____

SKILL FACTORS

19. Formal schooling:

None	19.1_____
Less than 1	19.2_____
7-9	19.3_____
10-11	19.4_____
12	19.5_____
College	19.6_____
Doesn't know	19.7_____
1-2	19.8_____
3-4	19.9_____
5-6	19.0_____

20. Languages spoken fluently: English   20.1_____
(Check as many as apply. Specify   Spanish   20.2_____
any which do not appear.)   Other   20.3_____

21. Languages read well: English   21.1_____
(Check as many as apply. Specify   Spanish   21.2_____
any which do not appear.)   Other   21.3_____
                                        None   21.4_____

22. Special vocational training: None or doesn't know   22.1_____
(Check as many as apply   Trade courses in high school   22.2_____
provided ".1" is not   Vocational school   22.3_____
checked.)   Special on-job training   22.4_____
                                Vocational training   22.5_____
                                Rehabilitation training   22.6_____

23. Type of vocational training: None or doesn't know   23.1_____
                                    Skilled nonfarm   23.2_____
                                    Semi-skilled nonfarm   23.3_____
                                    Clerical-sales   23.4_____
                                    Farm skilled   23.5_____
                                    Divergent skills   23.6_____
                                    Prop. and manager   23.7_____
                                    Service occupations   23.8_____

JOB BACKGROUND LAST YEAR

One year from date of interview beginning with present job. Note under "method job obtnd," "SEO"=state employment office; "For Ch"=formal channels; and "Inf Ch"=informal channels. Limit number of jobs to six.

job	employer	address	length time	method job obtnd		
				SEO	For Ch	Inf Ch

24. Pattern of job experiences last year: 24_____
25.   (Cols. 24 thru 26 to be abstracted from above job   25_____
26.   history with the help of informant as a means of   26_____
      increasing reliability. See Code Sheet for symbols.)

27. Average lentgh of time above jobs held during said year:

Less than a week	27.1_____
More than a wk but less than a mo	27.2_____
More than a mo but less than 6 mos	27.3_____
More than 6 mos but less than 12 mos	27.4_____
Had same job a yr or more ago	27.5_____

28. Pattern of obtaining jobs last year:

(Check only
one unless
".8" checked,
and then in-
terviewer
must be
sure that
there are no
contradic-
tions.)

SEO predominately used	28.1_____
For Ch predominately used	28.2_____
Inf Ch predominately used	28.3_____
SEO and For Ch predominate and equal	28.4_____
SEO and Inf Ch predominate and equal	28.5_____
For Ch and Inf Ch predominate and equal	28.6_____
All three used about the same	28.7_____
SEO not used at all	28.8_____
Not known	28.9_____

29. Probe pattern of job background ten years ago: 29_____
    (See Code Sheet for symbols)

30. To be used for further analysis of Col. 29:   30_____
    (See Code Sheet for symbols)

31. Probe work pattern of supporting parent or guardian or most
32. influential person in informant's life:

Farm equipment operator	31.1_____
Harvest hand labor	31.2_____
Farm hand labor general	31.3_____
Farm supervisor	31.4_____
Farm owner or leasor	31.5_____
On reservation subsistence	31.6_____
Nonfarm skilled	31.7_____
Nonfarm semi-skilled	31.8_____
Nonfarm unskilled	31.9_____
Clerical-sales	31.0_____
Own or operate business	32.1_____
Professional	32.2_____
Service occupations	32.3_____
Military	32.4_____
Doesn't know	32.5_____
Sub farmer	32.6_____

Tenant and sharecrop farmer	32.7	_____
Farm services	32.8	_____
Self employed	32.9	_____
Crew leader (independent)	32.0	_____
On reservation subsistence and off reservation farm work	32.11	_____

STRUCTURAL-CIRCUMSTANTIAL FACTORS

33. Motor vehicle and telephone: (check one item in each category)

Owns no car	33.1	_____
Owns car but can't be used to commute	33.2	_____
Owns car but not sure of its dpndablty	33.3	_____
Owns car that can be used commute dly	33.4	_____
Cannot be reached easily by phone or ?	33.5	_____
Can be reached easily by phone	33.6	_____

34. Residence, commuting and migration pattern for worker as determined by the last calendar yr from date posted on his interview schedule:

NOTE: "Residence Household" consists of co-dependents who:

1. are members of the same nuclear family; 2. whom the worker supports substantially or with whom he integrates his income on a regular and frequent basis; and 3. with whom he lives on a regular and frequent basis. (Regular and frequent are interpreted as approximately monthly.)

In the case of a worker who claims the above but to whom the three criteria do not *all* apply, he is, for our purposes, his own household.

"+" signifies combined household or aggregate
"−" signifies single, "self" household or isolate

Permanent residence on farm where working at time of interview 34.1 _____ (Where worker has maintained his household a yr or more– not necessarily in exact same house)

Permanent residence off farm where working at time of interview 34.2 _____ *and commutes daily* (Where worker has maintained his household a yr or more–not necessarily in exact same house–and from which he commutes daily to this job)

Permanent residence off farm double commutes (Where worker 34.3 _____ has maintained a household a yr or more–not necessarily in exact same house–which is too great a distance from job to commute daily. Worker therefore lives alone closer to job but maintains contact with dependents as specified above)

Dual residence (Where worker has moved household back and 34.4 _____ forth between two fixed places of residence–not necessarily in exact same house–each of which he has "occupied" in this fashion for more than a yr and in which he has lived at least once in the last 13 mos.)

Circular migration (Where worker has moved household to 2 34.5 _____ or more locations in last yr but returned to a kind of hub residence–not necessarily exact same house–which he has "occupied" more than a yr in this fashion, having set up housekeeping in it at least once in the past yr)

Anomic migration (Where worker has moved household to 2 or 34.6_____
more locations in the last yr having not returned to any of the
places of residence within the last 13 mos. If worker has moved
household to only 2 locations in the last yr, he must also have
lived in the original place of residence—i.e., the place he was
occupying a yr ago—less than a yr continuously)

Immigration (Where worker has moved household to 2 locations 34.7_____
or *fewer* in the past yr. If worker moved household 2 times he
must have occupied original residence—i.e., the place he was occupying a yr ago—for at least a yr continuously)
Indefinite and unclear as to worker's residence, commuting and 34.8_____
migration pattern.

Description of residence in which worker is now maintaining household

35. Rural-urban classification:

Farm hse free	35.1_____
Farm hse rent	35.2_____
Farm hse own	35.3_____
Urb frng free	35.4_____
Urb frng rent	35.5_____
Urb frng own	35.6_____
Urban free	35.7_____
Urban rent	35.8_____
Urban own	35.9_____
Rsv free	35.0_____
Rsv rent	35.11_____
Rsv own	35.12_____

36. Type construction:

Frame all wd	36.1_____
Frame stucco	36.2_____
Cncre pmce blk	36.3_____
Brick	36.4_____
Adobe blk	36.5_____
Jacal	36.6_____
Log	36.7_____
Mixed const	36.8_____
Open air	36.9_____
Metal	36.0_____
Canvas	36.11_____
Trailer	36.12_____

37. Household facilities:

Inside water, toilet, electricity, cold storage	37.1_____
Inside water, outside toilet, elect, cold storage	37.2_____
Outside water, (comm), electricity, cold storage	37.3_____
Outside water, (comm), no elect, cold storage	37.4_____
Outside water, (comm), electricity, no storage	37.5_____
Outside water, (comm), no elect, no storage	37.6_____

Outside water, (haul), electricity, cold storage   37.7_____
Outside water, (haul), no elect, cold storage   37.8_____
Outside water, (haul), electricity, no storage   37.9_____
Outside water, (haul), no elect, no storage   37.0_____

38. Number of rooms and people living in house or associated houses:

1 to 2 rms with 1 or 2 people   38.1_____
with 3 or 4 people   38.2_____
with 5 to 7 people   38.3_____
with 8 or more people   38.4_____
3 to 4 rms with 1 or 2 people   38.5_____
with 3 or 4 people   38.6_____
with 5 to 7 people   38.7_____
with 8 or more people   38.8_____
5 or more rms with 1 or 2 people   38.9_____
with 3 or 4 people   38.0_____
with 5 to 7 people   38.11_____
with 8 or more people   38.12_____

39. Daily commuting, miles to and from work:

Lives on place   39.1_____
Less than 20   39.2_____
20-29   39.3_____
30-39   39.4_____
40-59   39.5_____
60-100   39.6_____
More than 100   39.7_____

40. Daily commuting, most frequent method of getting to work: (Check more than one if apply)

Lives on place of work   40.1_____
Own or family car   40.2_____
Friend's car   40.3_____
Farm carrier, special   40.4_____
Farm carrier, "day haul"   40.5_____
Crew leader or crew foreman   40.6_____
Public transportation   40.7_____
Hitch hike   40.8_____
Walk   40.9_____

41. Personal property: (Check all which apply provided ".5" is not checked)

Home, real estate, or farm   41.1_____
Stove, refrigerator, or furniture   41.2_____
Special trade tools   41.3_____
TV   41.4_____
None   41.5_____

42. Obligations—number people in subsistence household besides
    self: None   42.1_____
    ("Subsistence Household" consists of those who   1-3   42.2_____
    have a regular paycheck-by-paycheck subsistence   4-6   42.3_____
    relationship either by integrated incomes or by   7-10   42.4_____
    being in a provider-dependent relationship. They   11-14   42.5_____
    may or may not be related otherwise.)   15+   42.6_____

43. Indebtedness—amount of money owed by   None   43.1_____
    subsistence household: (Dollars)   Less than 100   43.2_____
    (Includes all debts of all participants— 100-499   43.3_____
    whether dependents and providers,   500-999   43.4_____
    co-providers, or simply partners.)   1,000-1,499   43.5_____
                                             1,500-2,499   43.6_____
                                             2,500-3,999   43.7_____
                                             Not sure   43.8_____
                                             4,000-6,999   43.9_____
                                             7,000-9,999   43.0_____
                                             10,000+   43.11_____

44. Income estimated for the year past date Less than 600   44.1_____
    of interview: 600-1,199   44.2_____
                                             1,200-1,799   44.3_____
                                             1,800-2,399   44.4_____
                                             2,400-2,999   44.5_____
                                             3,000-3,999   44.6_____
                                             4,000-5,999   44.7_____
                                             6,000-7,999   44.8_____
                                             8,000+   44.9_____
                                             Has no idea   44.0_____

45. Reservation contacts last yr:
    (one only)
                    Live on reservation part of time   45.1_____
                    No longer live on reservation any time   45.2_____
                    Non-Indian, does not apply   45.3_____
                    No longer live reservation but visits   45.4_____
                    Live on reservation all time (commutes)   45.5_____

46. County Hospital: (Worker and/or dependents — other members
    sub household—one only)
                    Used the County Hospital last year   46.1_____
                    Did not use the County Hospital last
                        yr but has used it last 3-5 yrs   46.2_____
                    Has never used the County Hospital   46.3_____
                    Doesn't know   46.4_____
                    Getting reservation hospital benefits
                        (self or dependent)   46.5_____

47. Welfare (ADC, OAA, GA) and/or surplus commodities:
    Worker and/or other members of subsistence household—
    one only)

  Benefited by one or more of the above in the past year   47.1_____

  Not in the past year but has in the past 3-5 years   47.2_____

  Never benefited by any of the above—last 3-5 years   47.3_____

  Doesn't know   47.4_____

48. Other Benefits: (Specify any other Benefit Factors which   48_____

49. may fit informant's situation. Quantifiable and pertinent   49_____
    information to be coded later.)

VALUE FACTORS

50. Festivals attended last year: (one only)

None	50.1_____
1	50.2_____
2-3	50.3_____
4-6	50.4_____
6+	50.5_____
Non-Indian	50.6_____

51. Church affiliations:
    (Specify any not included)

None	51.1_____
Roman Catholic	51.2_____
Assembly of God	51.3_____
Pentecostal	51.4_____
Church of Christ	51.5_____
Baptist	51.6_____
Nazarene	51.7_____
Mormon	51.8_____
Seventh Day Adventist	51.9_____
Congregational	51.A_____
Presbyterian	51.B_____
Methodist and Episcopal	51.C_____
United Brethren	51.D_____
Lutheran	51.E_____
Evangelical	51.F_____
Christian	51.G_____
Apostolic	51.H_____
Jehovah's Witnesses	51.I_____
Church of God	51.J_____

52. Frequency of Church attendance:

Not all all	52.1_____
Biweekly	52.2_____
Weekly	52.3_____
Monthly	52.4_____

Seldom	52.5____
Active one place but not another	52.6____

53. Union membership:

Currently	53.1____
At one time	53.2____
Never	53.3____

Remaining IBM columns (54-80) reserved for following categories of information: Interviewer should discuss the following subjects and write the information using words that are as succinct and equable as possible. Quantifiable and pertinent information to be coded later.

54. What does worker do Saturday nights?

55. What does worker do Sundays?

56. What other affiliations? (recreational, political, civic, religious and/or tribal, etc.)

57. Ambitional: Tell instances of best jobs you've had, and what you liked about each. (List most important reason first and so on in order of importance. If this is not successful in evoking criteria then ask about what kind of job informant wants. Look for one of the following orientations):

rural or farm	_____
class or status	_____
folk or tribal	_____
independence or avoidance	_____
subsistence	_____

General Comment— regarding interviewee, conditions under which interview taken and rapport:

SPECIMEN OF CODE SHEET

Quantifiable and Pertinent Information Coded from Written Information in Worker Interviews

Coding instructions for
Columns 24, 25 and 26:

(Analysis of last year's or last six jobs)

— Insert one code symbol only in each column in the order of importance of that job pattern in terms of time spent.

— If 25 and 26 are left blank, that automatically means that they are not in effect—i.e., 24 job pattern is *the* only one for the year.

— If 26 alone is left blank, that means that only two job patterns approximately equal apply—viz. 24 and 25.

— If 24 is "Z" — "drifting or unstable" — then 26 is automatically left blank with 25 being in this case only a further analysis of the "drifter" in terms of longest *continuous* time last year spent at: . . .

Column 24:

Most time last year's or last six jobs spent as or in (insert one symbol only):

1 Farm owner
2 Farm supervisory I — Ass't. general foreman, general foreman, manager
3 Farm supervisory II — Row boss and foreman
4 Farm equipment operator and/or mechanic
5 Farm services — own hauling, custom tillage, etc.
6 Farm crew leader independent
7 Farm hand general — irrigator, ditch tender, etc. — all hand but year round
8 Harvest hand labor — seasonal activities involving massive amounts hand labor
9 On-reservation subsistence (excepting wage work)
A Professional and managerial
B Clerical and sales
C Service occupations
D Fishery — Forestry and kindred (excepting farm, nursery, gin, cannery)
E Skilled
F Semi-skilled
G Unskilled
H Own business
I Military
J Attending school
K Self-employed
L Housewife
S Unemployed
T Jail
Z Drifting or unstable pattern

Column 25:

Second most important job pattern for last year or last six jobs (insert one symbol only):
(Use identical key to Column 24)

Column 26:

Third most important job pattern for last year or last six jobs (insert one symbol only):
(Use identical key to Column 24)

Coding instructions for
Column 29:

Indicate most important job pattern for informant in "stable past" 10-15 years ago. For bases of judgment see "Definitions." (Insert one symbol only):
(Use identical key to Column 24 except symbol "M" added for pre-school)

Coding instructions for
Column 30:

To be used for further analysis of "29.1," "farm owner"; "29.8," "harvest hand labor"; "29.9," "on reservation subsistence"; and "29.E," "skilled":

"Farm owner" (one only):
    1 Subsistence farm (crops grown to be eaten primarily by owner's family)
    2 Small family farm — low income
    3 Sharecrop or tenant farm
    4 Large farm owner or leasor
    5 Not able to determine

"Harvest hand labor" (one only):
    A Citrus
    B Citrus plus other fruit (tree) crops
    C Lettuce
    D Lettuce plus other vegetable crops
    E Cotton
    F General (including cotton in most cases)
    G Shedworker lettuce

"On reservation subsistence" (one only):
    8 On reservation subsistence only (farming plus wage work)
    9 On reservation subsistence and off reservation farm work

"Skilled" — *Industries represented* (one only):
    H Mining — metal
    I Machine shop — machinist
    J Construction (carpenter, cement finisher, bricklayer, painter, plumber)
    K Mining — coal
    L Petroleum production
    M Automotive services (mechanic, body man, painting)
    N Cook
    O Automobile manufacturing
    P Non-ferrous metal (smelting and refining)
    Q Watchmaker
    R Iron and steel (smelting and refining)
    T Railroad
    U Sawmill

    Y Other (blaster)
    Z Unable to determine

Coding instructions for
Column 54:

Harvest hand labor pattern with reference to citrus, lettuce, and cotton for last year's or last six jobs. Informant being classed in any of these three crops if he worked in them for *any* length of time (check only *one*):
    1 Citrus
    2 Citrus and lettuce
    3 Citrus, lettuce and cotton
    4 Citrus and cotton
    5 Lettuce and cotton
    6 Lettuce
    7 Cotton

Coding instructons for
Column 58:

Attitude toward present vocational situation. This doesn't mean necessarily or simply informant is happy or unhappy with his job at the

moment — it means can he see himself doing this kind of job more or less on a permanent basis. (Check one only):
    1 Informant has no concept of "vocation"
    2 General rejection
    3 Ambivalent or mixed
    4 Passive or resigned acceptance
    5 Generally positive

Coding instructions for
Column 59:

General value orientation — focal point of informant's ambitions or satisfaction-giving "minimums" by which he seems motivated — the general locus of meaning to his "work-life." Unfortunately this admittedly rather vague concept had to be abstracted almost entirely from verbal behavior — it may, however, be illuminating in some cases (check one only):

1 *Folk-farm-rural*—farm and village and/or country life is inseparable from work-life — conscious of wages, to be sure, but just cannot envisage any way of working that does not involve the crop cycles, the outdoors, family unit together, being away from city, etc. *Work inseparable from way of life.*

2 *Class or status* — interested in "getting ahead" materially and/or prestigefully, and/or professionally and shows a vigorous interest to this end in his attitude. Farm may or may not be part of this depending upon where informant stands at the trough. He may have a good position in farm status systems prestige-wise and salary-wise — hence one could say that he is part of farm status system, but if his trough position changed he would go to another job — farm or *non*farm. Work tends to have class connotations.

3 Blank

4 *Independence and avoidance* — work a *means to the end of avoiding social commitment,* responsibilities, sedentary and domestic entanglements, daily routine, and family censure; perhaps adventure seeking — dysfunctional to a greater or lesser degree. Relatively high level of self confidence serves to differentiate this category from No. 5 — Subsistence.

5 *Subsistence* — work a *means to the end of meeting "minimal needs"* —food and/or drink. Degenerated stage of No. 4 in some cases, and apathetic stage of No. 1 in others. Dysfunction present to a greater degree.

ADDITIONAL DEFINITIONS OF QUESTIONS

Cols. 5-6

Present residence means the city, town, village, or community in which the informant is maintaining his "residence household" (as defined in Column 34 and described in Columns 35 through 38) at the time of the interview. The code number corresponding to the name of the city, town, village, or community will be entered in the blank. All types of farm-furnished housing will not have a code number. Therefore, code numbers will indicate independent housing only.

Cols. 7-8

A. This category though not a precise concept is nevertheless meaningful in that the informant, in most instances, will give the place with which he identifies himself—the place which accounts for his cultural background. In almost every case it is the place where he has spent the major portion of his life. Hence for an immigrant No. 7-8 may not be the place he was born, but rather the place in the U.S. where he was raised.

B. When a person's life is equally divided between two places give precedent to the last.

C. When time is so scattered that cannot really say where person from, e.g. 3 to 10 places, then put where *born*.

D. For naturalized citizens or aliens give, in addition, the place born.

Col. 15

A. Vet category is time in service of armed forces of *any* country.

B. If informant has married more than once, indicate his state at the moment of the interview—e.g. married, divorced, etc.

Cols. 16-17

A. "Mexican" means Mexican immigrants who have not yet achieved citizenship. They are green card or special-papers Mexicans—aliens still— who are presumably here to become U. S. citizens.

B. Anglo-Mexican is one of Mexican descent who claims U. S. citizenship.

C. When an individual is of mixed ethnicity, put him in the ethnic group which accounts for the highest percentage of blood. In cases of half-and-half, put him in the ethnic group of his father or the group with whom he identifies.

Col. 18

Checker is a harvest hand.

Col. 19

A. Last grade *fully* completed.

B. When the informant is confused between two grades, assign to *lower* grade.

Col. 20

A. The important thing here is, "How would the informant fare on a job where the language in question is spoken exclusively?" If this factor would be a serious limitation then he is not "fluent" in that language.

B. If it is necessary to conduct the interview in another language then that language is checked—not English.

C. In the case of bi-linguals, informant's say-so is accepted.

Col. 21

Language read *well* is determined by informant's say-so with his ability to read the newspaper cited as the criterion.

Col. 22

A. Special on-job training is defined as a formal training situation with special status as such and a formal period of time.

B. Training schools in military count as Vocational training provided they were not simply for combat training.

C. Completed correspondence courses are included under Vocational school.

Cols. 24-26, 29, and 31-32

A. The *Dictionary of Occupational Titles* (USDL 1949) is the basis for all of our occupational categories except the farm jobs.

B. Criteria for Drifting:

    1. Frequency of times jobs changed—three or more times a year.

    2. Length time jobs held—less than a month.

    3. Divergencies of types jobs—hand/skilled, farm/nonfarm.

    4. Long periods out of work—several months at a time.

    No. 3 in addition to any other, or anyone to an extreme is sufficient to categorize a worker as Drifting.

C. A crew leader is "independent" when he pays choppers or pickers instead of the farmer.

D. Farm equipment operator means running or operating equipment to the *full* extent of its use, e.g. tractor—using it to cultivate, till soil, plant, etc. for a reasonable length of time—time enough to establish worker as a tractor driver. Just driving a tractor to pull a trailer is *not* skilled.

E. In case of a tie in terms of amount of time spent, give precedence to the most recent job.

F. In heading of the job/time ratio as the main criteria as to whether second and third (25 and 26) should be used, if first job is something like 100 times as many days as second then do not check second. Stay at least 20:1 for jobs and 10:1 for unemployed time.

G. Unemployed and Drifting are not to be used together.

Col. 27

A. The number of jobs varies with the number of employers, not the various job tasks. The total number of jobs is divided into the total time these jobs were held. Omit unemployed time from the latter.

B. Average-length- time-job-held category does not really apply to a Papago who works for a farm a few months every year.

    1. If his work runs out but stays on same farm—*no* change.

    2. If he goes to reservation and back then *one* change.

    3. If he goes to another farm then *one* change.

C. School should be averaged in as a job.

Col. 28

A. State Employment Office (SEO) category counted when applying either through the SEO or being told by employer to go there and get card.

B. Formal category counted when applying to company's personnel office, to union, private employment service, an advertisement, or through green card (immigration) channels.

C. Informal means through contractors, friends, or simply asking an employee of a company.

D. SEO not used at all applies in the sense of informant presenting himself to SEO as an individual looking for a job—for the jobs he obtained.

Cols. 29-30

A. Job background ten years ago should be longer period time. The problem is comparing 20-year-olds with 70-year-olds. For younger than 40 it is informant's longest continuous period of employment around 1952. For 40 and over we look for a vocational identification in his background which may go as far back as 15 years.

B. Family farm is checked when a young man worked on his father's small farm.

Cols. 31-32

Give precedence to what informant says father did most of his life—if not this then go on what he said father did originally—if not this then give precedence to what came to informant's mind first.

Col. 34

A. Shifts within the year from one type of permanent residence to another—e.g. from on-farm to off-farm. The move is from one house to another in *same* area so does not shift classification from permanent residence to a movement pattern.

B. "Locating"—means in connection with a *job*—not vacationing or taking time off. If worker stopped to work at a *paying* job for any length of time or if he stopped to even *look* for work for a *month* or longer.

C. For determination of home or location of household while in military, determine his place of residence at time he joined the service.

D. Also stretching needed on man leaving wife and children for six weeks at a time for any *part* of year, e.g. while working for A Company in Salinas. (This was very seldom needed, perhaps half a dozen times.)

E. Residence—for those "on farm where works" but just moved there recently from nearby farm, mark "34.1" even though they may have just moved there. This provided they have been living on farm-where-works in same general area for at least a year.

F. Permanent residence on farm where works does *not* include semi-abandoned or "obsolete" farm labor camps even though the worker may at the moment be working for the company whose land the camp is on.

G. Permanent residence on farm where works most of time but was interviewed on another farm—still count on farm where works.

H. Anomic migration not really accurate for a person newly moved from a place of residence of long standing who went to work for a company which must move its people to several places. Put him in immigration with the stipulation of having worked for same company since located in the area.

I. Immigration in the case of part of a household who comes alone and has been here less than six weeks, count as an "aggregate" and describe household he left. In a sense he resembles double commuter except he hasn't established a pattern yet.

Col. 35

A. If worker owns housetrailer or camper mark "own" regardless of whether or not he rents space.

B. If someone in immediate family owns the house—grandparent, parent, child, or wife then the informant "owns." If anyone else owns the house in which informant is living with no charge then it is "free."

Col. 40

A. "Family car" marked for informant if owned by lineal relative; any other family is marked "friend."

B. Carpool is "friend's car."

C. "Day haul" category abandoned because it does not uniformly indicate type of transportation the company uses.

Col. 41

Check items which are part of grandparents', parents', children's and/or wife's if there is no nuclear family division—i.e. child married.

Cols. 42-47

It was necessary to handle income and indebtedness as observations pertaining to whole households rather than individuals because, in most instances, this information was available in no other fashion. Only in the case of isolates was it succinctly clear as to who earned what, who owned what, and who owed what. Most families are set up on an integrated income concept with the responsibility for indebtedness. Ownership of homes and property are shared among the working members of the family. The Anglo pattern is, of course, the joint income and ownership primarily of husband and wife.

The Mexican farm worker, generally with a much larger family, presents a much more confused picture. The pattern in the case of a working father and sons and daughters is for the unmarried children to turn their whole paycheck over to the mother. The mother in turn makes all payments for furniture, cars, etc., and buys the food. In many cases the car driven by the son will be in the mother's name, even though the son is paying for it. Yet in the case of the married sons and daughters, finances are kept separate from father, mother, and unmarried siblings.

The first task of the investigator was to delimit the subsistence household. This was done by establishing the number and identity of those who fit the subsistence household definition of which the informant was a member. Item No. 42 in the questionnaire entitled "number people in subsistence household besides self" has this purpose.

Col. 43

Indebtedness includes the total of the household within which the informant plays an integral subsistence role.

Col. 44

A. Income does not include perquisites, subsistence farming, or other non-wage means of subsistence.

B. *Gross* income *before* deductions.

C. Total income that is coming into informant's household regardless of who is making it — husband, wife, children, etc.

Col. 50

Festivals include any native, Anglo, or mixture of native and Anglo religious or secular observances for which it is customary for an Indian to take off work to attend.

Col. 52

For those who said "when I can" or "when I'm not working" we checked monthly — "52.4."

Col. 57

A. Subsistence

    1. Absence of material possession.

    2. Low wage-earning potential as illustrated by occupational or educational background.

    3. Dysfunction.

All must be present.

B. Independence

    1 and 3 present to a certain degree but not 2.

REFERENCES

Abshier, George S. and G. B. Wood
  1949   Prepackaging Lettuce. Lafayette, Purdue University Agricultural
          Experiment Station.

Archer, R. C.
  1948   Progress in the Mechanical Picking of Cotton. Lubbock, Report of
          the Proceedings of the Second Annual Beltwide Cotton Mechaniza-
          tion Conference, sponsored by National Cotton Council of America.

Arizona Fruit and Vegetable Standardization Service
  1962   Annual Report Arizona Fruits and Vegetables, Crop Year 1961-62.
          Phoenix.
  1963   Annual Report Arizona Fruits and Vegetables, Crop Year 1962-63.
          Phoenix.

ASES (Arizona State Employment Service)
  1950   Arizona Cotton Harvest 1950. Phoenix, Farm Placement Division.
  1951   Arizona Post-Season Farm Labor Report for 1950. Phoenix, Farm
          Placement Division.
  1952   Arizona Post-Season Farm Labor Report for 1951. Phoenix, Farm
          Placement Division.
  1953a   Arizona Cotton Harvest 1952. Phoenix, Farm Placement Division.
  1953b   Arizona Post-Season Farm Labor Report for 1952. Phoenix, Farm
          Placement Division.
  1954   Arizona Post-Season Farm Labor Report for 1953. Phoenix, Farm
          Placement Division.
  1955   Arizona Post-Season Farm Labor Report for 1954. Phoenix, Farm
          Placement Division.
  1956   Arizona Post-Season Farm Labor Report for 1955. Phoenix, Farm
          Placement Division.
  1957   Arizona Post-Season Farm Labor Report for 1956. Phoenix, Farm
          Placement Division.
  1958   Arizona Post-Season Farm Labor Report for 1957. Phoenix, Farm
          Placement Division.
  1959   Arizona Post-Season Farm Labor Report for 1958. Phoenix, Farm
          Placement Division.
  1960a   Arizona Cotton Production Survey 1959-1960 Harvest. Phoenix,
          Farm Placement Division.
  1960b   Arizona Post-Season Farm Labor Report for 1959. Phoenix, Farm
          Placement Division.
  1961   Arizona Post-Season Farm Labor Report for 1960. Phoenix, Farm
          Placement Division.
  1962a   Arizona Lettuce Production Survey. Phoenix, Farm Placement
          Division.

1962b   Arizona Post-Season Farm Labor Report for 1961. Phoenix, Farm Placement Division.
1963   Arizona Post-Season Farm Labor Report for 1962. Phoenix, Farm Placement Division.
1964a   Arizona Seasonal Employment in Cotton Harvest Activities for Peak Periods 1950-1963. Phoenix, Farm Placement Division, unpublished.
1964b   Arizona Post-Season Farm Labor Report for 1963. Phoenix, Farm Placement Division.
1964c   Number of Green Card Men by County from November 1, 1963 to May 15, 1964. Phoenix, Farm Placement Division, unpublished.
1964d   Personal Communication Oct. 13, 1964. Phoenix, Farm Placement Division, unpublished.

Barnes, Kenneth K.
1963   A Mechanization Case History . . . Cotton. Implement & Tractor, Vol. 78, No. 11:44, 52.

Brandow, G. E.
1961   Interrelations among Demands for Farm Products and Implications for Control of Market Supply. Pennsylvania State University Agricultural Experiment Station Bulletin 680, August 1961.

Burma, John H.
1954   Spanish-Speaking Groups in the United States. Durham, Duke University Press.

Burnham, James
1941   The Managerial Revolution. New York, The John Day Company.

California Citrus League
1963   Picking, Hauling and Packing Costs for California-Arizona Citrus, 1961-1962 Season, Mimeograph, April 1963.

Cannon, M. D.
1964   Personal Communication, May, 1964. Tempe, University of Arizona Cotton Research Center.

Castetter, Edward F. and Willis H. Bell
1942   Pima and Papago Indian Agriculture. Albuquerque, The University of New Mexico Press.

Colwick, Rex F.
1953   Mechanization of Cotton Production. Washington, United States Department of Agriculture, Bureau of Plant Industry, Soils and Agricultural Engineering. Southern Cooperative Series, Bulletin No. 33.

Cooper, Martin R., Glen T. Barton and Albert P. Brodell
1947   Progress of Farm Mechanization. Washington, United States Department of Agriculture, Miscellaneous Publication No. 630.

Cowhig, James D.
 1963   Education, Skill Level, and Earnings of the Hired Farm Working
         Force of 1961. Washington, United States Department of Agricul-
         ture, Farm Population Branch, Economic and Statistical Analysis,
         Economic Research Service, Agricultural Economic Report No. 26.

Davis, Allison and John Dollard
 1940   Children of Bondage. Washington, American Council on Education.

Davis, Allison, Burleigh B. and Mary R. Gardner
 1941   Deep South. Chicago, The University of Chicago Press.

Dobyns, Henry F.
 1950   Papagos in the Cotton Fields. Tucson, The University of Arizona
         (mimeographed).

Dollard, John
 1949   Caste and Class in a Southern Town. Doubleday Anchor Books,
         Garden City, Doubleday & Company, Inc. (originally published
         1937).

Dozier, Edward P.
 1964   Folk Culture to Urbanism. The Case of the Mexicans and Mexican-
         Americans in the Southwest. Unpublished.

Enochian, R. V., F. J. Smith and L. L. Sammet
 1957   Cost and Efficiency in House Packing Western Head Lettuce. Ber-
         keley, California Agricultural Experiment Station, Giannini Foun-
         dation of Agricultural Economics Mimeograph Report No. 199.

Gallardo, Lloyd L.
 1963   The "green carder." Employment Security Review, Vol. 30, No.
         1:25-27.

Gamio, Manuel
 1930   Mexican Immigration to the United States. Chicago, The University
         of Chicago Press.

Goldschmidt, Walter
 1955   Social Class and the Dynamics of Status in America. American
         Anthropologist, Vol. 57, No. 6, Part 1:1209-1217.

Haury, Emil W.
 1950   The Stratigraphy and Archaeology of Ventana Cave. Tucson, The
         University of Arizona Press.

Higleman, Robert H.
 1964   Personal Communications, January, 1964. Tempe, The University
         of Arizona Citrus Experimental Farm.

Hill, James S. and Jimmye S. Hillman
 1964   Some Economic Aspects of the Arizona Citrus Industry. Unpub-
         lished.

Horne, R. L. and E. G. McKibben
1937   Changes in Farm Power and Equipment: Mechanical Cotton Picker. Washington, Works Progress Administration, National Research Project Report, No. A-2.

Jones, Don L.
1948   Accomplishments and Problems in the Mechanization of Cotton and Related Crops in the Southwest. Lubbock, Report of the Proceedings of the Second Annual Beltwide Cotton Mechanization Conference, sponsored by National Cotton Council of America.

Jones, D. L., W. M. Hurst and D. Scoates
1928   Mechanical Harvesting of Cotton in Northwest Texas. College Station, Texas Agricultural Experiment Station, Circular No. 52.

Jones, H. A. and E. L. Garthwaite
1925   The Growing and Handling of Head Lettuce in California. Berkeley, University of California, College of Agriculture, Agricultural Experiment Station, Circular 295.

Knott, J. E. and A. A. Tavernetti
1944   Production of Head Lettuce in California. Berkeley, University of California, College of Agriculture, California Agricultural Extension Service, Circular 128.

Landsberger, Henry A.
1958   Hawthorne Revisited. Geneva, W. F. Humphrey Press Inc.

Lewis, Oscar
1960   Mexico Since Cardenas. *In* Social Change in Latin America Today. The Council on Foreign Relations, New York, Harper & Brothers.
1962   Five Families. New York, Science Editions, Inc.
1964   Pedro Martinez: A Mexican Peasant and His Family. New York, Random House.

Malinowski, Bronislaw
1942   Man's Culture and Behavior. Sigma Xi Quarterly, Vol. 30, No. 1:66-78.
1961   The Dynamics of Culture Change. New Haven, Yale University Press (originally published 1945).

Mayo, Elton
1960   The Human Problems of an Industrial Civilization. New York, The Viking Press (originally published 1933).

McGinty, R. A.
1923   Head Lettuce in Colorado. Fort Collins, Colorado Agricultural College, Agricultural Division, The Colorado Experiment Station, Bulletin 283.

McGowan, Joseph C.
1961   History of Extra-Long Staple Cottons. Master's Thesis, Tucson. The University of Arizona, published by SuPima Association of American and Arizona Cotton Growers Association.

Mississippi State College
1949   The Labor Supply and Mechanized Cotton Production. Jackson, Agricultural Experiment Station, Bulletin 463.

Neighbour, Leonard
1948   Progress in the Mechanical Stripping of Cotton. Lubbock, Report of the Proceedings of the Second Annual Beltwide Cotton Mechanization Conference, sponsored by National Cotton Council of America.

Padfield, Harland
1961   The Arizona Seasonal Farm Worker: Some Theoretical and Practical Problems. Arizona Review of Business & Public Administration, Tucson, Bureau of Business & Public Research, University of Arizona, Vol. 10, No. 4.

Park, Joseph F.
1961   The History of Mexican Labor in Arizona During the Territorial Period. Unpublished Master's Thesis, Tucson, The University of Arizona.

Perlo, Victor
1953   The Negro in Southern Agriculture. New York, International Publishers.

Platenius, Hans
1940   Handling and Shipping Lettuce in New York. Ithaca, Cornell University Agricultural Experiment Station, Bulletin 723.

Redfield, Robert
1960   The Little Community. Phoenix Books, Chicago, The University of Chicago Press.

Roethlisberger, F. J. and William J. Dickson
1943   Management and The Worker. Cambridge, Harvard University Press.

Rose, Arnold
1961   The Negro in America. Boston, The Beacon Press (originally published 1948).

Seltzer, R. E. and E. E. Pfuehler
1959   Prices and Production of Arizona Farm & Ranch Products. Tucson, The University of Arizona, Agricultural Extension Service and Agricultural Experiment Station, Special Report No. 1.

Smith, Frank J.
1961   The Impact of Technology on the Marketing of Salinas Lettuce. Unpublished Ph.D. dissertation, Department of Agricultural Economics, Berkeley, University of California.

Smith, H. P. and D. L. Jones
1948   Mechanized Production of Cotton in Texas. College Station, Texas Agricultural Experiment Station, Bulletin 704.

Stollsteimer, John F.
 1960   Bulk Containers for Deciduous Fruits: Cost and Efficiency in Local Assembly Operations. Berkeley, California Agricultural Experiment Station, Giannini Foundation of Agricultural Economics Mimeograph Report No. 237.

Street, James H.
 1957   The New Revolution in the Cotton Economy. Chapel Hill, The University of North Carolina Press.

Underhill, Ruth
 1939   Social Organization of the Papago Indians. New York, Columbia University Contributions to Anthropology 30.

University of Arizona
 1954   Unpublished data, File No. 3158, Department of Agricultural Economics. Tucson.
 1962   Arizona Agriculture 1962. Tucson, Agricultural Experiment Station and Cooperative Extension Service, Bulletin A-21.
 1963   Arizona Agriculture 1963. Tucson, Agricultural Experiment Station and Cooperative Extension Service, Bulletin A-25.
 1964a   Arizona Agriculture 1964. Tucson, Agricultural Experiment Station and Cooperative Extension Service, Bulletin A-31.
 1964b   Unpublished data, Project 489, Department of Agricultural Economics, Tucson.

USDA (United States Department of Agriculture)
 1962a   Lettuce Prepackaged at Shipping Point: A Preliminary Market Survey. Washington, Agricultural Marketing Service, Transportation and Facilities Research Division and Fruit and Vegetable Division.
 1962b   Charges for Ginning Cotton, Costs of Selected Services Incident to Marketing and Related Information, Season 1961-62. Washington, Economic Research Service, Marketing Economics Division and Agricultural Marketing Service, Cotton Division.
 1963a   Agricultural Statistics 1962. Washington, United States Government Printing Office.
 1963b   Charges for Ginning Cotton, Costs of Selected Services Incident to Marketing and Related Information, Season 1962-63. Washington, Economic Research Service, Marketing Economics Division and Agricultural Marketing Service, Cotton Division.
 1963c   Statistics on Cotton and Related Data 1925-1962. Washington, Economic Research Service, Economic and Statistical Analysis Division, Statistical Bulletin 329.
 1963d   Farm Labor, October 1963, La 1(10-63), Washington, Statistical Reporting Service.

USDC (United States Department of Commerce)
1959   Agricultural Census, Washington, Bureau of the Census.
1960   Arizona, General Population Characteristics, Washington, Bureau of the Census.

USDJ (United States Department of Justice)
1961   Annual Report of the Immigration and Naturalization Service. Washington.
1963   Annual Report of the Immigration and Naturalization Service. Washington.

USDL (United States Department of Labor)
1949   Dictionary of Occupational Titles. Washington, Bureau of Employment Security, Division of Occupational Analysis, United States Employment Service, Vols. I and II.

Vanvig, Andrew and James S. St. Clair
1954   Costs of Harvesting Upland Cotton in Arizona. Tucson, University of Arizona, Agricultural Experiment Station, Bulletin 259.

Voegeli, Lawrence J., Edgar F. White, Bryce Masters and P. L. Breakiron
1955   Packing and Shipping Lettuce in Fiberboard Cartons and Wooden Crates. Washington, United States Department of Agriculture, Agricultural Marketing Service, Marketing Research Report No. 86.

Vogt, Evon Z.
1955   American Subcultural Continua as Exemplified by the Mormons and Texans. American Anthropologist, Vol. 57, No. 6, Part 1: 1163-1171.

Wagley, Charles and Marvin Harris
1955   A Typology of Latin American Subcultures. American Anthropologist, Vol. 57, No. 3:428-451.

Warner, Lloyd W.
1960   Social Class in America. Harper Torchbooks, New York, Harper & Row (originally published 1949).

INDEX

Adverse effect ruling, 20
Aggregate, defined, 151
Ahijida, -o *See* Compadrazgo
Anglo-Aggregate, defined, 180-81 *See also* Aggregate
Anglo-Isolate, 14; subculture, defined, 181; described, 218-30
  See also Isolate

Bin-forklift system, described, 28-34
Bin-trailer system, described, 17-28, 115
Bin-truck-forklift system, described, 116, 118
Bin-truck system, discussed, 114-15
Bi-vocational family, described, 198, 213-17
Bracero, attitude toward, 204, 210, 229; defined, 192
  See also Public Law 78
Bulk system, defined, 13
Bulk-trailer system, described, 23-28
Bulk-truck system, described, 17-23

Comadre *See* Compadrazgo
Compadrazgo, described, 186-87
Compadre *See* Compadrazgo
Composite institution, discussed, 282
Cotton scrapper, effect of, 90
Culture, role of, 7

Demand function, 125
Demise focus, defined, 227
Domestic labor, attitude toward, 257; green carders as, 72
Dry pack *See* Field pack

Elasticity *See* Price elasticity
Equilibrium, economic, defined, 2, 129; social, discussed, 282-92

Farm harvest system *See* Composite institution
Field box, defined, 12; system described, 13-17, 115
Field pack, described, 46-49, 51-65, 65-76, 120-22
Field wrap, described, 51-65, 73-76
Firm theory, described, 107-08, 111, 251
Formal management structure, defined, 3-4
Formal organization, defined, 5, 265
Functional illiterate, defined, 148

Green carder, attitude toward, 195-96, 259; defined, 72, 192;
  described, 192-97 *See also* Mexican-American, Public Law 114

Harvest system, defined, 267 *See* Bin-trailer system,
  Field pack system, etc. *See also* Composite institution

Harland Padfield is a native Arizonan who grew up on a farm near Chandler, Arizona, where he attended school. Following service in the Navy, he did his undergraduate work at San Diego State College, and took an M.A. at Arizona State University in 1952. Several years of teaching in private and public schools followed. In 1964 he received his Ph.D. from the University of Arizona where he is now assistant professor of anthropology.

A continuing interest in rural populations was stimulated by his farm background. It was this interest, combined with his knowledge of farming, that led Dr. Padfield and his co-author to undertake the research which resulted in this volume.

A native of California, William E. Martin grew up on a farm near Modesto. His undergraduate work was done at the University of California at Davis, where he received his B.S. in 1954. Four years of service in the Navy followed, after which he enrolled for graduate work at the University of California, Berkeley, where he received his doctorate in agricultural economics in 1961. Since that time he has been at the University of Arizona, where he is now associate professor of agricultural economics.

Dr. Martin's particular interest is production economics. He is currently cooperating on a study of the economic value of water to the Arizona economy.